W9-BQU-167

THE
unofficial GUIDE®
TO Maui

4TH EDITION

THE *unofficial* GUIDE®
TO Maui

4TH EDITION

MARCIE *and* RICK CARROLL

WILEY

Please note that prices fluctuate in the course of time, and travel information changes under the impact of many factors that influence the travel industry. We therefore suggest that you write or call ahead for confirmation when making your travel plans. Every effort has been made to ensure the accuracy of information throughout this book, and the contents of this publication are believed correct at the time of printing. Nevertheless, the publishers cannot accept responsibility for errors or omissions or for changes in details given in this guide or for the consequences of any reliance on the information provided by the same. Assessments of attractions and so forth are based on the authors' own experiences, and therefore, descriptions given in this guide necessarily contain an element of subjective opinion, which may not reflect the publisher's opinion or dictate a reader's own experience on another occasion. Readers are invited to write the publisher with ideas, comments, and suggestions for future editions.

Published by:
John Wiley & Sons, Inc.
111 River Street
Hoboken, NJ 07030-5774

Produced by Menasha Ridge Press

Cover design by Michael J. Freeland

Interior design by Vertigo Design

For information on our other products and services or to obtain technical support, please contact our Customer Care Department within the United States at 800-762-2974, outside the United States at 317-572-3993 or fax 317-572-4002.

Wiley also publishes its books in a variety of electronic formats. Some content that appears in print may not be available in electronic formats.

ISBN: 978-0-470-37998-1

Manufactured in the United States of America

5 4 3 2 1

CONTENTS

LIST *of* MAPS

ACKNOWLEDGMENTS

Mahalo Nui Loa, Maui . . .

With delight we thank island sources who helped with this fourth edition of *The Unofficial Guide to Maui*. This guide is not only the result of our personal experiences over three decades, but also the latest collective knowledge of many others, including:

- Marsha Weinert, Hawaii Tourism Authority
- Kelii Brown, Maui Visitors Bureau
- Nancy Daniels, Outrigger, Hawaii
- MaryLou Foley, Outrigger, Hawaii
- Mary Charles, Hotel Lanai
- Lori Abe, McNeil Wilson, Honolulu
- Kim Kessler, Ritz-Carlton, Kapalua
- Lacy Colley, Four Seasons Lanai
- Wendy Harvey, Fairmont Kea Lani
- Nane and Candy Aluli, Napili/Kapalua
- Caroline Bhalla, Hana
- Yvonne Biegel, Wailea
- Bonnie Friedman, Grapevine Productions, Wailuku
- Keoni Wagner, Hawaiian Airlines, Honolulu
- Luly Unemori, Wailea and Makena
- Caroline Witherspoon, Becker & Associates

And we thank editor Molly Merkle for enabling us to present this fresh, critical, journalistic perspective of Maui, Molokai, and Lanai.

Further, we pay respect to storytellers, interpreters, and authors, living and dead, for their keen observations: Ben Keau Sr. and Ben Keau Jr., Emmett Aluli, George Kanahele, Katharine Luomala,

Duke Kahanamoku, Charmian K. London, Mary Kawena Pukui and Samuel H. Elbert, Jack London, Isabella L. Bird, Mark Twain, Joana McIntyre Varawa, Robert Louis Stevenson, MacKinnon Simpson, Fletcher Knebel, Michel Tournier, Gian Paolo Barbieri, Charles Nordhoff, and Simon Winchester.

We acknowledge the sources of some of our personal anecdotes, sidebars, and marginalia: *Great Outdoor Adventures of Hawaii; Chicken Skin True Spooky Tales of Hawaii; Hawaii* magazine; *Successful Meetings* magazine; *San Francisco Chronicle; Seattle Times;* and Oceanic Cable's **www.hawaii.rr.com.**

We are honored to dedicate this book to the late Fred and Wanda Keeble of Carmel, who loved Maui longer and better than any other travelers we know.

And last, we thank you for choosing *The Unofficial Guide to Maui.*

Mahalo nui loa!

Marcie and Rick Carroll
Wailea, Maui 2009

ABOUT *the* AUTHORS

RICK CARROLL, author of *IZ: Voice of The People* (the first biography of legendary Hawaiian singer Israel Kamakawiwo'ole), is the best-selling creator of *Hawaii's Best Spooky Tales* series, *Madame Pele: True Encounters with Hawaii's Fire Goddess,* and *In the Path of Night Marchers.*

A former daily journalist at the *San Francisco Chronicle,* Carroll wrote award-winning travel and feature stories about Hawaii and the Pacific for the *Honolulu Advertiser* and covered Hawaii and the Pacific for United Press International.

MARCIE RASMUSSEN CARROLL, former communications director for the Hawaii Convention and Visitors Bureau, has written and edited political, environmental, and other news for the *San Francisco Chronicle, San Jose Mercury News,* and UPI in Atlanta. She was a Journalism Fellow in Asian studies at the University of Hawaii and in energy studies at Stanford University. She has been a freelance writer for many publications specializing in Hawaii travel stories.

Together, the Carrolls, who moved to Windward Oahu in 1983, collected and edited *Travelers Tales Hawaii: True Stories of the Island Spirit,* now in its second edition, an anthology praised as "the best collection of contemporary Hawaii travel stories." They are also the authors of the *Unofficial Guide to Hawaii.*

THE *unofficial* GUIDE® TO Maui

4TH EDITION

INTRODUCTION

The **MAGICAL ISLANDS** of **MAUI**

"MAUI NO KA OI." Anyone who has been to Maui can probably tell you what that means—"Maui is the best!" Not the cheapest, or the most Hawaiian, but the island where culture and nature and golf and beaches come together just right under the tropical sun to create the vacation dream most visitors envision.

For reasons we spell out for you in this guide, Maui is the perennial favorite place to visit in the Hawaiian Islands, other than Honolulu, where most visitors by necessity have to arrive and depart because of flight schedules. Not only is Maui the most visited of the Hawaiian Islands after Oahu, but it has also been voted the best island anywhere, year after year, in multiple travel magazine reader polls. Ever noticed how many people say proudly they're going to Maui? Not just to Hawaii, but to Maui. It's the heart of the Hawaiian Islands. Maui's nearby sibling islands, Molokai and Lanai, in contrast, are the least visited of the major islands in the Hawaiian chain. And while a fourth island, mysterious Kahoolawe, beckons on the horizon, this former U.S. Navy bombing range is off-limits for visitors altogether.

Together these islands form the realm of Maui County, jewel of the Hawaiian chain. They could hardly be more different, and yet they are linked by the geologic fundamentals they share under the aegis of towering Haleakala, the "House of the Sun" and largest dormant volcano in the world.

What is it about Maui that makes it so popular? One pilgrim, an Oklahoma restaurateur whose eyes light up just as much today at the thought of a Maui trip as they have every year for the past decade, puts it this way: "On Maui, you just know you're going to have fun."

The Hawaiian Islands

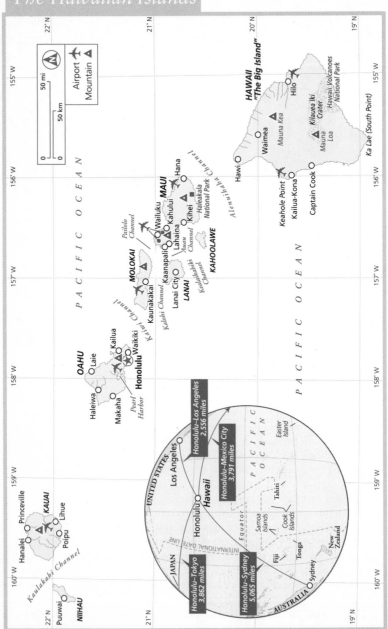

Myth has it that the demigod Maui, the merry prankster of Polynesian legend, fished up the Hawaiian Islands from the middle of the Pacific Ocean then lassoed the sun to slow its progress and let it shine longer on his namesake, the island of Maui, thus ensuring long, bright days to accommodate all the things there are to do.

Maui's islands offer rejuvenation to suit any visitor, from relaxing on a massage table at the spa to careening down the volcano on a specially built bike. And the Pacific is always nearby, offering the thrill of windsurfing, the promise of tanning on the beach, and the wonder of watching giant whales or spinner dolphins frolic in the waves. The important thing is to count on kicking back. This isn't New York, or Kansas, or even Waikiki. These are country islands where tourism is replacing sugar, pineapple, and ranching on huge spreads of land and where clever marketing lent an air of sophistication that somehow became fact.

If the Hawaiian song "Maui No Ka Oi" sounds vaguely familiar, it should. The melody is based on the early American children's song "My Boat Is Sailing," introduced to Hawaii by missionaries in the 1800s. The Rev. Samuel Kapu of Maui took the melody, composed Hawaiian lyrics praising Maui, and changed the title to create the island anthem, according to George Kanahele in *Hawaiian Music & Musicians*. Steel-guitar virtuoso Jerry Byrd and slack-key artists Sonny Chillingworth and Raymond Kane made "Maui No Ka Oi" a local hit.

ABOUT *This* GUIDEBOOK

PERHAPS THE GREATEST HELP A GUIDEBOOK can be is in tailoring your expectations to the reality you are likely to find at your destination. Prepare to enjoy the people of Maui, Molokai, and Lanai and their easy way of living. Lighthearted island attitudes, the surprising generosity of spirit from people who go out of their way for you, and the sense of extended family soon begin to melt even the most hardened urban refugees and suburban road warriors. Remember that this isn't West Coast West, but a former Polynesian kingdom inhabited by a fairly exotic mix of people. Slow down, and be prepared for unfamiliar accents and customs, unexpected pleasures like the sight of a whale breaching as you drive along, and upheavals in your plans. Brief yourself by reading this book, prowling the Internet, and talking to friends. Those who come to the Islands with advance knowledge and plenty of patience are bound to have delightful encounters. Bring your *keiki* (kids) and *kupuna* (elders). They'll have a good time in this family-oriented haven.

On the subject of reasonable expectations, know that you won't necessarily find movie-set huts by the sea on Maui's islands, and although there are plenty of beautiful, fanciful resorts, they're not all on the shore. At the Kahului airport, you're more likely to be met by lines at the rental-car facilities than maidens bearing a lei of flowers, unless you have already paid for the greeting service or are being met by a friend who lives there. However, the welcome at many hotels includes lei of fresh orchids for guests when they arrive to check in.

Last, just because you're on a Hawaiian Islands vacation doesn't mean you're immune to misfortune. Maui, Molokai, and Lanai are generally safe destinations, but try not to tempt fate. If you leave valuables unattended on your beach mat or in your rental car, locked or not, chances are they will vanish before you return. If you hike in a waterfall valley, watch out for cloudbursts, or you could be washed away. You can fall off those beautiful sea cliffs, so hike *akamai* (wisely). The sea sets its own rules, so keep your challenges within your limits.

We're here to help you make the most of your trip to Maui and perhaps even augment your agenda with some serendipitous experiences. They're really hard to miss on Maui, but we want to help make sure you don't. It's hard for the "official" folks to recommend one of their members or sponsors over another. But it's easy for us to sort through the publicity. We tell you our favorites, and then we try to present a realistic view, pointing out pitfalls as well as don't-miss experiences. We'll provide some important details in advance, so that you'll be free to enjoy your entire vacation.

We aim to help you determine what suits you best among the dizzying array of hotels, condominiums, vacation rentals, and bed-and-breakfasts to   find the best deals. You'll get an up-to-date review of the best adventures, attractions, beaches, hotels, clubs, and restaurants. You'll gain insights into local customs and learn a few Hawaiian words and phrases that make you feel more like a *kama-aina* ("child of the land," a longtime or native-born resident).

Along the way, we'll examine questions like these:

- When is the best time to go?
- Where are the best beaches?
- What hiking trails can the family handle?
- Where do we find the best luau?

One Maui hotelier told a guest that a guidebook recommendation for his hotel is equal to a word-of-mouth rave review by a friend. Think of your authors as friends. We've lived in and written about Hawaii for many years and welcomed many friends and strangers as guests. Our own introductions to Maui were unforgettable adventures with family and friends. When we give our recommendations, we tell you what we tell our guests: what we like best and what we think would appeal to your special interests. Seniors, families, singles, honeymooners, European windsurfers, foodies, neo-hippies, and music lovers will all find something to love on Maui.

You want to be at the right place at the right time, enjoying the best Maui, Molokai, and Lanai offer, especially if it is your first trip. For those of you who have been to the Islands of Maui before and are ready to dig deeper, this book will suggest new possibilities. So mix up a mai tai, put on your favorite Hawaiian music, and launch your Maui adventure with *The Unofficial Guide to Maui*.

E komo mai! Welcome. Read on.

HOW *UNOFFICIAL GUIDES* ARE DIFFERENT

Our goal at *The Unofficial Guides* is to help you make informed decisions about how to pursue the Islands vacation you dreamed about, how to enjoy it best, and perhaps make a new discovery along the way. We try to tell you enough details about Maui, Molokai, and Lanai so that you can decide whether your family will be happier at Kaanapali or Wailea beach resorts, whether you want top-of-the-line hotel accommodations or camping, and whether you want haute cuisine or down-home local fare.

The Islands offer more things to do and see than you could pack into a lifetime of vacations. If you have only a week or two and you really just want to relax on a palm-fringed, gold-sand beach, no problem. We'll suggest—in a concise, easy-to-read format—that perfect beach and provide the information you need to enjoy it.

The Unofficial Guide to Maui, written for repeat and first-time visitors alike, addresses typical planning concerns ("Can I leave my coat and tie at home?" or "Should we visit the Maui Ocean Center?"). You'll find the answers to those questions and more in these pages.

Our Philosophy

If it matters to you, then it matters to us. From the beginning, the people behind *The Unofficial Guides* have worked diligently to deliver honest, straight-up reviews of major destinations and U.S. cities. The authors of this book are former San Francisco daily newspaper journalists who have lived in Hawaii and written about the Islands for two decades. They combine local knowledge with the ability to evaluate experiences from the visitors' point of view.

Special Features

The Unofficial Guide includes these special features:

- Insightful introductions to Maui, Molokai, and Lanai, highlighting the islands' special appeal and character
- A brief look at the Hawaiian Islands' fascinating history, from discovery by early Polynesians and other explorers to today's multicultural, mid-Pacific reality
- Local customs and styles

- Candid opinions on the best and worst of Maui, Molokai, and Lanai, including accommodations, beaches, restaurants, attractions, shows, clubs, and shops
- Practical information on driving distances and how to avoid crowds, dodge traffic jams, and park cheaply on Maui; or, alternatively, how to visit without a car
- Suggested itineraries for travelers based on their interests
- A guide to Maui's best golf courses

COMMENTS AND SUGGESTIONS FROM READERS

WE WELCOME YOUR SUGGESTIONS and comments about all our *Unofficial Guides*, including this book. Should you find any errors or omissions, we would appreciate hearing from you. Some of the best suggestions come from our readers.

How to Write the Authors:

Rick and Marcie Carroll
The Unofficial Guide to Maui
P.O. Box 43673
Birmingham, AL 35243
unofficialguides@menasharidge.com

Be sure to put your return address on your letter as well as on the envelope. And remember, our work takes us on the road for long periods of time, so please forgive any delayed response.

Reader Survey

At the back of this guide you'll find a reader questionnaire that will help you express your satisfaction/dissatisfaction with both this book and your visit to the Maui County islands. This survey will also help us make improvements to future editions of this guide. Please clip out the survey along the dotted lines and mail it to the above address.

HOW INFORMATION IS ORGANIZED

TO GIVE YOU QUICK ACCESS TO INFORMATION about the best of Maui, Molokai, and Lanai, we've organized material in a subject-matter format. Sections of this guidebook are dedicated to:

HOTELS So many hotels, condos, and bed-and-breakfasts seek your business that choosing the right one can be daunting. We offer easy-to-read charts, maps, and rating systems, as well as pertinent information on room size, cleanliness, service, amenities, cost, and accessibility to the beach.

ATTRACTIONS There's a lot more to do in Maui County than loll around on the sand—although there are plenty of beaches, and we highlight those, too. Besides thorough descriptions, our attractions overview includes author ratings and ratings by age group to help you determine what to include on your itinerary.

RESTAURANTS A highlight of every Hawaiian vacation is sampling Island cuisine. The menu is vast, ranging from simple local favorites like plate lunches to extravagant gourmet repasts and Hawaii's own regional cuisine. We take you to the best restaurants, out-of-the-way bistros, and roadside stands.

THE OUTDOORS Natural splendor is a big part of Maui's appeal. We tell you where to hike, camp, surf, bike, and more—making the Maui outdoors accessible.

GOLF The chance to play the fabled golf courses of Maui and Lanai is a major draw for many visitors. To help you choose the right one, we detail the vital stats of the top courses, including the scenic championship layouts that appear on televised professional tournaments in winter, when most duffers are confined to their living rooms, as well as others you might not find without us.

ENTERTAINMENT AND NIGHTLIFE Most visitors want to see live entertainment, Hawaiian style, during their stay. We review shows you shouldn't miss and the nightlife you're likely to find on Maui, Molokai, and Lanai.

THE GEOGRAPHIC REGIONS OF MAUI COUNTY

- West Maui
- Central Maui (and the North Shore)
- South Maui
- Upcountry Maui (and Haleakala)
- Hana (and East Maui)
- Molokai
- Lanai

Kahoolawe

Please note that the Island of Kahoolawe is technically part of Maui County, but we have not listed it as a place you can visit. For decades, Kahoolawe, the red dirt island that seems to be bleeding across the channel from South Maui, just beyond the snorkel haven of Molokini Crater, was a target for U.S. Navy bombing practice. Now it is in the process of being transformed into a Hawaiian cultural preserve, but visitors won't be permitted there for a long time to come, for a very good reason: the federal cleanup effort hasn't yet removed all the munitions that could still explode in the ground. The uninhabited island is off-limits, except by special invitation. So for now, most of us can only imagine what Kahoolawe Island will be like when all its wounds are repaired.

Maui and Central Maui

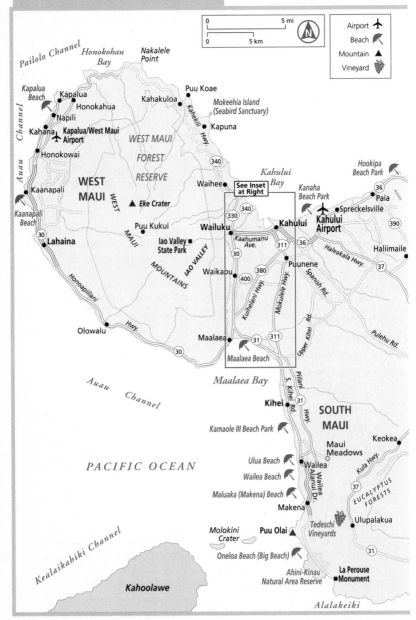

	0		5 mi
	0		5 km

Airport ✈
Beach 🏖
Mountain ▲
Vineyard 🍇

Pailolo Channel

Honokohau Bay

Nakalele Point

Puu Koae

Mokeehia Island (Seabird Sanctuary)

Kahakuloa

Kapuna

Kapalua Beach
Kapalua
Honokahua
Napili
Kahana
Kapalua/West Maui ✈ Airport
Honokowai

Channel
Auau

WEST MAUI FOREST RESERVE

Kehekili Hwy.

340

Kahului Bay

Kanaha Beach Park

Hookipa Beach Park

Waihee

Kaanapali

Kaanapali Beach

30 Lahaina

▲ Eke Crater

Puu Kukui

330
340

Wailuku

Kahului

Kahului Airport ✈

Spreckelsville

Paia 36

390

Iao Valley ■ State Park

IAO VALLEY

Kaahumanu Ave.

311 36

Haleakala Hwy.

Haliimaile

WEST MAUI MOUNTAINS

30

Waikapu

380

Puunene

37

See Inset at Right

400

Kuihelani Hwy.

Mokulele Hwy.

Spanish Rd.

Olowalu

Honoapiilani Hwy.

30

Maalaea

31 311

Pulehu Rd.

Maalaea Beach

Auau Channel

Maalaea Bay

Upper Kihei Rd.

Kihei 31

Piilani Hwy.

SOUTH MAUI

Kamaole III Beach Park

Maui Meadows

Keokea

PACIFIC OCEAN

Ulua Beach
Wailea Beach

Wailea
Wailea Alanui Dr.

Kula Hwy.

37

Maluaka (Makena) Beach

Makena

S. Kihei Rd.

EUCALYPTUS FORESTS

Tedeschi Vineyards 🍇

Ulupalakua

Molokini Crater

Puu Olai ▲

Oneloa Beach (Big Beach)

31

Kealaikahiki Channel

Kahoolawe

Ahini-Kinau Natural Area Reserve

La Perouse ■ Monument

Alalakeiki

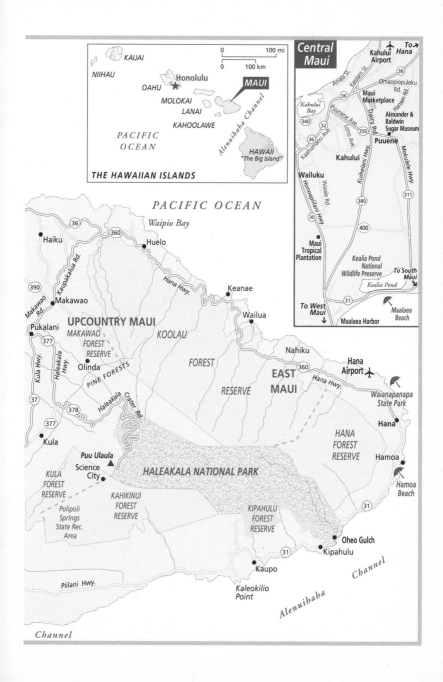

West Maui: Lahaina to Kaanapali Accommodations and Attractions

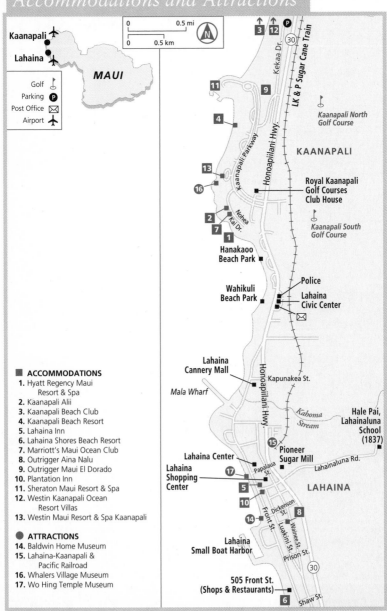

ACCOMMODATIONS
1. Hyatt Regency Maui Resort & Spa
2. Kaanapali Alii
3. Kaanapali Beach Club
4. Kaanapali Beach Resort
5. Lahaina Inn
6. Lahaina Shores Beach Resort
7. Marriott's Maui Ocean Club
8. Outrigger Aina Nalu
9. Outrigger Maui El Dorado
10. Plantation Inn
11. Sheraton Maui Resort & Spa
12. Westin Kaanapali Ocean Resort Villas
13. Westin Maui Resort & Spa Kaanapali

ATTRACTIONS
14. Baldwin Home Museum
15. Lahaina-Kaanapali & Pacific Railroad
16. Whalers Village Museum
17. Wo Hing Temple Museum

Kaanapali
Lahaina
MAUI

Golf
Parking
Post Office
Airport

0   0.5 mi
0   0.5 km

N

LK & P Sugar Cane Train
Kekaa Dr.
Honoapiilani Hwy.
Kaanapali Parkway
Kaanapali North Golf Course
KAANAPALI
Royal Kaanapali Golf Courses Club House
Kaanapali South Golf Course
Nohea
Kai Dr.
Hanakaoo Beach Park
Police
Wahikuli Beach Park
Lahaina Civic Center
Lahaina Cannery Mall
Mala Wharf
Kapunakea St.
Honoapiilani Hwy.
Kahoma Stream
Hale Pai, Lahainaluna School (1837)
Pioneer Sugar Mill
Lahainaluna Rd.
Lahaina Center
Lahaina Shopping Center
Papalaua St.
LAHAINA
Dickinson St.
Front St.
Wainee St.
Luakini St.
Prison St.
Lahaina Small Boat Harbor
505 Front St. (Shops & Restaurants)
Shaw St.

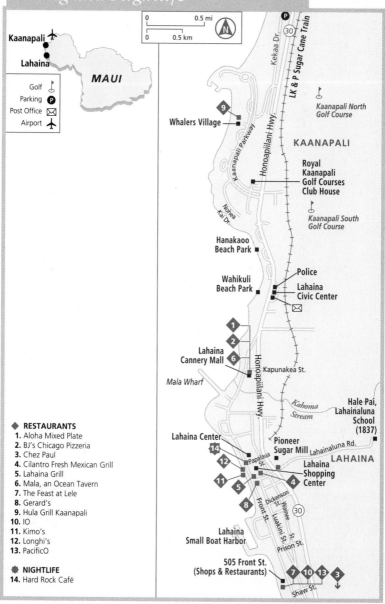

West Maui: Lahaina to Kaanapali Dining and Nightlife

Kaanapali ✈
Lahaina
MAUI

Golf ⛳
Parking Ⓟ
Post Office ✉
Airport ✈

0   0.5 mi
0   0.5 km

Ⓟ
30
LK & P Sugar Cane Train
Kekaa Dr.

Whalers Village — 9

Kaanapali North
Golf Course

Kaanapali Parkway

Honoapiilani Hwy.

KAANAPALI

Royal
Kaanapali
Golf Courses
Club House

Nohea Kai Dr.

Kaanapali South
Golf Course

Hanakaoo
Beach Park

Wahikuli
Beach Park

Police
Lahaina
Civic Center
✉

1
2
Lahaina
Cannery Mall   6
Honoapiilani Hwy.   Kapunakea St.

Mala Wharf

Kahoma Stream

Hale Pai,
Lahainaluna
School
(1837)

Lahaina Center
14
Pioneer
Sugar Mill   Lahainaluna Rd.
12
Papalaua St.
11
5
Lahaina
Shopping
Center
4
LAHAINA

8

Dickenson St.
Wainee St.
Front St.
Luakini St.
Prison St.
30

Lahaina
Small Boat Harbor

505 Front St.
(Shops & Restaurants)
7   10   13   3

Shaw St.

◆ RESTAURANTS
1. Aloha Mixed Plate
2. BJ's Chicago Pizzeria
3. Chez Paul
4. Cilantro Fresh Mexican Grill
5. Lahaina Grill
6. Mala, an Ocean Tavern
7. The Feast at Lele
8. Gerard's
9. Hula Grill Kaanapali
10. IO
11. Kimo's
12. Longhi's
13. PacificO

● NIGHTLIFE
14. Hard Rock Café

West Maui: Honokowai to Kapalua

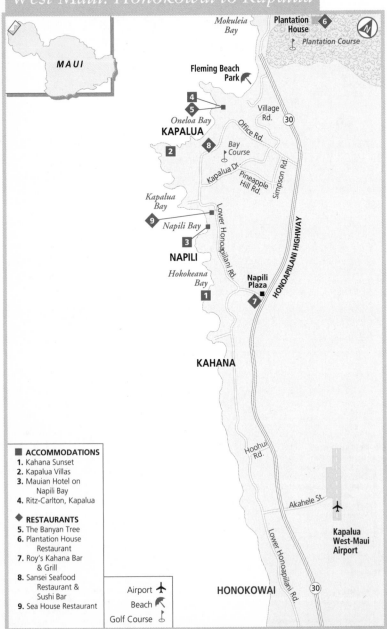

MAUI

Mokuleia Bay

Plantation House **6**

Plantation Course

Fleming Beach Park

4
5

Oneloa Bay

KAPALUA

Village Rd.

Office Rd.

30

2

8

Bay Course

Kapalua Dr.

Pineapple Hill Rd.

Simpson Rd.

Kapalua Bay

9

Napili Bay

3

Lower Honoapiilani Rd.

NAPILI

Hokokeana Bay

1

Napili Plaza

7

HONOAPIILANI HIGHWAY

KAHANA

Hoohui Rd.

Akahele St.

Kapalua West-Maui Airport

Lower Honoapiilani Rd.

HONOKOWAI

30

■ **ACCOMMODATIONS**
1. Kahana Sunset
2. Kapalua Villas
3. Mauian Hotel on Napili Bay
4. Ritz-Carlton, Kapalua

◆ **RESTAURANTS**
5. The Banyan Tree
6. Plantation House Restaurant
7. Roy's Kahana Bar & Grill
8. Sansei Seafood Restaurant & Sushi Bar
9. Sea House Restaurant

Airport ✈

Beach ⚲

Golf Course ⛳

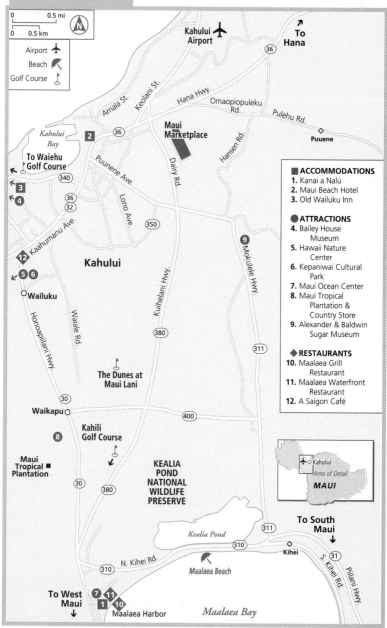

Central Maui

0   0.5 mi
0   0.5 km

Airport ✈
Beach 🏖
Golf Course ⛳

Kahului Airport ✈

To Hana

36

Hana Hwy.

Amala St.

Keolani St.

Omaopiopuleku Rd.

Pulehu Rd.

Kahului Bay

36

Maui Marketplace

Hansen Rd.

Puuene

To Waiehu Golf Course

Puunene Ave.

2

340

36
32

Lono Ave.

Dairy Rd.

350

Mokulele Hwy.

9

Kaahumanu Ave.

Kahului

12

5 6

Wailuku

Honoapiilani Hwy.

Waiale Rd.

Kuihelani Hwy.

380

311

The Dunes at Maui Lani

30

Waikapu

400

8

Kahili Golf Course

Maui Tropical Plantation

30   380

KEALIA POND NATIONAL WILDLIFE PRESERVE

Kealia Pond

311

To South Maui

310

Kihei

N. Kihei Rd.

Maalaea Beach

S. Kihei Rd.

Piilani Hwy.

31

To West Maui

7 11
1 10

Maalaea Harbor

Maalaea Bay

■ ACCOMMODATIONS
1. Kanai a Nalu
2. Maui Beach Hotel
3. Old Wailuku Inn

● ATTRACTIONS
4. Bailey House Museum
5. Hawaii Nature Center
6. Kepaniwai Cultural Park
7. Maui Ocean Center
8. Maui Tropical Plantation & Country Store
9. Alexander & Baldwin Sugar Museum

◆ RESTAURANTS
10. Maalaea Grill Restaurant
11. Maalaea Waterfront Restaurant
12. A Saigon Café

Kahului
Area of Detail
MAUI

South Maui Accommodations

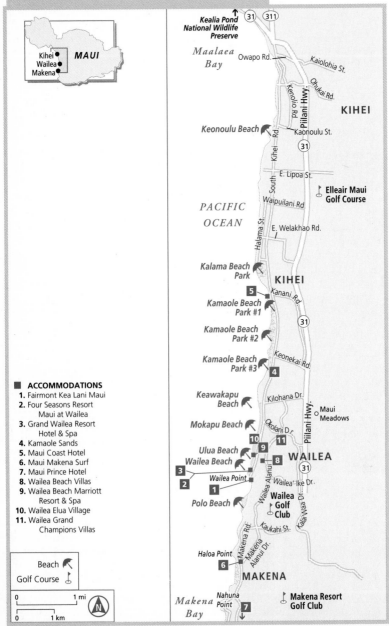

Kealia Pond
National Wildlife
Preserve

31 311

*Maalaea
Bay*

Owapo Rd.

Kaiolohia St.

Ohukai Rd.

Kenolio Rd.

Piilani Hwy.

KIHEI

Keonoulu Beach

South Kihei Rd.

Kaonoulu St.

31

E. Lipoa St.

Elleair Maui
Golf Course

*PACIFIC
OCEAN*

Waipuilani Rd.

Halama St.

E. Welakhao Rd.

Kalama Beach
Park

KIHEI

5

Kanani Rd.

Kamaole Beach
Park #1

31

Kamaole Beach
Park #2

Keonekai Rd.

Kamaole Beach
Park #3

4

Keawakapu
Beach

Kilohana Dr.

Maui
Meadows

Mokapu Beach

Okolani Dr.

10   11

Piilani Hwy.

Ulua Beach

9

Wailea Beach

8   **WAILEA**

3

31

2

Wailea Point

Wailea Alanui

Wailea 'Ike Dr.

1

**Wailea
Golf
Club**

Polo Beach

Kalai Waa Dr.

Kaukahi St.

Makena Rd.

Makena Alanui Dr.

Haloa Point

6

MAKENA

*Makena
Bay*

Nahuna
Point

7

Makena Resort
Golf Club

ACCOMMODATIONS

1. Fairmont Kea Lani Maui
2. Four Seasons Resort
   Maui at Wailea
3. Grand Wailea Resort
   Hotel & Spa
4. Kamaole Sands
5. Maui Coast Hotel
6. Maui Makena Surf
7. Maui Prince Hotel
8. Wailea Beach Villas
9. Wailea Beach Marriott
   Resort & Spa
10. Wailea Elua Village
11. Wailea Grand
    Champions Villas

Beach

Golf Course

0   1 mi

0   1 km

Kihei
Wailea   *MAUI*
Makena

South Maui Dining and Nightlife

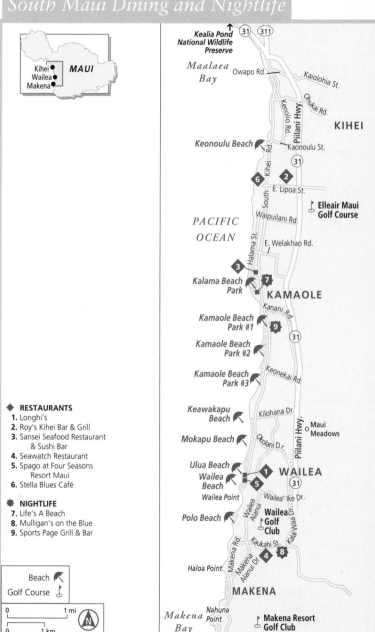

RESTAURANTS
1. Longhi's
2. Roy's Kihei Bar & Grill
3. Sansei Seafood Restaurant
   & Sushi Bar
4. Seawatch Restaurant
5. Spago at Four Seasons
   Resort Maui
6. Stella Blues Café

NIGHTLIFE
7. Life's A Beach
8. Mulligan's on the Blue
9. Sports Page Grill & Bar

Beach
Golf Course

0   1 mi
0   1 km

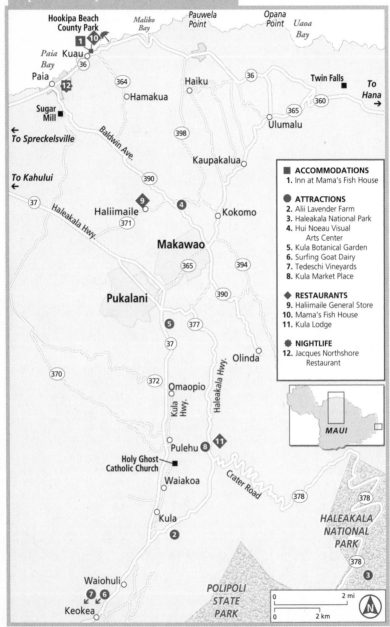

Upcountry and East Maui

Hookipa Beach County Park
Maliko Bay
Pauwela Point
Opana Point
Uaoa Bay

Paia Bay
Kuau
Paia
36
364
Hamakua
Haiku
36
Twin Falls
To Hana →

Sugar Mill
Baldwin Ave.
360
365
Ulumalu

To Spreckelsville ←

To Kahului ←
37
398
Kaupakalua

Haleakala Hwy.
390
Haliimaile
371
9
4
Kokomo

Makawao

365
394

Pukalani
390

5
377

37
Olinda

370
372
Omaopio

Kula Hwy.
Haleakala Hwy.

Pulehu
8
11
Holy Ghost Catholic Church
Waiakoa
Crater Road

378
378

Kula
2

HALEAKALA NATIONAL PARK

378
3

Waiohuli
7 6
Keokea

POLIPOLI STATE PARK

0   2 mi
0   2 km

ACCOMMODATIONS
1. Inn at Mama's Fish House

ATTRACTIONS
2. Alii Lavender Farm
3. Haleakala National Park
4. Hui Noeau Visual Arts Center
5. Kula Botanical Garden
6. Surfing Goat Dairy
7. Tedeschi Vineyards
8. Kula Market Place

RESTAURANTS
9. Haliimaile General Store
10. Mama's Fish House
11. Kula Lodge

NIGHTLIFE
12. Jacques Northshore Restaurant

MAUI

Hana

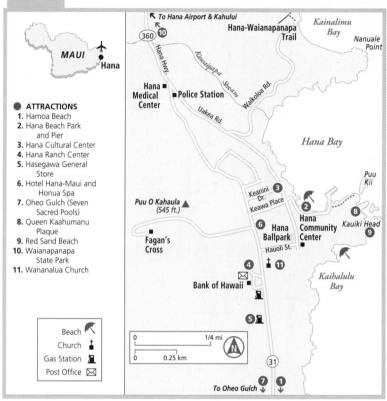

MAUI ✈

● Hana

● **ATTRACTIONS**
1. Hamoa Beach
2. Hana Beach Park and Pier
3. Hana Cultural Center
4. Hana Ranch Center
5. Hasegawa General Store
6. Hotel Hana-Maui and Honua Spa
7. Oheo Gulch (Seven Sacred Pools)
8. Queen Kaahumanu Plaque
9. Red Sand Beach
10. Waianapanapa State Park
11. Wananalua Church

Beach 🏖
Church ✝
Gas Station ⛽
Post Office ✉

↖ To Hana Airport & Kahului

360 10

Hana-Waianapanapa Trail

Kainalimu Bay

Nanuale Point

Hana Hwy.

Kawaipapa Stream

Waikoloa Rd.

Hana Medical Center ■ ■Police Station

Uakea Rd.

Hana Bay

Puu O Kahaula (545 ft.) ▲

Keanini Dr. 3
Keawa Place
2

Puu Kii

6 Hana Ballpark

Hana Community Center
Kauiki Head
8
9

Fagan's Cross ■

Hauoli St.

4 ✝ 11

Kaihalulu Bay

Bank of Hawaii ✉
⛽

5 ⛽

0 ———————— 1/4 mi
0 ———— 0.25 km
N

31

To Oheo Gulch ↓ 7   1 ↓

Molokai

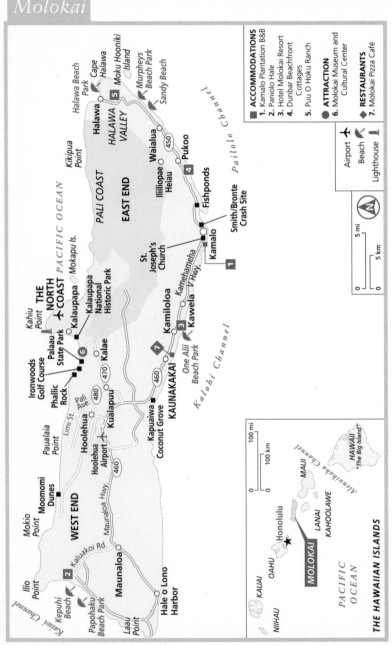

ACCOMMODATIONS
1. Kamalo Plantation B&B
2. Paniolo Hale
3. Hotel Molokai Resort
4. Dunbar Beachfront Cottages
5. Puu O Hoku Ranch

ATTRACTION
6. Molokai Museum and Cultural Center

RESTAURANTS
7. Molokai Pizza Café

Airport ✈
Beach 🏖
Lighthouse 🚩

THE HAWAIIAN ISLANDS

Lanai

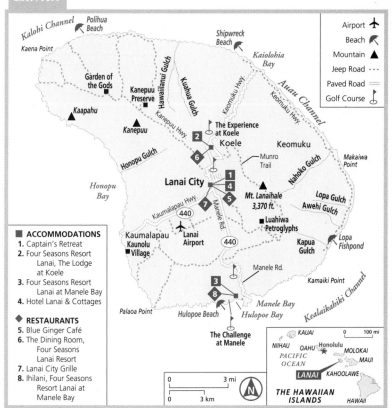

Legend:
- Airport ✈
- Beach 🏖
- Mountain ▲
- Jeep Road ---
- Paved Road ▦
- Golf Course ⛳

Map labels:
Kalohi Channel, Polihua Beach, Kaena Point, Shipwreck Beach, Kaiolohia Bay, Garden of the Gods, Kanepuu Preserve, Hawaiilanui Gulch, Kuahua Gulch, Keomuku Hwy., Auau Channel, Kaapahu, Kanepuu, Kanepuu Hwy., The Experience at Koele, Koele, Keomuku, Makaiwa Point, Honopu Gulch, Munro Trail, Nahoko Gulch, Honopu Bay, Lanai City, Mt. Lanaihale 3,370 ft., Lopa Gulch, Awehi Gulch, Kaumalapau Hwy., 440, Manele Rd., Luahiwa Petroglyphs, Kaumalapau, Kaunolu Village, Lanai Airport, 440, Kapua Gulch, Lopa Fishpond, Manele Rd., Kamaiki Point, Palaoa Point, Hulopoe Beach, Manele Bay, Hulopoe Bay, Kealaikahiki Channel, The Challenge at Manele

■ ACCOMMODATIONS
1. Captain's Retreat
2. Four Seasons Resort Lanai, The Lodge at Koele
3. Four Seasons Resort Lanai at Manele Bay
4. Hotel Lanai & Cottages

◆ RESTAURANTS
5. Blue Ginger Café
6. The Dining Room, Four Seasons Lanai Resort
7. Lanai City Grille
8. Ihilani, Four Seasons Resort Lanai at Manele Bay

THE HAWAIIAN ISLANDS
KAUAI, NIIHAU, OAHU, Honolulu, MOLOKAI, MAUI, LANAI, KAHOOLAWE, PACIFIC OCEAN, HAWAII

0 — 100 mi

0 — 3 mi
0 — 3 km
N

PART ONE

GETTING ACQUAINTED *with* MAUI

MAUI NUI: *Centerpiece of the Hawaiian Feast*

THE ISLANDS OF MAUI INCLUDE MAUI, Molokai, and Lanai. All are part of Maui County, politically speaking. This diverse trio comprises one of the best Hawaiian holiday destinations.

The Maui County islands are believed to be the tips of a single, sunken island, legendary Maui Nui, or Big Maui. You can see the geologic theory at work on Maui as you fly into Kahului Airport—the two main parts of the "Valley Isle" are mountains linked by a low-lying isthmus or valley, covered with fields of waving green sugarcane and Kahului Airport. If Maui were to sink much more over the coming geologic eons, or if the ocean were to rise dramatically, modern-day Maui could become two islands, one around the base of 10,000-plus-foot Haleakala and the other circling the mile-high West Maui Mountains. Intact and familiar for the foreseeable ages, however, Maui is the second largest of the major islands (next to the neighboring Big Island) at 729 square miles, 48 miles long, and 26 miles across at the widest point, with 81 accessible beaches spread along a shoreline of 120 miles.

They may be joined at the base, but each of the Maui islands is quite different from the next. You can get the big picture from the air, on the descent into Honolulu International Airport from the Mainland. Look out the left side of the aircraft during the last 30 minutes, when flight attendants announce the final stage of your transpacific flight. After more than 2,300 miles of open sea, the first sight of land is the two hulking volcanoes of the Big Island, and then across the water after a moment, the cloud-wreathed peak of 10,023-foot Haleakala, the summit of Maui. Sometimes you can see into the crater at the top, a burnt, cindery vista that looks like a misplaced chunk of Arizona.

Next comes Molokai, its steep, green slopes continuing out to sea in reefs visible near shore and its flattened, dry West End ringed with golden beach. Finally you'll see the little red-dirt Island of Lanai, once the world's biggest pineapple plantation and now a luxury retreat. The three islands in the middle of the Hawaiian chain are the core of the archipelago, each with its own appeal. Maui is an island of sophisticated resorts and fine dining, championship golf courses, and great beaches, among other attractions. But its little historic towns add an air of reality and recall the sweet past of sugar plantations and a farming heritage. Molokai is part open grassland, part lush valleys and ancient fishponds, part small farm. It is totally laid-back, with little in the way of tourism facilities, but plenty of spectacular scenery to offer visitors who can get along without resorts. Lanai is an exclusive retreat that draws honeymooners and folks with deep pockets who like the great outdoors. From dawn at the summit of Haleakala until the sun sets behind Lanai, your sojourn to Maui's islands can be packed with enough diversions to create a lifetime of memories.

CHOOSING *an* ISLAND

THE CHOICE DEPENDS ON WHAT YOU SEEK: beaches and water sports, rest and relaxation, action and adventure, hip shops and nightlife, historic homes and ruins, romantic evenings with champagne and chocolate, nature and culture, hiking and camping, championship golf, or just lazy days under the tropical sun.

A stay on Maui promises warm beaches, great golf on championship courses, winter whale-watching, snorkeling and sailing, hikes, sunrise at Haleakala Crater, and quiet nights outside of Kihei and Lahaina. People come to Maui to have fun—with their lovers, their families, their business associates, their school friends and cruise mates, their best pals and fellow travelers. But all that popularity means you will share Maui with lots of others. If you're looking for a getaway, consider those other little-known islands across the water, Molokai and Lanai.

Maui is the most accessible and offers the most action, hotels, shopping, restaurants, golf, and beaches. Molokai offers the least of those features and the least-disturbed tropical landscape. Lanai, a secluded luxury retreat for the most part, offers some of both: great hotels, golf, dining, and wide-open spaces to explore.

The following passages give an overview of each island, describing Maui in keeping with the geographical divisions used throughout the book: West Maui, Central Maui, South Maui, Upcountry Maui, and Hana. Besides providing an introduction to the physical and cultural geography of Maui County's distinct regions, the passages will help you determine where to focus your vacation. All of Maui County will be within reach during your stay (though interisland travel can be costly and time-consuming). However, if you know you want to spend your time at the beach, it doesn't make sense to stay Upcountry. Targeting a particular resort, city, or region can save you lots of transit time, thus leaving more play time. However, these are small islands, and day trips are an easy way to enjoy attractions, restaurants, and beaches outside the area you have chosen as home base.

■ MAUI: *Island of Adventure*

MAUI IS HAWAII'S MOST FAMOUS ISLAND, thanks to the popularity of the sunny resorts and golf courses on its southern and western coasts. Maui's two volcanic masses are joined by a slender valley and ringed with golden beaches and blue sea. Haleakala Crater's sheer bulk anchors the isle. Its slopes covering more than half Maui's land, Haleakala towers like a guardian spirit above the whole, particularly the South Maui resort coast, which it shields from wind and rain. What draws everyone to Maui, we suspect—besides its natural diversity, great beaches, and endless summer weather—is location: Smack dab in the middle of the inhabited Hawaiian chain with a clear view of neighboring islands. Mainlanders and people who live landlocked lives somehow feel comforted by the presence of other islands in plain sight. We don't know why this is; we only know that to be all alone on the vast Pacific is an isolation only solo sailors crave. In the empty ocean, even migratory whales seek out one another around Maui. The West Maui Mountains are mysterious, a series of steep valleys that lead to peaks lost in clouds, lending haunting beauty to the sloped fields of cane and pineapple behind the seaside West Maui resorts. Maui combines a hint of Honolulu's cosmopolitan flash, the genuine country pace of a rural plantation island, and the sophisticated influence of its luxury spreads and the people who frequent them.

With nearly 19,000 visitor units, ranging from less than $100 to more than $10,000 a day, and more than a dozen golf courses, Maui accommodates wide-ranging tastes. Elegant luxury hotels cater to the wealthy and free-spending corporate incentive winners, but Maui also offers some affordable bargains, particularly in tough economic times when the tourism industry competes even harder for every visitor's attention.

Maui delights people who like living it up at swanky beach resorts and those who prefer bedding down in rustic park cabins and camps; people who like hiking cool upland trails or exploring remote bays by kayak and those content to watch from the beach and pool; people who like to shop international boutiques in shorts and those who crave the awesome beauty of natural vistas. Getting rowdy in Lahaina is a century-old tradition, and young visitors crowd the historic streets nightly to keep the whalers' heritage alive in their own way. More than a few Maui travelers are drawn by the mystic powers attributed

MAUI FACTS	
Flower: Lokelani (rose)	Population: 129,471
Color: Pink	Highest Point: Haleakala (10,023 feet)
County Seat: Wailuku	Coastline: 120 miles
Area: 729 square miles	Airports: Kahului Airport, Central
Length: (east–west) 48 miles	Maui and Kapalua, West Maui
Width: (north–south) 26 miles	

to Haleakala, "House of the Sun," and then find themselves caught by the misty magic of the West Maui Mountains. Whatever the draw, visitors with myriad interests regularly return to Maui, and Maui eagerly embraces its tourists, more than 2 million a year from around the world. They mean jobs and prosperity for a large share of Maui residents and Molokai commuters, many of whom would otherwise find it tough to make ends meet on these tiny dots in the middle of the North Pacific, the most remote island chain in the world.

CENTRAL MAUI

MAUI'S UPLAND **Iao Valley** flanks the West Maui Mountains on the east, dipping to the slender lowlands that bridge Maui's two massive mountain structures. This low, flat stretch is Central Maui. To most visitors, Central Maui is just a corridor through which they travel after landing at **Kahului Airport** on the North Shore, turning right when they reach the opposite shore en route to resorts in West Maui (via Kuihelani and Honoapiilani highways) or left to South Maui (via Mokulele and Piilani highways). The roads through Central Maui flank fields of waving sugarcane, punctuated by the smokestack of the **Puunene Sugar Mill,** still at work even though sugar mills have shut down across most of the Islands.

WEST MAUI

A WORLD TO THEMSELVES, the towns and resorts of West Maui ring the lower slopes around Puu Kukui, topped by **Eke Crater.** It's a leisurely hour's drive from Kahului Airport to **Maalaea** and on to **Lahaina** (longer if you stop to watch the passing whales in winter) along the shoreline on Honoapiilani Highway (Route 30) through open country—dry slope on one side and ocean and beach on the other. From bustling, historic Lahaina town, it's 3 miles farther to the verdant, parklike setting and popular midrise hotels and condos of **Kaanapali Beach Resort.** The developed coast continues north 7 more miles to elegant **Kapalua Resort,** with its high-end hotel and residences, working plantation buildings, golf courses spreading up to meet pineapple fields, and beaches down below. Then the buildings dwindle away and the wild nature of Northwest Maui takes over. The road leads on for the brave, getting ever slimmer and more tortuous as it snakes along the coastal cliffs and stream valleys, past inspiring **Kahakuloa** and steep countryside dotted with periodic ranches and remote housing developments, ending up eventually in a Wailuku suburban neighborhood.

SOUTH MAUI

BEGINNING AT THE SOUTHEASTERN END of the isthmus valley at **Kihei,** South Maui spills down around the base of Haleakala like a newly unfolding map. A through-traffic upland highway, in addition to the shoreline road, makes it easy to get around. First comes the beach resort town, **Kihei,** a crowded strip of shops, restaurants, and older condos along **Kamaole Beach Parks I, II,** and **III,** which draw aspiring surfers and whale-watchers alike. South of Kihei is the world-famous, manicured and leafy **Wailea Resort,** where visitors find luxury rooms, high-end shopping, five beautiful beaches separated by low lava reef headlands, a shoreline trail, a tennis stadium, and three golf courses. Then come the least known, most remote of Maui's destinations, **Makena Resort** and finally **Makena State Beach Park,** before the road runs out around the bend in lava-flow wilderness at **La Perouse Bay.**

UPCOUNTRY MAUI

HALEAKALA NATIONAL PARK IS THE centerpiece of Upcountry Maui and its primary draw. The park stretches from the sea (at Oheo Gulch, beyond Hana) in the east to the crater at the summit, though most visitors arrive via **Kula,** not so much a town as a linear community of farms, houses, churches, and a few stores on the 3,000-foot shoulder of **Haleakala.** Upcountry offers a respite from Maui's tropical heat, and there's even a winery, **Tedeschi Vineyards,** at Ulupalakua Ranch, south of Kula. Pineapple wine and other vintages, including sparkling wines, are available to sample and buy at the tasting room. To the north, surrounded by cane and pineapple fields, are **Makawao,** a ranching and rodeo town with colorful Western-style storefronts; the working plantation village of Haliimaile, home to the deceptively named restaurant, **Haliimaile General Store;** the rural hilly hamlet of **Haiku;** and **Paia,** a former plantation town that is now a bustling, picturesque tourist shopping village. Few visitors spend a night in Upcountry Maui, although they can do so in a tent inside the crater or on the slopes of Haleakala. However, Kula offers the quaint **Kula Lodge** and a variety of bed-and-breakfast rooms or vacation rentals. A few rentals and bed-and-breakfasts in and around Haiku are favorites of the windsurfing jet-setters who come for the waves at Hookipa.

HANA

THE TWISTY ROAD TO HANA takes you winding by magnificent sea views, waterfalls, and botanical gardens on a skinny lane for 52 miles, away from the here-and-now and deep into old Hawaii. Time hasn't changed much in the remote cattle ranch village of Hana, even though visitors make day trips just to experience the drive and celebrities fly in and out of their retreats there, living alongside Hawaiians who actively practice their culture. Exclusive **Hotel Hana-Maui,** venerable veteran of many owners and facelifts, remains a glorious tropical getaway. Its restaurant is the only one in town open nightly for dinner, although dinner is served twice a week and takeout food and lunch are available across the way at the **Hana Ranch** restaurant. A few condos and vacation rentals offer shelter, but most visitors return at night to the brighter lights on the other side of the mountain.

Count on two to three hours each way for the drive to Hana on Maui's most famous road, depending on how many times you stop to swim in waterfall pools or admire the view. The rich and famous fly to Hana in small planes, and you can, too. There is a small airport served by planes from Kahului.

HANA REDUX

We spent our first summer in Hana 30 years ago. We stayed in a big old beach house near the police station, where Keith Keau then served as one of Hana's two policemen. Their chief mission seemed to be rescuing tourists in rental cars who had missed a turn while admiring the scenery. That summer, we swam in five icy pools, with one eye on the sky in case of a cloudburst, shook breadfruit out of trees, ate poi pancakes with tree-ripe bananas from our yard, dug an *imu* (pit) for a *luau* (barbecue party) of *kalua* pig, picked *opihi* (limpets) on the reef, hiked to the white cross on the hill, visited Lindbergh's grave, learned half a dozen old Hawaiian songs, made lei of flowers so big they looked unreal, attended Sunday services sung in Hawaiian, hiked to Red Sand beach, bodysurfed at Hamoa Bay, set reef nets at sunset and plunged into the sea at sunrise to pick *pupu* (appetizers) of bright, tropical fish, and, of course, shopped Hasegawa General Store.

It was the best of times in Hawaii, that summer in the 1970s in Hana. And, wonder of it all, three decades later, Hana remains this vestige of old Hawaii. Oh, there have been a few changes—Hasegawa's burned down and rose from the ashes at a new location. The Hana Hotel closed and reopened and closed and reopened. There's a paved parking lot at Kipahulu now, and by noon it resembles a rental-car lot. Wild pigs don't run across the road as often, but you can still buy those juicy mangoes for giveaway prices at roadside stands—and everyone smiles if you do. Life in Hana is still wonderful.

MOLOKAI: *Friendly Isle,* *Accidental Destination*

PEOPLE GO TO MOLOKAI to wrap themselves in its abundant, unencumbered nature and Hawaiian ways, or possibly by mistake, since the history of Molokai tourism seems to involve unintended, serendipitous discoveries. Among its first Western visitors were two daring airmen who flew from the Mainland bound for Honolulu, 26 more miles across the sea, and almost made it. When they ran out of fuel and crashed on Molokai, they discovered a gentle island, now somewhat lost from view compared to its neighbors. Look for the historic plaque along Kamehameha V Highway on the island's East End, denoting the 1927 Smith-Bronte flight. Molokai, content with relative obscurity, suffered tourism rather than sought it, and even in the face of spiraling welfare and agricultural setbacks, an antitourism contingent continues to fight any proposal that opens the island more. Formed by two volcanoes, the long, narrow island is the result of a merger that didn't quite work out. One side is hot, dry, and flat; the other is lush, green, and steeply peaked like Tahiti. It's a schizophrenic island that's always described in negatives: Molokai has no resorts (just a defunct one), no fancy restaurants, no stoplights, no malls or Golden Arches, and no buildings taller than a coconut tree. And many people feel that's all for the good, for less is more on Molokai, Hawaii's last raw outpost (if you don't count Niihau or Kahoolawe—and we don't). The simple life, wilderness beauty, and absence of contemporary American landmarks is what attracts those in search of the "real" Hawaii on the Friendly Isle. Although a distinctly unfriendly contingent recently caused the demise of the largest employer and landowner, 65,000-acre Molokai Ranch, and its excellent ecotourism facilities on the West End, the majority of the 7,000 residents display warm hospitality and a willingness to share their culture. One condo-hotel and a smattering of condos, cottages, and bed-and-breakfasts still welcome travelers, and a few activities devoted to visitors are interesting and different, such as the switchback mule ride down a steep sea cliff to a historic former leper colony at Kalaupapa.

For better or worse, Molokai, an island with a long tradition of sorcery that even modern people continue to mutter about, has avoided the usual definition of "progress." The island sustained devastating economic hits over recent decades—sugar and pineapple production ceased, residents snuffed new hotel and tourism proposals, federal agriculture officials killed all the cattle in the 1980s. The one resort, Kaluakoi Resort and golf course on the West End, closed, but new Molokai Ranch owners were working to reopen it. However, after cattle ranching and tourism operations had resumed

MOLOKAI FACTS

Flower: White kukui blossom	Width: 10 miles
Color: Green	Population: 7,404
Villages: Kaunakakai and Maunaloa	Highest Point: Kamakou Peak
Area: 260 square miles	(4,961 feet)
Length: 38 miles	Coastline: 88 miles

elsewhere on the huge ranch, a development squabble in 2008 triggered bankruptcy and even more unemployment. The ranch shut down its cattle operations, roster of rugged outdoor activities, beautiful upland visitor lodge and beach camping village, most facilities in the ranch town of Maunaloa, and efforts to reopen Kaluakoi.

Islanders continue to grow prized produce, such as watermelons, sweet potatoes, boutique miniature veggies, honey, coffee, and macadamia nuts. Molokai folks are country folks, uncommonly down-home and honest. Once we inadvertently left a usable airplane coupon ticket at the rental car counter in Molokai's tiny airport. Three days later, it was still there—not far from the sign reminding passengers not to place watermelons in the overhead racks.

The island is not a destination for everyone, especially those who crave creature comforts, of which there are just enough to be adequate. The beaches are wild and empty, but not generally safe or desirable for swimming. The greatest natural features, the world's tallest sea cliffs and the jungle valleys of the North Shore, are virtually inaccessible wilderness. The most famous, and poignant, attraction is **Kalaupapa National Historic Park,** where leprosy victims were banished by royal edict in the 1860s.

Adventurers who love the great outdoors: Molokai holds challenge for you. The Nature Conservancy runs preserves and hike programs at **Moomomi Dunes** and at **Kamakou** in the high cloud forest filled with rare native plants. Hikers have been known to trek through scenic **Halawa Valley** wilderness on the East End, although the ancient Hawaiian settlement was declared off-limits to visitors by the private owner. Ask locals about its status when you visit.

Sightseers find an odd assortment of natural and historic sites, such as ancient fishponds, **Mapalehu Mango Grove,** and **Iliiliopae Heiau,** temple ruins of an ancient school of sacrificial rites. The frontier-like town of **Kaunakakai** is a sleepy crossroad with a handful of stores and a celebrated bakery.

LANAI: *The Plantation Island*

SMALLEST AMONG THE MAIN ISLANDS, Lanai is a world removed. Your arrival at Lanai Airport after a short hop by air from Honolulu or Maui will prove it. The plane touches down in **Palawai Basin** on an empty, bright landscape of rusty earth and green scrub that truly looks like the middle of nowhere—no trees or buildings in sight except for the cheery little terminal, the state's newest. Then you are met by the unlikely sight of uniformed hotel staff who guide you to a shuttle bus and whisk your bags aboard for the short ride through fallow fields to your lodging. You hear echoes in your mind, "Da Plane! Da Plane!" But this fantasy island is real.

At your hotel, you are wrapped up in a Hawaiian welcome and presented with a glass of pressed pineapple cider. Soon you are itching to shed travel clothes, jet lag, and your adult years and get out there to discover freedom in this compact near-wilderness playground—on foot, horseback, golf cart, off-road four-wheel drive, rental car, resort shuttle, or boat. Unlike most destinations, there are few places here you cannot go, whether or not you use one of the three paved roads, and it's all within the secure confines of a nearly private island.

Lanai is no tropical wonderland; its deep gorges and eroded plains speak of a hard agricultural life. But there's beauty to its hinterlands, headlands, and wide-open red valley touched only by blue sky and puffy white clouds. While prowling the 100 miles of four-wheel roads, explorers can find historic sites like a crumbled sugar town, an ancient king's summer fishing residence, strange rock formations, and petroglyphs etched into lava rocks by ancient artists. On a clear day, from the **Lanaihale** summit, you can see most of the main Hawaiian islands. Hunters come to pursue wild (introduced) game: turkeys, pigs, mouflon sheep, and small axis deer, which outnumber people on this island.

Lanai, in Maui's rain shadow, is dry and hot around the lower edges but cool and misty on the slopes of 3,366-foot Lanaihale, thanks to an unlikely crown of tropical pines planted on the mountain ridge long ago to snag passing clouds and milk their moisture. The genius responsible for altering the climate was an early plantation manager, George Munro from New Zealand. The summit trail is named for him.

Lodging on the island is available at two fabulous luxury hotels, a charming old lodge, and a few rentals. If the sky's the limit, reserve a butlered suite. You'll find them at both **Four Seasons Lanai, Manele Bay** and **Four Seasons Lanai, Lodge at Koele.** As your personal concierges, butlers will ease your arrival and departure and greet you personally, make your reservations, bring you anything you like, take care of any wrinkles in your trip, and send you a good-bye note when you leave.

With access reined in by a history of insularity, luxury rates, and limited rooms, the island remains secluded. The people of Lanai still enjoy a quiet lifestyle that is rapidly vanishing throughout Hawaii. It is an island of anomalies, isolated and yet worldly. Former immigrant

LANAI FACTS	
Flower: Kaunaoa	Width: 13 miles
Color: Orange	Population: 3,164
Village: Lanai City	Highest Point: Lanaihale (3,366 feet)
Area: 141 square miles	Coastline: 47 miles
Length: 18 miles	

fieldhands who retrained as hotel workers and old Hawaiian families are neighbors now with celebrity travelers and wealthy residents who wanted to stay longer under their own tin roofs. It's red-dirt rural with a good supply of decent red wines. In former times, the days started with a plantation whistle before 5 a.m. Now, days in the sun begin with more discreet wake-up calls.

Shopping's a bit limited, but you can catch the Expeditions ferry over to Lahaina to shop and play. Nightlife is nonexistent except for evening entertainment performed by Island dancers and musicians in the hotels. A very few less-pricey alternatives exist for visitors, including the Hotel Lanai & Cottages, a historic 11-room lodge built in 1923, and some neighboring plantation houses and vacation rentals. Day-long snorkel-sail trips from Maui are a good way to see Lanai overland and underwater, without paying dinner prices for breakfast. Hats off to Lanai's new owners for figuring out how to turn its riffed, rutted, abandoned plantation roads into adventure trails for the gentry.

Hawaii's Privately Owned Islands

In Hawaii, where land is finite and costly, it may seem odd that any one person could own an island in the chain. Yet it is possible, because Hawaii once was a kingdom, and the king sold land (sometimes a whole island) when he needed cash. Most of Lanai and all of Niihau are privately owned, one by heirs of a New Zealand family, the other by a self-made California tycoon. Dry, barren Niihau, formerly known as the "forbidden" island because travel there was once prohibited, is owned by the Robinson family, who raise sheep and cattle and otherwise keep the island (and its Hawaiian-speaking residents) unchanged. No telephones, no jail, no paved roads, and no uninvited guests or tourists exist in Puuwai (population 226), the island's lone settlement. The Robinsons are descendants of Eliza Sinclair of New Zealand, who traded her piano and $10,000 in gold in 1864 to acquire the island from King Kalakaua. Her grandson, Charles Gay, paid $200,000 for Lanai in the late 1800s, but his farming enterprise failed.

Lanai was eventually sold to James Dole, who turned the island into the world's largest pineapple plantation. In the 1980s, entrepreneur

Lanai is perhaps most interesting because of its history of defeating nearly all who set foot on the island—early Polynesians, fierce Hawaiian kings, European explorers, even Mormons, among the most steadfast Pacific missionaries. Ancient Hawaiians believed Lanai was haunted by "spirits so wily and vicious that no human who went there could survive," according to Ruth Tabrah, author of the history *Lanai*.

In 1778, Big Island King Kalaniopuu invaded Lanai in "the war of loose bowels." His men slaughtered every warrior and set fire to everything except a bitter root that gave them dysentery. When, 14 years later, Captain George Vancouver sailed by what he wrongly termed "Ranai," he noted in his journal: "It seems thickly covered with shriveled grass in a scorched state." King Kamehameha the Great had a summer house on Lanai in the early 1800s, yet only stacked rocks remain. In 1802, Wu Tsin tried to harvest wild sugarcane on Lanai, but failed. New England missionaries arrived in 1820 and used Lanai as a prison for women convicted of adultery. Walter Murray Gibson looted the Mormon treasury, bought half the island, and founded a cult in 1866; it lasted three years. Charles Gay subsequently acquired 600 acres of Lanai at auction and planted pineapple; a three-year drought bankrupted him. Others tried cotton, sisal, sugar beets, a dairy, sheep, and pig farms. All failed.

Harry Baldwin, a missionary's grandson, may be the island's first success story. He bought Lanai for $588,000 in 1917, developed a 20-mile water pipeline, and five years later sold the island to Jim Dole for $1.1 million. Dole planted 18,000 acres of pineapple and enjoyed great success for a half century. However, even Dole was eventually vanquished; cheaper pineapple production in Asia ended Lanai's plantation heyday.

The island today might seem to be slipping back in time, resembling old photographs of itself in the glory days of Dole, except, of course, for two notable exceptions: A pair of hotels built for $400 million. The engines of Lanai's new tourism industry are so deliberately nostalgic they appear to have been here all along. Any minute now, you half expect to look up and see old Jim Dole himself rattling up the road in a Model T truck with a load of freshly picked pineapples. Only now there is a new lord of the manor, and his name is David Murdock. He gambled, successfully, that people like you would pay big bucks to visit his "private island." And, maybe while you are there, buy one of his $1 million vacation retreats, too.

David Murdock gained control of Dole Food Corporation in a merger acquisition, and he discovered that as majority stockholder he owned Lanai. He closed the moribund pineapple plantation and opened two ritzy resorts, moves that had been envisioned by his predecessors.

So, **HOW'S** *the* **WEATHER?**

MAUI ENJOYS ONE OF THE WORLD'S most agreeable climates. The norm is blue skies, trade winds, temperatures in the 70s and 80s, and almost 12 hours of daylight every day of the year. The reason is geographic. Maui sits in the middle of the Hawaiian chain, in the middle of the Pacific, 1,700 miles north of the equator and just inside the Tropic of Cancer (between 154° 40′ and 179° 25′ west longitude and 18° 54′ to 28° 15′ north latitude, to be precise).

Cold northeast winds, which propelled New England whalers and sailors to Lahaina from the West Coast and earned the name "trade winds," still sweep down the North Pacific, softening as the water warms, so that the tamed breezes arrive as natural air-conditioning. All islands have a cooler, wetter "windward" side, which receives the trades and their showers first, and a hotter, drier "leeward" side where the sun bakes the land. The line between is a northeast–southwest diagonal echoing the trade-wind flow.

On Maui, the hottest spot is Lahaina, named for its ovenlike heat. The coolest place on the resort coast is Kapalua, where the trades blow in directly. The coolest place of all is up—the higher the altitude, the lower the temperature. On Molokai, the East End gets the welcome showers to nourish its green landscape, while the West End is drier. Lanai, situated in the rain shadow of Haleakala, is lucky to get any rain.

Cooling trade winds are always welcome. But on the Island of Maui, they are often blustery, especially in the isthmus valley in the afternoons when they cause some bumpy rides for planes and on the windward northwest coast. Now and then, the winds die off in what is called *kona* (leeward) weather, hot and still and fretful, and the smudgy haze off the volcano, called "vog," creeps northward from the Big Island, obscuring the normally clear views.

Reflections on Water

We once spent a summer away from Hawaii, traveling in Asia, and what we came to miss most was not the singular beauty of the place, or the soft tropical air, but the water. It wasn't only the cobalt-blue Pacific Ocean surrounding the Islands that we missed, but rather the embracing wetness of the place. You might say we missed the climate, but our yearning went beyond that. We missed the waterfalls and the ceaseless waves, the light rain everyone calls a blessing, and the sudden summer squalls. We missed what Hawaiians call the *wai* (fresh water) and the *kai* (salt water). Sitting in Tokyo on a gray day that summer in Asia, we found ourselves dreaming of the soft, warm rain that drizzles down on Hana. We could close our eyes and see all the great bays (Kaneohe, Kailua, Mamala, Kealakekua, Hilo, and Hanalei) and the little pretty ones (Hanauma, Kahana, Hamoa,

Wailea, and Kapalua). Our eyes ached to see again the amazing variations on the color blue, from turquoise to deep purple, with shades of sapphire, cobalt, mulberry, and indigo for effect. We could almost feel the foggy dew of Manoa and the fine mist raised by Akaka Falls. We could hear the roar of North Shore surf in winter. We yearned to snorkel the green tidepools on Maui's black lava coast. Out there in Asia, it all seemed like a dream, and we suppose in a way it is. The wonderful waters of Hawaii—the wai and kai—are so otherworldly that we suspect they must be two of the essential elements of paradise.

Maui's year-round average temperature of 77°F is one of the most agreeable anywhere. The difference between winter and summer, and between night and day, is about 5 to 10°F on the islands' shorelines, with normal daytime highs in the 80s, although they can be lower in winter, when storms hide the sun, or rise into the low 90s in steamy August and September. Nights are in the 70s in summer and 60s in winter, with rare dips into the 50s. The rest of the thermometer seems superfluous, until you travel up. Temperatures drop as the altitude rises—about 3.5°F for every 1,000 feet, meteorologists estimate. Each of these islands has at least one mountain in the middle, so if the heat gets you down, rise up and cool off. You may need a jacket or sweater and a blanket at night at Kula, Maui, and Lanai City, Lanai, even in the warmer months. The weather atop Haleakala can be downright alpine; a winter dusting of snow is not unusual.

A word about showers: Don't worry too much about getting wet in the trade-wind showers that often blow through. It's just more of the natural air-conditioning system. If it rains while you're on the beach, jump in the water or get under a beach mat or Hobie Cat trampoline. The shower will probably be gone in a minute or two. With the ubiquitous Hawaiian "pineapple juice" showers that drift over while the sun shines brightly, everyone just gets wet one moment and dries off the next. Showers are considered blessings.

COLORFUL HISTORY

ONCE YOU TOUCH THE *aina* (land) of the Valley Isle, you will begin to see why more than 2 million people find their way here each year. It isn't only the sea breezes and golf greens that bring them back again. They come to roam the volcanic peaks, gaze at the spectacular scenery, and draft dream messages announcing they won't return as planned. A whole parade of adventurers, entrepreneurs, heroes, and scoundrels have done so throughout Island history. Since the Hawaiian Islands were settled in about AD 650 by Polynesian seafarers, all kinds of people have washed ashore.

Born of fire in the middle of the sea, the Island of Maui has a most interesting history, with tales of legendary gods, fierce kings, and fabled explorers, whalers, missionaries, sugar planters, immigrants, and travelers from around the world.

The island gets its name from the demigod Maui, a multitasking Polynesian superman.

The first Hawaiians most likely sailed to the Big Island from the Marquesas. Some later crossed the Alenuihaha Channel to Maui, where they settled coastal villages and farmed taro in narrow stream valleys like those at Iao and Kahakuloa. To worship their gods, they built *heiau* (temples), including the massive Piilani Hale, now the site of an archaeological dig on the Hana coast. They buried their dead in sand dunes in places like the Kapalua and Wailuku shores and held sacred the jumping-off places for the spirits of the deceased, like Black Rock on Kaanapali Beach. These adventurers from the South Pacific, seeing the Island of Molokai a short distance across the Pailolo Channel from northwest Maui, probably set sail for the island's calm south shore, where they built a complex of fishponds that still line the coast and constructed Iliiliopae Heiau, a kind of early university for sorcerers. Molokai gained a reputation for sorcery. According to some historians, Molokai was also the island where the Hawaiian dance was first performed on the summit of Mount Kaana, known today as "the birthplace of the hula."

Adventurers also wandered to neighboring Kahoolawe, which served as a prison for a time, and to Lanai, which gained a reputation of being haunted by cannibal spirits so fearsome no mortal man could survive a night there—until a brave prince proved them wrong. Bad spirits continued to plague the island. Lanai was the scene of one of the first and bloodiest battles in the royal effort to unify the islands into one kingdom in the late 1700s. Most of the residents were killed, and the island was burned by a raiding party from the Big Island that included the future king Kamehameha. The battle was decisive, and Lanai never quite recovered its Hawaiian populace or its original landscape.

CAPTAIN COOK AND LA PEROUSE

IN 1778, BRITISH EXPLORER JAMES COOK reported sighting Maui and Molokai but sailed on by, bound for the Big Island, where he was later killed. Cook's explorations inspired many others, including Jean-François de Galaup, known as Admiral La Perouse, the first recorded European to land on Maui. In 1785, the king of France commissioned La Perouse to head an expedition to explore Pacific whaling and fur prospects, map the islands more precisely, and establish French claims. With two ships, the *Astrolabe* and the *Boussole,* and a crew of 114, including scientists, draftsmen, naturalists, and a mathematician, La Perouse sighted the peak of Haleakala on the morning of May 28, 1786. As the French ships sailed past Maui, La Perouse was "enchanted by its beauty" and fascinated to find waterfalls and coastal villages of grass houses built in "the same shape as the thatched cottages found in certain parts of France."

"Imagine the feelings of the poor sailors, who, in this hot climate, had been reduced to a water ration of one bottle a day, when they saw the mountains clothed in vegetation, the homes surrounded by green banana trees," he added in his journal. But the surf was too strong to land, and they sailed on to a safe anchorage on "a shore made hideous by an ancient lava flow." That was the tip of South Maui, a place now known as La Perouse Bay.

> *When we were in sight of Maui about two hundred canoes came out from the shore to meet the frigates. All the canoes were loaded with pigs, fruits, and fresh vegetables which the natives conveyed to us on board and forced us to accept as gifts. The wind then became stronger and speeded us on our way, preventing us from further enjoying the picturesque view of the island and the great gathering of canoes, which as they moved about, provided us with the most exhilarating and exciting scenic spectacle imaginable.*

> —The Journal of Dr. Rollin, ship's surgeon aboard Boussole, *Voyages & Adventures of La Perouse,* 1786.

Now that Maui was on the map, the inevitable began to occur: Others found the island, including lusty New England whalers spoiling for shore liberty and, soon after, prim Boston missionaries. They found themselves at odds in, of all places, Lahaina.

In 1812, the first whalers sailed into Lahaina. They found eager women and ready grog, and their behavior gave Lahaina a wild reputation as word spread that there was "no God West of the Horn." Presumably, Pacific humpbacks they hunted elsewhere were right offshore breeding and raising their young and cruising as they do today, but it seems the whalers went to the strategic mid-Pacific stop for other reasons—to restock their ships and go ashore in search of rowdy times. They did, however, begin to kill whales in Maui waters, a practice that died off when the whales stopped coming around.

In the whalers' heyday, 1840 to 1860, several hundred whaling ships anchored in Lahaina Roads. The sailors preferred Lahaina to Honolulu because of its easy-access harbor, low fees, and, most of all, the warm embrace of the local folks. When 20 or more whaling ships dropped anchor at once and the whalers went ashore, the people of Lahaina prospered. The whaling era gave rise to tourism with all the usual good and bad results. Missionaries took a dim view of the whalers' onshore diversions, which involved alcohol, gambling, and sexual excess.

Thriving Lahaina became the royal capital of the Hawaiian kingdom in 1840, only to surrender political clout to Honolulu four years later. In 1871, whaling was halted by the discovery of petroleum oil in Pennsylvania. Whale oil for lamps became obsolete. Lahaina, once the wealthy port of call, dozed in the hot sun, safe in the hands of Bible-toting missionaries. The now-civilized seaport began to trade with merchant ships. The missionaries stayed on and acquired land and power.

Maui is very foreign and civilized, and although it has a native population of over 12,000, the natives are much crowded on plantations, and one encounters little of native life.

—Isabella L. Bird, *Six Weeks in the Sandwich Islands*

Kalaupapa's Sad Legacy

Over on Molokai, authorities conducted a forced immigration to remote Kalaupapa Peninsula, 5,000 acres at the foot of imposing sea cliffs that served as a natural prison for victims of leprosy. The only ways in or out of Kalaupapa were by sea or on foot, via the three-mile trail down a 1,664-foot cliff with 26 switchbacks—still one of the most spectacular, if daunting, hikes in the Pacific. Leprosy victims were hunted throughout the Islands, rounded up, and exiled to live and die on Kalaupapa. Some 800 sufferers were there in 1873 when a Belgian priest, Father Damien de Veuster, was dispatched to tend to the ailing souls. He stayed until his own death on April 15, 1889, after he contracted the disease. Leprosy, or Hansen's disease, was eradicated decades ago with sulfa drugs, and Kalaupapa is now a lonely National Historical Park. Father Damien is currently a candidate for sainthood.

SWEET SUCCESS

IN 1876, A GERMAN IMMIGRANT named Claus Spreckels arrived on Maui from San Francisco and changed life on the island. He became pals with King Kalakaua, bribed him with $10,000 cash, loaned him $40,000, plied him with champagne, and acquired vast tracts of

Maui. He irrigated the land, planted it with sugarcane, and made a fortune refining the sugar in California.

"Never in the history of the Hawaiian kingdom had money been used to procure official favors from the king," according to Ralph Kuykendall, author of *The Hawaiian Kingdom*. The idea of "owning" land was a Western concept, not understood by Hawaiians until foreigners introduced it to the royalty earlier in the 1800s. Hawaiians' family-held lands, uncertain in title and boundaries, were often simply taken by the enterprising foreigners to amass the acres needed for sugar plantations.

Not enough Hawaiians could be found to tend the sugar, so owners like Spreckels imported immigrants from Japan and China, and later Korea, the Philippines, Portugal, Puerto Rico, and other areas of Europe and Asia, who worked cutting and hauling cane for a pittance and a home. They lived on plantations, tied to the company house and the company store in a kind of contracted servitude. Samuel Alexander and Harry Baldwin, descendants of New England missionaries, later acquired the Spreckels plantations and pioneered an island company that continues today.

Sugar governed the Hawaiian economy from the 1860s to the 1980s, with Wailuku and Paia/Makawao among the major centers. Life was sweet, and sugar was king of the Hawaiian economy, drawing thousands of immigrants who saw it as a way to escape harsh conditions in their homeland and seek a new life. As soon as many of them could work off their debt, they started to leave the plantations and pursue their fortunes in other endeavors. Other nationalities were recruited to take their place.

In another, perhaps more surprising, saga of royal patronage with a sugary episode, the arid Island of Lanai passed from the pocket of one foreign lord after another through history and is still largely owned by one man's company. It may seem odd that a private owner could control a whole island in the chain. But when the Islands were a kingdom, the king sold land when he needed cash. In 1864, New Zealander Eliza Sinclair traded her piano and $10,000 in gold to acquire the Island of Niihau from King Kalakaua. (She decided not to purchase Waikiki, then a mosquito-choked swamp.) Then in the late 1800s, her grandson, Charles Gay, paid $200,000 for Lanai. But his farming enterprise there failed, as had cultivation attempts 30 years prior by Mormons, who came to the island in the 1850s but were thwarted by insects and droughts. Lanai eventually was sold to a young American named James Dole, who dug into the rich red dirt and, in a sense, struck gold.

Dole turned the island into the world's largest pineapple plantation, some 20,000 acres fenced by an ocean, featuring the golden fruit that became Hawaii's icon. But competition from other nations' pineapples eroded the market, and Lanai's influence dwindled.

In the 1980s, Southern California entrepreneur David Murdock gained control of Dole Food Corporation—and discovered that as majority stockholder, he owned the Island of Lanai. He closed the pineapple operations, an institution for 65 years, recycled Filipino fieldhands into chambermaids and waiters, and opened two swanky resorts, now the Four Seasons Resort Lanai, Lodge at Koele and Four Seasons Resort Lanai, Manele Bay, with two equally remarkable golf courses. He built new tracts of million-dollar estates and began cultivating well-heeled tourists. Microsoft billionaire Bill Gates got married on Lanai; Oprah Winfrey stayed a week with her personal fitness trainer and hairdresser in adjoining private suites.

I have visited Haleakala, Kilauea, Wailuku Valley—in a word, I have visited all the principal wonders of the Island, and now I come to speak of one which, in its importance to America, surpasses them all. A land which produces six, eight, ten, twelve, yea, even thirteen thousand pounds of sugar to the acre on unmanured soil! There are precious few acres of unmanured ground in Louisiana— none at all, perhaps—which yield 2,500 pounds of sugar; there is not an unmanured acre under cultivation in the Sandwich Islands which yields less. This country is the king of the sugar world as far as astonishing productiveness is concerned.

—Mark Twain, September 10, 1866

WARTIMES

THE AMERICAN CIVIL WAR OFFICIALLY ended in 1866. Meanwhile in Hawaii, sugar mills began to falter, but the industry stumbled on, through crippling strikes and the rise of competing imported sugar at cheaper prices. Eventually, the plantations closed on several islands, ending a way of life that created the Hawaii of today in several ways. However, Maui's cane fields are still producing and being harvested, even after those of other islands long since went fallow or became housing tracts. Above Kapalua Resort, Maui pineapples are still harvested as well.

When the Japanese attacked Pearl Harbor on Oahu in 1941, Maui County turned out the lights and pulled down the blinds. All islands were placed under martial law, and blackouts were mandatory so the enemy could find no easy targets. Many Japanese Americans on Maui volunteered for army duty and served heroically in Europe and the Pacific. On the day after the Pearl Harbor attack, the U.S. Navy began dropping bombs on Kahoolawe, across the Alalakeiki Channel from South Maui. (Target practice continued into the mid-1990s, when President George H. W. Bush finally stopped it.)

Maui became a major training ground for jungle fighters during the war. Thousands of American troops came to Maui, marching off navy ships to prepare to fight the bloody battle of Okinawa in

April 1945. Maui boomed while the troops bivouacked, but when World War II ended and the military camps closed, the island economy sank. Many postwar Mauians left the island to seek jobs on the West Coast.

But in 1946, a new wave of people flooded the Islands: the last major immigration of 6,000 new plantation workers came from the Philippines aboard the SS *Maunawili,* a converted U.S. troopship. They were brought in from Ilocos Sur by the Hawaii Planters Society to work the cane fields of Maui and other islands. It was an effort to bring the fields back to life. Immigrants from Japan and China had been outlawed, and would-be recruits from Korea, Puerto Rico, Spain, Portugal, and other European countries were too scarce. Filipino plantation workers went to all the islands, including Lanai in more recent times.

The Hawaiian Islands boomed again as an R&R destination for Vietnam warriors and their wives and sweethearts. Tour buses began to rumble on island roads, and jets brought in a new age of tourism. While condos began to sprout all along Kihei's scalloped beaches, a group of West Maui sugar planters decided to devote a chunk of unprofitable coastal scrub land to create Hawaii's first master-planned resort, Kaanapali Beach Resort. They drew up plans for golf courses, shops, lodging, and restaurants, all along a picturesque beach. First came the Royal Lahaina in 1962. In 1963, the Sheraton Maui opened as the first luxury hotel on Maui, on the very site where Maui's King Kahekili took daredevil leaps off *kapu* (forbidden) Puu Kekaa (Black Rock) almost two centuries prior. As more and bigger chain resort hotels, like Marriott, Hyatt, and Westin, opened on Kaanapali Beach, Maui began to entertain a new breed of visitor who spent small fortunes in upscale fantasy resorts full of exotic macaws, parrots, and swans.

▌ GOLDEN PEOPLE

ONE OUTSTANDING FEATURE OF HAWAII is the diversity of its people. Throughout the 50th state, no ethnic group comprises a majority of the population. People who declare themselves of mixed race are the largest group, followed by Caucasians, Japanese, and Filipinos. Pure Hawaiians are in short supply, but part-Hawaiian heritage is shared by many.

Each ethnic group has made its mark on Island culture, contributing foods, arts, music, and customs to Hawaii's melting-pot community.

The Chinese were the first immigrants. More than 200 workers from southeastern China came to the Islands in the mid-19th century after signing five-year contracts to work the sugar plantations.

These laborers were provided food, clothing, shelter, and a salary of $3 a month. Most of the Maui Chinese lived in Lahaina.

The first Japanese immigrants arrived in 1868. By the beginning of the 20th century, more than 60,000 Japanese laborers and their families lived in Hawaii. Like all immigrants, Japanese faced racial prejudices, but far more so after Japan's attack on Pearl Harbor. Many Japanese Americans were taken away to internment camps on the Mainland, and many more lost their family businesses, even though not a single case of Japanese American treason or sabotage was ever documented. But they rebounded strongly in Hawaii after the war, gained prominence in politics and education, and integrated Japanese customs and design into everyday life. Today, Japanese Americans are a major presence in Hawaii, and most residents embrace at least a degree of Japanese custom, including removing shoes before entering a home. Rice, sushi, sashimi, *mochi,* and miso soup are staples at the Hawaii local table.

In 1903, the first Koreans arrived to work on the plantations. Ambitious and hardworking, Koreans have the highest education and income level per capita of any ethnic group in the Islands.

A group of 15 Filipino laborers began working on Island plantations in 1906; by mid-century, that number had swelled to 125,000. Every summer, the Filipina Fiesta festivals held throughout the state celebrate the colorful traditions and customs of the Filipino culture. Dishes such as chicken adobo, *pancit,* and *lumpia* are favorites on any local menu.

Later immigrants included Southeast Asians, some of them refugees of the Vietnam War, and Pacific Islanders from throughout Polynesia, mostly Tonga and Samoa.

Endangered Species

Hawaiians are a vanishing minority in their own land. When Cook "discovered" Hawaii in 1778, the native population was estimated at 20,000 to 30,000, although some historians believe the population may have reached 800,000. Today, there are fewer than 8,000 pure Hawaiians left. Diseases brought by foreigners, destruction of habitat, broken spirit, and changing times contributed to the decline. Reflecting the plantation immigrations of the past, the resident population of Hawaii today is a cosmopolitan cultural mix of Pacific Islander, Portuguese and other Caucasian, Japanese, Filipino, Chinese, Korean, and Southeast Asian. No one race achieves a majority rank. Most modern Hawaii natives are *hapa*—half Hawaiian and half Caucasian or something else—or, more often, a sum of many racial ingredients. It's a heritage often referred to locally as "chop suey." Many Hawaii residents believe the most important contribution the Islands make to humankind is not the promise of unparalleled vacation beaches but the reality of a multiracial culture where, by and large, people get along.

THINGS *the* LOCALS
Already KNOW

THE LEI TRADITION

A HAWAIIAN FLOWER LEI IS ONE of the most extravagant presents in the world. Some leis take more than a thousand flowers and quite a bit of time and artistry to make. They fade and perish within hours or days of their creation. Often they are worn only once.

Lei giving is one of the most colorful traditions in Hawaii. You'll see it first at the airport. But it isn't an embarrassing designation of a newly arrived tourist. Lei is a sign of honor for a family member, friend, or special guest of either gender.

Having a garland placed around your neck is a special welcome, farewell, or congratulations, usually followed by a hug or kiss on the cheek, especially if you know the donor. A lei greeting remains Hawaii's most tangible expression of aloha. Local tradition is to drape loved ones up to their noses with leis at graduations; they are also given for anniversaries, birthdays, and other special celebrations. They're great icebreakers with local strangers who want to admire the lei and congratulate you on your special occasion. It's also customary to share the lei around after you wear it for a while (take it off and give it to someone else to wear).

Hawaiian language advisory: The word *lei* is singular and plural; there is no "s" in the Hawaiian language.

The tradition of lei giving may have originated with Hawaii's earliest settlers, who brought flowering plants to use for adornment. Early Hawaiians offered lei to their gods during religious ceremonies.

Today, long lei are also draped over the statues or images of important people in Hawaiian history, or over the bows of victorious racing canoes, or on anything worthy of commemoration. Each June, the King Kamehameha Day celebration kicks off with a colorful lei-draping ceremony at the King Kamehameha statue in downtown Honolulu.

Writer-poet Don Blanding initiated Lei Day, a May 1 celebration held since 1928. The biggest event is held at Kapiolani Park in Waikiki, where floral creations by the state's top lei makers are displayed.

Before World War II, I never saw lei presented to all and sundry accompanied by a kiss. True, our greeting was the honi, kiss, almost like the hongi of the Maoris of New Zealand, but we did not greet everybody that way with a lei—and so I wondered how a kiss with lei giving began. One day, I wondered out loud at the Waikiki Camouflage Unit where I worked shortly after the beginning of World War II. A worker, who was a cutter in the Camouflage Unit by day and a USO entertainer at night, heard me and laughed. She then told me that while entertaining one evening, her fellow musicians dared her to kiss a homely officer sitting nearby. She could not just barge up to kiss him, so she sat thinking a while until an idea came. When there was a little recess, she walked up to him, removed her lei, placed it on his shoulder, and said loud enough for those about to hear, "This is a Hawaiian custom," and implanted a kiss upon the man's cheek. Thus a neo-Hawaiian custom was born.

—Mary Kawena Pukui, *Aspects of the Word Lei: Directions in Pacific Traditional Literature* (Bishop Museum Press)

Fresh-flower lei can be purchased throughout Hawaii, at every major airport and many supermarkets as well as florists. Home style is to make your own, and many families still do. You'll find lei made of all kinds of flowers, including plumeria, gardenias, ginger, orchids, pakalana, roses, ilima, and carnations, as well as fragrant maile leaves, braids of ti leaves, kukui nuts, seashells, flowers made of dollar bills, and, for the kids back home, even candy and gum.

Lei costs range from a few dollars for a simple crown flower or sweet-smelling tuberose lei to $40 for an intricately crafted rope lei. One of the most popular new lei is the cristina, an expertly sewn garland made of purple dendrobium orchids ($25 to $30).

Often people try to keep a lei alive by refrigerating it. Here's another suggestion: Drape it over a doorknob or lampshade in your hotel room or some other place where it cheers you to see the flowers and smell the fragrance.

A Tip about Tipping

Many service workers in Hawaii depend on tips for their living. At the airport, tip a porter at least two dollars per bag. Taxi drivers receive a 15 percent tip of the total fare plus 25¢ per bag or parcel. At the hotel, tip the bellhop $5 for transporting your luggage to and from your room, and give the parking valet a couple of dollars. Tip your room housekeeper a dollar or two for each day of your stay. For dining, tip 18 to 20 percent of the bill.

LOCAL CUSTOMS AND PROTOCOL

- When going to the *lua* (restroom) make sure you know the difference between *kane* (man) and *wahine* (woman), since many restrooms are only identified in Hawaiian.

- Here's a sign of friendship: Close your middle three fingers of either hand while keeping your thumb and pinky finger fully extended. Shake your hand a few times in the air. That's the *shaka*, a gesture expressing acknowledgment, goodwill, or appreciation, suitably made to children and adults. That, and maybe the universal thumbs-up, are the only finger signals we suggest you make.

- Technically speaking, Fridays are Aloha Friday throughout Hawaii and in the Maui Islands, a tradition like casual Fridays on the Mainland except it calls for wearing aloha shirts and muumuu or other colorful Island wear. But actually, on rural islands where shorts and sandals are de rigueur, aloha wear is dressing up. Many invitations to weddings and other events call for "aloha attire" or even sometimes "evening aloha attire." It's what to wear to the luau, along with flowers in your hair. Women, if you don't have a muumuu or plan to buy one, that colorful pareo (sarong-like wrap) makes a great aloha skirt. If you can't get a plumeria or other small flower to stay in your hair, try sticking a toothpick down the throat of it and pinning or placing the toothpick base. The first aloha shirt was sold in the mid-1930s in Honolulu, where boys wore shirts made from Japanese prints, and the idea caught on. The origin of the muumuu traces to missionary days when the missionary wives sewed "Mother Hubbard" nightgowns to hide the bodies of half-dressed Hawaiian women.

- If you are invited to a *kamaaina* (local) home, remember to bring a small gift and, in most cases, remove your shoes before entering the house. The tangle of loose shoes in front of the door is your first clue.

- Local people of all kinds share a deep reverence for the *aina* (land), although all that litter along Hawaii's roads can't be from visitors alone. This is a beautiful place that deserves respect. Please don't trash it.

STATE HOLIDAYS

IN ADDITION TO ALL MAJOR U.S. HOLIDAYS, Hawaii celebrates three state holidays.

- **Kuhio Day** (March 26). This holiday honors Prince Jonah Kuhio Kalanianaole (1871–1922), a statesman and member of the royal family who served in the U.S. Congress in the early 1900s.

- **King Kamehameha Day** (June 11). Hawaii's great king, Kamehameha I, united the islands into a kingdom under one rule. An imposing figure (some reported him as tall as eight feet), the Big Island–born monarch died in May 1819, when he was believed to be in his early 60s, and his bones were hidden at a secret location, perhaps on the Kona Coast. Modern islanders celebrate the life of Kamehameha with colorful festivities, including lei-draping ceremonies, parades, and *ho'olaule'a* (public parties).

- **Admission Day** (third Friday in August). On August 21, 1959, U.S. President Dwight D. Eisenhower signed the proclamation welcoming Hawaii as the 50th state, following a long, often emotional campaign for statehood that originated more than a century earlier. Many expected Hawaii to be named the 49th state, but that distinction went to Alaska in 1958. Today, "Hawaii—49th State" memorabilia, ranging from record labels to buttons, is highly prized by collectors.

You may not know a papaya from a *puakenikeni* (one's a juicy fruit, the other's a sweet-smelling South Pacific flower), but everybody knows these Hawaiian words and expressions. Test your vocabulary here:

Aloha (ah-low-hah) noun, verb: All-purpose Hawaiian word: "hello," "good-bye," "I love you." Not to be shouted like a tour-bus driver, but said softly with feeling.

Mahalo (mah-haw-low) noun, verb: Appreciative Hawaiian remark: "thanks," "thank you." *Mahalo nui loa* means "thank you very much."

Ohana (oh-hah-na) noun: Old Hawaiian for "family" or "kin group," "da gang."

Keiki (kay-kee) noun: Old Hawaiian word meaning "child," "offshoot," "young-ster," "tot," "little one." *Keiki o ka aina* literally means "a child of the island."

Mele (mehl-lay) noun: Old Hawaiian for "song," "anthem," or "chant." Also "merry," as in Mele Kalikimaka, "Merry Christmas."

Talk story (tawk sto-ree) noun, verb: Pidgin expression for storytelling, the oral tradition of Polynesia. "Let's talk story."

Kaukau (cow-cow) noun: Food, though often referred to more specifically using *ono, grinds,* or *pupu.* **Ono** (oh-no) is a Hawaiian/pidgin hybrid, adjective or noun meaning "good" or "good food." Ono appears on local menus as "onolicious," Hawaiian/*haole* for "real good." **Grinds** (grines) means "meal," "entree," "breakfast," "plate lunch," or any dinner less than a luau. Derived from the act of mastication, chewing, or grinding food. "Dis mahi ono grinds, brah." **Pupu** (poo-poo) means "finger food," "snacks," "small bites of kaukau"—Hawaiian for "hors d'oeuvres." *Plenny* pupu may amount to grinds, but grinds typically is *moah* kaukau than pupu.

Alii (ah-lee-ee) noun: Old Hawaiian for "king," "monarch," "chief," or "com-mander." Also means *haimaukamauka–kine folks,* or "uncommon people."

Kupuna (coo-poo-nah) noun: Old Hawaiian for "grandparent," "ancestor," "elder." Like **tutu** (too-too), or one who's supposed to know all the answers.

Kane/wahine (kah-nay/vah-hee-nay) nouns: Old Hawaiian terms for "male" and "female," respectively, often seen on public bathroom signs. If you don't know the difference by now, *plenny pilikia,* but that's one 'nother story, brah.

All pau, now. Live aloha. For more information and definitions, see *The Hawaiian Dictionary,* by Mary Kawena Pukui and Samuel H. Elbert.

A WORD ABOUT DIRECTIONS

WE TRY TO ORIENT YOU SOMEWHAT with the familiar directions of north, east, south, and west. But these words won't be terribly helpful in Hawaii. Local usage has little to do with the compass. The words you want to know are *ma uka* (uphill, inland, toward the mountains) and *ma kai* (toward the sea). The other directions are identified by a bewildering variety of local landmarks.

SAYING IT *in* HAWAIIAN

IN HAWAII, ENGLISH AND HAWAIIAN are both official languages. The Hawaiian alphabet has only 12 letters—the vowels *a*, *e*, *i*, *o*, and *u* and the consonants *h*, *k*, *l*, *m*, *n*, *p*, and *w*. A diacritical mark called the *okina*, pronounced as a glottal stop, is almost as vital as a letter, so that those vowels can do extra duty. The language takes practice and patience. The most authoritative Hawaiian language book is the *Hawaiian Dictionary*, by Mary Kawena Pukui and Samuel H. Elbert.

Here are some general rules of thumb for you to remember:

- Vowels are pronounced this way: *a* as "uh," as in "lava"; *e* as "ay," as in "hay"; *i* as "ee," as in "fee"; *o* as "oh," as in "low"; and *u* as "oo," as in "moon."

- All consonants are pronounced as in English except for w, which is usually pronounced as "v" when it follows an *i* or *e*. Example: Ewa Beach is pronounced as "Eva" Beach. When following a *u* or *o*, *w* is pronounced as "w." When it is the first letter in the word or follows an a, there is no designated rule, so the pronunciation follows custom. Which means *Hawaii* and *Havaii* are both acceptable.

- Some vowels are slurred together in a diphthong, forming single sounds. Examples: ai as in "Waikiki," au as in "mauka," ei as in "lei," oi as in "poi," ou as an "kou," and ao as in "haole."

- Some are separated by a glottal stop, or *okina,* an upside-down and backward apostrophe that emphasizes a separate vowel sound, acting like another consonant, and keeps identically spelled words from being confused. For instance, *pau* means "finished," but *pa'u* is a skirt worn by women horseback riders. *Pau* is pronounced as "pow," and *pa'u* is pronounced as "pah-oo."

- A macron, or *kahako*, designates a long vowel. A macron is marked as a line directly over the vowel. Logically enough, long vowels last longer than regular vowels. The macron, however, is used less frequently than the okina, in part because it isn't as often needed to distinguish between words. This book, like most English publications from Hawaii, excludes macrons. However, don't be surprised if you see them over the *i*s in Waikiki. They indicate that the word is correctly sounded "why-kee-kee" rather than "why-kiki."

- Every Hawaiian syllable ends with a vowel. Thus, every Hawaiian word ends with a vowel. Therefore, the word *Hawaiian* isn't a Hawaiian word.

- If a word contains no macrons, the accent usually falls on the next-to-last syllable. Examples: a-LO-ha, ma-HA-lo, ma-li-HI-ni, and o-HA-na.

PIDGIN

YOU MAY HEAR PEOPLE TALKING in what sounds like abbreviated English, except that it's more colorful. Hawaii-style pidgin, the local patois, is the third language of the Islands. It combines words and syntax of several languages and was developed so that multicultural plantation people could communicate. Although it is a true creole language and not simply slang, it's definitely not an official tongue.

> *The term aloha used either in music, poetry, or social behavior, is regarded as, perhaps, the singularly most important word in Hawaii today. The idea of love, affection, openness, generosity—all connoted by the term—is most readily associated with Hawaiians; that is, ethnic Hawaiians and their culture, of which the songs of aloha are a part.*

> —George Kanahele, *Hawaiian Music and Musicians;*
> *An Illustrated History*

The pros and cons of pidgin have long been debated by local educators and cultural experts. Some say that the practice should not be encouraged because it is not an acceptable manner of speech, whereas others insist that pidgin is a treasured cultural asset that should not be looked down on. In Hawaii, it's not uncommon for a kamaaina to speak perfect English in an office setting, then pick up the phone and speak pidgin to a friend. Following are some commonly used pidgin words and phrases you might hear during your stay.

TWENTY WORDS EVERY HAWAII VISITOR SHOULD KNOW

IF YOU CAN PRONOUNCE "AIEA," "KEEAUMOKU," and "Anaehoomalu" correctly and know "hapa" from "hapai," then you are *akamai,* brah. No need to read da kine. If you no can understand a word up there, mo bettah you read da kine.

Da kine is one of 20 words or phrases every Hawaii visitor should know. So are *akamai* and *pau.* When you go pau reading da kine, you will be akamai, li'dat.

Welcome to Hawaii, the linguistically rich and confusing Islands with not one but two official languages—Hawaiian and English— where the 12-letter alphabet has 7 consonants and 5 vowels, and everybody speaks a little pidgin. No other archipelago has such an eclectic array of words that look and sound so foreign. You probably can get by with a now-and-then "aloha" and a mumbled "mahalo," but to understand what's really going on in Hawaii, you need to know a few basic words like *da kine, howzit,* and *mo bettah.*

Everyone knows *wahine* from *kane* and *mauka* from *makai,* but what about *akamai, kokua,* and *holoholo*? Most *haoles* (that's you, *seestah* and *bruddah*) have trouble saying Hawaiian words because they are repetitive, have too many vowels, and look like the bottom line of an eye chart, e.g.: Kaaawa, Kuliouou, and Napoopoo. A good example of all the above is *humhumunukunukapuaa,* the state fish. To haole eyes, honed on brittle consonants, Hawaiian looks impossible. Once spoken, the way Hawaiian was intended, the soft, round, soothing vowels are music to your ears.

Banned by New England missionaries, who crudely translated into English what they thought they heard, the native tongue survived underground to carry a nation's culture down through generations in warrior chants, hula lyrics, and talk story. And then there is pidgin, the local patois originated by Chinese immigrants to do business with an easy-to-understand lingo. The root word of "pidgin" is, in fact, "business." A caveat: Before you go to Hawaii and put your foot in your mouth, it's probably a good idea to clip and save this lexicon for future review. Or, as any local might put it: Good t'ing, brush up on da kine, brah, so no make A.

Here are 20 words, common in everyday Hawaiian usage, that you should know. Fo' real. They'll also help you make sense of the passage above.

1. **kokua** (ko-coo-ah) *verb, noun:* Help, as in help, assist, (please kokua), or contribute (kokua luau), a gentle reminder. "Your kokua is appreciated."

2. **pau** (pow) *noun:* All gone, no more, time's up. Used every Friday (when you go pau hana), finish work, when you finish kaukau ("All pau"), when your car or other mechanical object breaks down ("Eh, dis buggah pau"). Not to be confused with make (mah-kay), which means dead, a permanent form of pau.

3. **malihini** (mah-ly-hee-nee) *noun:* Nonderisive old Hawaiian word, meaning the opposite of kamaaina, or local. If first time come Hawaii, that's you, brah: a stranger, tourist, someone who wears socks and shoes instead of rubbah slippahs and eats rice with a fork, not chopsticks. You remain a malihini until you use "used to be" landmarks as directional aids.

4. **mo bettah** (mow bedder) *adjective:* A contemporary pidgin self-descriptive term meaning excellent, outstanding, the best. Often used for comparison of ideas, objects, or places, as in "Dis beach mo bettah." Sometimes spelled "moah bettah."

5. **no ka oi** (nok caw oy) Hawaiian phrase, a sequence of words that serves as an appositive, can only follow nouns as in "Maui no ka oi" (Maui is the best), a superlative expression, bragging rights, the best, similar to mo bettah.

6. **hana hou** (hah-nah ho) *interjection:* Hawaiian expression of joy, a cry for more, the local equivalent of "encore." Most often heard at music concerts after Auntie Genoa Keawe sings.

7. **to da max** (to dah macks) *interjection:* Pidgin expression of boundless enthusiasm, meaning no limits, to the moon, give it your all, knock yourself out. Also, the partial title of a popular book, *Pidgin to da Max* by Douglas Simonson, Ken Sakata, and Pat Sasaki.

Commonly Used Hawaiian Words and Phrases

aina Land, earth

aloha Love, kindness, or goodwill; can be used as a greeting or farewell

e komo mai Welcome!

hale House

hana hou Do again, repeat, or encore

haole Formerly any foreigner; now primarily anyone of Caucasian ancestry

holoholo To go out for a walk, ride, or other activity

hoolaulea A big party or celebration

hooponopono To correct or rectify a situation

ikaika Strong, powerful

ilima A native shrub bearing bright yellow or orange flowers; used for lei

kahuna Priest, minister, expert

kala Money

kamaaina Native-born or longtime Island resident

kanaka Person, individual

kane Male, husband, man

kapu Taboo

keiki Child

kohola Humpback whale

kokua Help, assistance, cooperation

kolohe Mischievous, naughty; a rascal

kupuna Grandparent

kuuipo My sweetheart

8. **akamai** (ah-kah-my) *noun, adjective:* Smart, clever, locally correct in thought, common sense as opposed to intelligence, or school smarts. "Many are smart but few are akamai." Also the name of a high-tech Mainland computer outfit.

9. **chance 'em** (chants em) *verb:* Take a chance, go for it, try. Also a rally cry. Often heard in Las Vegas at blackjack tables and in Aloha Stadium late in the fourth quarter when the Warriors are behind. "Fourth and inches on the five. Coach June Jones says, 'Chance 'em.'"

10. **chicken skin** (chee-kin skeen) *noun:* Descriptive pidgin term, the local version of goose bumps, for a frisson or shiver of excitement. Also the title of best-selling local spooky book by favorite author. "Oh, dat spooky kine stuff gives me chicken skin."

lanai Porch, verandah

lua Toilet, bathroom

luau A Hawaiian feast

luna Foreman, boss, leader

mahalo Thank you

makahiki Ancient Hawaiian harvest festival with sports and religious activities

makai Toward the ocean; used in directions

malihini Newcomer

mana Spiritual power

mauka Inland direction, toward the mountain

me ke aloha With warm regards pumehana

mele Song

Menehune Legendary small people who worked at night, building fish-ponds, roads, and temples; according to legend, if the work was not completed in one night, it was left unfinished.

muumuu Loose-fitting Hawaiian gown

ohana Family

ono Delicious

pau Finished, done

pupu Hors d'oeuvre, appetizer

tutu Grandmother

wahine Female, wife, woman

11. **laters** (lay-derz) *noun:* Salutatory remark, often substituted for "good-bye," pidgin for see you later, *sayonara,* adios, after while crocodile.

12. **howzit?** (house it) *interjection:* A greeting, always a question, friendly contraction of "How is it?" The inquiry is directed at your state of mind at the time. The preferred response is, "It's good, brah!" Or maybe, "I'm feeling junk" (pidgin for "poorly").

13. **shaka brah** (shah-kah brah) *interjection, noun:* A contemporary pidgin phrase similar to "hang loose," used as a casual form of agreement that everything is cool. The first word, *shaka,* refers to a hand signal made with thumb and pinkie extended, index, middle, and ring fingers closed, and a brisk horizontal flip of the wrist. This public sign that all is well often follows the phrase "life is good, brah," and is seen nightly on local TV news sign-off. The second word, *brah,* is a truncation of *brother.*

Commonly Used Pidgin Words and Phrases

an den?	So? And then?
bra	Brother or friend, short for "braddah"
bumbye	Do it later
bummahs!	That's unfortunate!
da kine	The kind of, that thing
fo real?	Really?
garans	Guaranteed
geev um!	Go for it!
go fo broke	Give it your all (famous motto of the 442nd Battalion in WWII)
how you figgah?	How do you think that happened?
howzit!	How are you?
laytahs	See you later
lidat	Like that
minahs	Minor; no problem; don't worry about it
mo bettah	Better
no shame	Don't be shy or embarrassed!
nuff already!	That's enough!
shaka	Greetings; good job; thank you
small keed time	Childhood
soah?	Does it hurt?
stink eye	Disapproving glance, a dirty look
talk story	Converse, talk, or gossip
tanks, eh?	Thank you
whatevahs	Whatever
who dat?	Who is that?
yeah, no?	That's right!

14. **holoholo** (hoe-low-hoe-low) *verb:* An old Hawaiian word meaning to go out for pleasure on foot or in a car or boat, a stroll to check things out, with emphasis on going out for fun. Not to be confused with similar sounding *halohalo* (hah-low-hah-low), the classic Philippine dessert made with ice cream and chopped fruit.

15. **wikiwiki** (wee-key-wee-key) *adjective, noun:* An old Hawaiian word and the name of the Honolulu International Airport shuttle bus, originally meaning to go fast, move rapidly, hurry (a concept missing on the islands

of Molokai and Lanai). Not to be confused with hele (hell-lay), which means to go, or let's go, as in "Hele on."

16. **mauka/makai** (mao-cah/mah-kigh) *noun:* Two of the four key directions on Oahu, *mauka* and *makai* are used on all Hawaiian Islands. *Mauka* means inland or toward the mountain, and makai means toward the ocean. Other Oahu directions are Ewa (eh-vah) and Diamond Head (die-mohn hed), meaning toward the Ewa plain or Waikiki's famous crater, known in Hawaiian as *Leahi* (lay-ah-hee) or tuna brow. On Maui, Upcountry same t'ing mauka, brah.

17. **kapu** (kah-poo) *noun:* An old Hawaiian word meaning taboo, off limits, no trespassing, keep out, forbidden, sacred. Often seen on signs in high-crime areas, danger spots, and geothermal plants.

18. **hapa-haole** (hah-pa-howl-ee) *noun, adjective:* If you're not *kanaka* (kah-nah-kah), that's you: literally a person with no breath. *Ha* is breathe, *ole* is nothing. Haole is what early Hawaiians called the first European visitors, who looked pale as death, or breathless. *Hapa* is Hawaiian for half, not to be confused with *hapai* (hah-pie), meaning one and a half, or pregnant. *Hapa-haole* is half white. When used derogatorily, *haole* is generally prefaced by adjectives like "stupid" or "dumb."

19. **da kine** (dah khine) *adjective, interjection:* Pidgin slang literally meaning "the kind," implying something perfectly understood but not exactly defined. A one-size-fits-all generic expression used when two or more people know what they are talking about but nobody can think of the right word, as in "Cannot explain, you know, da kine."

20. **li'dat** (lye daht) *adverb:* Existential pidgin phrase, from "like that." Agreement or confirmation that an idea, concept, or statement is what it is. Similar to English "uh-huh" and Japanese *honto des*.

▌ **PROBLEMS** *in* **PARADISE?**

NONE OF THESE POTENTIAL DIFFICULTIES would keep you from coming, but be prepared.

WINDS The same gusty trades that make North Shore Maui an international windsurfers' joy can rock your landing jet and sting your skin with sand at the beach, not to mention kicking up the channel waters under your snorkel cruiser. It's a natural phenomenon. Nearly constant tradewinds accelerate when they funnel through Maui's isthmus valley or whistle down the interisland channels. If you are an iffy sailor, go in the mornings when it's calmer.

CLOUDS Takeoffs and landings can be delayed by low-cloud conditionson the Island of Lanai.

SUNBURN Don't underestimate the power of the tropical sun. It's strongest from 9 a.m. to 3 p.m. Do what you want when you want, but slather everyone with high-potency waterproof sunscreen before you go out and often during your activity, and use sunglasses and hats as well. If you do get scorched, slather even more with aloe vera gel.

SHARKS Shark attacks are rare in Hawaii, but sharks are not. Attacks have occurred off Maui beaches. Those clear blue waters harbor a variety of the creatures, which, by Hawaiian legend, are more revered than feared as *aumakua,* or family guardian spirits.

FOODS Maui's cornucopia of restaurants and food stores dries up on the smaller islands. Molokai is one of those places where you don't nap into dinnertime, or you might miss it if you wait too late. Molokai receives milk and staples by once-a-week barge from Honolulu. If you shop the Island markets and cook your own meals, plan dinner around what there is to buy. Although U.S. Department of Agriculture rules restrict movement of fresh produce between Hawaii and other places, anything goes interisland. If you're renting a condo for a family of fussy eaters, you may want to consider buying some groceries on Oahu or Maui and carrying them to Molokai. In Lanai City, wines and limited groceries are available in the plantation general stores, and a few of Lanai City restaurants serve breakfast and lunch. Otherwise, you eat at the hotels only, which are excellent, if costly.

WATER Maui, Molokai, and Lanai are fragile, isolated ecosystems with few resources and little margin for error in tight times. Even the abundant rainfall of wetter areas drains away quickly, leaving water problems for the increasing population of Maui.

Now and then, water gets out of control. Rogue waves and riptides can sweep you out to sea, and occasionally threats are posed by rough surf and even tsunami, or tidal waves, as well as flash-flooding that occurs when tropical rainstorms, usually brief and intense, meet mountains. The runoff down steep slopes poses flash-flood dangers in a downhill waterfall valley or across a road that briefly becomes a raging waterfall course. If you get caught in a storm while hiking by a stream, go immediately to high ground. If driving, park before you get to deep water on a road and wait an hour or two. It will all be gone as soon as the water flows out to sea.

PESTS Bugs love the climate, too. You may see huge red or black centipedes (several inches long by an inch wide) and smaller blue ones (they bite, painfully); delicate, small scorpions (their sting is like a bee sting, according to one victim); several species and sizes of terrorizing cockroaches that don't bite; fast, hairy cane spiders (harmless); several sizes of ants; your average fly and superfly; little black pineapple bugs; and mosquitoes that seem to prefer tender flesh fresh from the Mainland. Mosquitoes will breed in vases of flowers and the rain held by a leaf overnight. Imported and hitch-hiking plants and animals also thrive in the tropical air, usually at the expense of a former arrival. The history of the Islands is a tale of one species crowding another toward extinction—particularly risky for the rare and delicate native inhabitants, including the vanishing race of pure Hawaiians.

TRAFFIC This is not a problem on Molokai or Lanai, but the Maui roads are inadequate for large crowds, as you'll discover if you land on a loaded jumbo jet flight at local commute time. One of the traffic problem areas is the three miles between Lahaina and Kaanapali Beach Resort. Allow extra time on airport runs, or plan to take a breather if the traffic is bugging you.

You may also encounter crowds at rental-car stands when big jets arrive. The best policy is to slow down and cool off. Allow more time. Strike up a conversation. Hawaiian time just isn't as *wikiwiki* (speedy) as you're used to, so relax and enjoy it.

POPULATION Maui County grew by 28 percent in the decade before the 2000 census and is now estimated at 141,320 people. The influence of new residents, many of them from California, and increasing economic reliance on tourism has changed the once-insular social culture of islands formerly devoted to agriculture, mostly sugar and pineapple plantations. The multicultural populace of Maui County, like the rest of Hawaii, is a harmonious racial rainbow most of the time, but clouds do appear.

COST OF GOODS Prices are relatively high for food, gas, and other items. On the other hand, the advent of big discount stores and increased retail competition has helped diminish the high costs and increase the choices, at least on Maui. In populations as small as Molokai and Lanai, shoppers are limited to what the ships bring in once a week or what they can buy on shopping sprees to Maui or Oahu and what they can make, grow, or catch at home.

These remote islands share many of the same problems that burden other American communities: drugs, crime, and traffic. But open-hearted strangers are welcome, and local people largely rely on kindness, respect, and humor to get along. The skies and seas are truly blue way out here, and there is plenty of spectacular scenery to soothe the soul.

Important Phone Numbers

Here's a list of phone numbers that may come in handy during your stay. For interisland calls, use the area code ☎ 808 before the number. Be aware these calls generally are charged long-distance rates.

- Police, fire, ambulance 911
- Directory assistance 411
- Weather and marine forecast 866-944-5025
- Kahului Airport 872-3803, 872-3893

- Kapalua Airport 669-0623
- Hana Airport 248-8208
- Molokai Airport 567-6140
- Kalaupapa Airport 567-6331
- Lanai Airport 565-6757
- Office of Consumer Protection 984-8244

Safety Tips

Hawaii is a peaceful state with few violent crimes. Much is invested in the safety of tourists, the state's biggest industry, but the state is not crime-free. We urge you to use the same common sense and self-protective measures you would at home.

- Carry only as much money, in cash or traveler's checks as you need for the day.
- Never leave your luggage unattended until you arrive at your hotel.
- Never display large amounts of cash during transactions, such as at automated teller machines.
- Beware of pickpockets, especially in crowds.
- Carry your purse close to your body.
- Carry your wallet in a front pocket rather than a rear pocket.
- Never leave valuables in your rental car.
- If your vehicle is bumped from behind at night, do not stop; instead, proceed to the nearest public area and call 911 for assistance.
- Leave your hotel room key with the front desk when going out.

PART TWO

PLANNING *your* VISIT

▌█ WHEN *to* GO

YOU CAN GO TO MAUI WHENEVER you feel like it—when you see the best bargains, when your frequent-flyer mileage has to be claimed, when school's out, or if you live on the West Coast, when you can get away for a long weekend with your sweetie.

There is no "tourist season" on these islands because nothing shuts down for the winter or even for the weekend. This is the land of eternal spring, according to some poets, or perpetual summer, according to others. Tourism is the most important business, and you are always welcome. So timing your trip will depend on other factors.

Travel industry experts in Maui report that the "booking window," or the period between reservations and actual travel, has narrowed dramatically, accelerating a trend that emerged over recent years. Not as many people are planning their trips far in advance, and more people are taking advantage of last-minute deals offered by airlines, hotels, and rental-car firms anxious to fill empty spaces. The entire picture became clouded in late 2008 by worldwide economic concerns that caused many vacationers to postpone or restrain their plans and caused providers to cinch up operations, lay off staff, delay construction completion, and the like. While we all suffer the changes, if you are able to continue with your plans, you will have much-improved chances of getting what you want, when you want, at the price you want to pay.

WEATHER, OR NOT

MORE PEOPLE WANT TO HEAD FOR HAWAII, the only American tropical state, when their weather at home is awful or when they can bring the family, so that relatively speaking, rates go up and availability goes down in winter and summer. That makes spring and fall the easiest and best value seasons. As for the weather on Maui, Molokai, and Lanai, temperatures around the shoreline vary only slightly from one time of year to another, with winter months being the coolest and wettest. In a real cold snap, daytime highs can sometimes dip below 80°F at beach level. Cool night winds and higher elevations can inspire you to seek a sweatshirt. The winter storms that sweep across America often visit the 50th state first, making winter the rainiest time of year.

Perhaps the strongest argument for visiting Maui in winter is the migration of Pacific humpback whales to Hawaiian waters, with the peak time being January through April, and the peak place being the federally protected waters off Maalaea Bay in the center of Maui's resort coast. Winter is also the season for big surf, major golf events, visually stunning squalls rolling across the horizon, and, sometimes, snow dusting the top of Haleakala. It's the rainier, often less-breezy time between the holidays and late March, when the hills are particularly green. Winter isn't brown or leafless in the Islands, although there are some deciduous trees that drop their leaves for six weeks and grow them right back. Some tropicals bloom and ripen any time of year, on their own schedules—bananas and orchids, for example.

Summer in the Islands, on the other hand, is the time of ripe mangoes (the Yee Orchards in Kihei grow an incredible variety and sell them at a stand by the road), the sweet scent of jasmine, calmer seas on north shores, and bigger surf on south shores. Hurricanes and tropical storms march west across the Pacific in summer, yet it's generally warmer and drier, with an explosion of flowers—not that there weren't plenty in winter. The Southern Cross and Perseid meteor showers appear in the skies in late summer. Rates for airfare and accommodations may or may not be lower, since summer weather in the Islands is often kinder and gentler than the steamers at home, and it's a time when school's out and families head west for fun in the sun.

If you just want to kick back at any time of year, watch travel ads and the Internet and catch the next plane that suits your budget and schedule.

GET A HEAD START

THE FACT THAT YOU'RE READING THIS *Unofficial Guide* suggests you're a savvy traveler who already recognizes the value of planning ahead. Though most people arranging a Maui vacation plan to enjoy the famous laid-back Islands attitude, preparedness is still important. In fact, there's nothing more frustrating than sitting in traffic or standing in line at a car-rental counter when you expected to be lounging on the beach. And wouldn't you rather read a novel on the beach than luau brochures from the hotel lobby? A few hours' research in advance of your trip will really pay off in Maui, helping you relax and get the full value of your vacation.

GET A MAP

THE BEST MAPS OF MAUI, MOLOKAI, AND LANAI are created by cartographer James A. Bier and published by the University of Hawaii Press. Each topographic map includes Island highways, roads, and trails as well as large-scale inset maps of towns with significant populations. They include points of natural, cultural, and historic interest; parks and beaches; sea channels; peaks and ridges (with altitudes); and Hawaiian words spelled with all their accent marks. The maps, printed on heavy paper, cost $3.95 for Maui and $3.95 for Molokai and Lanai, and fold to fit easily into a carry-on bag or backpack.

If your bookstore doesn't carry these maps, you can order them from several Internet sites or directly from the Marketing Department, University of Hawaii Press, 2840 Kolowalu Street, Honolulu, HI 96822. Specify which island map you want. You can also request a free catalog of great books about Hawaii and the Pacific. Call the University of Hawaii Press at ☎ 808-956-8255 for more information.

RECOMMENDED READING

EVERY TRAVELER TO MAUI, MOLOKAI, OR LANAI should read about these fascinating destinations before going. Check your local bookstore or library (you can also visit Booklines, the biggest distributor of books in Hawaii, on the Internet at **www.booklines.com)**.

Acquaint yourself before you go to Maui with these essential books:

- *Beaches of Maui,* by John R. K. Clark; published by University of Hawaii Press, 1999. Guide to 50 of Hawaii's best beaches.

- *Camping Hawaii,* by Richard McMahon; published by University of Hawaii Press, 1997. The only guide to 120 campgrounds in the Aloha State.

- *50 Thrifty Maui Restaurants: Dining on a Budget, Island-Style* by Yvonne Biegel and Jessisca Ferracane, 2006. How and where to eat like the locals do.

- *Hawaiian Heritage Plants,* by Angela Kay Kepler; published by Fernglen Press, 1998. Thorough presentation of Hawaii's native plants. Full-color photos.

- *The Colony: The Harrowing True Story of the Exiles of Molokai* by John Tayman; published by Scribner, New York, 2006. Tayman tells the sad and shocking stories of victims of the infamous 19th-century leper colony at Kalaupapa.

- *Hawaii: True Stories of The Island Spirit,* edited by Rick and Marcie Carroll; published by Travelers Tales, San Francisco, 1999. This is an anthology of essays by a divergent group of contributing authors, some famous, others unknown, all insightful.

- *Na Kuaa Ina: Living Hawaiian Culture* by Davianna Pomaikai McGregor; published by University of Hawaii Press, 1997. Explores four places where Hawaiian culture thrives, including Hana.

- *Hawaii's Best Golf,* by George Fuller; published by Island Heritage Publishing, 1999. Hawaii's best golf courses, profiled and photographed in full color.

- *IZ Voice of the People,* by Rick Carroll; published by Bess Press, Honolulu, 2006. Award-winning biography of late, legendary Hawaiian singer of "Over the Rainbow" fame.

- *Maui Hiking Trails,* by Craig Chisolm; published by Fernglen Press, 1999. Detailed look at 50 of the best hiking trails on Hawaii's six major islands.

- *Fragile Paradise: The Impact of Tourism on Maui, 1959–2000* by Mansel Blackford; published by University Press of Kansas, 2001. A thoughtful look at the good, bad, and ugly of selling an island for tourist dollars so successfully that its soul is at risk.

- *Molokai: An Island in Time,* by Richard Cooke III, photographer and longtime resident; published by Beyond Words, Honolulu, 1984.

- *No Footprints in the Sand: A Memoir of Kalaupapa,* by Jenry Nalailelua with Sally-Jo Bowman; published by Watermark Press, 2006. The biography of a leprosy survivor of Kalaupapa.

- *Shoal of Time: A History of the Hawaiian Islands,* by Gavan Daws; published by University of Hawaii Press, 1994. A history book that reads like a novel.

- *Sites of Maui,* by Elspeth Sterling; published by Bishop Museum Press, 1998. The single resource for information on the prehistory of Maui.

- *The Delicate Art of Whale Watching,* by Joana McIntyre Varawa; published by Sierra Club Books, 1991. Keen ocean watcher reveals how to really see whales.

- *The Island of Lanai,* by Kenneth Pike Emory; published by Bishop Museum Press, 1924. First archaeological field study of the island.

- *Under a Maui Sun: The Valley Isle,* by Cheryl Chee Tsutsumi; published by Island Heritage, 2000. Souvenir photo book with bright text by longtime Island writer.

Newspapers and Magazines

Maui News Island's only daily newspaper. Call ☎ 808-244-3981 or visit the Web site at **www.mauinews.com** for information.

Maui Time Weekly Scrappy weekly pulls no punches in efforts to reveal what's really going on in Maui. Read all about it online at **www.mauitime.com**

Maui No Ka Oi Magazine A slick quarterly celebrates Valley Isle personalities, issues, restaurant reviews, and events, and is published by Haynes Publishing Group on Maui. Call ☎ 808-871-7765 to subscribe. The Web site is **www.mauinokaoimagazine.com.**

Maui, Molokai, and Lanai are featured often in travel magazines like *Condé Nast Traveler, National Geographic Traveler, Travel+Leisure,* and *Arthur Frommer's Budget Travel Magazine* and airline in-flight magazines, but only a few feature magazines devote full coverage to the Islands.

Hawaii magazine, a bimonthly featuring articles on Island people, culture, arts, history, and travel, is published in Honolulu and is available at major newsstands. See more at **www.hawaiimagazine.com**

SURF THE INTERNET

SEARCH FOR THE WORD "MAUI" and you'll find a virtual tsunami of matches, too much to surf in a lifetime. More Maui Web sites appear every day.

VISIT MAUI The Maui Visitors Bureau Web site, **www.visitmaui.com,** makes you want to pack right now. It offers lots of solid information and useful links, including seven remote cameras (one focuses on Hookipa windsurfers) with Island scenes. You can check out the surf report and daily temperatures, order a free Maui Vacation Planner, book a B&B, and tour beach resorts. It links to **www.hawaii .com.** Check out **www.maui.net,** too, for an independent review of Maui information put together by Maui's primary Internet service provider.

SURF MOLOKAI Going to Molokai is like "landing in rural Arkansas sometime back in the 1930s or 1940s," novelist Fletcher Knebel once said. "I've had the feeling that if I turned on a radio, I'd hear Eddie Duchin on the piano, FDR in mid-fireside chat, or perhaps the Japanese bombing Pearl Harbor." Things haven't changed that much since Fletcher's day. However, old-fashioned Molokai has a big Internet presence, with plentiful home pages, from molokai-hawaii.com, the Molokai Visitors Association's official information roundup, to Monkey Pod Records (**www.monkeypod.com**), which promotes local musicians. One site details the somber history of the Kalaupapa National Historic Park, where victims of leprosy were once banished, and the way to get there—the Molokai Mule Ride (**www.muleride.com**).

LOOK AT LANAI Find lots of details at **www.visitlanai.net** on what there is to see and do and where to eat and sleep on the old plantation isle. At **www.fourseasons.com/lanai,** you can get a look at the exclusive resorts of Lanai. Several sites, including **www .lanaipropeties.com,** list real estate for sale in high-end developments. Don't miss **www.hotellani.com** to find details about Hotel Lanai & Cottages, the small historic (and affordable) plantation hostelry in Lanai City. Check out **www.lanairental.com** to see a vacation rental prospect, the Captain's Retreat.

FIND KAHOOLAWE The devastated Island of Kahoolawe presents quite a challenge to the Hawaiians working to restore it and create a cultural preserve because the U.S. Navy used it for bombing practice for half a century. You can learn more at **www.kahoolawe.org** and also at **www.hawaiiforvisitors.com**

MAUI VISITORS BUREAU

IN THE EARLY 1900S, several of Hawaii's hoteliers created the world's first tourist bureau to attract travelers and foster dreams of visiting the Islands. The boosters later hired Mark Twain to extol the virtues of a Hawaii vacation and sent entertainers on the road, a practice that continues today as the next best thing to being here. Now, the Hawaii Visitors and Convention Bureau spends millions of dollars globally to promote Hawaii as a top world destination. Part of that job belongs to its offspring, the Maui Visitors Bureau, which spreads the word about Maui, Molokai, and Lanai activities, accommodations, restaurants, and events. The statewide HVCB Web site is another source of information and links (**www.gohawaii.com**).

HAWAII VISITORS AND CONVENTION BUREAU
2270 Kalakaua Avenue, 8th Floor
Honolulu, HI 96815
☎ 808-923-1811 or 800-GO-HAWAII
www.gohawaii.com
Request a free copy of *The Islands of Aloha,* the Hawaii Visitors and Convention Bureau vacation planner.

MAUI VISITORS BUREAU
1727 Wili Pa Loop
Wailuku, HI 96793
☎ 808-244-3530 or 800-525-MAUI
www.visitmaui.com, www.gohawaii.com
Call or write for a free copy of *Maui, The Magic Isles,* a travel planner featuring Maui, Molokai, and Lanai.

DESTINATION LANAI
P.O. Box 700
Lanai City, HI 96763
☎ 808-565-7600 or 800-947-4774
www.visitlanai.net, www.gohawaii.com

MOLOKAI VISITORS ASSOCIATION
P.O. Box 960
Kaunakakai, HI 96748
☎ 808-553-3876 or 800-800-6367
www.molokai-hawaii.com, www.gohawaii.com

INTERNATIONAL CONTACTS

UNITED KINGDOM
Hawaii Tourism Europe
Colechurch House, 1 London Bridge Walk
London SE19EU
England
☎ 44-207-367-0900
Hawaii-tourism.co.uk

AUSTRALIA
Hawaii Tourism Australia
Level 6, 117 York Street
Sydney, NSW 2000
☎ 61-2-9286-8951
info@hawaiitourism.com.au

NEW ZEALAND
Hawaii Tourism New Zealand
Level 7, Citibank Building
23 Customs Street East
Auckland, New Zealand
☎ 64-9977-2234
info@hawaiitourism.com.nz

▌ PACK LIGHT

NO MATTER THE SEASON, PACK LIGHT. Think summer casual, without the chilly nights of California. The most you'll need at lower elevations is a light (not wool) sweater or windbreaker. In the cooler high country, the temperatures will seem like spring, so dress accordingly. If you have colorful aloha shirts and sarongs, bring those. If you yearn to hike those green trails, bring appropriate shoes and light socks.

Golfers, Island pro shops sell great tropical-weight duds for the links, and you can play in shorts on many courses. Windsurfers, you'll probably want to bring money for the new gear you'll be tempted to buy. If you're planning to ride horses, bring covered footwear and jeans, and hang onto your hat. If you're going camping, you can bring or rent gear, according to your preference and the amount of time you plan to camp. A night or two? Rent. A month? You might prefer your own.

A word to the wise: Besides sands of many colors on the beaches, these Islands are full of red dirt that stains clothing such as white tennies and shorts. Bring clothes that won't get in the way of a good time.

What men need: shorts, T-shirts and informal tops, a favorite Hawaiian shirt, swim trunks, lightweight slacks, a light jacket or sweatshirt for Upcountry, and sandals, sports shoes, or loafers. No ties or suits needed, unless your trip will involve a funeral or full-dress wedding. Most restaurants' dress codes run to requiring footwear rather than formal wear.

What women need: sundresses or shifts, swimsuits, bathing-suit coverups, shorts or cropped pants or skirts, tops, light sweater or jacket, sandals, sports shoes, and maybe a muumuu for the luau. Hemlines and styles vary at will here, and skin is in. No urban power-wear. Unless you're staying in butlered digs, minimize high-maintenance clothes, although many hotel rooms do come equipped with iron and board.

If you pack wisely for the tropical climate, you can put all your lightweight clothes in one case and bring an empty tote for all the gifts you'll bring back.

Staying in Touch

If a laptop computer is attached to your arm, bring it. The airport security process requires you to take it out of its carrying case and put it through the scope in a basket; be sure to recover it at the other end. Most hotels in the Islands have phones in the rooms. Many hotels provide high-speed Internet access, usually for a daily fee. Some offer free wireless connections throughout their buildings or in certain places like the lobby or business center. Some have rentable computer game gear.

WHAT NOT TO BRING

CERTAIN ANIMALS AND PLANTS ARE BANNED, and most are restricted from entering Hawaii. Entry into rabies-free Hawaii by pet cats and dogs is no longer subject to a mandatory six-month quarantine but does require strict injection timing schedules and documentation before the pet arrives. Check directly with the state Department of Agriculture **(http://hawaii.gov/hdoa/ai/aqs/ info)** at least four months before planning to bring a cat or dog to Hawaii. Snakes end up in the zoo or dead (the Islands have no wild land snakes and want none).

Exotic flora and fauna negatively affect Hawaii's fragile ecosystem. By the same token, the U.S. Department of Agriculture bans shipping many tropical fruits, plants, and other items from Hawaii to prevent the spread of fruit flies and other insects. Pineapples and coconuts are okay. Bananas, avocados, mangoes, and uncertified papayas are not. For specific information, call the USDA's Plant

Quarantine Branch at ☎ 808-586-0844 or the Animal Quarantine Branch at ☎ 808-483-7171.

▌■ WORTH *the* LONG FLIGHT

THE FLIGHT TO HAWAII IS ABOUT FIVE HOURS from the West Coast, eight from Dallas, nine from Atlanta, and 11 hours in the air from New York. Most major U.S. and several international airlines serve the Islands regularly, as do charters. Hawaii-based Hawaiian Airlines connects the Islands with various West Coast cities and Phoenix and Las Vegas (a frequent destination for Hawaii residents).

Honolulu International Airport (HNL) on Oahu is one of the nation's busiest airports, with 200 daily operations by some 40 airlines, many of them international, and more than 20 million passenger arrivals and departures annually. Most Mainland-to-Hawaii flights touch down in Honolulu, and passengers for Maui, Molokai, or Lanai then must transfer to the Interisland Terminal for short hops to those islands. Maui County airports are Kahului Airport, Hana Airport, and Kapalua–West Maui Airport on Maui; Hoolehua Airport on Molokai; and Lanai Airport on Lanai.

You can find direct service to Maui on several Mainland airlines from several Mainland cities, often at competitive prices, both scheduled and charter flights. Hawaiian Airlines flies nonstop to Maui from Seattle and Portland. United Airlines has daily Maui flights from Los Angeles and San Francisco. Delta Airlines and American Airlines fly nonstop to Kahului from Los Angeles.

All schedules are subject to change. Call toll-free numbers above for updated information.

If you have a bumpy ride over the Pacific, consider, please, the flight of Commander John Rodgers, the first pilot to almost fly to Hawaii. A 1908 Naval Academy graduate, Rodgers, the grandson of Commodore Matthew Perry, learned to fly from Wilbur and Orville Wright in 1911. On August 31, 1925, Captain Rodgers, age 44, lifted off from San Francisco in a Boeing PN9-1 seaplane named the *Flying Dreadnought* with 40 ham sandwiches and a crew of four. The seaplane's twin Packard V-8 engines ran out of gas 25 hours and 23 minutes after takeoff, and Ridges downed the plane at sea about 300 miles off Maui. When no rescuers arrived, the crew rigged a sail and made 50 miles a day in their "mutant square rigger"—as historian MacKinnon Simpson wrote—until they spotted Oahu's jagged Koolau peaks, but they were unable to stop. Wind and sea sent them sailing on to Kauai, where they arrived September 10, after a nine-day sea leg. Total voyage: 1,870 miles by air, 450 by sea. Rodgers's feat is memorialized in a bronze plaque at Honolulu International Airport, which is officially named for him.

Hawaii has its own time zone, known as Hawaii Standard Time or HST. On standard time, noon in San Francisco is 10 a.m. in Honolulu. Hawaii time is two hours earlier than the West Coast and five hours earlier than the East Coast. During Daylight Savings Time on the Mainland, March to October, Hawaii is three hours behind the West Coast and six hours behind the East Coast.

With an average 12 hours of sunshine daily, year-round, Hawaii has lots of daylight—and no need to "save" it. Hawaii's longest day, on June 21, is 13 hours and 26 minutes long. Its shortest day, on December 21, is 10 hours and 50 minutes.

HOW TO BOOK

BOOKING YOUR VACATION THROUGH A TRAVEL AGENT may save you time and money, since the agent can plow through myriad fares and rates to find you the best airfares, lodgings, and car rentals, and take advantage of specials offered just to agents. But you may also have to pay a fee, because most agents are charging customers as well as providers for their services. You can book your vacation yourself on the Internet or the telephone, although it consumes time and tries your patience. Internet fares are often discounted. The best plan is to research on your own to acquaint yourself with what's available and also find out what an agent can do for you, and then decide.

If you make the arrangements on your own, here are some tips and advisories on finding a good deal on airfares, hotels, and travel packages:

- Check out the travel-booking Web sites: **expedia.com, travel.yahoo .com, travelocity.com, orbitz.com, hoteldiscount.com, cheaptickets .com,** and others. Most charge a small fee for your tickets or reservations. Several Island providers will also book your whole trip if you choose. Look up hotels, cars, and airlines by name if you prefer or plan to cash in mileage awards.

- Be flexible in your travel planning until you choose dates and times for your round-trip flights. Then try not to change them; whether you paid in money or mileage, you are likely to face costly penalties for any changes. The best airfare deals are usually for travel on certain days of the week or hours of the day. Investigate how you might save money by leaving a day or two earlier or later, or taking a different flight. These days, travel agents will charge a fee (and airlines often do, too) if you make reservations with their agents. So, the least expensive option is for you to do the ticketing yourself on the Internet or on an automated phone line. That means you have to learn how to be your own travel agent. Check the Internet and familiarize yourself with the process and the fares several days before you actually commit to a ticketing plan. You can hold your reservation on most airlines for

AIRLINES SERVING KAHULUI AIRPORT	
Air Canada	☎ 888-247-2262
American Airlines	☎ 800-223-5436
America West/US Airways	☎ 800-428-4322
Continental Airlines	☎ 800-784-4444
Delta Airlines	☎ 800-325-1999
go! Airlines	☎ 888-435-9462
Harmony Airlines	☎ 866-868-6789
Hawaiian Airlines	☎ 800-367-5320
Island Air	☎ 800-652-6541
Northwest Airlines	☎ 800-225-2525
Pacific Wings	☎ 888-575-4546
United Airlines	☎ 800-864-8331
West Jet	☎ 888-937-8538

a day or so before you are charged for the ticket. Reserve rental cars in advance on the Internet as well, but check your guaranteed rate before your trip because the best-available rates may drop, and you can rebook to take advantage of them. You do not have to pay in advance for reservations made through rental-car companies.

- If your travel itinerary falls into a busy flight period, book early. Flights, cars, and rooms during holidays may sell out months ahead of time.

- Many discount fares are nonrefundable and usually nontransferable. If you want to change your discounted booking, you will pay more if that fare is not available on the new flight.

HOW TO AVOID JET LAG

START BEFORE YOU DEPART TO COMBAT JET LAG—"circadian desynchronization," in scientific terms. Whatever its name, it is that zonked feeling that occurs after flying across several time zones, especially when flying east. It is a physical and mental condition lasting a few hours to a few days. You are sleepy, disoriented, and a little out of sync—waking when you should be asleep and vice versa.

Here are some practical tips:

- Avoid coffee for a day or two before and after your flight and drink water, lots of it, rather than coffee, sodas, or alcohol, on the plane. Alcohol can intensify jet lag. Drink water to prevent dehydration—an eight-ounce glass for each hour of flight, according to our doctor. This will also help to combat the colds passengers often give one another.

- During flight, remove shoes to improve circulation. Flex your feet, ankles, and legs often. If possible, stroll through the cabin and stand for awhile.

Contacting Hawaii's Air Carriers

GO!

Toll-free: ☎ 800-I-FLY-GO2
www.iflygo.com

HAWAIIAN AIRLINES

Toll-free: ☎ 800-367-5320
Oahu: ☎ 808-838-1555
Maui: ☎ 808-871-6132
Big Island: ☎ 808-326-5615
Kauai: ☎ 808-245-1813
Molokai: ☎ 808-553-3644
Lanai: ☎ 808-565-7281
www.hawaiianair.com

ISLAND AIR

Toll-free: ☎ 800-652-6541
Lanai: ☎ 808-565-6744

MOKULELE AIRLINES

Toll-free: ☎ 866-260-7070,
☎ 808-426-7070
www.mokuleleairlines.com

PACIFIC WINGS

Toll-free: ☎ 800-575-4546
Maui: ☎ 808-873-0877
www.pacificwings.com

PARAGON AIR

Toll-free: ☎ 800-428-1231
Maui: ☎ 808-244-3356
www.paragon-air.com

Molokai: ☎ 808-567-6115
www.islandair.com

- Adjust your watch to Hawaii Standard Time when you board the plane. This prepares you mentally to adjust to Hawaii time. Think of time as it is where you're going, not where you've been. Then, on the ground, get acclimated to local time as soon as possible. Stay up until bedtime in the Islands if you can, even though you may feel extremely tired.

- Go for a swim or a long soak. It will replenish moisture lost during your flight and soothe tired muscles and nerves.

INTERISLAND FLIGHTS

MAUI IS LINKED TO HONOLULU AND OTHER ISLANDS by frequent, efficient jet service all day, from sunrise to late evening. It is provided by the full-service Honolulu-based airlines Hawaiian Airlines and go!, which entered the interisland fray in 2006 and sparked a fare war. go! is operated by Mesa Airlines of Phoenix, Arizona, one of the nation's largest regional carriers. The competition, plus spiraling fuel prices, led to the bankruptcy and closure in 2008 of longtime island-based international Aloha Airlines. Nonetheless, another hopeful, Kona-based Mokulele Airlines, launched interisland service in early 2009 serving all three Maui County islands.

The jet airlines share the Interland Terminal at Honolulu Airport; the smaller aircraft of the interisland airlines that fly to smaller airports on Molokai and Lanai, as well as Maui's

Kapalua/West Maui airport, are based at the commuter terminal at Honolulu Airport. Hawaiian Airlines also flies to the small airports of Molokai, Lanai, and Kapalua, as well as Kahului. Island Air flies twin-engine planes to Kapalua and Kahului on Maui, as well as Molokai and Lanai.

Hawaiian jets have small first-class seating areas. But the interisland flights take only 25 minutes, so the chief advantage, besides bigger seats and more service, is that you can board and deplane first. Check with the airline for baggage rules. Boogie boards, surfboards, coolers, skateboards, and strollers are not allowed in the cabin.

When booking your interisland flight, ask about special promotions that may lower your fare. And check the Web sites.

CAR RENTALS

IT'S POSSIBLE TO ENJOY MAUI, MOLOKAI, AND LANAI without rental cars. The larger Maui resorts have free shuttles to link your lodgings with airports, beaches, and golf courses, as well as a full array of other amusements. But to explore Maui and Molokai the way they deserve, you have to rent a vehicle.

Likewise on Lanai: A resort shuttle will take you to most sites, but one of Lanai's more popular activities is to explore the back roads in a Jeep four-wheel-drive rental, allowing you to discover wild country and island history on your own. People talk of driving "around the island," but you can't really do that around the entire coastline of any of the islands. Yet, given their small size, each island can be traversed end-to-end in a relatively brief trip.

Carry in your rental car as little as possible that might appeal to thieves. We leave ours empty and open; no sense paying for a broken window.

Car rentals are available on all islands. The costs average less than in many large cities, plus fees and taxes (rates tend to be higher on Molokai and Lanai, where there are fewer cars and customers). Rental-car rates are lower in the Islands than the nation as a whole. Shop for rates by telephone or on the Internet, if making your own arrangements. Try Expedia, Priceline, Travelocity, and other Internet travel discounters (you will have to prepay in full on some of these, so be sure to read the rules), as well as the car company sites (pay when you return the cars). You are less likely to find bargain rates during busy holidays.

Most major car-rental firms offer special rates and include car rentals in money-saving travel packages with airfare and accommodations. Check with a travel agent or call the car-rental agencies for details before you go. Again, be sure to try the Internet travel discount sites for special package deals. When making interisland flight reservations, check the Internet or ask the airlines for any

Contacting Hawaii's Car-rental Agencies

ALAMO RENT-A-CAR
Toll-free: ☎ 800-327-9633
www.goalamo.com

MAUI:
Kahului Airport: ☎ 808-871-6235
Kaanapali Transportation Center:
☎ 808-661-7181

AVIS RENT-A-CAR
Toll-free: ☎ 800-331-1212
www.avis.com
MAUI:
Kahului Airport: ☎ 808-871-7575
Kaanapali: ☎ 808-661-4588
Ritz-Carlton Kapalua:
☎ 808-669-5046

BUDGET RENT-A-CAR
Toll-free: ☎ 800-777-0169
www.budgetrentacar.com
MAUI:
Kahului Airport: ☎ 808-871-8811
Kaanapali: ☎ 808-661-8721
MOLOKAI:
Molokai Airport: ☎ 808-567-6877

DOLLAR RENT-A-CAR
Toll-free: ☎ 800-367-7006
www.dollarcar.com

MAUI:
Kahului Airport: ☎ 808-877-2731
Hana: ☎ 808-248-8237
Kaanapali Transportation Center:
☎ 808-667-2651
MOLOKAI:
Molokai Airport: ☎ 808-567-6156
LANAI:
Lanai City ☎ 808-565-7227

HERTZ RENT-A-CAR
Toll-free: ☎ 800-654-3011
www.hertz.com
MAUI:
Kahului Airport: ☎ 808-877-5167
2580 Kekaa Dr.: ☎ 808-661-7735
Westin Maui: ☎ 808-667-5381

NATIONAL CAR RENTAL
Toll-free: ☎ 800-CAR-RENT
www.nationalcar.com
MAUI:
Kahului Airport: ☎ 808-871-8851
Kaanapali Transportation Center:
☎ 808-667-9737

special deals on flights or flights packaged with rental cars. They often partner with car agencies in promotional fly/drive packages. All sorts of discounts can lower your rates: you may get a break of 5–15 percent for association memberships, credit cards, frequent-flyer clubs, and coupons. Web sites (provided below) offer up to 20 percent off regular rates.

All the major car-rental agencies are located at or near Maui's airports, and many have reservations desks at various resorts or stores. Budget and Dollar are the only car-rental agencies at the Molokai Airport, and Dollar is the only car-rental option for Lanai. On Maui, besides Kahului Airport and the hotels, many car-rental agencies operate near Kapalua Airport in West Maui at the Kaanapali

Transportation Center (30-1 Halawai Drive), a five-minute free shuttle ride from the Kapalua terminal.

Maui is just the kind of place you might want to splurge and rent a convertible or a fancy sports car. Most car-rental agencies have a fleet of vehicles ranging from economy cars and luxury sedans to four-wheel-drive Jeeps and shiny red roadsters. Luxury wheels and Harley Davidson motorcycles are also available for rent on Maui.

As with car rentals in any destination, you can rent a car after you arrive, presuming one is available, but you'd do better to reserve a car before you go, especially on these small islands. Courtesy phones and free shuttles in airport terminals connect you to their nearby offices. Rental rates are based on the number of cars available, so they constantly fluctuate. Since you don't have to pay up front, you can always book one early and recheck rates later.

Expect to see the rental fee jump by the time you sign for the car, since several charges will be added. Car rentals are subject to a $2-per-day state road tax and a nominal vehicle license tax (17¢–45¢ per day). In addition, transactions that take place at an airport are subject to an airport concession fee of 7.5 percent. Web reservations will reflect the rates and taxes but not the prepaid fuel option, one you should take with car agencies that charge you only for what you use.

Optional insurance rates vary by car-rental agency. Remember that your own car insurance, and often your major credit card, provide coverage on you while driving rental cars. Check before you leave. Hawaii is a no-fault insurance state.

Gas prices will look astronomical on Maui, Molokai, and Lanai, compared to almost any Mainland location. But think about where you are. Fortunately, rental cars today are rarely gas-guzzlers, and the Islands are small enough that you seldom rack up major mileage.

About Island Driving: These islands don't have a lot of roads. Most roads are two lanes and have lower speed limits than roads in other states. Island driving manners are such that people will let you merge into their lane, turn left in front of traffic, or stop briefly to pick up or dispatch a rider without protest, often with a wave. Take it slow, signal, look, smile a lot, and wave your thanks. Leave your aggressive driving habits at home.

ISLAND HOPPING: *Pro or Con?*

ON PAPER, IT LOOKS EASY TO HOP AT WILL between Maui, Molokai, Lanai, and Honolulu—and it used to be. But today's increased airport security requirements, flight schedules, and slow ticket counters, especially in Kahului Airport, can consume hours of your precious vacation time. If you're staying on Maui and want to see Lanai, one pleasant way to go is by boat. The sailing cruises are fun, and some include an island tour. The Expeditions passenger

Now you can go *holoholo* in Hawaii just as early Islanders did, on double-hulled oceangoing vessels. Those ancient Polynesian outrigger canoes were remarkable, but today's modern double-hull, 350-foot Hawaii Superferry, *Alakai*, is simply awesome. It holds 800 passengers, sports a first-class lounge, throws a huge wake from four 12,000-hp jet engines, and carries vehicles (a first in Hawaii). You can bring a car aboard, even a rental car, and fill it with people and luggage to journey between Honolulu and Kahului, Maui, for less than the cost of a jet ride with multiple car rentals. It's also a lot more fun than cooling your heels at yet another airport. Go early in the day, when you have the best chance for smooth sailing in the big water of the mid-Pacific. If you're prone to motion sickness, choose seats amidship rather than in the first-class lounge in the bow of the ship. Take anti-seasick pills, avoid the breakfast bento with spam and Portuguese sausage, get out in the open air, and enjoy the ride.

The $75-million ferry sails to Maui from Honolulu Harbor's new $4-million interisland ferry terminal at Pier 19 and lands at the port of Kahului. The three-hour voyage offers sea and island vistas you can't see any other way, as well as cushy reclining armchairs, televisions, food, beverages, and shopping.

Plans are to expand the ferry service with a second ship to sail from Honolulu to the Big Island.

The vessels, built in Alabama in a joint venture between Bender Shipbuilders of Mobile and Austral Ltd. of Australia and funded by Silicon Valley venture capitalists, carry 280 vehicles and travel up to 45 mph.

For fare, schedule, and ticket information, call ☎ 877-443-3779 or visit **www.hawaiisuperferry.com.**

Editor's note: The Hawaii Superferry ceased operations, at least temporarily, in March (just before press time) following an unfavorable court ruling regarding its environmental review. If your plans include a sail on the big car ferry, be sure to check the operator's Web site or call to determine whether the ship is under way again or still dead in the water by the time of your visit.

ferry that links Lanai and Lahaina is inexpensive, scenic, and takes less than an hour dock to dock.

When you do fly between islands, the flights are only half an hour or so and the airlines are efficient, but the transfers are time-consuming and plane tickets are expensive. Most interisland hops go through Honolulu, even if your destination is right next door. Before you leave home, ask your agent or airline about discounted interisland rates.

The quickest way to see the Islands is a scenic flight on a helicopter or twin-engine airplane. Several companies offer low altitude half-day and full-day scenic tours over the main islands. One is **Pacific Wings:** ☎ 808-873-0877; **www.pacificwings.com.**

Norwegian Cruise Lines offers one-week Hawaiian cruises aboard the *Pride of America* with port calls on several islands. Call ☎ 800-327-7030 or visit **www.ncl.com.**

SUGGESTIONS *for* TRAVELERS *with* SPECIAL INTERESTS

Singles

BEST ISLAND TO VISIT Maui

THINGS TO SEE AND DO Ride with a bike tour down Haleakala or take a snorkel cruise to Molokini or Lanai. Drive to Makawao and Paia and poke around the villages. If you're a golfer, pro shops are often looking to fill up a foursome on the links. Head Upcountry to Kula and stop to taste Tedeschi Wines at the winery at Ulupalakua Ranch. The best places to party are Lahaina and Kihei, where the few bars with live music and dancing are easy to find and the action commences after 10 p.m.

COMMENTS If you're traveling solo, Maui has the most social appeal, the most single visitors of various ages to meet, and the most places to meet them. You won't feel uncomfortable eating alone in restaurants or signing up for activities by yourself.

Couples

BEST ISLANDS TO VISIT Lanai and Maui

THINGS TO SEE AND DO On Lanai, divide your time between the seaside Four Seasons Resort Lanai at Manele Bay, where you can wake up to warm breezes and spinner dolphins in the waters out front, and the inland Four Seasons Resort Lanai, Lodge at Koele, where evenings are chilly enough to cuddle, and not much else is on the agenda after dinner. Hike to Sweetheart Rock, take a four-wheel-drive vehicle out to the secluded hinterlands, or ride horses through the woods. Paddle a kayak for two through snorkel-garden waters.

On Maui, get up early to see the spectacular sunrise over Haleakala, then relax with massages for two in tents by the sea and take a stroll on Wailea Beach. If you seek solitude, just go to Hana to see how romantic Maui really is.

COMMENTS If you love the one you're with, you won't need our help for suggestions on romance and entertainment. Maui will do it for you, and Lanai is so indulgent of privacy that the world seems to fall away, leaving just you and the soft tropical nights and the starry skies.

Families

BEST ISLAND TO VISIT Maui

THINGS TO SEE AND DO Lanai and Molokai have great appeal for families as well, but Maui is the place the kids most want to go. It has the most family-oriented attractions designed to educate as well as entertain, such as the Maui Ocean Center at Maalaea and the Whale Museum at Whalers Village Shopping Center in Kaanapali Beach Resort. That is, if you can tear them away from the water-park pools at hotels through-out Kaanapali and Wailea resorts—the most elaborate being the Grand Wailea Resort Hotel & Spa water complex, with pools, canyons, slides, and a water-driven elevator. Smaller kids can learn about the Islands and make new friends at hotels' supervised children's programs while their parents enjoy some adult time. Hawaii Nature Center programs in Wailuku offer a chance for kids to discover denizens of the rain forest.

COMMENTS Kaanapali Beach in West Maui is considered the most popular family destination, but all three islands are excellent family choices. Maybe the best thing about Islands vacations *en famille* is that they happen *en famille*—rather than as simultaneous individual vacations—because Hawaii's activities and attractions have broad appeal. Bring everybody, from tots to nephews to grandparents, and spend some real quality time together. If the family group is one parent and child, exploring Maui, Molokai, and Lanai together will be the experience you hoped for. Plenty of discoveries await families on these islands, and you'll be surprised how many the children make first.

Bikers

BEST ISLANDS TO VISIT Maui

THINGS TO SEE AND DO You won't forget the thrill of coasting down 10,000-foot-high Haleakala on a specially built bicycle, 38 miles to the sea on a guided cruise. The air is cold in the early morning at the sum-mit, but warms as you descend the slope. There are frequent stops to shed clothes and admire the scenery that starts with alpine lavascape and ends with tropical wonderland. You are awed by the majesty of the sleeping volcano. If your notion of bike cruising runs to Harleys, your ride awaits at the nearest rental spot. Be forewarned: The biker bars have already been discovered, largely by prowling CEOs who like to hang incognito with the folks. Bicycles are available to guests at several hotels, including the Hana-Maui, where the grounds have gentle slopes and shady paths. Lanai and Molokai activities also include mountain biking.

COMMENTS Equipment rentals are readily available, the terrain is challeng-ing, and the scenery is mesmerizing. What a terrific way to experience the Islands.

Nature Lovers

BEST ISLANDS TO VISIT Molokai and Maui

THINGS TO SEE AND DO On Maui, go directly up—to Haleakala National Park to look for rare silversword plants and the endangered Hawaiian nene goose, or to hike in the cloud forest at Polipoli State Park. Or head along the north shore toward Hana; the crooked road leads through some of the most beautiful scenery waterfalls and exotic plants can produce. Stop at Waianapanapa State Park for a short stroll to a jet-black beach. Go for a guided hike in any of the forested hills. Drive on your own on the Upcountry road through Kula and continue past Ulupalakua Ranch for a few miles on a new road that takes you through an incredible variety of mini-climate zones without a building in sight.

Molokai has more nature than man-made attributes. It varies from verdant fern valleys and coconut groves on the east end to vast empty stretches of dryland ranch on the west end. Investigate the Nature Conservancy preserves in the high-country bog and lowland sand dunes, and sign up for a guided tour to hear about the extraordinary nature of Hawaii's rare species that abound there.

Lanai's landscape is wild and open, and nature is reasserting itself after nearly a century of pineapple plantation agriculture. The pine-lined uplands offer forest trails up the flank of Lanaihale, the old volcano that anchors the island.

COMMENTS Hawaii's natural beauty is legendary; its native wildlife (Monk seals, nene geese, and native Hawaiian birds) may be endangered, but you will not be disappointed by the great outdoors. Maui's fabled Hana is a prime destination for people who like to feel overwhelmed with the majesty of nature. If you're lucky, you may win admission to the Puu Kukui nature preserve atop the West Maui Mountains. For details, see "A Rare Hike between Heaven and Earth," page 234.

PLAN TO CAMP?

If you intend to camp at national or state parks and other popular spots, you may have to compete before you arrive for inexpensive reservations for rustic cabins and tent sites. (See camping section, page 241.)

Golfers

BEST ISLANDS TO VISIT Maui and Lanai

THINGS TO SEE AND DO On Maui alone, 13 golf courses beckon to you, so how can you lose? Your choices include the world-famous sites of pro golf classics telecast each winter, such as the Mercedes PGA Championship Tournament at Kapalua, and courses relatively obscure to all but the Island golfer. The newest is Maui Lani near Wailuku. Lanai has only two, but what a pair—upland, The Experience at Koele, with its signature hole in the middle of a forest, across water, between trees, and 200 yards from the tee, and the oceanfront Challenge at Manele, its very beauty a hazard to the distractable golfer.

COMMENTS Golf doesn't get much better, or more beautiful, than the Golf Coast of Maui and the courses of Lanai.

Gays and Lesbians

BEST ISLANDS TO VISIT Maui and Molokai

THINGS TO SEE AND DO Tolerant attitudes, a Polynesian tradition that recognizes a "third sex" (*mahu*), and plenty of outrageous natural beauty make Maui equally popular with gay and straight visitors. Few places cater specifically to gay travelers, but most places accept visitors of all persuasions. Try a few days on Molokai: quiet, private, and low-key, with a local gay tradition.

Ocean Swimmers

BEST ISLANDS TO VISIT Maui and Lanai

THINGS TO SEE AND DO Maui's best swimming/snorkeling beaches include Kapalua Beach and Napili Bay Beach, fronting the Mauian and other small hotels and condos on the northern end of the resort coast, and Wailea Beach, fronting the Four Seasons and Grand Wailea on the southern end. In the center, surfers and swimmers head for Kamaole Beach County Park III in Kihei. The black-and-white sands of Hamoa Beach in Hana are scenic and the waves just right for bodysurfing much of the time. Maluaka Beach in Makena, across a small sand hill from the Maui Prince Hotel, is another satisfying choice.

We like these beaches because the waters are clear and buoyant, the bottoms sandy, the waves gentle and fun, and the swimming safe. The bay and cove beaches with finite edges of lava reef, such as those at Kapalua and Wailea resorts, lure swimmers to do laps, particularly on calm mornings. Snorkeling is good off the lava rocks that form the bays.

At Lanai's scenic, palm-shaded Hulopoe Beach, below Four Seasons Resort Lanai at Manele Bay, the waters are usually fine for swimming and snorkeling. There is also a pool carved into the lava on one side, just right for little kids to splash around safely.

COMMENTS Oddly enough, a lot of visitors and residents don't go in the ocean waters. It's a shame, for there's no finer place to swim in the sea.

Active Seniors

BEST ISLANDS TO VISIT Maui

THINGS TO SEE AND DO Seniors can do anything they like on Maui's islands, often at a discounted rate. Able elders find most Maui facilities to be easily accessible, including view points. Van groups will have the most sightseeing choices on Maui. Attractions include the Maui Tropical Plantation, where visitors ride trams through sample fields of Island crops, which they can then pick up at the produce market. The National Tropical Botanical Gardens, the only such federally chartered research gardens, are definitely worth a visit near Hana, where the 125-acre Kahanu garden of Pacific Island plants also includes the state's largest archaeological site, Piilanihale Heiau. Plenty of privately operated botanical gardens are sprinkled throughout the Islands, too.

COMMENTS Anyone with gray in their hair tends to be viewed with respect in the Islands. You are considered a wise *kupuna* (elder), especially if you take advantage of senior discounts that shave the costs of activities, attractions, meals, and even merchandise in some stores—sometimes but not always on certain days of the week. For instance, Outrigger Hotels Hawaii offers a substantial break from published room rates for visitors over 50 years and members of the American Association of Retired Persons (AARP), a group that also offers organized tour travel packages to members. Several airlines offer a discount for passengers 65 and over. Elder Hostel stages affordable, stimulating educational travel programs in Maui County and elsewhere for travelers

55 and older. The healthy seniors who live in the Islands surf, dance, play golf, and swim daily—and so can you.

Visitors with Disabilities

BEST ISLANDS TO VISIT Maui

THINGS TO SEE AND DO Haleakala National Park, Maui Tropical Plantation, and Maui Ocean Center on Maui—all of which accommodate disabled visitors.

COMMENTS The *Aloha Guide to Accessibility*, published by the Commission on Persons with Disabilities, provides detailed information on accessibility features of Island hotels, attractions, beaches, parks, theaters, shopping centers, transportation services, and medical and support services. Write the commission at 919 Ala Moana Boulevard, Room 101, Honolulu, HI 96814, or call ☎ 808-586-8121. You can visit their Web site at **www.hawaii.gov/health/cpd.**

Hawaii Centers for Independent Living provides useful information for the disabled at **www.assistguide.com.**

Business Travelers

BEST ISLANDS TO VISIT Maui and Lanai

THINGS TO SEE AND DO Business does happen on Maui's islands, even though they seem devoted to pleasure. Most hotels offer fitness and business centers, handy in-room dataports for laptop computers or high-speed Internet access, and complete understanding when it comes to 24-hour business anxiety, even on vacation. Corporate meeting groups flock to the luxury resorts of Maui and Lanai whenever the economy permits. Situated in the middle of the Pacific, the Aloha State is the only place in the world where you can talk and transact live with New York, Japan, China, and Hawaii all on the same business day.

The Maui County islands are favorites for corporate groups meeting for fun and profit, rewarding top performers, top customers, and top prospects. The extensive choice of luxury resorts and outdoor sports, imaginative team-building events, al fresco parties, and other features draws groups back year after year. The remote setting, extensive international air service in nearby Honolulu, and controlled access (nearly everyone flies in or out), plus the relatively safe and secure environment, add to the appeal of the Maui islands for diplomats, scientists, politicians, and economic leaders, among others.

COMMENTS When it comes to high-tech, the Islands are always on the cutting edge—the latest technology links them to the rest of the world and customers demand it. Technology is keen on Maui, where the fiber optics system linking the island to the West Coast is one of the best in the world, thanks to the presence of an air force supercomputer. This supercomputer complex at Kihei includes a program where businesses and scientific groups and other organizations use the computer's research and data-banking powers for a fee.

Art Aficionados

BEST ISLAND TO VISIT Maui

Musing about Maui: Romantic Suggestions

HE: Remember our first trip to Maui? When we were young, in love, and spontaneous?

SHE: What you are is mature, married, and in trouble. What makes you think you have to be young to be in love and spontaneous?

HE: Well, you don't, but it helps.

SHE: So does going to Maui.

HE: You're absolutely right. Even the climate is right for romance—steamy days, soft breezes, warm seas.

SHE: Cool waterfalls and red sunsets and the sweet perfume of flowers in the air . . . and the hula, and of course, the aloha spirit. Aloha means love, doesn't it?

HE: I thought it meant hello and good-bye.

SHE: I wonder why there aren't more romance novels set on Maui? And movies? Hollywood should love Maui because it's so gorgeous—and all the stars like to go there.

HE: Forget the movies, let's go see the real thing.

SHE: Great idea. Our anniversary's coming up. We can start by finding a secluded beach . . . there's that secret snorkeling cove near Makena.

HE: Or we could fly to Lanai and laze under the palms at **Hulopoe Beach,** or search for fishing floats at **Shipwreck Beach.**

SHE: Let's go to **Molokai.** We could find that little golden beach on the East End, have a picnic, and watch the moon rise over the West Maui Mountains across the water . . . and swim in the moonbeams.

HE: What about skinny-dipping at **Kaihalulu,** the red-sand beach at **Hana** on Maui?

SHE: Sunburned and arrested, too? I'll just wait for you in our private hot tub at the **Hotel Hana-Maui.** Now, there's a romantic spot.

HE: You know, if I really wanted to impress a girlfriend, I'd charter a yacht and take her out to watch the whales . . . and then head for the **Grand Wailea Resort Hotel and Spa.** We'd stay in the biggest suite, dance half the night, and have massages by the sea.

THINGS TO SEE AND DO Maui has a thriving arts and crafts community, with galleries in Lahaina, Wailea, and Kahului, as well as Hana, Paia, Upcountry, and in the northwest area of Kahakuloa. Other options include the Maui Arts and Cultural Center and Hui Noeau Visual Arts Center. The quality, popularity, and price of Island art have increased in recent years, and works by artists from other places are also featured in several galleries.

SHE: Girlfriend!?

HE: It's entirely theoretical, anyway, since that suite runs about $10,000 per night. Where would you want to go to enjoy a romantic dinner?

SHE: Can we afford dinner at Wolfgang Puck's showplace at the **Four Seasons Wailea?** I can hear the waiter now: "More champagne, Mrs. Carroll?"

HE: We'd have to eat plate lunches the rest of our trip.

SHE: I thought money was no object when it came to our anniversary? A candlelight dinner for two at **Banyan Tree** at the **Ritz-Carlton, Kapalua,** on the terrace under the stars. Or the **Wailea Beach Marriott,** dinner for two on the oceanfront lawn, breeze ruffling my linen dress, stars peeking through the trees.

HE: The prices aren't really coming down.

SHE: OK, affordable, but it has to be oceanfront with a sunset view.

HE: I think **Hula Grill** at **Kaanapali Beach** would be perfect. So beachfront you can dig your toes in the sand at the **Barefoot Bar.**

SHE: Or, we could skip the view for once and concentrate on the food—put a little spice in our life, compliments of **Sansei** at **Kihei** or **Kapalua.**

HE: Nothing like some wasabi to bring a romantic tear to your eye. And for dessert, fresh **Kula strawberries** dipped in **Hawaiian Vintage Chocolate.** Or we can just have a romantic picnic under the wild avocados at **Tedeschi Vineyard.** Did you know it used to be called **Rose Ranch?**

SHE: Perfect.

HE: The next day, we could rent a Harley and ride around the lonely side of **Haleakala.** Or, we could ride horses down into Haleakala crater and spend the night. In a rustic cabin or a tent, by a campfire, just the two of us in the wilderness.

SHE: As long as I'm with you, on Maui, with the moonlight sparkling on the sea, it really doesn't matter where we go or what we spend—we'll have a terrific time.

COMMENTS Crafts fairs and crafts booths at other fairs are a good place to see and buy local handicrafts. Fairs are held frequently on the Maui Islands, and local artisans demonstrate and display their work at resorts and hotels, as well. For instance, you don't have to go to the Kingdom of Tonga to find examples of Tongan basketry, some of the best in the Pacific, because a friendly Tongan family participates in the weekly crafts "fair" at Napili Shopping Center, and at Maui Ocean Center.

Hawaiian Culture Seekers

BEST ISLANDS TO VISIT Maui and Molokai

THINGS TO SEE AND DO Hawaiian cultural arts, dances, music, and crafts are in the spotlight year-round in the resorts and communities of Maui, Molokai, and Lanai. Perhaps the most emphasis on Hawaiiana comes in the fall, during the annual Aloha Festivals. Colorful parades and pageantry and special performances of music and dance are among the features. The islands each have their own programs during the statewide Aloha Festivals, which occur during September and October. Resorts support Hawaiian culture, hosting traditional performances and showcasing arts and crafts. Hawaiiana is the way of life on Molokai, where an annual spring festival celebrating the birth of the hula is particularly festive. Maui Arts and Cultural Center, the island's premier showcase, presents a rich cultural array of talent from local hula halau to world-class entertainers. Check the schedule at **www .mauiarts.org.**

COMMENTS Look for *hula halau* (school) fundraisers, church and community luau, music festivals, holiday festivities, and talk story events for a real look at the Hawaiian culture. Or just tune the radio to a Hawaiian music station and get in the groove.

Gourmets

BEST ISLANDS TO VISIT Maui and Lanai

THINGS TO SEE AND DO Superb fine dining is abundant on Maui. Hawaii Regional Cuisine chefs Bev Gannon, Roy Yamaguchi, and Peter Merriman have restaurants on the island, but they are not the only creative chefs in action on the Valley Isle. Make room on your agenda for less-formal dining in a variety of indoor and outdoor locations, where you will enjoy fine, funky, and fusion versions of Japanese, Chinese, Thai, Vietnamese, Swiss, Korean, French, Italian, American, and Latino cuisines. There's a gourmet luau, The Feast at Lele, where chef James McDonald applies his skill to Pacific Island dishes you're unlikely to have anywhere else. Lanai's two hotels offer first-rate restaurants, and the village of Lanai City offers Lanai City Grille for excellent dinners, plus plantation and other small restaurants as popular alternatives.

COMMENTS Be sure to treat your palate to a taste of Hawaii Regional Cuisine. (See Part Eight, Dining and Restaurants, page 271.)

History Lovers

BEST ISLANDS TO VISIT Maui

THINGS TO SEE AND DO Maui's historic preservation plum is Lahaina. Not only have missionary-era homes, a Chinese temple, and other buildings been restored and granted National Historic Landmark status, but plans are under way to unearth and restore an ancient royal Hawaiian palace site currently buried beneath a ball field. Don't miss the Bailey House Museum in Wailuku, housing a collection of artifacts that help tell Maui's story in a restored missionary home. The Piilanihale Heiau dig near Hana will appeal to archaeology buffs.

On Lanai, you can drive and hike to petroglyph rocks on a hill over Palawai Basin, or pilot a vehicle over rough roads to Kaunolu, King Kamehameha's summer fishing camp, or Keomoku, a deserted sugar village.

COMMENTS Buildings crumble rapidly under the assault of tropical sun, rains, bugs, and verdant jungle, so the few that have been restored and maintained are all the more precious. All you'll find of ancient Hawaiian buildings are the lava-rock foundations of homes and temples, but these are revered. On Molokai, seek out the huge Iliiliopae Heiau.

GOING *to* MAUI *to* MARRY?

MAUI HAS LONG BEEN ONE OF AMERICA'S FAVORITE honeymoon destinations. But increasingly, couples choose to hold wedding ceremonies on the Valley Isle as well. Sometimes the whole entourage comes for the wedding, meaning a Maui vacation for all. Sometimes just the lucky pair appears for the ceremony, escaping the family dynamics back home. As soon as the vows are spoken, the couple is already on their honeymoon. Weddings have become a thriving business on Maui and Lanai. Lots of planners are available to handle the details. Hotel concierges and wedding consultants can be helpful. Plenty of Internet sites offer information and services. Lovers can get married at sunset on a scenic golf course overlooking the sea, barefoot on the beach at dawn, on a knoll by a tumbling waterfall, underwater amid tropical fish, in special wedding chapels and churches old and new, on sailboats, and even in midair while skydiving. Or pick your favorite location when you get there. Your selection runs from free-of-charge at public beaches to $10,000 to rent a popular chapel, such as the Grand Wailea's.

Today, thousands of couples are wed each year on Maui. Some hotel chapels average multiple weddings daily. But in old Hawaii, marriage ceremonies were reserved only for high-ranking *alii* class. The first Christian marriage took place in 1822, two years after the arrival of the American missionaries. For a time, it was illegal for non-Christian marriages to be held in the Islands.

Lanai is another prized wedding location, famous as the place where Bill and Melinda Gates were married some years ago. Its elegant resorts, great outdoors to explore at will, private and secure atmosphere, and scenic backdrops comprise a dream setting for a bride and groom.

Molokai isn't fancy, but it offers picturesque historic chapels and natural settings for couples who enjoy ecotourism activities or find comfort in the homey atmosphere.

HOW TO GET MARRIED IN THE ISLANDS

GETTING A MARRIAGE LICENSE IS RELATIVELY EASY in the Aloha State, since there are no residency, citizenship, or blood-test requirements. The legal age to marry is 18. However, with the written consent of both parents or guardians and a family court judge, bride and groom may be married at 15. Consent forms may be obtained from a marriage license agent. Teenagers 18 and under must bring a certified copy of their birth certificates, and people over 19 should have proof of age in the form of a military ID or driver's license. Cousins may legally marry. Formerly married participants should be prepared to provide the date and location of divorces or deaths of prior partners on their new marriage license application. The names of each partner's parents and places of birth must also be provided.

You can review the rules and download a marriage license application from the State Department of Health (**www.state.hi.us/ health/records/vr_marri**) before you arrive or pick up an application at a marriage license office after you get to the Islands.

Both bride and groom must be 19 years or older and present to file the application for a license with a Maui County licensing agent. The fee is $25 in cash. Once approved, the license is issued then and there, good for getting married within 30 days anywhere in Hawaii.

To plan the actual event, you have a choice of more than three dozen wedding coordinators on Maui. You can find out what several have to offer on the Internet—just search for "weddings" in combination with Maui, Molokai, and Lanai.

After the wedding, your officiant will file the necessary paperwork and you will get a copy of the marriage certificate, the document that proves your legal marriage, but be advised that it may take two or three months to receive your certificate at home by mail. If you need a copy faster, or additional copies in the future, the State Health and Human Services/Vital Records division offers specific instructions online at the above Internet address.

You can obtain a license in Honolulu at the State Department of Health's Marriage License Office, 1250 Punchbowl Street, Honolulu, HI 96813. A free "Getting Married" pamphlet is also available from Hawaii's Marriage License Office. Write to the address above or call them at ☎ 808-586-4544. The Marriage License Office is open Monday to Friday from 8 a.m. to 4 p.m. (closed on holidays).

Call the registrar on these Maui County islands for information on contacting a marriage agent:

- Lanai: ☎ 808-565-6411
- Maui: ☎ 808-984-8210
- Molokai: ☎ 808-553-3663

You can also ask your hotel concierge or wedding coordinator to help you find the nearest agent.

The Hawaii Visitors and Convention Bureau has a list of wedding planners on all islands at **www.gohawaii.com.**

ROMANTIC WEDDING SETTINGS

Maui

HAMOA BEACH, HOTEL HANA-MAUI, HANA Down on the sands, with ocean breezes teasing your veil and waves for your sound track: make it a Hawaiian-style wedding in Hana, with wedding lei, a traditional service, hula, and a luau to celebrate with your family and friends. Then later, steal away to your Sea Ranch Cottage with its private hot tub on the deck and contemplate your future. Contact Hotel Hana-Maui, ☎ 800-321-4262.

OVERLOOK AT KAPALUA BEACH Picture this: Watching the sun set on a grassy point overlooking the sea, Molokai in the background, beautiful beach below, pineapple fields forever up the slopes behind the gracious hotel with its lush tropical gardens and huge trees. If it's wintertime, look for the spouts of party-crashing humpback whales out in the channel. Nature's done all she can. The rest is up to you. Contact Ritz-Carlton, Kapalua, ☎ 808-699-6200.

WAILEA GOLF CLUB High on a hill, with a breezy view and a fiery sun setting into the sea, or outdoors on the course, or on the clubhouse deck: scenic grandeur adds an element to your wedding preparations that could even upstage the loving couple. Contact Wailea Golf Club, ☎ 800-888-MAUI.

WATERFALL GARDEN, THE MAUI PRINCE HOTEL, MAKENA RESORT The peaceful waterfall pool garden in the open-air atrium, a patch of green surrounded by black-lava tide pools where golden Japanese carp splash, is a popular wedding site in South Maui for local and visiting brides-to-be. Contact Maui Prince Hotel at Makena, ☎ 808-874-1111.

Lanai

THE CONSERVATORY AT KOELE Exchange vows amid thousands of exotic orchids in the glass-paned Conservatory, then dance your wedding waltz in the Lodge at Koele, a most romantic setting for weddings and honeymoons. Contact Four Seasons Resort Lanai, The Lodge at Koele, ☎ 808-565-7300.

A **CALENDAR** *of* **FESTIVALS** *and* **EVENTS**

MAUI COUNTY LOVES A PARTY, and the list of annual cultural, sports, food, and entertainment events gets longer every year, making it much easier to include a local event in your travel plans.

Following is a sampling of what's coming up in the future. Ongoing cultural activities with changing programs and dates also merit attention—for instance, musical and arts programs at the Maui Arts and Cultural Center (☎ 808-242-7469; **www.mauiarts.org**) and continuing resort programs, such as The Fairmont Kea Lani Maui Food and Wine Masters series in Wailea (☎ 800-659-4100). Maui Ocean Center has a summertime schedule of special events for children (☎ 808-270-7000).

Please note: The event timing in our calendar is approximate, based on traditional and advance schedules, but future events may have different dates. We've tried to include community celebrations with the flavor and culture of the Islands. If you plan your trip around a special interest or a specific event, or just want to see what's happening during the time you want to be on Maui, Molokai, or Lanai, confirm dates with event organizers or look at the online calendar maintained by Maui Visitors Bureau, **www.visitmaui.com.**

January

MERCEDES CHAMPIONSHIPS PROFESSIONAL GOLF ASSOCIATION TOURNAMENT Kapalua Resort Plantation Course, West Maui. A $5 million purse attracts the world's best golfers in the PGA Tour season opener, held the first week after New Year's. ☎ 808-666-9160.

MOLOKAI MAKAHIKI FESTIVAL, KAUNAKAKAI, MOLOKAI This cultural celebration of hula, Hawaiian arts and crafts, games, and food re-creates the spirit of the ancient makahiki harvest festivals. ☎ 808-553-3673.

February

CHINESE NEW YEAR AND LION DANCE Lahaina, West Maui. Dance with the lion at historic Wo Hing Temple on Front Street in Lahaina, center of the annual celebration, which includes fireworks, food booths, and arts and entertainment. ☎ 808-667-9175.

WENDY'S CHAMPIONS Skins Game—Wailea Gold Course. Legendary Champions Tour golfing pros compete for $600,000 in South Maui. ☎ 888-328-MAUI or 808-875-7450.

WHALE WEEK ON MAUI Wailea-Kihei, South Maui, and Whale Quest, Kapalua. Maui honors its biggest, most-famous visitors, the humpback whales, in mid-February at the height of their winter migration. Events include parade, run, regatta, and annual Whale Fest Celebration in Kalama Park in Kihei, with Hawaiian entertainment, gourmet food booths, a crafts fair, and a carnival. If you want to watch whales for a reason, volunteer to join Pacific Whale Foundation's annual count from shore. In Kapalua, lectures, exhibits, and interpretive walks celebrate the leviathans. ☎ 808-879-8860.

March

HAIKU FLOWER FESTIVAL Upcountry Haiku blooms with a Hoolaulea (street party) and flower demonstrations, farmers' market, food, crafts, and entertainment. ☎ 808-573-3573; **www.haikumaui.org.**

PRINCE KUHIO CELEBRATION March 26, a statewide holiday in the Islands, is the birthday of Prince Jonah Kuhio Kalanianaole, one of Hawaii's last royals and its first congressman in the early 1900s.

April

CELEBRATION OF THE ARTS Ritz-Carlton, Kapalua, Kapalua Resort, West Maui. Celebration of the people, arts, and culture of the Islands; workshops, demonstrations, and entertainment, on Easter weekend. ☎ 808-669-6200; **www.celebrationofthearts.org.**

DA KINE HAWAIIAN PRO AM WAVESAILING CHAMPIONSHIP Hookipa Beach, Central Maui. Top wave sailors compete on the Maui stop of the Professional Windsurfing Association's World Tour. ☎ 800-827-7466.

DAVID MALO DAY Lahainaluna High School, Lahaina, West Maui. Celebrate Hawaii's most famous scholar by attending this community luau with hula performances in early April in lieu of the commercial ones down the road. ☎ 808-662-4000.

EAST MAUI TARO FESTIVAL Hana Ball Park, Hana. Ancient Hawaiians believed man descended from taro (*kalo* in Hawaiian), so essential was the plant to the culture. This festival celebrates the taro tradition with exhibits, lectures, demonstrations, food booths, and entertainment, in mid-April. ☎ 808-248-8972; **www.tarofestival.org.**

May

ANNUAL WAILEA OPEN TENNIS CHAMPIONSHIP Wailea Golf and Tennis Club, South Maui. Free to spectators, this tournament features players of world renown in several divisions. ☎ 808-879-1958.

INTERNATIONAL FESTIVAL OF CANOES Front Street, Lahaina, West Maui. The mighty oceangoing canoe is the star of this weeklong cultural festival featuring master canoe carvers from around the Pacific, a parade of canoes, cultural demonstrations, and a concert. ☎ 888-310-1117.

KAIWI CHALLENGE ONE-MAN CANOE RACE Kaunakakai, Molokai. International relay teams paddle a tough route from Molokai to Oahu in a race of one-person outrigger canoes. ☎ 808-969-6695.

MAY DAY, ANNUAL LEI FESTIVAL AND COMPETITION Marriott Wailea Beach Resort and Fairmont Kea Lani Maui, Wailea, South Maui. The Marriott Wailea sponsors a flower lei competition with Hawaiian entertainment and an appearance by the Aloha Festival Royal Court to mark the statewide floral explosion. ☎ 808-879-1922. At the southern end of Wailea, the Fairmont Kea Lani Maui displays flower, feather, and kukui nut lei, also with Hawaiian entertainment. ☎ 808-875-4100. A Hawaiian musical concert and hula by the Brothers Cazimero with Leinaala Heine follow May 2 at the Maui Arts and Cultural Center in Kahului (because the Caz, as they're known, perform every May 1 at the Waikiki Shell).

MOLOKAI KA HULA PIKO Papohaku Beach Park, Molokai. Annual cultural festival celebrates the hula, which by legend was born on Molokai, with pageantry, hula performances, lectures, storytelling, Hawaiian food, games, and crafts. ☎ 808-658-0662.

JAPANESE SUMMER FESTIVAL Market Street, Wailuku, Central Maui. Here's a good excuse to spend some time on Market Street in quaint Wailuku, complete with cultural festivities, food, crafts, and displays, in early June. ☎ 808-270-7414.

June

KING KAMEHAMEHA DAY FLORAL PARADE AND HOOLAULEA Front Street, Lahaina, West Maui; Molokai Civic Center, Kaunakakai, Molokai. June 11 is a statewide holiday honoring King Kamehameha I, who united the Islands into a kingdom two centuries ago. See colorful flower floats and elaborately costumed riders on parade, cultural performances, entertainment, food, and crafts festivals in Lahaina, ☎ 888-310-1117, and Kaunakakai, ☎ 808-567-6027.

MAUI FILM FESTIVAL Wailea Resort, South Maui. Cinephiles give it two thumbs up as one of the best small film festivals, for independent film premieres and location, location, location: outdoors under the stars at Wailea. The weeklong mid-June event draws celebrity guests and Hollywood directors and producers. One popular event at the film festival is the Wild on Water Awards, which honors extreme sports athletes and filmmakers with the Wowwy Award. ☎ 808-572-3456 or 888-999-6330.

UPCOUNTRY FAIR Eddie Tam Community Center, Makawao, Upcountry Maui. Annual country fair features a 4-H livestock auction, farmers' market, games, crafts, plants and flowers, ethnic dances, entertainment, and food.

KAPALUA WINE AND FOOD FESTIVAL Kapalua Resort, West Maui. Winemakers from around the world conduct formal tasting seminars and panels, then pair their wares with the creations of local and visiting chefs to create tasty informal events. Restaurant professionals attend the sessions at the Ritz-Carlton Kapalua, and wine lovers will learn interesting things from the discussions as well as the tasting; held during a four-day weekend in June or early July. ☎ 808-669-0244.

July

FOURTH OF JULY Kaanapali Beach Resort and Lahaina, West Maui. Kaanapali celebrates Independence Day with live music and children's special activities throughout the day. After dark, look to the Lahaina skies for fireworks. ☎ 808-661-3271.

LANTERN BOAT CEREMONY/BON DANCE LAHAINA Jodo Mission, West Maui. A colorful Buddhist ceremony honors ancestors by symbolically setting their spirits free to float to sea in tiny lantern boats; accompanied by a traditional O Bon celebration and dance. ☎ 808-661-4304.

MAKAWAO RODEO AND ANNUAL PANIOLO Parade Makawao, Upcountry Maui. You'll never see another July Fourth parade like this one, replete with flowers trimming the cowboy hats, horses, and riders of all ages—definitely worth getting up early on Parade Day (rarely on the actual 4th) to go Upcountry, park at the Rodeo Grounds, and shuttle to town to celebrate Independence Day, down-home Maui style. A rodeo follows at Oskie Rice Arena, usually after the Fourth. ☎ 808-572-2076.

PINEAPPLE FESTIVAL Lanai City, Lanai. Lanai's heritage as home of the golden fruit is celebrated with pineapple eating and cooking contests, entertainment, arts and crafts, and fireworks. ☎ 808-565-7600.

EPIC MOLOKAI WORLD CHAMPIONSHIP Paddleboard racers rely mostly on superhuman arms to power their sleek longboards across the 37-mile channel from Molokai to Oahu. Some paddle very long boards while standing up, using a canoe paddle for propulsion, while others kneel and paddle by hand. It's a grueling workout either way, topping a busy island race schedule. Also in July, the Naish Annual International Paddleboard Championships race is staged along 9 miles of the North Shore of Maui from Maliko Gulch past Hookipa and Paia to Kahului Harbor. ☎ 808-575-7409.

August

ADMISSIONS DAY August 21 is Admissions Day, a statewide holiday marking Hawaii's anniversary as a state. The Aloha State was admitted to the United States on August 21, 1959.

MAUI ONION FESTIVAL Whaler's Village Shopping Center, Kaanapali Beach Resort, West Maui. Behold the Maui onion, so sweet and good you could just eat it like an apple ("kula apple" is its Upcountry nickname). Or you could cook it in a dozen different ways, as they do in this annual celebration with chef demonstrations, entertainment, and an onion-recipe contest. ☎ 808-661-4567.

September

ALOHA FESTIVALS Maui, Molokai, and Lanai. A cultural celebration of the music, dance, and history of Hawaii, with observances on every island between late September and mid-October. Check on Molokai, ☎ 800-852-7690; Lanai, ☎ 808-852-7690; and Maui, ☎ 808-878-1888.

ANNUAL NA WAHINE O KE KAI Papohaku Beach, Molokai. During this race, one of the Islands' two biggest paddling events, the wahine (women) speed 40 miles from Molokai to Oahu in six-person outrigger canoes; late September. ☎ 808-259-7112.

HANA RELAYS RACE Kahului to Hana. Relay teams take on Maui's famous, 52-mile crooked Hana Highway in this annual mid-September run. ☎ 808-871-6441.

MAUI MARATHON Kahului to Kaanapali, Central and West Maui. This annual late-September race begins at Queen Kaahumanu Center and heads 26.2 miles to Lahaina, with a prize purse of more than $10,000. ☎ 808-871-6441.

MAUI CHEFS PRESENT Lahaina Civic Center, West Maui. This annual food festival shows off the talents of local chefs, beginning with an elegant dinner and continuing with cooking demonstrations, wine tasting, entertainment, and a kids' zone. ☎ 888-310-1117 or 808-667-9194.

ST. JOHN'S KULA FESTIVAL St John's Episcopal Church, Keokea, Kula, Upcountry. Fall festival with live entertainment, food, plants, produce, crafts, auction, and other events. ☎ 808-878-1485.

October

HALLOWEEN IN LAHAINA Lahaina, West Maui. Everyone takes to Front Street in search of fun, masked and costumed, for the so-called Mardi Gras of the Pacific. ☎ 888-310-1117 or 808-667-9194.

MAUI COUNTY FAIR War Memorial Complex, Wailuku, Central Maui. Parade, arts and crafts, ethnic foods, amusements, rides, and a grand orchid show highlight this tropical fair. ☎ 808-270-7626.

MOLOKAI HOE CANOE RACE Molokai. The men's annual 40-mile Molokai-to-Waikiki championship race in six-person outrigger canoes; an October classic. ☎ 808-259-7112.

XTERRA WORLD CHAMPIONSHIP Makena Resort, South Maui. Triathlon plus shorter runs. ☎ 877-751-8880.

November

CHRISTMAS HOUSE Hui Noeau Visual Arts Center, Makawao, Upcountry. Shop for handcrafted items, made on Maui, for your holiday gift list. ☎ 808-572-6560.

HULA O NA KEIKI Kaanapali Beach Hotel. Young hula students from throughout the Islands compete each year for solo honors in this children's dance festival at Kaanapali Beach Hotel. Awards are given for language, music, costume, adornment, and *oli* (traditional chant). ☎ 808-661-0011.

December

CHRISTMAS LIGHT PARADE Kaunakakai, Molokai. A light parade launches the holidays on Molokai with Santa's arrival. ☎ 808-567-6180. Wailea Resort, South Maui. Santa doesn't find too many chimneys in Hawaii, so he tends to show up by other means, such as paddling onto Wailea Beach in an outrigger canoe in early December. You can explain that one to your *keiki* (children). ☎ 808-879-1922.

GALA TREE-LIGHTING CEREMONY Ritz-Carlton, Kapalua, West Maui. Launch the holiday season early with special dinners, brunches, a life-size gingerbread house, children's hula performances, and a tree-lighting. Held in early December. ☎ 808-669-6200.

MELE KALIKIMAKA! HAUOLI MAKAHIKI HOU! Merry Christmas! and Happy New Year! What better present could you receive than to spend the holidays on Maui, Molokai, and Lanai?

NA MELE O MAUI (THE SONGS OF MAUI) Kaanapali Resort, West Maui. Festival to perpetuate Hawaiian culture includes children's song contest and holiday arts-and-crafts fair. ☎ 808-661-3271 or 800-245-9229.

PART THREE

ACCOMMODATIONS

▌ **WHERE** *to* **STAY**

YOUR CHOICES RUN THE GAMUT from top of the line to bare basics among the 200-plus hotel, condo, and bed-and-breakfast choices in the Maui County islands. Most are in the resort areas of West Maui and South Maui, on or near a beach, but others beckon from the cool uplands and forests.

The Maui Visitors Bureau counts 18,469 visitor units, including hotels, vacation villas and condos, time-shares, and bed-and-breakfasts—and 2.3 million visitors a year to stay in them all. In recent years, increases occurred in both Maui-bound visitors and the huge investments spent to appeal to them with ever more luxurious lodging. But few places are more susceptible to worldwide economic influences than the little islands of Maui County. In 2008, multi-million-dollar upgrades and new construction met a sudden drop in visitor traffic due to fuel prices and financial jitters. The last time this happened in Hawaii, in the early 1990s, travelers who did proceed with Island vacation plans found a variety of extravagant upscale properties competing for their business with lower rates and greater incentives. While rough on the captive Island travel industry, uncertain economic times open many doors for Maui visitors—so shop for deals and go enjoy them. Everyone's anxious to greet you.

Trends include emphasis on high-end "residential" tourism—where frequent vacationers buy their hotel room (expanded to include kitchens, etc.) or villa unit and enjoy a new home with resortlike amenities. They can elect to live there, hold it for their own use, or put it in a rental pool. It seems a natural outgrowth of the popular time-share concept that has blossomed on Maui. Now, "fractional ownership" is making its Hawaii debut. The opulent 62-unit Ritz-Carlton Club, Kapalua Bay is scheduled to be complete by 2009 on the site of the former Kapalua Bay Hotel, along with 84 multimillion-dollar condos. Buyers can purchase a three-week interval owner-ship for $300,000 and up, with annual maintenance fees of about $15,000—or buy a unit for $4 million and up. The neighboring Ritz-Carlton hotel, fresh from a $180-million renovation, sports 107 new "residential suites" now among its 463 rooms as well.

Meanwhile down at Wailea Resort, Baccarat is busy building on the site of the former Wailea Renaissance to create Baccarat Resort and Residences, with 193 units in 14 low-rise buildings by 2011. The units will sell for roughly $2–$10 million, can be pooled for rentals or held for owners, and will have restaurants and a spa among the amenities. Just up the trail, 98 capacious, brand-new Wailea Beach Villas offer similar enticements, plus private plunge pools and out-door private showers, with rates of $1,800 and up. Upslope behind Grand Wailea Resort Hotel & Spa, 120 large (3,200–4,000 square feet) two-story townhouses have been built on 30 acres, a gated development known as Hoolei at Grand Wailea. Rentals range upward from $1,600 per night in season.

Many famous hotel and condo management firms—Starwood, Westin, Hyatt, Marriott, Prince, Sheraton, Ritz-Carlton, Four Sea-sons, Fairmont—are well represented on Maui, as well as locally owned independents.

You know what to expect from the Four Seasons and the Ritz-Carlton, and these luxury establishments will not disappoint you. But if your budget has limits not recognized by your taste in vacation spots, we've included the hotels or condos we consider to be hidden jewels among the better known and more expensive options at each resort.

Chances are your choice of resort defines your experience as much as the individual hotels within it. So here is a recap of each of Maui County's regions and the resorts that make each distinct.

WEST MAUI

THE CLASSIC PLANNED RESORT, **Kaanapali Beach Resort,** first emerged in the 1960s and is still a pacesetter. With its mid-rise array of luxury hotels, condos, and time-shares, as well as private homes, golf and tennis facilities, shopping, and restaurants, it is the engine that has driven Maui tourism for decades, just past **Lahaina,** the historic party town. Farther north are the mid-rise condo clusters of **Honokowai** and **Kahana.** They are generally newer than their counterparts around Kihei, although beach and swimming conditions are better in Kihei. Next comes the lesser known enclave of small condo complexes around **Napili Bay.** Finally, West Maui resorts end with exclusive **Kapalua Resort,** along the shoreline of a vast pineapple plantation. Kapalua is home to the Ritz-Carlton, Kapalua and a number of condo villas dating from the 1970s, with plans for 146 new ultra-luxury units on the site of the demolished former Kapalua Bay Hotel. Shops, restaurants, two world-class golf courses, a tennis stadium, a chapel, and resort homes complete Kapalua visitor facilities. A drive down lanes lined with towering Island pines also reveals the tidy red buildings of the working plantation.

Lahaina

Lahaina, the old whaling capital, missionary outpost, and heart of the ancient royal kingdom from 1820 to 1845, is a colorful waterfront village with a lively past, echoed in its quaint preserved buildings. Lahaina has gone to some effort to recapture and celebrate its history, which lends charm to the raffish collection of old wooden structures on the shores of the harbor. A few small inns are scattered among the shops and galleries full of art, jewelry, souvenirs, T-shirts, and Hawaiian crafts that compete for attention with bars, restaurants, and showrooms along tiny, crowded streets and malls.

You can elect to stay at the century-old **Pioneer Inn** for a real taste of history. It was once the hangout of lusty whalers on R&R, until disapproving missionaries came to town. Lahaina also offers lodging in the **Lahaina Inn** and **Plantation Inn** and condo resorts, including the newly redone **Outrigger Aina Nalu** (formerly Maui Islander) and beachfront **Lahaina Shores,** as well as vacation rentals.

But Lahaina is primarily a fun zone, where people congregate to shop, eat, drink, and meet. The area is surrounded by residential neighborhoods, an old sugar mill, and an active harbor with a large fleet of tour vessels. Sheltered by neighboring Lanai across the waters of Auau Channel, the Lahaina shoreline is protected and calm, not much of a place to swim, but a safe anchorage—which is why the Lahaina Roads has been a favorite mooring spot for centuries. Once upon a time, whaling ships and sailing barks anchored offshore for the winter. Nowadays, winter cruise ships stop here in abundance, and this has triggered a new kind of traffic jam: passengers awaiting rides on the lighter vessels that ferry them between ships and shore.

Lahaina is a fine place to stop and watch the sunset, memorable when the sun starts dropping like a fireball behind Lanai and the boats in Lahaina harbor. It's a welcome moment in Lahaina, which is by nature hot and dry. Its name means "cruel sun," and its streets swelter in the daytime. Perhaps that's why it has always been a popular nightspot. Most of West Maui nightlife is based here. Other amusements are also found in Lahaina, notably the best live theatrical show in the Islands, *Ulalena,* at the Maui Myth and Magic Theater; other productions; some noteworthy restaurants; and a couple of good luau, the **Old Lahaina Luau** and **The Feast at Lele.**

Kaanapali Beach Resort

Kaanapali is the prize-winning role model for an Islands master-planned resort, invented in the 1960s by a group of visionaries as a promising way to develop some excess sugar lands along the beach. Like most of its successors, the resort is a cluster of individual hotels and condo resorts, all thriving on the same beaches, restaurants, shops, and golf courses. You'd never guess its age. The success of the resort stems from brilliant early marketing. No one outside Hawaii could master the name "Kaanapali." So instead, the resort was promoted in campaigns that aimed to make a household word out of a name much easier to pronounce: Maui. As in "Here today, gone to Maui" and other catchy slogans. By promoting the Island of Maui, the resort at the center of local tourism flourished, and everyone else did, too.

Kaanapali is three miles north of Lahaina, but when the traffic is heavy, the drive can take more than half an hour. Once you get there, the resort is a pleasing parklike spread of lawns, trees, a curving boulevard, and mid-rise beachfront hotels and condos separated by trees and gardens of lush tropical plants. After 40 years and many prizes for its pioneering design, Kaanapali continues to reinvent itself and remains a popular destination. Its hotels are popular with corporate groups, as well as families, honeymooners, and all who like the active resort atmosphere. Kaanapali Beach is a four-mile strand punctuated in the middle by a lava headland known as **Black Rock,** and the rest of the resort stretches up the slopes to the highway and beyond. Kaanapali beachfront properties on the southern end include **Hyatt Regency Maui Resort & Spa, Marriott's Maui Ocean Club** (time-shares), **Kaanapali Alii** (condos), **Westin Maui Resort & Spa,** and **The Whaler on Kaanapali Beach** (condos). Beyond Whalers Village Shopping Center are **Kaanapali Beach Hotel** and **Sheraton Maui Resort.** All these properties are linked by a beachfront promenade and a resort shuttle. Beyond **Black Rock,** the **Royal Lahaina Resort** commands the principal setting to the north, followed by the hillside **Outrigger Maui Eldorado,** and more beachside properties—**ResortQuest Maui Kaanapali Villas,** luxurious new time-shares Westin and Westin Kaanapali Ocean Resort Villas North, **ResortQuest Kaanapali Shores, ResortQuest Mahana at Kaanapali,** and **Westin Kaanapali Ocean Resort Villas Norta.**

The 600-acre resort has two golf courses, executive resort homes, restaurants with a full range of open-air, ocean-view, and ocean-front dining, and the beachfront **Whalers Village Shopping Center.** The center offers upscale European and American boutiques in addition to art galleries, a whale museum, and an array of Maui goods. Kaanapali also has beachfront tennis courts, public access-ways, and beach parks, as well as a shuttle that connects to **Kapalua/West Maui Airport.** It's convenient to visit, but parking is no longer free. Guests are issued cards to get in and out during their stay. Public beach-access parking is very limited. Three entries from the highway lead to parts of Kaanapali Beach Resort, but they don't all connect. The southernmost entry leads to the lion's share of facilities, including lodging, restaurants, golf, and shopping.

Kaanapali is an ideal place to bring a family, especially one with teenagers. They can find plenty to check out, without needing a car or driving parent, but little real trouble to get into unless they have a credit card. Activities *en famille* are easy and fun, from Hawaiian crafts at the **Kaanapali Beach** to excursions that leave from the beach. You can jump on a resort shuttle and go off to Lahaina to play. Kaanapali succeeds because it still fills the bill, providing visitors a good value and memorable experience. It's not the newest, swankiest, or most serene resort, but it is one of the best maintained, and it far exceeds the normal American definition of vacation resort.

The smaller-craft Kapalua/West Maui Airport is a few miles farther north, about ten minutes away from either Kaanapali to the south or Kapalua Resort to the north and an alternative to the commute to busy, understaffed Kahului Airport.

Kahana/Napili Beach

Farther still to the north, the coastal route, Lower Piilani Highway, leads past restaurants, some shops, and beach parks mostly used by surfers, plus a dizzying forest of midsized condo towers from Honokowai to Kahana—some of them with beachfront access but otherwise hard to distinguish. An attractive low-profile standout is the **Kahana Sunset.** Then without fanfare, after a series of residential oceanfront neighborhoods, comes one of Maui's great little secrets— Napili Bay, a handful of affordable small hotel and condo complexes along a golden beach and its rocky lava promontories. Comfortable (if not fancy) properties located on the beach or rocky reefs include the deluxe 162-unit **Napili Beach Club.** There you'll have a choice of hotel rooms or suites with kitchen facilities and adjoining Sea House Restaurant, the smaller **Mauian Hotel** on the beach next door (with recently revamped studio units), and the smaller-still **Hale Napili,** plus a collection of condo resorts. The beach has picturesque charm and a view of Molokai. For a change of scene, you can walk north to the public accessway for **Kapalua Beach** or up along the road to **Kapalua Resort.**

Kapalua Resort

The signature Cook and Norfolk Island pines marching along roads and ridges denote luxurious **Kapalua Resort.** Kapalua is more edge-of-the-world than end-of-the-road, situated at the lowest slope of a 23,000-acre pineapple plantation. The spiky gray-green plants carpet red-dirt hills on up to the high forests below the summit of 5,871-foot-high Puu Kukui, the tallest peak in the West Maui

Mountains. To the north, an open vista stretches for miles. This is the most beautiful part of West Maui, a setting framed by wild lands and open seas.

Kapalua is home to the **Ritz-Carlton, Kapalua**—plus three postcard beaches, several clusters of villas and homes, three standout golf courses, a small shopping complex, and several restaurants, including **Sansei Seafood and Sushi Restaurant,** one of Maui's brightest fusion-food stars. The tidy, prim red buildings of the adjacent still-functioning pineapple plantation share this hilly setting at the base of Puu Kukui. The Honolua General Store, church, and plantation managers' home have been restored for resort use. Kapalua-bound guests can fly from Honolulu to West Maui Airport in smaller aircraft and avoid the congestion of Kahului. The hotel will send a shuttle to meet you at the airport. Shuttles also go to Lahaina, ten miles away. At Kapalua, especially at the Ritz and northward beyond the sheltering influence of Molokai across the water, the weather is more windward, meaning gustier trades, cooler temperatures, and more passing showers than at the resorts to the south.

Beyond Kapalua, development stops and the road leads along Maui's great northwest coast. Still undiscovered by most visitors, this is some of the island's finest territory, with huge ranches spreading from mountains to sea; popular surfing beaches and sheltered snorkeling bays; coastal lookouts like **Nakalele Point,** where you might see the great pod of spinner dolphins that pirouette and play in these waters; and the tiny settlement at **Kahakuloa Head,** the 636-foot-high coastal rock landmark where you'll find a gallery of made-on-Maui arts and crafts. The road is not for the fast-paced or faint-hearted, with stretches of crooked one-lane track clinging to the coastal slopes and few pullouts for passing, but it is interspersed with better pavement and engineering at some places. Eventually, the coastal ranches give way to mini-estate subdivisions and residential communities around urban Wailuku and Kahului.

Our Choices in West Maui

BEST ON THE BEACH AT ANY PRICE **Sheraton Maui Resort** has a great blend of Hawaiian-style romantic charm, fun features, and elegant architecture, but most importantly, commands the best beach and waterfront location, at Kaanapali Beach Resort's Black Rock.

BEST VALUE ON THE BEACH The 44-studio **Mauian Hotel** on Napili Beach is intimate and low-key with a very Hawaiian spirit; it's so popular with return guests that some families rent several units at a time.

BEST CONDO ON THE BEACH **Kaanapali Alii,** situated in a garden setting front and center on Kaanapali Beach, has luxury units in which families enjoy the same great views with more room and privacy than at surrounding hotels.

BEST CONDO VALUE ON THE BEACH Napili Kai Beach Resort, with its spacious, kitchen-equipped studios and suites (ask for renovated rooms) and hotel-style services, is a comfortable perch on an uncrowded beach with everything at hand for a good vacation experience.

BEST-KEPT SECRET Outrigger Aina Nalu in Lahaina, an oasis of serenity redone with first-class boutique interiors and party-house lanai by the infinity pool, ample parking, and lush landscaping, is within walking distance to the waterfront and noisy pleasures of Lahaina. Stay five nights and you get one free, plus a gift card for groceries and a reusable green tote to carry them.

CENTRAL MAUI

THE WAILUKU/KAHULUI/PAIA STRETCH of the **North Shore** in Central Maui isn't a resort at all, but there are a few interesting places to stay for a different kind of Maui experience, and plenty of outdoor adventures at your fingertips. Budget beachfront hotels on the Kahului waterfront and a B&B inn in Wailuku are good for tight airplane connections and thrifty business stays. On the other end of Maui's central valley, nearly a dozen condo resorts are clustered on the beach and reef at **Maalaea,** near the Maui Ocean Center and Maalaea Harbor area, with restaurants and cruises galore. Everyone who drives from Kahului to the southwestern shore sees them, but most drive on, much farther, to seek a more crowded and expensive version of much the same thing. Those who stop tend to stay awhile; ask about the monthly rates. Keep in mind that Maui's famous winds funnel through the Central Valley most afternoons and may sand-blast your exterior on that five-mile beach.

Kahului/Wailuku

Departing Kahului Airport, you run a gauntlet of familiar commercial landmarks (Costco, Wal-Mart, Barnes & Noble). But there is a Maui, if you persist. Wander farther into Kahului and you'll find more interesting shops around the harbor, where the interisland cruise ships make weekly port calls. Close at hand are the **Queen Kaahumanu Mall,** with more than 100 shops (see Shopping, page 329), a number of smaller malls, and the neighborhoods of Kahului, a waterfront town with a busy port and three small, clean, affordable bayfront hotels frequented by budget travelers. They are the **Maui Beach, Maui Palms,** and **Maui Seaside,** and while you won't want to spend your vacation there, they are close to the airport and handy for early-morning and late-night departures.

The famous windsurfing beach areas, **Kanaha** and **Hookipa beaches,** are beyond the airport, on the North Shore road toward Hana.

In the opposite direction, up beyond Kahului, is the county seat of **Wailuku,** historic and quaint, and the scenic rain forest at

Iao Valley State Park. *Akamai* (in-the-know) travelers check into **The Old Wailuku Inn at Ulupono,** a 1920s-vintage former plantation manager's house that offers ten private rooms, well appointed with plush towels, clawfoot tubs, Aveda room amenities, and a breakfast to rival that of any five-star hotel.

Maalaea

Maalaea, on the resort coast at the other, southwest, end of Maui's central valley, is home to the island's best paid attraction, the **Maui Ocean Center,** and principal harbor of the snorkel-sailing, whale-watching, reef-cruising fleet. Migrating Pacific humpback whales spout and breach and spy-hop everywhere around Hawaii January through April, but nowhere more abundantly than in Maui's **Maalaea Bay,** once a whale-hunting ground and now a national marine sanctuary. Clusters of condos rise up along the shore of Maalaea and across the isthmus, at **Sugar Beach,** where families enjoy an affordable waterfront location, just before the congestion of **Kihei.** Swimming is better at Kihei beaches, but the waters here are popular for surfing.

Our Choices in Central Maui

BEST PLACE TO STAY AT ANY PRICE   Old Wailuku Inn is far from a beach but handy to Iao Valley, the airport and North Shore, the road to Hana and Upcountry, and old Wailuku. A true inn, its rooms are charming and bright and breakfast is delicious, but it's the hospitality of Janice and Thomas Fairbanks that puts it at the top of our list.

BEST CONDO ON THE BEACH   Units at the **Kanai A Nalu,** designed so that all face the sea, or at **Hono Kai** are hard to beat for price and proximity to the beach, both at Maalaea Bay Village.

BEST CONDO VALUE ON THE BEACH   In South Kihei, **Punahoa Beach Condominiums** offer 15 studio, one-, or two-bedroom units, all with kitchens. They are lovingly maintained and share an unbeatable location, beachfront *lanai* (patios), and views of Lanai, Kahoolawe, and Molokini Crater. They are close to shops and restaurants on a quiet side street to the beach. Call ☎ 808-879-2720.

BEST-KEPT SECRET   Mama's Fish House, near Hookipa Beach on the windy North Shore, offers **Mama's Beachfront Cottages,** six units in a small space next to the restaurant, under coconut palms looking out to a sandy beach. The neighbors are pretty close by—restaurant on one side, residences on the other, highway behind—but attractive appointments and a discount at the pricey fish house make this appealing.

SOUTH MAUI

DEVELOPMENT IN SOUTH MAUI runs from **Kihei** south to La Perouse Bay, where the road terminates. In the busy beach town Kihei, condo-dwelling vacationers and local residents share shopping, restaurants and bars, golden beaches, good swimming, and rolling surf.

Below Kihei, **Wailea Resort** can claim status as the premier Maui resort and certainly the top South Maui destination. Developed mostly during the 1980s, this luxurious spread of green contains five hotels and several condo complexes of varying settings, from hillside to oceanfront. Wailea enjoys easy access at the end of a bypass highway, reliably good weather, the **Shops at Wailea** (the largest, newest, and fanciest of the resort shopping areas), three notable golf courses, a tennis complex, homes, and condo choices for varying budget levels.

Just down Wailea Alanui Drive is **Makena Resort,** home of the **Maui Prince Hotel,** two condo resorts, and two golf courses. The resort, located near a former ranching village, has a laid-back air, perhaps because the road ends nearby and few visitors, save guests, pass through.

Kihei

If you're after sun on a budget, go straight to Kihei. It is a sprawling beachside shopping, dining, and entertainment strip, lined with some 50 vacation condo complexes—first popular in the 1960s with Canadian snowbirds who would bunk in for four months at a time to escape winter—and new residential neighborhoods. A newer hotel, **Maui Coast Hotel,** is located across the street from **Kamaole Beach Park I** at the western end of Kihei. Many of the condos are pretty basic shelter, but **Hale Kamaole** is recommended, especially for its location across from **Kamaole Beach Park III,** as well as the **Resort-Quest at the Maui Banyan, Kihei Kai Nani,** and **Mana Kai Maui,** all of which enjoy good beach access.

Kihei suffers the ill effects of strip zoning and sometimes seems like one long traffic tie-up, easily avoided now that a highway bypasses the whole place. But Kihei has beautiful swimming/surfing beaches with public parks, not to mention good restaurants, some of them located on the beach, and fun bars. It is the nightlife district for South Maui. In the daytime, its surfing breaks call to a burgeoning number of surfing-school students, so that visiting kids can learn to be surfa' guys and surfa' girls and get out there with the locals. Outrigger canoe clubs practice in Kihei waters, and humpback whales winter there. Just like the Canadians who first put affordable Kihei condos on the map, the whales leave the cold north each year and head for Maui waters to spend several months lolling about and cavorting in the tranquil seas.

Kihei is also the home of many people who work in the neighboring resorts, as well as the **Air Force Super Computer** technology complex nearby, which gives it an air of reality as opposed to the too-good-to-be-true refined resort atmosphere of neighboring Wailea.

The town fronts a ten-mile coast indented by black lava reefs that frame some excellent pocket beaches and broad beach parks alike. Most popular is **Kamaole Beach III** in the heart of Kihei, with a shaded grass picnic area and park, views of Lanai and Kahoolawe, and free parking. Canadians and Europeans still come to Kihei to stay as long as they can. Families like the freedom and extra space of condo units by the beach. We have California friends who loved Kihei for most of their long lives and won't stay anywhere else. Judging by the crowded bustle of Kihei, in good tourism times or bad, they are not alone.

Wailea

Verdant **Wailea Resort** used to be "the other" resort on Maui—other than Kaanapali, that is—but now it claims top billing as the destination for the luxury-resort crowd. Recently created as a planned resort, this is a groomed, green oasis on the sunny coast, where lavish hotels and condos and public accessways share five desirable beaches defined by lava headlands. The low-rise condos and mid-rise hotels are largely hidden by landscaping and the beachcliff setting on the last leg of Haleakala's southern slope before it drops into the sea. Other features include a high-end boutique shopping center with galleries, shops, and restaurants, exceptional spas, a competition tennis stadium complex, and three velvety golf courses, plus on-beach and off-beach condo complexes and executive homes. When money's no object, or the boss is paying, or you're pining for a spectacular golf fix, Wailea is the place to be.

A 1.5-mile public coastal walking and jogging trail along the resort waterfront affords stunning views of Kahoolawe, Molokini, and Lanai, as well as occasional whales, outrigger canoe races, and other marine travelers. The trail ties Wailea together—from its north end where Baccarat is building a new hotel on the site of the former **Renaissance Wailea Beach,** past the **Wailea Marriott Beach Resort** (fresh from a $60-million upgrade), fronting the new ultra-luxurious **Wailea Beach Villas,** followed by **Grand Wailea Resort Hotel and Spa, Four Seasons Maui Resort at Wailea,** and clifftop **Wailea Point** luxury units. At the southern end, just beyond thriving native-plant gardens and the ruins of an ancient hillside village, the trail drops to beach level in front of the Arabian fantasy–styled **Fairmont Kea Lani Maui.** Along the route are a variety of waterfront condo homes and resorts, some with units close to the beach. The long-established Marriott has great charm and a relaxed atmosphere, and its oceanfront units are near the sea. The same is true of the oldest condos, the **Ekahi** units. Behind the Marriott and the new **Wailea Beach Villas, The Shops at Wailea,** and **Elua** with architecture every bit as grand as the hotels, house retail shops ranging from esoteric European boutiques to coffee stands, plus exceptional galleries and a choice of appealing restaurants.

Grand Wailea features a multimillion-dollar art collection (much of it commissioned for the hotel), a renowned spa, a busy wedding chapel, and an elaborate water complex with miniature river canyons, slides, dives, waterfall caves, and a water-powered elevator so swimmers (and not just kids) don't have to walk back up to the top to start over. Despite the theme-park appointments, Grand Wailea earns national distinction, like the elegant neighbor with which it shares Wailea's best beach, the Four Seasons. Though not exactly condos, Fairmont Kea Lani Maui offers all suites and villas fronting a fine beach. **Diamond Resort** is an all-suite resort, too, high up the slope, set apart from the others on the southern end of Wailea Resort.

Wailea perfects the master-planned resort trend that Kaanapali started in the 1960s. Its beaches are more swimmable, its location closer to Kahului airport, its setting less dominated by cars, and it is more than twice as large, at 1,500 acres. Wailea properties are linked by a resort shuttle, which also serves to bring customers to The Shops at Wailea from neighboring Makena.

Makena

Want more solitude and less bustle? That would be serene **Makena Resort** at Maui's southern end. On its 1,800 mostly natural acres, **Maui Prince Hotel** rises among the scrubby kiawe and other greenery like a mirage. It is ringed by splendid, underpopulated wild beaches and two excellent golf courses. South Maui is punctuated by Puuolai, a cinder-cone peninsula that juts into the sea just beyond the Prince. Some residential development is occurring at the border between Wailea and Makena, but far from sight of the hotel.

Makena is actually an old village where cattle from the upland Ulupalakua Ranch, directly above, were once herded down the mountain and into the water to swim to the ships that would take them to market. They were hoisted aboard in giant slings. Cowboys flapped their hats to ward off sharks. The tiny community today has a picturesque Hawaiian-language church, **Keawalai Congregational,** by the sea.

The road ends where Haleakala's last eruption spilled lava down to the sea, south of Makena, more than 200 years ago. Horseback riding, a sporting-clay shooting range, and hiking add to Makena's appeal. But it is isolated from the rest of the island, making dinner out an expedition. Fortunately the food in the hotel is good.

Our Choices in South Maui

BEST ON THE BEACH AT ANY PRICE **Four Seasons Resort Maui** at Wailea is classy from top to bottom without being ostentatious, quiet without being deadly. Rooms, food, setting, and service are all great.

BEST BEACHFRONT CONDOS Sample the high-end residential vacation trend at **Wailea Beach Villas** in one of its 98 spacious two- and three-bedroom units (Building A is closest to the beach). Ground-level units feature private plunge pools and outdoor showers, built-in barbecues on the lanai, and swanky interiors to match the rates, ranging from $1,800 to $5,000 per night.

BEST VALUE ON THE BEACH Fairmont Kea Lani Resort is hardly inexpensive, but the value comes in the family comforts found in this all-suite hotel, with spacious rooms and a separate children's pool, not to mention homey villas (a three-bedroom, two-story unit with kitchen and plunge pool near the ocean is half the price of the same type unit at Wailea Beach Villas—but older and less plushy too).

BEST CONDO VALUE Grand Champions Golf and Tennis Villas—Wailea amenities on one side, Kihei amusements on the other, the beach a short walk downhill.

BEST-KEPT SECRET Diamond Resort sits high up the hillside, with capacious units and large, open-air *onsen* (Japanese soaking tubs) with sweeping views, plus authentic Japanese food and style.

UPCOUNTRY MAUI AND HANA

FROM KAHULUI, A HIGHWAY RUNS UP THE BASE of Haleakala and becomes a country road as it winds through the cool, pastoral community of **Kula,** where, at 3,000 feet, exotic protea, roses, and carnations grow in the fields and the blue jacaranda trees bloom in late spring. Visitors can stay in a rustic chalet at **Kula Lodge** or in a variety of bed-and-breakfast accommodations up here on the shoulder of the mountain. Kula is a stop on the way up to **Haleakala National Park.** You can keep going to reach the summit or remain closer to Kula. It's a place to escape from the tropical heat of the shoreline, with a rural landscape featuring ranches, a botanical garden, flower farms, a lavender farm, and a winery at Ulupalakua Ranch, **Tedeschi Vineyards.** Pineapple wine and other vintages, including sparkling wines, are available to sample and buy at the tasting room. A cool, grassy setting under wild avocado trees is fine for picnics. But then you must turn around and retrace your route, since the road doesn't connect to the Wailea-Kihei shoreline below.

Upcountry roads do come down to the sea on the opposite, North Shore end. Descending Haleakala, you pass **Makawao,** a ranching and rodeo town with colorful Western-style storefronts; the working plantation village of **Haliimaile,** site of one of Maui's best Hawaii regional-cuisine restaurants, the **Haliimaile General Store; Haiku,** a rural area with bed-and-breakfast lodging mostly used by windsurfers; and **Paia,** a former plantation town now transformed into a busy, picturesque tourist shopping village.

If someone tries to tell you of Hana that getting there is half the fun, don't believe it. Getting there is still an adventure—less so than it used to be now that the road is maintained—but Hana itself is still the most magical Shangri-la on Maui. The arduous 52-mile switchback Hana road, with more than 600 hairpin turns along Maui's northeastern shore, is less scary than it used to be, since it has been properly paved in many areas. However, being in Hana is more than worth the drive that serves to keep the world at least somewhat at bay. The little ranch village and its exclusive hotel define unabashed, old-Hawaii aloha and romance. The **Hotel Hana-Maui and Honua Spa** has undergone a restoration to its former glory, offering cottages and suites with new amenities, including the spa with an ocean view. Besides the hotel, which is expensive, and its restaurant, tourist facilities are limited to a few rooms and condos and state park camping cabins.

Our Choices in Upcountry Maui and Hana

BEST ON THE BEACH AT ANY PRICE The luxurious Hotel Hana-Maui's oceanfront **Sea Ranch Cottages,** some with indoor/outdoor shower gardens as well as private hot tubs on the decks, get our vote for Maui's most wonderful resort. The best beaching is a shuttle ride away at Hamoa Beach.

BEST VALUE ON THE BEACH Four miles out of Hana, 120-acre **Waianapanapa State Park** offers 12 cabins plus tent-camping sites. Where else can you overnight at one of Hawaii's most picturesque black-sand beaches for free (in tents) or in inexpensive cabins that sleep six? But bring insect repellent and book six months ahead in writing. For details see National and State Parks on page 238.

BEST CONDO ON THE BEACH **Hamoa Bay Bungalow** has a Balinese-style cottage for two (and a house for up to four) within walking distance of black-and-white-sand Hamoa Beach.

BEST CONDO VALUE ON THE BEACH Not exactly on the beach, but beside a lava rock stream that runs to the sea, 18-unit **Hana Kai-Maui Resort** is the closest and only beach-area condo in Hana. Clean, modern studios and one-bedroom units that sleep four range from $145 to $255 per night with daily maid service. Write 1433 Uakea Road, P.O. Box 38, Hana, HI 96713; call ☎ 800-346-2772 or 808-248-8426; or visit **www.hanakaimaui.com.**

BEST-KEPT SECRET Hidden behind the famous restaurant Mama's Fish House (Mile 8 on the Hana Highway past Paia), are a cluster of four comfortably furnished apartment-cottages with lanai near a picturesque cove. Prices range from $175 for a garden studio to $575 for a beachfront haven. Write Inn at Mama's, 799 Poho Place, Paia, HI 96779; Call ☎ 808-579-9764; **www.Mamasfishhouse.com**

MOLOKAI

THE LEAST DEVELOPED OF HAWAII'S MAIN ISLANDS, Molokai can be described by what it doesn't have: traffic lights, shopping malls, action, or resorts. The lifestyle is slow and unpretentious, and people pride themselves on being a more traditional Hawaiian community than most in the Islands today. Restaurants and bars and rental cars are few and funky on Molokai, and the airport is as down-home and unassuming as the island itself.

Head east from the airport on Kamehameha V Highway and you'll find the lush, green, and tropical **East End,** with ancient fishponds along a palm-lined coast. Head in the other direction and you'll encounter the **West End,** arid and spiked with cacti. Condo resorts, bed-and-breakfasts, and vacation-rental beach houses in a range of budgets are available in either direction.

Most of the available hotel and condo rooms are aging but well kept. Molokai Ranch, once a 65,000-acre spread encompassing a third of the island and the only modern tourist facilities, closed completely in 2008. **Kaluakoi Resort,** once a favorite weekender for Honolulu residents, is also closed, along with its golf course. Several adjacent independent condo complexes have continued to operate in lonely splendor.

Our Choices on Molokai

BEST VALUE ON THE BEACH Two cottages, **Puunana** and **Pauwalu,** sit like sisters on their own gold-sand beaches on Molokai's East End, just past mile marker 18 on Kamehameha V Highway. If you are lucky enough to reserve one of Kip and Leslie Dunbar's green-and-white two-bedroom, plantation-style cottages, you'll have the ideal spot on Molokai. If Pauwalu cottage were any closer to the beach, it would be in the water. Rates are $170 per night, with a three-night minimum. Call ☎ 800-673-0520 or 808-558-8153; or visit **www.molokai-beachfront-cottages.com.**

BEST CONDO AND BEST CONDO VALUE ON THE BEACH **Paniolo Hale,** with appealing and comfortable units, is on Molokai's West End next to defunct Kaluakoi Resort and a short walk across a golf green from a three-mile golden sand beach.

BEST-KEPT SECRET On Molokai's far East End, a good hour's drive from Kaunakakai at mile marker 25, is **Puu O Hoku (Hill of Stars) Ranch,** secluded by 14,000 acres of conservation land. Besides an organic produce farm, the retreat features an historic 11-room lodge and cottages with a view of the Pacific. Two rustic cottages with awesome views can be rented separately from the lodge—the four-bedroom, three-bath Grove House ($160 a night for two, $20 per extra person up to eight, three-night minimum) and two-bedroom, two-bath Cottage with full kitchen ($140 per night or $840 per week). In winter you can see whales from the living room. Cleaning fees and a refundable security deposit will be charged. For more information, write to P.O. Box 1889, Molokai, HI 96748; call ☎ 808-558-8109; or visit **www.puuohoku.com/cottage.**

LANAI

LODGING ON LANAI IS YOUR CHOICE of two fabulous and recently redone luxury hotels, a charming historic lodge, some plantation cottages, and a few other rentals, some humble, some high-end. Up in the cool highlands surrounded by towering Norfolk and Cook pines, quaint plantation cottages are still clustered in the ambitiously named village, **Lanai City,** topped by the small historic inn **Hotel Lanai & Cottages,** built in the 1920s for plantation guests. Nearby, the elegant 100-room **Four Seasons Resort Lanai, Lodge at Koele** commands a cool Upcountry estate-like setting, while eight miles below on the coast, the lavish Mediterranean-style, 250-room **Four Seasons Resort Lanai at Manele Bay** nestles on a sunny coastal hillside and features a conference center for small groups. The Lodge sits on a hill at the end of a pine-lined lane and looks so important that you think a royal retainer might greet you instead of a hostess with a flower lei. It is cool at night here, which makes it a favorite with weekending Honolulu residents who love to dress up in sweaters and sit by a roaring fire. Downhill, beside the Island's only safe swimming beach at **Hulopoe Bay,** the Manele Bay hotel simmers in splendor around its pool, a lobby full of European and Asian art, and tropical gardens lining a man-made stream.

At Lanai's resorts, amenities include stables, tennis courts, and croquet lawns, fine dining that features dishes made with fresh produce and venison from Lanai, and a special brand of hospitality. These are not snooty resorts, but gracious places where the staff, from boss to busboy, actually seems to care whether everything is right for you.

Golfers can play either of the island's two magnificent 18-hole courses: the oceanside **Challenge at Manele** or the upland **Experience at Koele,** possibly the most beautiful course anywhere. Yet while visitors are signing up for substantial fees, local golfers choose the little nine-hole upland **Cavendish Golf Course,** where fees are paid on the honor system in a drop box.

Visitors can explore at will the private wilderness prized by hunters and fishermen, divers and sailors. Four-wheel-drives and other rental vehicles are available through the hotels and a Dollar Rent A Car office. But if you don't want to drive at all, resort shuttles link the resorts, airport, village, and best beach. Honeymooners, this is your island, so long as you can forgo boogie bars. Nightlife is limited to whatever amusements the hotels have lined up in terms of Island music and hula.

Our Choices on Lanai

BEST ON THE BEACH AT ANY PRICE Simple. If you care about being next to the beach and sea, pick **Manele.** If you are intrigued by the thought of cool Upcountry in tropical Hawaii, pick **Koele.** Or stay at both.

BEST VALUE **The Hotel Lanai & Cottages** above Lanai City is quaint and charming, with good food. You can live the plantation village life in a hotel room or one of five larger cottages and take the resort shuttle down to the beach.

BEST-KEPT SECRET Wedding? Reunion? Golf shoot-out? Lanai Hui's **Captains Retreat,** a contemporary 3,000-square-foot cedar house in the uplands near Lanai City, may fill the bill. The vacation rental, which sleeps eight, runs $4,000 per week minimum, $500 a day thereafter. Call ☎ 808-268-1834 or visit **www.lanairental.com.**

GREAT PLACES *to* STAY *that* SUIT YOUR INTERESTS

THE FOLLOWING ARE SOME OTHER RECOMMENDATIONS to consider, based on what you most want from a Maui vacation.

Hopelessly Romantic

HOTEL HANA-MAUI AND HONUA SPA, MAUI In misty green, tropical Hana, this idyllic inn by the sea offers private cottages with bubbly hot tubs on the deck, private outdoor shower gardens, and thick towels to get dry again. Your tropical fantasies come to life in this exclusive 66-room, 67-acre, old-Hawaii setting. Explore the neighborhood on foot or horseback—this area is all part of a large ranch. Call ☎ 800-321-HANA or visit **www.hotelhanamaui.com.**

FOUR SEASONS RESORT LANAI AT MANELE BAY OR LODGE AT KOELE, LANAI You don't have to indulge in a luxury blowout to prove your love, but then again, why not? This setting is dedicated to your privacy and enjoyment—as hassle-free as possible, classy but not intimidating. Your worst dilemma is choosing the mountains (Koele), where it's cool enough to snuggle, or the sea (Manele), where the warm sun bakes away inhibition. But you can go to both in the same trip. Call ☎ 800-321-4666 or visit **www.fourseasons. com/lanai.**

RITZ-CARLTON KAPALUA, MAUI Hawaii's only Ritz commands the last outpost of resort life in West Maui, which ensures unmatched views up the wild northwest coast and out to sea. Its caring management and celebrations of Hawaiian culture and art add to its romantic setting, on an old pineapple plantation at the foot of the West Maui Mountains. You can get married in the historic little church on the grounds. An oasis of calm with old-fashioned Hawaiian hospitality: at this Ritz, it's your pleasure. Call ☎ 800-262-8448 or visit **www.ritzcarlton.com.**

Great for Families

FAIRMONT KEA LANI MAUI, WAILEA, SOUTH MAUI With its white towers and turrets, like something out of *Arabian Nights,* the luxury Fairmont Kea Lani Maui hotel delivers far more than fantasy. All the rooms are well-equipped suites with iPod docks and kitchens, and the townhouse-style private villas add more bedrooms and private plunge pools. Kea Lani has a great beach and interesting, varied restaurants. Kids are so welcome that they get their own pools with a slide; there's also one for adults only. Find the hotel at the south end of Wailea Resort, within walking distance on the coastal trail of neighboring shops and restaurants. Call ☎ 800-659-4100 or visit **www.kealani.com.**

WESTIN MAUI RESORT & SPA AT KAANAPALI BEACH RESORT, WEST MAUI This open, airy beachfront hotel, now partly devoted to time-share units, looks like a Disney fantasy—tropical jungle foliage, waterfalls, and parrots everywhere inside the open atrium, and Kaanapali Beach outside. Kids love the aquatic playground with 128-foot slide, the easy-breezy feeling, and year-round summer camp–like fun. Big kids like it, too. Call ☎ 800-937-8461 or visit **www.westinmaui.com.**

Great Historic Traditions

HOTEL LANAI & COTTAGES, LANAI CITY Built in 1923 for the pleasure of James Dole's guests, this little ten-room upland inn was the only place to stay on Lanai, the world's biggest pineapple plantation, until everything changed in 1990. The plantation shut down, and two world-class hotels and residential development started up, but the little hotel and Lanai City stayed pretty much intact. New owners have added five plantation cottages scattered around the village to accommodate families or couples traveling together. The hotel features a fine restaurant for dinner. It's cool up here under the tall Cook pines, so the Hawaiian quilts come in handy. Call ☎ 808-565-7211 or visit **www.hotellanai.com.**

PIONEER INN, LAHAINA, MAUI Overlooking Lahaina Harbor, the Pioneer Inn turned 100 years old in 2001, holding on nicely after a $5-million face-lift. This once-rowdy sailor's haunt, now run by Best Western, is a relic fit for all who "collect" old hotels and prefer tradition over trend. Call ☎ 800-457-5457.

The first time we checked into the Pioneer Inn in the 1970s, a second-story room overlooking Lahaina Harbor went for $20 and included a can of Raid. The screen door was rusty, the ceiling fan was broken, and the bed sagged almost to the floor. None of that mattered; what mattered is that the pile of old green wood still stood—and still stands today, the oldest inn on Maui, sole survivor of an era long past.

Great Bargain

THE MAUIAN HOTEL AT NAPILI BAY, MAUI Long owned and still operated by a Hawaiian family, this small 44-unit beachfront complex has to be the deal of them all on Maui. It has a perfect position on Napili Bay, a scenic and swimmable cove with a beckoning beach and Molokai on the horizon across the channel. Its newly upgraded boutique studios cost substantially less than their neighboring counterparts or nearby luxury hotels that would have benefited from this prime location. The ambience is low-key (TVs, DVDs, phones, and internet access are all available in the common meeting room where continental breakfast is served). The grounds are lovingly tended, and the units brightened with private lanai and stylish interiors that include kitchenettes. Call ☎ 800-367-5034 or 808-669-6205 or visit **www.mauian.com.**

Great Escape

HUELO POINT FLOWER FARM Perched on a spectacular, secluded, 300-foot sea cliff near a waterfall stream, yet only about 20 minutes driving time beyond Paia on the Hana road, this vacation rental estate puts you in a Maui setting beyond your most romantic dreams. Four architecturally stunning contemporary homes are available in a lush tropical garden setting, accommodating up to 18 people altogether. Six people can share the artfully designed main house; there is also a studio cottage with three walls of glass so as not to miss a view, a carriage-house apartment with glass walls facing the sea that sleeps four, and a two-bedroom guesthouse with soaring (18-foot ceiling) interiors. A group can rent the whole two-acre estate that claims incredible ocean views. Rentals are monthly. Amenities include a pool and three hot tubs, not to mention a garden where guests can help themselves to vegetables, fruit, and flowers. The homes are completely equipped. It's enough to make you want to thank the hosts for sharing such a splendid retreat. Call ☎ 808-572-1850 or visit **www.mauiflowerfarm.com.**

DIAMOND RESORT & SPA, WAILEA RESORT, SOUTH MAUI Diamond Resort, 15 acres on a hill above Wailea's Blue Golf Course, is an unexpected find: 72 terraced suites and a full-on Japanese *onsen* (soaking tub), with separate men's and women's large, open-air soaking pools that have extraordinary panoramic views of islands and ocean to contemplate while you soak, plus the most unusual spa treatments this side of Beppu. The resort began life as a private Japanese club, but now has gone public and welcomes Western guests. If you appreciate Japanese design, food, and onsen, you'll like this. The rooms are Western style, not tatami, each with a deep soaking tub, separate bedroom and living room, private lanai, kitchenette, wireless access, and bathrobes. The sushi bar is authentic. Call ☎ 800-800-0720 or 808-874-0500 or visit **www.diamondresort.com.**

GETTING *a* GOOD DEAL *on a* ROOM

NOW THAT YOU'VE HAD A PREVIEW of some of Hawaii's great places to stay, here are some ways to get the best deal.

- Check for special Internet rates and browse the hotel sites carefully. Then call the hotel to confirm your choice, and their cancellation policies, with a reservation agent so that you get the price, view, and other amenities you expect.

- Go in spring or fall (April through early June, or September through November).

- Educate yourself on what you want and where and when you want it. If you use a travel agent, they may have suggestions that alter your plan, but they'll surely do a better job if you narrow the search for them. Most agents now charge customers a fee for their services, as well as collect a percentage of the booking as their commission. In Hawaii, hotel and condo commissions are usually 10 percent. Ask about your agent's fee policies in advance.

- Ask a travel agent to research package rates and other specials that combine your lodging with sports and spa facilities, car rentals, and other features. They have access to information you won't find as a consumer.

- Call the hotel to see what rate you can negotiate. Current economic times dictate slashed rates and plenty of extras. Ask for the best rate they can offer. Ask about renovations and the condition of the room you reserve.

- Pursue discounts for corporate travel, seniors, kids staying in your room, military, travel clubs, and other special-status travel. And see what frequent flyer mileage you may gain from your hotel stay.

- Book early and make a priority list of what you want before you book.

Several factors determine a hotel room rate: demand, location (including island and resort area), season, availability, view, grade of room, and proximity to beach, shopping centers, and entertainment. Hawaii room rates are traditionally highest from late December through late March, when everyone wants to escape winter, and in mid-summer when families are visiting. Average hotel room rates on Maui are higher than the rest of the state.

Hawaii's visitor industry provides a quarter of the state's gross state product, a quarter of the state's tax revenue, and one-third of the jobs. Hawaii's dependency on tourism is unlikely to shrink. That means competitive rates and good deals are possible for you.

WHERE THE DEALS ARE

NEWSPAPER TRAVEL SECTIONS Check the travel sections of major U.S. newspapers for good room deals and airfare, hotel, condo, and car combinations.

SURF THE INTERNET If the search is part of your journey, surf the Internet. You can preview islands, beaches, and golf courses, as well as hotels, condos, and vacation rentals. The Internet and this guidebook, which highlights Web sites, will make your search easy.

MONEY-SAVING SUGGESTIONS FOR BOOKING A ROOM Many hotels and condos offer their own periodic package deals with value-added amenities like a free rental car, food-and-beverage credits, rounds of golf, spa treatments, extra-special treatment for honeymooners (chocolates and champagne) and families, free nights if you stay a certain number of nights, and free or cheaper second rooms when you book the first room. Off-beach properties are cheaper; so are mountain- or garden-view rooms. Ask if kids can stay in your room free.

TRAVEL PACKAGES Travel packages save money, provide value, and eliminate the search for separate deals for airlines, rooms, and car rentals. In recent years, they have become very flexible and include a wide range of rates and places to stay, usually resort hotel rooms or condo units. Be a good shopper by knowing what your cost would be for each component of the package, and be sure the package total is cheaper and, hopefully, includes extras.

These packages have a single inclusive rate, but they differ from tour travel. On a tour, you are escorted by a guide who handles everything on the trip for you (including bags, airport transfers, and other annoying necessities). Travel packages are for independent travelers.

IF YOU MAKE YOUR OWN RESERVATION If you hunt your own bargains, call the hotel directly instead of the toll-free number. The toll-free clerk may be in Iowa, unaware of special local rates. The quoted, or "rack," room rates—the ones printed once a year for brochures in a lobby rack—are nothing if not flexible. Virtually no one has to pay the full rack rate, except perhaps at Christmas and other peak travel times. Don't be shy about inquiring about lower rates, especially during the low season, when your bargaining position is improved. Ask for the lowest and best rates available to you. Hotels would rather fill rooms at discounted prices than leave them empty.

- Be wary of deals that are too good to be true. If you suspect something's amiss, check directly with the airline, rental-car company, or lodging provider in Hawaii.

- Don't be pressured into accepting a rate on the spot—but be aware that discounted airfares, for example, can disappear very quickly. Question any requests to send money immediately. Do not provide your credit card number or bank information over the phone unless you know the company.

- Ask questions. Find out what's covered in the total cost. Ask if there are additional charges, such as daily resort fees. Ask about cancellation policies and refunds.

- Get all the information in writing before you agree to purchase a travel package, and read it.

CORPORATE RATES Many hotels provide corporate rates (up to 20 percent off regular rack rates). Ask your hotel about them. Some hotels require a written request on company letterhead, while others will guarantee the rate regardless of your work status.

TRAVEL CLUBS Travel clubs are not a major factor in Hawaii travel, but they may offer discounts with restrictions, particularly on transportation. They generally apply on a space-available basis and are not available in blackout periods. Some may apply only on certain days of the week.

Most travel clubs or half-price programs charge an annual fee. When you join, you receive a membership card and directory of participating hotels. These travel-club programs offer lodging in Hawaii:

Encore ☎ 800-638-0930

Entertainment Publications ☎ 800-285-5525

International Travel Card ☎ 800-342-0558

Quest ☎ 800-638-9819

TOUR WHOLESALERS Tour wholesalers annually purchase blocks of hotel rooms at a low, negotiated rate. They resell rooms during the coming year to travel agents and the public. Wholesalers sometimes offer rooms at bargain prices to avoid returning unsold rooms to the hotel. They prefer that you reserve packages through your travel agent. Dozens of tour wholesalers offer Hawaii travel packages, including these:

All About Hawaii ☎ 800-274-8687, **www.allabouthawaii.com**

Classic Vacations ☎ 800-221-3949 or ☎ 800-635-1333,
www.classicvacations.com

Creative Leisure ☎ 800-426-6367, **www.creativeleisure.com**

Pleasant Holidays ☎ 800-742-9244, **www.pleasantholidays.com**

INTERNET WHOLESALERS The dot-coms of travel—**orbitz.com, travelocity.com, hoteldiscount.com, travel.yahoo.com, expedia.com, cheaphawaiitickets.com,** to name a few of the best-known—offer good rates for Hawaii trips. They put travel packages together like the tour wholesalers and charge travelers minimal fees.

OTHER WAYS *to* STAY:
Condos and B&Bs

CONDOMINIUMS

CONDO UNITS, THE BUILDING BLOCKS of Maui tourism, can be the perfect way to go for family trips, couples traveling together, or anyone seeking more space, privacy, and value than a hotel room can offer. Good condo resorts exist on all the islands except Lanai. Together, they form a pool of thousands of choices for you, at all budget levels. The most recent additions tend to be very expensive units affording luxury, privacy, and security for about $550 per night per bedroom, and up.

Often located beachfront with many of the services offered by hotels, condo resorts range from standard to super, with all the comforts home may lack. They come in small clusters or large buildings, often with lobbies, front desks, and daily maid service. Frequently, they are located in major resort areas with the full menu of extras, including golf, tennis, pools, restaurants, and shuttles. The difference between some resort condos and hotels, particularly suite hotels, is hard to discern as a guest, other than the additional space and homelike facilities of condos. The units are individually owned, but the rentals are usually managed in a pool. Units in one complex may be managed by several different companies, some of them hotel firms (including locally owned ResortQuest Hotels and Resorts and Outrigger Hotels and Resorts), just to confuse it further, and individual owners may rent their own units, too.

Units usually range from 600 to 800 square feet for a one-bedroom unit to 3,000 square feet or more for a two- or three-bedroom unit. With kitchens, you have the option of cooking all meals or just putting together a quick breakfast or lunch, then having dinner in restaurants. A kitchen means you can sample fresh tropical fruit, Maui coffee, and other Island specialties, and it erases problems with fussy

Recommended Condo Reservations Agents

ResortQuest	Kapalua Villas
☎ 800-GO-RELAX	☎ 800-545-0018 or 808-669-8088
www.resortquest.com	**www.kapaluavillas.com**
Destination Resorts Hawaii	Kihei Maui Vacations
(Wailea Resort)	(affordable homes, too)
☎ 808-879-1595	☎ 800-541-6284 or 808-879-7581
www.drhmaui.com	**www.kmvmaui.com**
Hawaiian Condo Resorts	Outrigger Hotels and Resorts
☎ 800-487-4505 or 808-949-4505	☎ 800-688-7444
www.hawaiicondo.com	**www.outrigger.com**

eaters or special diets. Most condo units also have laundry facilities.

Ask about children's programs when traveling with the family. Outrigger, for instance, offers an "Island Explorer Kit" (free to kids ages 5 to 10 with a three-day minimum stay at any of Outrigger's three Maui condo resorts) to get families outdoors to discover Hawaii's special environment. The kit comes complete with a reef adventure guide (produced with Jean Michel Cousteau's Ocean Futures Society) with six lessons about ocean, reef, and shoreline life, and an explore-Hawaii guide—how to prepare for an Island hike, read a map, and identify creatures that live in the rain forest (developed by the University of Hawaii).

Maui condo unit prices can range up to more than $800 per night for a two-bedroom ocean-view, and twice that much for a four-bedroom penthouse, depending on the location, size of accommodation, and your dates of stay. Condos also may offer free nights, groceries, gas, and other incentives to encourage travel in tough financial times.

You can book through one of the dozens of condo reservations agencies to find units that suit your needs. State your preferences on location, size, price, amenities, ambience, and the number in your party, and what activities you want to enjoy during your stay, and you'll receive a list of properties from which to choose. Some condo representatives offer extra services, like car rentals and lei greetings, and some handle private resort home rentals as well.

Kapalua Resort on Maui is one of several luxury resorts with on-site management operations, handling some 200 luxury units and homes at the resort. Destination Resorts Hawaii at Wailea is another, handling a wide variety of condo units at Wailea, from unassuming to palatial.

If you go condo shopping on your own, you'll find plenty of condo travel packages are available in the same way that hotel packages are offered, with car, flights, activities, and special services or gifts included. Watch the ads, use the Internet, ask your friends, and keep on top of special offers. Also, individual owners may rent their units through the Internet and ads in magazines or newspapers.

Terms and policies differ. A deposit is usually required, payable by a major credit card. It's wise to book several weeks in advance, although late bookings are entirely possible. Holidays and other high-demand periods, like spring break, are the most competitive times.

RECOMMENDED CONDOS

BELOW ARE SOME recommended condos to check out, chosen for their locations and special features. See page 118 for the "$" conversion chart.

South Maui

2095 South Kihei Road, Kihei, HI 96753;
☎ **800-822-4409 or 808-879-5445**
www.kamaolesands.com

kids Kamaole Sands $$$

Across the street from Kihei's best beach park, Kamaole Sands is at the quiet Wailea end of this busy little beach town, near good restaurants and Wailea's upscale shops and resort amenities, and, of course, the beach. Ask about the condition and specifics of your unit when you reserve it. One- and two-bedroom units with open lanai overlook the lushly landscaped courtyard with adult and child swimming pools, pool house with snack bar, hot tub, and outdoor barbecue grill. You may bump into someone famous at Kamaole Sands because Maui Arts and Cultural Center lodges its visiting entertainers here.

3600 Wailea Alanui Drive, Kihei, HI 96753;
☎ **866-384-1366 or 808-891-6200;**
fax 808-874-3554
www.drhmaui.com/ wailea-elua-village.php

kids Wailea Elua Village $$$$

Just a lawn away from irresistible Ulua Beach, these luxury units spread across 24 acres that include two pools, a pavilion for entertaining, paddle-tennis court, putting green, and whirlpool tub. Designer furnishings grace one-, two-, and three-bedroom units with spacious lanai. Guests in the 152 units get special golf and tennis rates at Makena and Wailea resorts.

3750 Wailea Alanui Drive, Kihei, HI 96753;
☎ **866-384-1366 or 808-891-6200;**
fax 808-874-3554;
www.drhmaui.com/grand champ/index.asp

Wailea Grand Champions Villas $$$

Off-beach but next to tennis courts and golf greens, this newer complex at the south end of Wailea is attractively decorated and well appointed but substantially less dear than the oceanfront Wailea condos. Two great Wailea beaches—Ulua and Keawakapu—are a short downhill walk or drive away. Destination Resorts handles reservations for 188 one-, two-, and three-bedroom units. Another agency, Maui Condo and Home Realty, handles 30 units, but often at lower rates (☎ 800-822-4409 or 808-879-5445, or visit **www.resortquestmaui.com**).

kids Maui Makena Surf $$$$$

Blissful seclusion, fantastic views, and high-ticket luxury await guests at these oceanfront and beachfront units. They were built on the toe of a lava flow that divided sandy beaches beyond Wailea in remote, quiet Makena. Golf, tennis, restaurants, and shopping are within a few minutes' drive. Various rental agents handle the 200-unit (primarily large two-bedrooms and some three-bedrooms) low-rise, gated property.

93 Makena Road, Kihei, HI 96753;
☎ 866-384-1365;
fax 808-874-3554;
www.drhmaui.com/
maui-makena-surf.php or
www.maui.cc/vmakena
surf.html

West Maui

kids Kaanapali Alii $$$$$

Beachfront, between the Marriott Maui Ocean Club and Westin Maui, this award-winning 11-story luxury complex of 264 one- and two-bedroom units is just like a resort hotel, only nicer and with bigger units. Planning a blowout celebration? Get one of the palatial premier suites with a wraparound view and watch the whales, all of them, from your deck chairs. Amenities include free or valet parking, beachside barbecue grills and entertaining pavilion, kids' programs, pools with free scuba instruction, grocery deliveries and nightly turndown service on request, lighted tennis courts, daily maid service, reception and porters, and a concierge to arrange your activities, plus 1,500–1,900 square feet of oceanfront space for up to six of you to kick around in.

50 Nohea Drive, Lahaina, HI 96761;
☎ 800-642-6284 or
808-667-1400;
www.kaanapali-alii.com

kids Kahana Sunset $$

Terraced into a bowl-like cliff on a horseshoe curve in the shoreline road near its northern Napili end, this low-rise cluster of 79 one- and two-bedroom units enjoys a secluded, beautiful beach. Units are roomy and handsomely appointed (ask for a renovated unit) with large lanai or, at the lower edge, patios on the beach.

4909 Lower
Honoapiilani Road,
Lahaina, HI 96761;
☎ 800-669-1488 or
808-669-8011;
fax 808-669-9170;
www.kahanasunset.com

kids The Kapalua Villas $$$

Luxurious, spacious villas are set in low-rise clusters with good views near the beach or on a hillside. The 280 units include one, two, and three-bedroom

500 Office Road,
Kapalua, HI 96761;
☎ 800-545-0018 or
808-669-8088;
www.kapaluavillas.com

villas updated with designer furnishings and feature equipped kitchens and laundries. Bring the whole clan and party on.

kids Outrigger Aina Nalu $$$

660 Wainee Street, Lahaina, HI 96761; ☎ 800-367-5226 or 808-667-9766; fax 303-661-3733; www.outrigger.com

Outrigger put a sleek new shine on a nice old shoe in renovating this low-rise complex of studio, one-, and two-bedroom units, an oasis among palms and gardens just outside the main business district. Tasteful interiors feature slate walk-in showers and floors, large sepia-toned Hawaiian photographs, geometric carpets that suggest ancient kapa patterns, bronze fixtures and black accents in a modern Eurasian design. Larger condos in the deluxe 92-unit resort (walking distance from Front Street and the harbor) have full kitchens and laundry facilities.

kids Maui Eldorado Resort $$$

2661 Kekaa Drive, Lahaina, HI 96761; ☎ 800-688-7444 or 808-661-0021; fax 303-369-9403; www.outrigger.com

These 204 spacious studio and one-bedroom units with views are spread over a green hillside setting, wrapped by Kaanapali Golf Course, accessible by the middle of three resort entry roads. The resort holds lots of appeal for families, including daily maid service, pools, grassy play areas, shops, and barbecue areas. They offer the comforts you need for a stay at Kaanapali Resort.

Central Maui

kids The Inn at Mama's Fish House $$$

799 Poho Place, Paia, HI 96779; ☎ 800-806-4852 or 808-579-8594; www. mamasfishhouse.com

One- and two-bedroom hideaway duplex cottages snuggle next to the restaurant, just a lanai away from the sands of picturesque Kuau Cove on the North Shore near Hookipa Beach. Coco palms à la central casting dot this beach; swimming and snorkeling are possible in the reef-protected waters before the famous winds come up in the afternoons. The six units are tastefully decorated with tropical styling, terra-cotta floors, and gas grills on the lanai. Guests get a discount off Mama's pricey lunches and dinners. Mama's also has two studios and a one-bedroom cottage six minutes up the road in an Edenlike private tropical garden. Guests are invited to sample the flowers and fruit in "Mama's Secret Garden," off the beach.

kids Kanai A Nalu (at Maalaea Bay Village) $$

250 Hauoli Street, Maalaea, HI 96793; ☎ 866-626-6367 www.kanai-a-nalu.com

These 80 two-bedroom units, each with an ocean view, have direct beach access to a strand that goes for miles across the isthmus. Stay longer, and the daily rates are cheaper. Whales play out front in winter. The units are done in tropical pastels with two baths and laundry facilities. A heated pool by the sea and barbecue facilities beckon outside your room.

Molokai

kids Paniolo Hale $$$

P.O. Box 190, Maunaloa, HI 96770; 800-367-2984 or 808-552-2731; www.paniolohaleresort.com

Wrapped by Kaluakoi Golf Course, beside golden Kepuhi Beach, this architecturally appealing ranch-style retreat is the most interesting of the low-rise condo complexes at Molokai's west end. The resort is closed, but not Paniolo Hale, which operates independently. It is close to the beach and one of the best ways to stay on Molokai. The studio and one- and two-bedroom units have laundries, kitchens, and color TVs inside; a pool, paddle-tennis courts, barbecue grills, picnic tables, and free parking outside. Long walks along the sea cliffs may flush a few wild turkeys.

BED-AND-BREAKFASTS

A HAWAII-STYLE BED-AND-BREAKFAST can offer a satisfying personal Island experience, like staying at a friend's home. It can also be a disappointment with spare-room ambience and little privacy. Either way, this option may soon vanish, since county governments on various islands are busy trying to outlaw bed-and-breakfasts in residential areas. Some vacation rentals are already licensed, however, and remain good alternatives to traditional hotels and condos.

You should do some investigating before you book, checking, for instance, where the units have private baths and entries. You can often preview your choice on the Internet before you reserve it.

On the Mainland, a "bed-and-breakfast" usually means a refurbished mansion or historic house. In Hawaii, it's often a studio or a cottage with some kitchen facilities or a guest room in a private home.

You won't get a home-cooked breakfast at most of the in-house bed-and-breakfasts, thanks to restrictive laws. But you can expect a continental buffet or a basket of tropical fruit, breads, and Island coffee.

Beach properties are usually booked year-round, often by return guests. Plan to make reservations two or three months in advance, more for holiday periods.

Per-night prices range upward of $100 per night and average $250 per night for two people by the beach, cheaper off-beach. Most operators require a minimum three-night stay for bed-and-breakfasts, small inns, and hotels and a seven-day minimum for vacation rental homes.

To book, you can call the hosts directly or use a reservation service; we've provided a list of the largest, most reputable services, which have units on Maui and Molokai. Independent listings on Lanai are often vacation rental homes. Rental terms, minimum stays, and policies vary. Personal checks and credit cards are generally accepted. Deposits are refundable (minus a service fee) if you cancel your reservation at least two weeks prior to your arrival date. You will receive a confirmation letter shortly after your deposit is received, followed by a welcome letter, a map, and a brochure.

Bed-and-Breakfast Reservations (Statewide)

All Islands Bed-and-Breakfast
☎ 808-753-3445
www.all-islands.com

Bed-and-Breakfast Hawaii
☎ 800-733-1632
www.bandb-hawaii.com

Hawaii's Best Bed-and-Breakfasts
☎ 800-262-9912 or 808-263-3100
www.bestbnb.com

RECOMMENDED VACATION RENTALS

Here are a few of our favorite vacation-rental houses and cottages:

Molokai

Dunbar Beachfront Cottages
HC 01 Box 738
Kaunakakai, HI 96748
☎ 800-673-0520 or 808-558-8153
Molokai-beachfront-cottages.com

Lanai

Dreams Come True
P.O. Box 525
Lanai City, HI 96763
☎ 808-565-6961 or 800-566-6961
www.dreamscometruelanai.com

HOTELS: *Rated and Ranked*

WE'VE RANKED MORE THAN 20 HOTELS on Maui, Molokai, and Lanai based on room quality (cleanliness, spaciousness, views, amenities, visual appeal), value, service, and location. These are our ratings, independent of any travel organization or club.

The first number of stars in a rating applies to a property's overall quality. The second applies to the quality of rooms only.

For details on a specific property, see hotel profiles in this chapter.

HOW TO MAKE THE RATINGS WORK FOR YOU

THE CHIEF FACTORS WE USED TO RATE HOTELS are location (on the beach or nearby), views, service, amenities, character, price, and value. However, not every room at a given resort is the same; some are superlative, while others are lackluster. When you choose your lodging, ask whether construction or other noisy endeavors are going to be happening nearby, whether your room was recently renovated, whether it has one of the outdoor patios Hawaiians call lanai, what extras are included in the rate (in-room coffeemaker, newspaper, movies, free Internet access, minibar, beach gear, continental breakfast), and whether airport transfers are available. Most deluxe hotel rooms and condo units come equipped with hair dryers, irons and boards, and safes; some have CD/DVD players and iPod docks with clocks. If these extras are important to you, ask.

Upscale travelers who appreciate value should inquire about the club floors. Rooms on these floors have keyed elevator access, a lounge with free drinks, free food including a continental breakfast, light buffet lunch, evening *pupu* (appetizers), and sinful fresh-baked cookies; plus club floors have a concierge to call their own. The rates are higher, but the buffets take care of breakfast, lunch, snacks, and cocktails, all costly at resorts. You can get your morning coffee and children's breakfasts fast and easy and take things back to your room on a tray if you want.

You don't have to go first class to get great service. Usually service at Hawaii hotels is friendly and courteous at every level, from maids to general managers, without regard to price levels. Staff members exhibit lots of aloha spirit and wear flowers and tropical uniforms. They may not all speak your language, but they are anxious to please you.

All lodging is subject to an 11.5 percent state tax.

What the Ratings Mean

★★★★★	Excellent
★★★★½	Very Good
★★★★	Good
★★★½	Average
★★★	Below Average
★★	Poor

Each hotel is rated for room quality and overall quality, both expressed on the five-star scale. As the terms imply, the former rating is specific to accommodations while the latter takes into account all facets of the hotel. The overall quality rating considers the entirety of the property. A hotel with prime location, excellent restaurants, or a gorgeous lobby might rank highly despite small rooms. Conversely, a property with elaborate rooms and little else may rank lower overall. The size of a room, the quality of its furnishings, and the level of cleanliness are the prime factors in room quality. *Unofficial Guide* researchers and writers also take pride in scrutinizing aspects of a hotel room that most guests only notice when something goes awry: noise levels, lighting, temperature control, ventilation, and security.

The value ratings, also expressed using a five-star scale, indicate a general idea of value for money—in other words, are you likely to feel that you get what you're paying for, particularly in comparison to other Maui County properties at the same level. At all price levels, some properties deliver more than others. Good deals—getting more than you'd expect for the price—are likely to be available at all levels because of current economic conditions, but are not reflected in the published yearly rates.

Cost Indicators

$$$$$	Above $500
$$$$	$400–$500
$$$	$300–$400
$$	$200–$300
$	$100–$200

Cost is expressed on a five-dollar-symbol scale. The scale was devised with Maui's typical room rates in mind: roughly, a hotel's cost indicator coincides with its star rating. In other words, expect to see as many dollar signs as stars. The rates are based on the rack rate for a standard ocean-view room (or suitable equivalent) during high season, from December through March. Don't be intimidated by the cost indicators. Lower and higher prices usually are available at each hotel, and rack rates are just the starting point for negotiating rates.

HOTEL PROFILES

MAUI

 Fairmont Kea Lani Maui $$$$$

OVERALL ★★★★★   ROOM QUALITY ★★★★   VALUE ★★★★   SOUTH MAUI

Hotels by Location

WEST MAUI

Hyatt Regency Maui Resort and Spa

Kaanapali Beach Club (formerly Embassy Suites)

Kaanapali Beach Hotel

Lahaina Inn

Lahaina Shores Beach Resort

Marriott's Maui Ocean Club

Mauian Hotel on Napili Beach

Plantation Inn

Ritz-Carlton, Kapalua

Sheraton Maui Resort

Westin Kaanapali Ocean Resort Villas

Westin Maui Resort and Spa

SOUTH MAUI

Fairmont Kea Lani Maui

Four Seasons Resort Maui at Wailea

Grand Wailea Resort Hotel & Spa

Maui Coast Hotel

Maui Prince Hotel

Wailea Beach Marriott Resort and Spa

CENTRAL MAUI

Maui Beach Hotel

HANA

Hotel Hana-Maui and Honua Spa

LANAI

Hotel Lanai & Cottages

Four Seasons Resort Lanai, The Lodge at Koele

Four Seasons Resort Lanai at Manele Bay

Hotel Lanai and Cottages

4100 Wailea Alanui, on Polo Beach, Wailea, HI 96753; ☎ 800-882-4100 or 808-875-4100; fax 808-875-1200; www.kealani.com

Maybe it's the large suites and villas with plentiful amenities and spacious lanai that make this hotel seem so comfy. There's a village feel to its open-air, family-friendly, green-leaning, Hawaiian culture–embracing ways. Maybe it's the embrace of kids as guests, or the presence of a deli, or the wonders of the morning canoe tour as an introduction to Maui. So the whole family can enjoy the experience—the Kea Lani also allows pets, one of the few Hawaii hotels that does (but check into quarantine rules before trying to bring yours from the Mainland).

SETTING AND FACILITIES

Location On Polo Beach at Wailea Resort's south end.

Dining The newest restaurant, Ko, highlights Maui's multinational plantation heritage—not in fusion dishes but in authentic choices from the six major ethnic cuisines, with recipes often from the chefs' own families. Nick's Fishmarket Maui is a popular seafood bistro. Caffe Ciao serves Italian cuisine in a garden setting. Put together a picnic with goodies from Caffe Ciao Deli. Breakfasts are served at the Kea Lani Restaurant, while the Polo Beach Grille and Bar offers poolside lunch.

How the Hotels Compare

HOTEL	OVERALL RATING	ROOM RATING	VALUE RATING	COST
MAUI				
Hotel Hana-Maui and Honua Spa	★★★★★	★★★★★	★★★★½	$$$$$
Ritz-Carlton, Kapalua	★★★★★	★★★★★	★★★★★	$$$$$
Four Seasons Resort Maui at Wailea	★★★★★	★★★★★	★★★★★	$$$$$
Fairmont Kea Lani Maui	★★★★½	★★★★★	★★★½	$$$$$
Grand Wailea Resort Hotel and Spa	★★★★½	★★★	★★★	$$$$$
Kaanalali Beach Club	★★★	★★★★	★★★	$$$$
Sheraton Maui Resort and Spa	★★★★	★★★★	★★★★	$$$$$
Westin Maui Resort and Spa	★★★★	★★★★	★★★★	$$$$
Westin Kaanapali Ocean Resort Villas	★★★★	★★★★	★★★★	$$$$$
Hyatt Regency Maui Resort and Spa	★★★★	★★★★	★★★	$$$$$
Wailea Beach Marriott Resort and Spa	★★★★	★★★★	★★★½	$$$$
Kaanapali Beach Hotel	★★★	★★★	★★★★	$$$
Maui Prince Hotel	★★★★	★★★★	★★★★	$$$$

Amenities and services Full-service spa and fitness center with personal trainers available, 3 swimming pools (one for adults only and two family swimming lagoons connected by a 140-foot water slide and swim-up beverage bar), tennis, golf, children's program, indoor/outdoor meeting and conference space.

ACCOMMODATIONS

Rooms Rooms 450, all suites, including 37 larger oceanfront villas with 2 or 3 bedrooms, and 11 suites for the disabled.

All rooms A/C, iPod dock, CD and DVD player, two flat-screen TVs, kitchenette facilities, sleeper sofa, private lanai, phone. High-speed Internet access available.

Some rooms Private pool, gourmet kitchen, sun deck, barbecue grill, extra bedrooms.

HOTEL	OVERALL RATING	ROOM RATING	VALUE RATING	COST
MAUI (CONTINUED)				
Plantation Inn	★★★★	★★★	★★★★	$$$
Marriott's Maui Ocean Club	★★★	★★★	★★★	$$$$
Lahaina Inn	★★★★	★★★½	★★★	$$
Mauian Hotel on Napili Beach	★★★★	★★★★	★★★★	$$
Maui Coast Hotel	★★★½	★★★	★★★	$$$
Lahaina Shores Beach Resort	★★★	★★★½	★★★★½	$$
Maui Beach Hotel	★★★	★★★	★★★★	$$
MOLOKAI				
Hotel Molokai	★★★	★★★	★★★	$$
LANAI				
Four Seasons Resort Lanai, The Lodge at Koele	★★★★★	★★★★★	★★★★★	$$$$
Four Seasons Resort Lanai at Manele Bay	★★★★★	★★★★★	★★★★★	$$$$$
Hotel Lanai and Cottages	★★★½	★★★	★★★	$

Comfort and decor Very spacious (840 square feet of suite and lanai), with separate bedroom and living room, exceptionally clean. Soft tropical colors provide cheerful ambience. Luxurious furnishings with Island-theme artworks. Large European marble bathroom with walk-in shower, soaking tub, and twin pedestal sinks.

RATES, RESERVATIONS, AND RESTRICTIONS

Family plan Four people can stay in a suite with no extra charge. For a third child, a rollaway bed is available.

Deposit 2-night deposit due upon booking. Cancellation notice must be given at least 14 days prior to arrival for refund.

Credit cards All major credit cards accepted.

Check-in/out 4 p.m./noon. Early check-in and late checkout available on request.

Four Seasons Resort Maui at Wailea $$$$$

OVERALL ★★★★★   ROOM QUALITY ★★★★★   VALUE ★★★★★   SOUTH MAUI

3900 Wailea Alanui; Wailea, HI 96753; ☎ 800-334-6284 or 808-874-8000; fax 808-874-6449; www.fourseasons.com/maui

Ever since it opened in 1991 and redefined the art of delivering Hawaiian hospitality in a glamorous understated setting, the Four Seasons Wailea has attracted devoted repeat travelers and earned AAA Five Diamond Award status. A honeymoon and Hollywood favorite, this gracious place has perfected pampering, from the Evian spritzes to cool off sunbathers by the pool to room service at the lounge chairs on the beach below. The spacious (600 square feet and up) rooms were recently refreshed in seashell colors of cream, coral, and sand. The Spa at Four Seasons offers indoor treatments and outdoor ocean-view massage huts. The breezy, open lobby is testament to the resort's Island-accented architectural design, which also includes commissioned reproductions of early Hawaiian furniture as well as paintings, sculptures, and other Hawaii-inspired artworks. Special features include a children's program, health club, game room, meeting facilities, and salon. Service is professional, warm, and courteous. It doesn't hurt a bit that in winter you can lounge on your ocean-facing lanai and watch humpback whales cruising by. To top off everything, the Four Seasons is located at Wailea Resort's best beach, with all the resort's features at hand—shopping, famous golf courses and tennis facilities, restaurants, and a beachfront trail. Overall, the Four Seasons perenially rates as one of the best hotels (if not the best) on Maui. Goldilocks would find it just right.

SETTING AND FACILITIES
Location On Wailea Beach.

Dining Ferraro's Bar e Ristorante offers Italian cuisine under the stars, while Spago presents Wolfgang Puck's contemporary California approach to Island fishes and Pan-Asian dishes. Pacific Grill serves breakfast and dinner (seafood and steaks).

Amenities and services Spa services, 24-hour room service, dry-cleaning and laundry service, workout facilities, business center, children's program, game room, salon.

ACCOMMODATIONS
Rooms 377, including 74 suites. ADA-approved and nonsmoking rooms available.

All rooms A/C, cable TV, CD/DVD player and library, lanai, iPod dock, in-room safe, hair dryer, coffeemakers with grinders and beans, iron and board, multiline phone and voicemail, high-speed Internet access, daily newspaper, twice-daily maid service, robes, free overnight shoeshine.

Some rooms Fax machine, extra bedroom.

Comfort and decor Very spacious (Maui's largest hotel rooms), exceptionally clean and well maintained. Decor in soft tropical pastels with white shutters; deep-cushioned rattan and wicker furnishings. Large bathrooms include marble counters and dual vanities. Elegant Island-themed artwork adds to the warm atmosphere.

RATES, RESERVATIONS, AND RESTRICTIONS

Family plan Children ages 17 and under stay free with parents if using existing bedding.

Deposit 2-night deposit at booking. Cancellation notice must be given 21–30 days prior to arrival.

Credit cards All major credit cards accepted.

Check-in/out 3 p.m./noon. For early check-in and late checkouts, the hotel will store bags and offer an Aloha Suite with TV and showers for freshening up.

kids Grand Wailea Resort Hotel and Spa $$$$$

OVERALL ★★★★★	ROOM QUALITY ★★★	VALUE ★★★	SOUTH MAUI

3850 Wailea Alanui Drive, Wailea, HI 96753; ☎ 800-888-6100 or 808-875-1234; fax 808-874-2411; www.grandwailea.com

Even if you don't stay here, it's worth a visit to see this opulent hotel, part of the Waldorf Astoria Collection today but originally designed as a Grand Hyatt fantasy hotel to lure incentives groups in the 1990s. Six major design themes—flowers, water, trees, sound, light, and art—define the ambience indoors and outdoors throughout the 40-acre property. Artworks valued at more than $100 million decorate the public areas, including commissioned bronzes of Hawaiian figures in places you'd never expect, like the middle of a fish pond. The resort has an artists-in-residence program as well, featuring local artists' works. Among the special features here are Camp Grande, a 20,000-square-foot children's facility; the 50,000-square-foot Spa Grande; a breathtaking wedding chapel with stained-glass windows; and a 2,000-foot-long swimming river and pool system that includes valleys, water slides, waterfalls, caves, grottoes, whitewater rapids, a Jacuzzi, sauna, and the world's only "water elevator," which lifts guests from the lower-level pool to the higher-level pool. While many love this place, others will find it over the top. But that's clearly part of the fun. It's worth joining an art-and-garden tour to walk through the collections. However if you want the amenities of Grand Wailea with a more expansive and exclusive lodging unit, look into Hoolei at Grand Wailea, the adjacent development of lavish townhouses.

SETTING AND FACILITIES

Location On Wailea Beach.

Dining Among 6 restaurants, the most dramatic is Kincha, which serves seafood buffets nightly in a traditional Japanese setting, embellished with 800 tons of rock from Mount Fuji. Bistro Molokini offers California and Hawaii cuisine for lunch and dinner. Cafe Kula presents lighter fare for breakfast, and on the edge of a man-made lagoon, Humuhumunukunuku-apuaa, named for the colorful state fish, specializes in fresh seafood (you can pick your lobster in the lagoon and have it served on your plate).

Amenities and services Room service, huge full-service spa and fitness center, squash/racquetball courts, extensive meeting facilities, business center, valet parking ($20 daily fee, in addition to $25 resort fee), Wailea resort shuttle to golf, tennis and shopping, scuba clinics, shops, art tours, children's program, babysitting, swimming pools, and fantasy water complex (including a water-powered elevator and pool-linking river-like "canyons" to speed up the ride) with swim-up bar and man-made beach beside the real one.

ACCOMMODATIONS
Rooms 761, including 51 suites, 10 ADA-approved rooms. Nonsmoking rooms available.

All rooms A/C, cable TV, lanai, in-room safe, Internet access, honor bar, iron and board, unlimited local and toll-free calls on 3 in-room phones, coffeemaker, hair dryer, turndown service, spa bath amenities, robes, slippers.

Some rooms Larger accommodations, extra bedrooms and baths.

Comfort and decor Pleasant rooms (average 640 square feet) with elegant decor. Warm colors and high ceilings add to the setting.

RATES, RESERVATIONS, AND RESTRICTIONS
Family plan Children ages 17 and under stay free with parents if using existing bedding. Maximum 4 people per room.

Deposit 2-night minimum deposit with 14 days' notice for cancellation (30 days for summer reservations), rises to 5-night minimum at Thanksgiving and spring break with 30 days' cancellation notice. For Christmas holidays, full payment required in advance with 90 days' cancellation notice prior to scheduled arrival for refund.

Credit cards All major credit cards accepted.

Check-in/out 4 p.m./noon. Early check-in and late check-out available on request.

Hotel Hana-Maui and Honua Spa $$$$$

OVERALL ★★★★★   ROOM QUALITY ★★★★★   VALUE ★★★★½   HANA

P.O. Box 9, Hana, HI 96713; ☎ 800-321-4262 or 808-248-8211; fax 808-248-7202; www.hotelhanamaui.com

What this cozy small hotel lacks (television and air-conditioning in most rooms, no need for either), it makes up for in romantic appeal, charm, location, and friendly, attentive service. The Hana-Maui sits on expansive landscaped gardens by the sea, and the ocean and mountain views are, like Hana, heavenly. Remote, quiet, romantic, this is the epitome of a honeymoon hotel. September is adults-only month. A weekly luau is held on the beach. Available outdoor activities include horseback riding, hiking, snorkeling, bike riding, and historical tours. Treatments at the Honua full-service spa (spa facilities are free to hotel guests) involve Hawaiian traditional methods and materials—ginger, coconut, or red sea-salt scrubs, kukui nut oil, slightly narcotic *awa,* and seaweeds. The Hana-Maui, built in 1946, is Maui's oldest hotel and one of its most expensive. New owners (owners of The Post Ranch in Big Sur and Cavallo Point in Sausalito) have tastefully refurbished it. Most units are one-story suites or cottages, clustered near the central hotel facilities. Plantation House is more removed, a two-bedroom Victorian-era house with full kitchen and wrap-around lanai, in private splendor on four acres of lush landscaping—ideal for weddings or small meetings. But perhaps the most spectacular are the Sea Ranch Cottages, in a dramatic sea cliff setting with private hot tub on the lanai.

SETTING AND FACILITIES

Location In Hana, on the east end of Maui. Shuttle available to Hamoa Beach.

Dining Pacific Island and Hawaiian regional flair characterize the fare at Kauiki, the hotel dining room. Executive Chef John Cox changes menus daily according to what's local and fresh from the fishermen and farmers. On Fridays, a Hawaiian buffet is followed by a live show featuring local musicians and dancers.

Nearby, the Hana Ranch Restaurant serves more casual ranch-style fare, highlighted by ranch beef.

Amenities and services Room service (breakfast only), flower lei greeting, dialup internet connections in room but no TV, radio or clock; laundry service, complimentary use of Honua spa and or exercise facilities, Hamoa Beach, and Hana airport shuttle, parking.

ACCOMMODATIONS

Rooms 66 spacious suites and cottages.

All rooms Wet bar, lanai, coffee and tea maker stocked with special coffee and teas, organic cotton linens. Welcome amenities include tropical fruit and banana bread.

Some rooms Jacuzzis.

Comfort and decor The Hana-Maui's luxurious brand of rustic decor features bleached hardwood floors, wicker and rattan furnishings, handmade quilts, wet bars, sitting and dining areas, and large private lanai. The oversize tiled baths open onto private shower gardens in some cottages.

RATES, RESERVATIONS, AND RESTRICTIONS

Family plan Children under age 18 free with parents if using existing bedding in cottages; up to six in Plantation House.

Deposit 1-night deposit required. Cancellation notice must be given 10 days prior to arrival for refund.

Credit cards All major credit cards accepted.

Check-in/out 4 p.m./noon. Early check-in and late checkout available on request.

Hyatt Regency Maui Resort & Spa $$$$$

OVERALL ★★★★ **ROOM QUALITY ★★★★** **VALUE ★★★** **WEST MAUI**

200 Nohea Drive, Lahaina, HI 96761; ☎ 800-233-1234 or 808-661-1234; fax 808-667-4497; maui.hyatt.com

The Hyatt Maui was the first of Hawaii's celebrated, larger-than-life "fantasy hotels," complete with an elaborate water playground with waterfall grotto, enclosed "lava tube" water slide, a suspended rope bridge, and other features designed to appeal to the kid in everyone. The atrium lobby is lush with tropical plants and exotic birds. Its nightly *Tour of the Stars* program gives guests a guided tour of the Hawaiian skies and allows them to peer through a state-of-the-art, computer-controlled 16-inch reflector telescope. A wildlife tour brings visitors face-to-face with penguins, swans, parrots, macaws, flamingos, and koi. You can also tour the tropical gardens (it's about a two-mile walk) or browse the $2 million art collection. This property offers something for travelers of all ages and interests. It's a favorite with meeting groups.

SETTING AND FACILITIES

Location On Kaanapali Beach.

Dining 5 restaurants, 6 lounges; Son'z Maui at Swan Court features fresh local fish and other fare and Maui products prepared with a contemporary flair and served by a pool where stately swans swim up for a handout. Spats Trattoria serves Italian food, and Cascades Grille and Sushi Bar offers fresh seafood and steak. Pavillion serves lunch and afternoon snacks. Weeping Banyan Café features coffee drinks, pastries, fruit, and juices to go in the mornings.

Amenities and services Full-service spa and Moana Athletic Club fitness center (free with mandatory $15 per day resort fee), tennis, golf, outdoor dinner theater, activities desk, children's program, babysitting, shops, meeting and convention facilities, multilingual staff, valet parking ($20 per day) or free self parking, rooftop astronomy program.

ACCOMMODATIONS

Rooms 807, including 31 suites and 4 rooms for the disabled.

All rooms Lanai, A/C, cable TV, two-line phone, honor bar, in-room safe, hair dryer, robes, coffeemaker, iron and board, daily news digest, video or voicemail checkout, high-speed Internet access, robes.

Some rooms Living room, dining area, wet bar, refrigerator.

Comfort and decor Spacious and clean, with warm earth and mauve Asian/Pacific tones reflecting stylish elegance. Furnishings are comfortable and wall hangings attractive.

RATES, RESERVATIONS, AND RESTRICTIONS
Family plan Children ages 17 and under stay free with parents if using existing bedding. Maximum 4 per room.

Deposit 2-night deposit due within 14 days after booking. Cancellation notice must be provided 72 hours prior to arrival for refund.

Credit cards All major credit cards accepted.

Check-in/out 3 p.m./noon. Early check-in and late checkout based on availability.

Kaanapali Beach Club (formerly Embassy Vacation Resort Kaanapali Beach) $$$$

OVERALL ★★★   ROOM QUALITY ★★★★   VALUE ★★★   WEST MAUI

104 Kaanapali Shores Place, Lahaina, HI 96761; ☎ 877-988-6284 or 808-661-2000; fax 808-667-5821; www.kaanapalibeachclub.com

Opened in 1988, this first all-suite Hawaii property is now a time-share resort. Ocean views, beach in front, waterfall pools, and above-average rooms are some of the attractions. A popular feature here is the 60-foot water slide, which plops you right into a one-acre swimming pool.

SETTING AND FACILITIES
Location On Kaanapali Beach.

Dining The oceanfront North Beach Grille serves catch of the day and Mediterranean favorites for dinner.

Amenities and services Laundry facilities, limited housekeeping service, front desk and security, concierge, room service, fitness center, barbecues, valet or self parking ($13 per day).

ACCOMMODATIONS
Rooms 413, all suites; 12 ADA-approved rooms.

All rooms Nonsmoking, A/C, high-speed Internet access, lanai, cable or satellite TV, DVD player, in-room movies, phone and voicemail, sleeper sofa, microwave, refrigerator, in-room safe, coffeemaker.

Comfort and decor Spacious (more than 800 square feet), with separate living-room area. Oversized soaking tubs, separate showers, walk-in closets, and dual marble vanities are popular features. Elegant and stylish with a cool tropical appeal, cheerful and airy.

RATES, RESERVATIONS, AND RESTRICTIONS
Family plan Up to 5 in a room, includes up to 4 children ages 17 and under who stay free with parents if using existing bedding.

Deposit 2-night deposit required. Cancellation notice must be given 72 hours prior to arrival for refund.

Credit cards All major credit cards accepted.

Check-in/out 4 p.m./11 a.m.

kids Kaanapali Beach Hotel $$$

| OVERALL ★★★ | ROOM QUALITY ★★★ | VALUE ★★★★ | WEST MAUI |

**2525 Kaanapali Parkway, Lahaina, HI 96761; ☎ 800-262-8450 or
808-661-0011; www.kbhmaui.com**

Located on one of the widest stretches of Kaanapali Beach, the Kaanapali Beach Hotel prides itself on being Maui's "most Hawaiian" hotel. The management and staff are dedicated to the aloha spirit, and their easygoing friendliness makes up for a lack of needed renovations. The spirit of this place is reminiscent of the romantic past, with its four wings like arms sheltering a ten-acre garden courtyard. A variety of Hawaiian activities—hula lessons, lei making, *lauhala* weaving, and ti-leaf skirt making—are held daily, and employees provide Hawaiian entertainment three days a week. They've released two music CDs, one a prize winner in the Hawaii Visitors and Convention Bureau's annual "Keep It Hawaii" awards. For visitors seeking a value hotel on Kaanapali Beach with a strong emphasis on Hawaiian hospitality, look no further.

SETTING AND FACILITIES

Location On Kaanapali Beach.

Dining The Tiki Terrace Restaurant serves continental and Island cuisine. The Kupanaha Dinner Show is held at 4:30 p.m., Tuesday–Saturday. The Polynesian show features magician Jody Baran and costs $79 for adults, $55 for ages 13–20, and $39 for ages 6–12 ($89 per person for Gold Circle seating at tables nearest the stage).

Amenities and services Laundry service, parking ($11 per day valet parking, $9 per day self parking), children's program.

ACCOMMODATIONS

Rooms 430, including 15 suites. Nonsmoking rooms and rooms for the disabled available.

All rooms A/C, lanai, cable TV, phone, in-room safe, refrigerator, iron and board, hair dryer, bath amenities, coffeemaker.

Some rooms More space, upgraded amenities.

Comfort and decor Rooms are comfortable, clean, and well maintained. Tropical green and golden sand hues accentuate the Hawaiian setting, along with Hawaiian quilt–design bedspreads, light tropical furniture, and local artwork.

RATES, RESERVATIONS, AND RESTRICTIONS

Family plan Maximum of 4 people to a room. Children ages 17 and under stay free with parents if using existing bedding.

Deposit 1- or 2-night deposit due within 10 days of booking (5 nights for Christmas holiday reservations). Cancellation notice must be given 3–14 days prior to arrival.

Credit cards All major credit cards accepted.

Check-in/out 3 p.m./noon. Early check-in and late checkout available on request.

Lahaina Inn $$

OVERALL ★★★★   **ROOM QUALITY** ★★★½   **VALUE** ★★★   **WEST MAUI**

127 Lahainaluna Road, Lahaina, HI 96761; ☎ 800-669-3444 or 808-661-0577; fax 808-667-9480; www.lahainainn.com

Lahaina Inn is proof that good things can come in small packages. Rick Ralston, founder and owner of the popular Crazy Shirts stores, restored the dozen rooms of this historic inn; pieces from his personal collection furnish each individually decorated room. Because of the valuable furnishings, children under the age of 15 are not allowed in the inn, but families may rent one of the larger Kaanapali cottages or Lahaina or Kihei condo units run by the inn (five-night minimum applies). The inn's location on Lahainaluna close to Front Street is a "good news, bad news" situation: it's good to be action central (Lahaina is Maui's most bustling town), but it also gets noisy. There are no television sets in the guestrooms (one is available in the community room), but who needs sitcoms when you have a view of Lahaina?

SETTING AND FACILITIES

Location In the heart of Lahaina, across from waterfront; no beach.

Dining Lahaina Grill, one of Maui's best restaurants, serves New American cuisine.

Amenities and services Parking ($7 per day).

ACCOMMODATIONS

Rooms 12 (two-person maximum), including 3 suites (three-person maximum). 1- to 3-bedroom rental cottages and condos also available.

All rooms Nonsmoking, A/C, ceiling fans, high-speed wireless Internet access, complimentary coffee, hair dryers, beach towels, iron and board.

Some rooms Lanai, full bath and shower, king-size bed.

Comfort and decor Rooms are smallish, but well maintained and clean, if dimly lit. Antique furnishings include restored brass and wood beds, period wall decorations, and armoires.

RATES, RESERVATIONS, AND RESTRICTIONS

Deposit One-night deposit (inn) or $300 (cottages) deposit required. Cancellation notice must be given 48 hours prior to arrival for refund, minus $25 fee for inn; for vacation rentals, balance due 60 days prior to arrival; cancellation fee is $150 before 60 days, full amount after unless rebooking occurs.

Credit cards All major credit cards accepted except Discover.

Check-in/out 1 p.m./11 a.m. Late check-out (until noon) on request.

 Lahaina Shores Beach Resort $$$

OVERALL ★★★   **ROOM QUALITY** ★★★½   **VALUE** ★★★★½   **WEST MAUI**

475 Front Street, Lahaina, HI 96761; ☎ 800-642-6284 or 808-661-4835; fax 808-661-4696; www.lahainashores.com

Location and value make up for less than perfect beaching. If you want to stay waterfront in the heart of Lahaina, this seven-story vacation condo, managed by Classic Resorts, is the place. Oceanfront rooms feature whale watching in winter and sunset views anytime from your own lanai. The airy lobby, with arched colonnades on either side, opens onto a panoramic sea view. The style is rambling, old-style plantation comfort. Families like its spacious rooms and central location. Tennis courts are across the street; shopping, restaurants, and entertainment right at hand.

SETTING AND FACILITIES

Location Beachfront, easy walking distance from downtown Lahaina. All rooms have views either of the West Maui mountains or the blue Pacific.

Dining Full kitchens, restaurants in walking distance.

Amenities and services Daily maid service, concierge, parking ($6/day), pool, whirlpool tub, gas grills, laundry facilities, babysitting referrals.

ACCOMMODATIONS

Rooms 199 studios, one-bedrooms, and one-bedroom penthouse suites, with magnificent ocean and mountain views.

All rooms Lanai, A/C, full kitchen, high-speed Internet access, daily complimentary in-unit coffee, in-room movies, TV with DVD/VCR player, iron and board, hair dryer.

Some rooms Sofa bed and second bath, extra space (penthouse units sleep up to 5).

Comfort and decor Tiled floors, tropical pastel decor, and rattan furnishings.

RATES, RESERVATIONS, AND RESTRICTIONS

Deposit $150 deposit required. Cancellation notice must be given 72 hours prior to arrival for refund.

Credit cards All major credit cards accepted.

Check-in/out 3 p.m./11 a.m.

Wailea Beach Marriott Resort and Spa $$$$

OVERALL ★★★★	ROOM QUALITY ★★★★	VALUE ★★★½	SOUTH MAUI

3700 Alanui, Wailea, HI 96753; ☎ 800-688-7444 or 808-879-1922; fax 808-874-7888; www.marriott.com/hotels/travel/hnmmc-wailea-beach-marriott-resort

Marriott recently spent $60 million renovating this deluxe hotel, which already enjoyed Wailea's best front-and-center location with ocean close at hand. It is the oldest in Wailea but well cared for by various managers since it opened in 1976 as the Maui Inter-Continental. It has a strong return-guest contingent and a comfortable Hawaiian air. The low-rise building design is a nice fit on 22 oceanfront acres, conveniently located near The Shops at Wailea and ample parking. Lei-making classes and craft demonstrations are offered regularly, and Hawaiian entertainment is provided nightly. Wailea Resort's three championship golf courses and tennis competition complex are a shuttle ride away, along with several fine restaurants. Overall, the Marriott Wailea Beach Resort is a gem suitable for families and couples, meeting groups, and individuals alike.

SETTING AND FACILITIES

Location At Wailea Resort, between two beaches.

Dining Mala Wailea serves breakfast and dinner, featuring Mediterranean and Pacific Rim cuisine. Kumu Bar & Grill serves lunch and dinner with live entertainment nightly. Honua Ula Luau Dinner Show features a Hawaiian luau buffet as well as the traditional live show.

Amenities and services Mandara Spa and fitness center, laundry service, heated infinity pool overlooking the sea (with over-water pool cabanas, hot tub, other pools, and slide), parking (self-parking $15 per day, valet $18 per day), full-service business center and 21 wireless meeting and banquet rooms, concierge, room service, game room; $25 daily resort fee.

ACCOMMODATIONS

Rooms 499, including 47 suites and 10 ADA-approved rooms.

All rooms Nonsmoking, lanai, newspaper, special bedding, A/C, flat-screen cable/satellite TV, in-room movies and games, CD player, safe, high-speed Internet access, refrigerator, coffeemaker, hair dryer, iron and board, robes and slippers.

Some rooms Oceanfront, more space, pull-out sofa bed.

Comfort and decor Spacious, clean, and well appointed, with sunny cream walls setting off light blue cushions, tropical woods, and minimal artwork.

RATES, RESERVATIONS, AND RESTRICTIONS

Family plan Children ages 12 and under stay free if staying with parents and using existing bedding.

Deposit 1-night deposit required. Cancellation notice must be given 72 hours prior to arrival for refund.

Credit cards All major credit cards accepted.

Check-in/out 4 p.m./noon

Maui Beach Hotel $

OVERALL ★★★   ROOM QUALITY ★★★   VALUE ★★★★   CENTRAL MAUI

170 Kaahumanu Avenue, Kahului, HI 96732; ☎ 800-367-5004 or 808-877-0051; fax 808-871-5797; www.elleairmaui.com

It's more motel-by-the-bay than Maui-of-your-dreams, but this recently renovated 145-room waterfront hotel by the harbor on Kahului Bay has something none of the dream resorts have—proximity to the Kahului Airport (three miles away, with a limited shuttle service) and the attractions of Upcountry, Iao Valley, and the North Shore. If you need an airport connection in a hurry or want to get the jump on all those other people headed up to the top of Haleakala or out to Hana, this is an option to consider. It is inexpensive and conveniently located near shopping malls (Queen Kaahumanu Center), sports activities (golf at Dunes at Maui Lani or Pukalani), the harbor, dining, entertainment (Maui Arts and Cultural Center), and attractions. The amenities include rooftop pool and sundeck, restaurants, cocktail lounge, and rooms with mountain or ocean views. There is a strip of sandy beach, unsuitable for swimming.

SETTING AND FACILITIES

Location Kahului, on Kahului Bay beach.

Dining Breakfast and Japanese dinner buffets at open-air Rainbow Terrace; or nearby restaurants; poolside lounge.

Amenities and services Daily maid service, 24-hour front desk, free parking, laundry facilities, sundries shop, pool, seven meeting rooms with outdoor function area.

ACCOMMODATIONS

Rooms 145, with pleasant tropical furnishings

All rooms Nonsmoking, A/C, cable TV, in-room movies, Internet access, phone, refrigerator, safe, hair dryer.

Some rooms Lanai.

Comfort and decor Cream walls, light woods, and deep teal, rose, or smoke spreads and upholstery.

RATES, RESERVATIONS, AND RESTRICTIONS

Deposit 1-night deposit required.

Credit cards All major credit cards accepted.

Check-in/out 3 p.m./noon.

Maui Coast Hotel $$$

OVERALL ★★★½   ROOM QUALITY ★★★   VALUE ★★★   SOUTH MAUI

2259 South Kihei Road, Kihei, HI 96753; ☎ 800-895-MAUI (6284) or 808-874-6284; fax 808-875-4731; www.mauicoasthotel.com

Kihei's only full-service hotel and one of Maui's few moderately priced hotels is across the street from a six-mile stretch of beaches, including Kamaole Beach Park I, and near Kihei restaurants, bars, shops, and golf courses, from pricey Wailea Golf Club to Ellair public course. Variety of room-and-car and activity packages are available, including golf at Dunes at Maui Lani.

SETTING AND FACILITIES

Location Off beach, Kihei near Wailea

Dining Spices Restaurant serves breakfast, lunch, and dinner; the poolside Tradewinds Café serves lighter fare and features live Hawaiian entertainment nightly until 10 p.m.

Amenities and services Room service, pool, two outdoor whirlpool tubs, children's wading pool, fitness center, lighted tennis court, gift shop, free parking, free laundry facilities, meeting room.

ACCOMMODATIONS

Rooms 265 smoke-free, including 1-bedroom suites; ADA-compliant rooms available.

All rooms A/C, cable TV, in-room movies, Nintendo system, safe, voicemail, lanai, ceiling fans, coffeemaker, mini-refrigerator, hair dryer, iron and board, high-speed Internet access on request.

Some rooms Whirlpool tubs and wet bars in suites.

Comfort and decor Recently renovated rooms feature tropical pastels and art.

RATES, RESERVATIONS, AND RESTRICTIONS

Deposit 1-night deposit required. Corporate rates available.

Family plan Children ages 17 and under stay free if staying with parents and using existing bedding.

Credit cards Major cards accepted.

Check-in/out 3 p.m./noon.

 ## Marriott's Maui Ocean Club (formerly Maui Marriott Resort) $$$$

OVERALL ★★★   ROOM QUALITY ★★★   VALUE ★★★   WEST MAUI

100 Nohea Kai Drive, Lahaina, HI 96761; ☎ 800-845-5279 or 808-667-1200; fax 808-667-8300; www.marriott.com/hotels/travel/ hnmmh-marriotts-maui-ocean-club/

This is a full-service time-share resort with a casual, family-oriented atmosphere and friendly service. Waterfalls, koi ponds, and tall coconut palms adorn the attractive grounds. A year-round children's program is available, as are Hawaiian craft lessons and a full menu of recreational sports and activities. The Marriott also has one of the island's best luau, held on the beach. Note: Major construction on this property is scheduled to continue through 2009. Some rates discounted.

SETTING AND FACILITIES

Location On Kaanapali Beach.

Dining Longboards Kaanapali serves American food for dinner. The poolside Beach Walk Market & Pantry deli is open for breakfast, lunch, and dinner.

Amenities and services Room service (until 10 p.m.), valet ($12 per day) and self-parking ($6 per day), nightly luau (except Monday), 2 swimming pools including fantasy "super pool" with slides and kids' shipwreck play area, 2 Jacuzzis, fitness center, coin-operated laundry service, wireless Internet access, babysitting available, newspapers, Barbecue area and grills, game room, Hale Mana Wellness Center spa by appointment.

ACCOMMODATIONS

Rooms 442 on nine floors, plus 77 on 12 floors in new Lahaina and Napili Villas.

All rooms Nonsmoking, A/C, cable TV, lanai, phone, refrigerator, microwave, in-room safe, coffeemaker, daily newspapers, evening reception, hair dryer, free local calls, DVD player, Internet access, sofa sleeper, iron and board.

Some rooms Larger lanai, separate dressing area, in-unit laundry, large jetted tub, separate dining area with table and chairs, second bedroom, third bath.

Comfort and decor Spacious 1-bedroom/2-bath and 2-bedroom/3-bath units with gourmet kitchens or kitchenettes, tasteful furnishings, warm, sunny colors, and Island artwork.

RATES, RESERVATIONS, AND RESTRICTIONS

Family plan Children ages 17 and under stay free with parents if using existing bedding. Maximum of 2 adults and 2 children per room.

Deposit 1-night deposit required. Cancellation notice must be given 14 days prior to arrival for refund.

Credit cards All major credit cards accepted.

Check-in/out 4 p.m./10 a.m. Early check-in and late check-out available on request (no guarantees).

Maui Prince Hotel $$$$

| OVERALL ★★★★ | ROOM QUALITY ★★★★ | VALUE ★★★★ | SOUTH MAUI |

5400 Makena Alanui, Kihei, HI 96753; ☎ 866-PRINCE-6 or 808-874-1111; fax 808-879-8763; www.princeresortshawaii.com

Situated on the lower slope of Mount Haleakala where it ends in lovely Maluaka Beach, this 1,800-acre resort is an isolated haven on the edge of a wilderness. The picturesque grounds surround a courtyard with a koi pond and waterfall, all of which add to the tranquil, understated atmosphere. All rooms face the ocean as well as the neighboring islands of Molokini Crater, Lanai, and Kahoolawe. The service here is impeccable. Snorkeling and scuba diving are among the outdoor activities available; there are six tennis courts at nearby Makena Tennis Club and a championship golf course. A hula show is presented at the oceanfront Molokini Lounge. Rooms were recently redone.

SETTING AND FACILITIES

Location In Makena in south Maui, short walk to Makena Beach.

Dining Award-winning Prince Court features contemporary Island cuisine with fresh seafood, steaks, and game dishes. Hakone serves traditional Japanese cuisine as well as Hawaiian/Japanese fusion dishes and fresh sushi. Café Kiowai, open-air and surrounded by koi ponds, serves breakfast, while light lunch is the fare at Makena Clubhouse. Maui Sunset Luau is staged on Tuesdays and Thursdays, 5–8:30p.m.

Amenities and services Room service, welcome baskets on arrival, laundry service, fitness center, parking, children's program, advance tee times and spa reservations through online concierge.

ACCOMMODATIONS

Rooms 310, including 19 suites. Nonsmoking rooms and rooms for the disabled available.

All rooms A/C, cable TV, lanai, in-room safe, mini-refrigerator with bottled water daily, phone, hair dryer, make-up mirror, iron and board, robes, high-speed Internet access, coffeemaker, nightly turndown service on request.

Some rooms Second bedroom.

Comfort and decor Spacious and clean rooms in what the Prince calls "retrocontemporary" style with warm colors, woven floral accents, and Island-theme artwork that create a modern, casual setting.

RATES, RESERVATIONS, AND RESTRICTIONS

Family plan Children ages 12 and under stay free with parents if using existing bedding, $60 charge per extra person.

Deposit 1-night deposit required. Cancellation notice must be given 72 hours prior to arrival for refund.

Credit cards All major credit cards accepted.

Check-in/out 3 p.m./noon. Early check-in and late checkout available on request.

The Mauian on Napili Bay $$

OVERALL ★★★★   ROOM QUALITY ★★★★   VALUE ★★★★   WEST MAUI

5441 Lower Honoapiilani Road, Napili, HI 96761; ☎ 800-367-5034 or
808-669-6205; fax 808-669-0129; www.mauian.com

Plain and simple, with a low-rise 1950s style on the outside and up-to-date boutique studios that have been tastefully redone inside, the Mauian endures with lots of homey Hawaiian spirit—from the heart, since it is Hawaiian-managed and was owned for most of its years by a local family. Two acres of manicured grounds feature fascinating flora, like jade vine used for lei making and Hawaiian medicinal plants, as well as bountiful bananas and other fruits that are served to guests. But the star attraction is Napili Beach, with Molokai and Lanai framing the scene. The Mauian occupies a central position on this swimmable stretch of golden sand with a few palms thrown in for atmosphere. If you care more about enjoying the beach in Island-style serenity than fancy bells and whistles, this is a very satisfying choice. Return guests get around the 350-square-foot studio size by renting multiple units for larger groups. It still comes out a deal. Casual and fine restaurants, golf, and tennis are a short walk or drive away. The Kapalua Airport and Napili Plaza supermarket are just up the hill. You skip all the fuss of a big hotel in exchange for carrying your own things, parking your own car, and making your own dinner if you choose. You'll also be making phone calls and using the wireless Internet access from the open-air *ohana* (family) lounge where the television and other amusements are located, but there's no charge for local calls. Fresh tropical fruit and juice, coffee, breads, and cereals are served buffet style for breakfast, and your room comes with a tray for your do-it-yourself room service. Being here is the next best thing to visiting a friend's comfy beach house.

SETTING AND FACILITIES

Location On Napili Beach.

Dining Continental breakfast buffet; units have fully equipped kitchen facilities.

Amenities and services Coin laundry, daily maid service, pool, presentation on marine environment every Monday morning, guest party with live entertainment Thursday evenings, free parking, beach towels and gear, courtesy phone (free local calls), lounge with books, games, wireless Internet access, DVD/VCR player and TV.

ACCOMMODATIONS

Rooms 44, mostly studios that sleep up to 3 people (6 hotel rooms available).

All rooms Refrigerator, stove, coffeemaker, kitchen.

Comfort and decor Updates such as tiled walk-in showers, granite counters, convection ovens, Tempur-Pedic beds, sleeper sofas, and new furnishings throughout put a bright new face on the units. But you still may want to spend all your at-home time on the lanai staring at the beach or ocean/island views in oceanfront units.

RATES, RESERVATIONS, AND RESTRICTIONS

Family plan Children ages 5 and under stay free. Rates are based on double occupancy; nominal charge per extra person.

Deposit $100 deposit required. Cancellation notice must be given more than 30 days before arrival for refund. Holiday reservations require $200 nonrefundable deposit and 5-night minimum.

Credit cards All major credit cards accepted.

Check-in/out 3 p.m./11 a.m. Early check-in and late check-out available on request.

Plantation Inn $$$

OVERALL ★★★★   ROOM QUALITY ★★★   VALUE ★★★★   WEST MAUI

174 Lahainaluna Road, Lahaina, HI 96761; ☎ 800-433-6815 or 808-667-9225; fax 808-667-9293; www.theplantationinn.com

Lahaina is fortunate to have two neighboring bed-and-breakfast inns, Lahaina Inn (described previously) and Plantation Inn, which also features an excellent restaurant on the premises and boasts even more appeal as a surprising refuge of peaceful sanity in the busy town. Quiet is one advantage of several at this property. The style is Victorian; the construction and amenities are modern, with a pool and whirlpool tub. The inn is a sister property to the Kaanapali Beach Hotel (described previously), and guests have beach and other privileges at the resort three miles up the road. Breakfast is served around the pool and at the guest pavilion.

SETTING AND FACILITIES

Location Off-beach in Lahaina.

Dining Gerard's is an excellent French dining spot, a longtime favorite serving what chef Gerard Reversade terms "contemporary Island French" cuisine. Guests get a discount on the price of dinner.

Amenities and services Free parking, pool and Jacuzzi, daily maid service, coin laundry, video library, outdoor pavilion for guests.

ACCOMMODATIONS

Rooms 19, including 4 suites, all nonsmoking.

All rooms A/C, ceiling fans, gourmet breakfast, private baths, TV/VCR, telephones, iron and board, hair dryer, refrigerator, safe, wireless Internet access, soundproofing.

Some rooms Lanai or balcony. Suites have kitchenettes. Most rooms have a private lanai.

Comfort and decor Rooms are well maintained, charming, and clean. Wood floors, antiques, canopy four-posters or brass beds, armoires, wicker, and the like set the mood.

RATES, RESERVATIONS, AND RESTRICTIONS

Deposit 2-night deposit required. Cancellation notice must be given 15 days prior to arrival for refund minus $25 fee; 7-night deposit required with 30 days' notice of cancellation for refund during the peak holiday week, Christmas Eve through New Year's Eve. Available packages combine a stay with dinner, whale-watching, rental cars, a dolphin cruise, and additional nights.

Credit cards All major credit cards accepted.

Check-in/out 3 p.m./noon. Late check-out on request.

 Ritz-Carlton, Kapalua $$$$$

OVERALL ★★★★★ ROOM QUALITY ★★★★★ VALUE ★★★★★ WEST MAUI

One Ritz-Carlton Drive, Kapalua, HI 96761; ☎ 800-241-3333 or 808-669-6200; fax 808-669-2028; www.ritzcarlton.com

This Ritz is a perennial AAA Five Diamond Award recipient, and it's easy to understand why. Everything here, from service to guestrooms to dining, is virtually perfect, even more so after a substantial $180-million renovation in 2008. Among the additions are the two-story Ritz Carlton Spa (which celebrates Hawaiian therapies and features outdoor shower gardens) and a new hotel choice, privately owned one- and two-bedroom Residential Suites that are available to guests to rent. The new look suggests Hawaii's ancient tropical glory—local art, lava-rock bar in the lobby, and wood floors in the rooms. Some room appointments are definitely high-tech (wireless, flat-screen TVs, and so on). The atmosphere remains elegant, but the new renovations heighten the Hawaiian sense of place and underline the hotel's longstanding support of local arts, culture, and environment. To the extent possible, as one observer put it, they have de-ritzed the Ritz. Well, maybe—except, perhaps, for options such as the seven luxury cabanas around the tri-level pool which come with flat-screen TV, wireless head phones, ceiling fan with light, iPod dock, high-speed Internet, refrigerator, electronic safe (in which to deposit bling when going for a swim), cell phone outlet, tropical fruit platter and beverages on arrival, personal attendant to bring more, cold towels, reading material, and $250 daily tab. The spa's features include an entry graced by bamboo groves and water-wall fountains and Hawaii's only coed, indoor-outdoor area where a whirlpool tub overlooks a taro patch. Set on 50 acres, the Ritz's two six-story wings reach down toward the sea (but are separated from it by an ancient burial ground) on Puukukui's lower slope. The Ritz Kids program allows children to learn about Maui's nature and heritage. Kapalua Resort has two championship golf courses, ten tennis courts, a general store, and several restaurants reachable by shuttle. The Ritz hosts several notable annual events, including the PGA Mercedes Championships (January), Celebration of the Arts (April), and the Kapalua Wine and Food Festival (June). The Ritz-Carlton, Kapalua, was the first Audubon Cooperative Sanctuary Resort.

The sand dunes of Kapalua nearby, where 1,200 Hawaiian bones were unearthed, are held in perpetual trust. Signs there read "Kapu"—no trespassing—where the hotel originally was to be built. It was moved when the graves were discovered. Often, we have seen unaware visitors walk across the old Hawaiian graveyard as if it were a lawn. Please respect this resting place.

SETTING AND FACILITIES

Location At Kapalua Resort in West Maui, a short walk to beach.

Dining The breezy Banyan Tree is the AAA Four Diamond–rated signature restaurant with a seasonal menu featuring fresh local ingredients. Kai Sushi is new and located off the lobby. Terrace Restaurant serves a popular buffet for breakfast and regional Pacific cuisine for lunch and dinner. The Pool Bar & Cafe serves a casual lunch. Beach House Grill & Bar down on the beach serves lunch and (in summer) an early dinner. Alaloa Lounge with lava rock walls and an onyx bar is located in the lobby.

Amenities and services 24-hour room service, twice-daily maid service, laundry service, fitness center, spa treatments, multilevel swimming pool, hydrotherapy pools, parking (free self-parking, valet $18 per day), business facilities, children's program, cultural history tours, arts and crafts, golf, tennis, ocean activities.

ACCOMMODATIONS

Rooms 463, including 107 residential suites. ADA-approved "barrier-free" rooms available.

All rooms Nonsmoking, A/C, flat-screen cable TVs with pay movies, luxury amenities in marble baths, 2 phones, large lanai, in-room safe, honor bar, hair dryer, iPod dock, DVD player, wireless high-speed Internet access, iron and board, bathrobes; $20 daily resort fee.

Some rooms Extra bedrooms, full kitchens and separate living rooms (residential suites); personal concierge service, complimentary food and beverages, dual phone lines (club floors).

Comfort and decor Comfortable rooms, beautifully appointed with wood floors, Hawaiian floral woven area rugs, Hawaiian prints on koa frames, new Travertine marble baths, large private lanai (80 percent of rooms have ocean views).

RATES, RESERVATIONS, AND RESTRICTIONS

Deposit 2-night deposit required. Cancel reservations 21 days prior to scheduled arrival for refund.

Credit cards All major credit cards accepted.

Check-in/out 3 p.m./noon. Early check-in and late check-out available on request (no guarantees).

Sheraton Maui Resort & Spa $$$$$

OVERALL ★★★★ ROOM QUALITY ★★★★ VALUE ★★★★ WEST MAUI

2605 Kaanapali Parkway, Lahaina, HI 96761; ☎ 800-500-8313 or 808-661-0031; fax 808-661-0458; www.sheraton-maui.com

The Sheraton Maui is an upscale beach destination, claiming the prime position on 23 acres on Kaanapali Beach. Its elevated lobby opens to a wide panoramic view of the Pacific Ocean and a spectacular 147-foot-long oceanfront, freshwater swimming lagoon. The resort is built atop and beside Black Rock, a lava-rock landmark. Children ages 5–12 can participate in the complimentary Keiki Aloha Club, which includes lei-making and hula lessons, beach activities, and field trips to historic sites. Locals regard Black Rock as one of the best snorkeling areas on Maui. At sunset, a torch-lighting and cliff-diving ceremony says aloha to another sunny day. The Hawaiian art on display throughout the public rooms is worth a look. A new full-service spa is expected to be completed in late 2008.

SETTING AND FACILITIES

Location On Kaanapali Beach.

Dining Black Rock Steak and Seafood is the place to be at sunset for dinner or prime rib buffet on Fridays and Saturdays. Kekaa Terrace serves breakfast and lunch. Teppan Yaki Dan offers five flavors of sake and Japanese contemporary cuisine with showmanship; chefs prepare meals while you watch. Drinks and cocktails are available at the poolside Sundowner Bar and Lagoon Bar (which also serve lunch) and Reef's Edge bar in the lower lobby.

Amenities and services Swimming pool, night-lit tennis courts, room service, cultural activities and crafts, laundry facilities, valet parking

($5 per day added to $25 resort fee), fitness center, spa, yoga and pilates classes, children's program, free first-night valet parking and self-parking thereafter, high-speed Internet access, Kaanapali Resort and Lahaina shuttle, Starwood shuttle to Westins (where Sheraton guests can sign dinner tabs to their rooms under "Stay at One, Dine At All" program) and downtown Lahaina.

ACCOMMODATIONS

Rooms 510, including 46 suites, 15 ADA-approved rooms. Most rooms are nonsmoking.

All rooms Lanai, A/C, cable TV, in-room movies, in-room safe, mini-refrigerator, coffeemaker, iron and board, hair dryer and makeup mirror, robes.

Some rooms Microwave, second TV, living room.

Comfort and decor Spacious, clean, well-maintained rooms have custom bedspreads and tropical furnishings, as well as large lanai. Hawaiian artworks adorn the walls.

RATES, RESERVATIONS, AND RESTRICTIONS

Family plan Children ages 17 and under stay free with parents if using existing bedding.

Deposit 1-night deposit due 10 days after booking. Cancellation notice must be given 72 hours prior to arrival for refund.

Credit cards All major credit cards accepted.

Check-in/out 3 p.m./11 a.m. Early check-in and late check-out available on request.

Westin Kaanapali Ocean Resort Villas $$$$$

OVERALL ★★★★   ROOM QUALITY ★★★★   VALUE ★★★★   WEST MAUI

6 Kai Ala Drive, Lahaina, HI 96761; ☎ 866-500-8313 or 808-667-3200; fax 808-667-3201; www.westinkaanapali.com

Kaanapali's newest property is a brand-new, all-villas luxury time-share spread in North Kaanapali, reached by a different access road than the older and larger portion of the resort. Starwood Hotels, which operates the Sheraton Maui, Westin Maui, and this two-part (Westin Kaanapali Ocean Resort Villas and adjacent Westin Kaanapali Ocean Resort Villas North) resort at Kaanapali Beach, links the three with shuttles and inter-changeable privileges, so that guests can dine, park, beach, or use the spa at the Westin Maui or Sheraton Maui if they choose.

SETTING AND FACILITIES

Location On Kaanapali Beach, north of Black Rock.

Dining Ocean Pool Bar and Grill offers breakfast, lunch, and dinner, children's menu, full bar, and a Wednesday Paniolo Island Barbecue feast. Pulehu features a breakfast buffet and a dinner grill menu with steak and seafood and a variety of tempting desserts Thursday–Monday with music on weekends. Kai Ala Market (Villas North) features a selection of snacks, groceries, fresh fish and meats to grill, fresh produce, espresso drinks, sundries, and hot meals to go. Puukollii General Store has deli items, fresh pizzas, baked goods, salads, and other treats. Pailolo features lunch and tropical drinks. Chefs are available for hire to make the dinner of your dreams at your villa.

Amenities and services Swimming pool with waterfall, tennis, children's program, spa services, market, general store, business center, game room, grills, free parking, resort shuttle, pre-arrival grocery order and delivery.

ACCOMMODATIONS

Rooms 280 studio, one- and two-bedroom villas, smoke-free. 250 more at neighboring property (Westin Kaanapali Ocean Resort Villas North).

All rooms Daily maid service, A/C, cable TV, in-room safe, fully equipped kitchen, laundry facilities, iron and board, hair dryer, high-speed Internet access, Bose stereo and DVD player, special bedding, pullout sofa bed, flat-screen TV.

Some Rooms Extra bedrooms.

Comfort and decor Spacious, with tasteful, Asian-influenced modern decor and warm neutral colors. Lots of stone countertops in kitchens and baths.

RATES, RESERVATIONS, AND RESTRICTIONS

Family plan Children ages 17 and under stay free with parents if using existing bedding. Maximum of 5 guests per room in studio, 6 in larger units.

Deposit 2-night deposit due within 15 days after booking. 72-hour cancellation notice required for refund.

Credit cards All major credit cards accepted.

Check-in/out 4 p.m./10 a.m.

Westin Maui Resort & Spa Kaanapali $$$$

OVERALL ★★★★   ROOM QUALITY ★★★★   VALUE ★★★★   WEST MAUI

2365 Kaanapali Parkway, Lahaina, HI 96761; ☎ 866-500-8313 or 808-667-2525; fax 808-661-5762; www.westinmaui.com

The Westin offers an elegant take on fun, with fantasy pools and waterfalls, swans and parrots, lush tropical gardens, and artwork throughout the property, 12 acres fronting Kaanapali Beach with two 11-story towers. An official Director of Fun makes sure of it (and the Director of Romance helps plan your wedding). The most notable feature is the resort's 87,000-square-foot aquatic playground, composed of five pools, three joined together by water slides and two divided by a swim-through grotto with twin waterfalls and a hidden Jacuzzi. One of the pools is designated "adults only" and features a swim-up bar. The Westin Kids Club provides supervised fun and games for the *keiki* (kids) during the daytime, while Night Kids Camp does the job from 6 to 10 p.m. Island-style entertainment plays nightly at various times and spots around the resort. For night owls, a side benefit of staying in Kaanapali is that it's just a five-minute drive to Lahaina, where most of West Maui's after-dark action takes place.

SETTING AND FACILITIES

Location On Kaanapali Beach.

Dining Tropica serves breakfast, lunch, and dinner, featuring fresh seafood and steak as well as Hawaiian Pacific flavors. Ono Bar & Grill serves food all day, from the breakfast buffet to casual tapas-style dinner. For breakfast, the fastest, cheapest solution is the Colonnade Cafe, serving Starbucks, fruit, juice, and pastries or rolls, with informal tables beside the waterfall pools. Sea Dogs sells hotdogs, pizza, and shave ice by the pool and beachwalk. Wailele Polynesian Luau is held weekly.

Amenities and services Full-service spa, room service, multilingual staff, laundry/valet service, parking, business center, meeting rooms and ballrooms, health club, wedding planning, special bedding, children's program; daily $25 resort fee includes various services, including an outdoor portrait photograph, fitness center, high-speed Internet access, self-parking, shuttles, bottled water daily, and souvenirs. Dogs are now allowed here, and dog amenities—including robes—are available (contact hotel for specific rules and be mindful of Hawaii quarantine laws).

ACCOMMODATIONS

Rooms 758, including 27 suites and 14 ADA-approved rooms.

All rooms Nonsmoking, A/C, flat-screen cable TV, lanai, special bedding, mini-refrigerator, safe, coffeemaker, iron and board, dual-line telephone, hair dryer, robes.

Some rooms Separate dining or parlor area, wet bar, sunken tubs, sleeper sofa, upgraded amenities.

Comfort and decor Newly renovated rooms are decorated in light neutrals and dark woods to create a modern tropical setting.

RATES, RESERVATIONS, AND RESTRICTIONS

Family plan Children ages 17 and under stay free with parents if using existing bedding. Maximum of 4 guests per room.

Deposit 2-night deposit due within 15 days after booking. 72-hour cancellation notice required for refund.

Credit cards All major credit cards accepted.

Check-in/out 3 p.m./noon. Early check-in and late checkout as available.

MOLOKAI

Hotel Molokai $$

| OVERALL ★★★ | ROOM QUALITY ★★★ | VALUE ★★★ | MOLOKAI |

Kamehameha V Highway, PO Box 120, Kaunakakai, HI 96748;
☎ **800-535-0085 or 808-553-5347; www.hotelmolokai.com**

Molokai's only hotel (after the 2008 shutdown of Molokai Ranch) makes the most of its beach setting on Molokai's east end, close to the town of Kaunakakai. Dark brown A-frame bungalows with steep Polynesian roofs contain newly repainted and upgraded units (condos; some are also rented by owners). This is a mixed bag—the retro architecture, waterfront locale, and down-home Molokai style can be charming, but the restaurant is iffy and the music from the popular bar wafts in on the breeze, causing some guests to bring ear plugs in order to sleep. Ask for oceanfront units—and kitchen facilities if you want to make your own meals. The beachfront location provides appealing views, but the water is shallow and the bottom is reef, so you'll need to drive farther east to find swimming beaches.

SETTING AND FACILITIES

Location Fronting Kamiloloa Beach with wide lawn and patio.

Dining Hula Shores Restaurant and Bar is a popular open-air waterfront restaurant and bar with live music nightly.

Amenities and services Free parking, coin laundry, small pool; function room accommodates up to 50 people.

ACCOMMODATIONS

Rooms 37.

All rooms Nonsmoking, ceiling fan, TV, lanai, coffeemaker, small refrigerator, high-speed Internet access.

Some rooms Oceanfront, kitchen or kitchenette, microwave, iron and board, hair dryer.

Comfort and decor Low-key atmosphere with open-air design to catch the tradewinds for cooling.

RATES, RESERVATIONS, AND RESTRICTIONS

Credit cards Visa, MasterCard, Discover, and American Express.

Check-in/out 4 p.m./11 a.m.

LANAI

Hotel Lanai & Cottages $

| OVERALL ★★★½ | ROOM QUALITY ★★★ | VALUE ★★★★ | LANAI |

848 Lanai Avenue, P.O. Box 630613, Lanai City, HI 96763; ☎ 800-795-7211 or 808-565-7211;
fax 808-565-6450; www.hotellanai.com

Opened in 1923 for visiting Dole Pineapple VIPs, the Hotel Lanai has always attracted a following to its perch on a hill overlooking the upland plantation village, Lanai City. Current owners, including owner-manager Mike Charles and restaurant manager Michelle Kommes, lured Maui celebrity chef Bev Gannon of Haliimaile General Store fame to oversee creation of the hotel's Lanai City Grille, working with Executive Chef

Mike Davis. If you can't afford to stay at The Lodge at Koele or Manele Bay, or don't want to, Hotel Lanai is your reasonable, genuine old-Hawaii alternative. Rooms are cheerful, comfortable, and naturally cooled by the Upcountry air; decor has been restored to simple plantation classic. Service is friendly, and you could meet some interesting local characters at the bar at *pau hana* (after work) time. An open-air tent behind the restaurant area becomes an entertainment and dancing venue on weekends, or a special-event area, with heaters and seating for 50.

SETTING AND FACILITIES

Location In Lanai City under stalwart century-old Cook pines; beach is a 20-minute shuttle ride away downhill at Hulopoe Beach.

Dining Lanai City Grille serves dinner. Continental breakfast buffet served in the lobby.

Amenities and services Free parking and wireless Internet access. No room service or laundry service.

ACCOMMODATIONS

Rooms 11, including attached one-bedroom cottage. Additional two- and three-bedroom plantation cottages in Lanai City will accommodate larger groups, with rates ranging to $329 per night for the largest cottage.

All rooms Nonsmoking, ceiling fans, phone, continental breakfast, hair dryer, iron and board, daily maid service.

Some rooms TV, bathtub, lanai, additional bedrooms, kitchens and other facilities in cottages.

Comfort and decor Medium-size, high-ceilinged historic rooms have pine floors and furniture, woven hala mats on the floors, ceiling fans, appliquéd Hawaiian quilts, local artists' work, and small modern baths in white board-and-batten rooms (and single wall construction—bring your iPod or earplugs if this is a problem). Some original photographs depict the island's plantation days.

RATES, RESERVATIONS, AND RESTRICTIONS

Family plan In hotel rooms, children ages 8 and under stay free with parents if using existing bedding. Additional person, $50.

Deposit Half of total stay due in advance on booking. Cancellation notice must be given 21 days prior to arrival for refund, minus a $25 processing fee. At holiday time, a 2-night deposit and stricter cancellation policy apply.

Credit cards Visa, MasterCard, and American Express.

Check-in/out 2 p.m./11 a.m. Early check-in and late checkout available on request.

Four Seasons Resort Lanai, The Lodge at Koele $$$$

OVERALL ★★★★★   ROOM QUALITY ★★★★★   VALUE ★★★★★   LANAI

P.O. Box 361380, Lanai City, HI 96763; ☎ 800-321-4666 or 808-565-4000; fax 808-565-4561; www.fourseasons.com/koele

Nestled on the island's cool highlands, the Lodge resembles a sumptuous English hill station from the colonial Raj, complete with spreading lawns for croquet, cozy fireplaces, afternoon tea, and a big pineapple mural on the front. Newly refurbished by new management Four Seasons, the changes are subtle but include air-conditioning and heating throughout the building, needed more for five-diamond status than guest comfort. Paintings, sculptures, and artifacts adorn the resort's interiors. Paths meander through flower gardens and past an English conservatory filled with orchids, a putting green, and an inviting swimming pool. The atmosphere is relaxed—roofed outdoor corridors are filled with oversized rattan chairs and ottomans placed to admire the views and maybe nod off; indoors, bountiful clusters of overstuffed couches and chairs in the soaring great hall and smaller lounges provide a quiet, restful retreat. But this is a rough and tumble island, and if you want to get out in it, you can hike up into the forests and along ridgelines, work out at the new fitness center, shoot at clay pigeons, explore the countryside on a mountain bike, ride a horse on a mountain trail, play tennis, rent a Jeep and head for unpaved adventures, or enjoy Lanai's awesome award-winning Experience at Koele championship golf course nearby, then return to the lodge and soak off all that red dirt in a deep tub. (P.S. Might want to leave your whitest sports gear at home.)

SETTING AND FACILITIES

Location Upcountry, among the tall tropical island pines; Hulopoe Beach and the hot sun are a short shuttle ride away.

Dining The award-winning Dining Room showcases Pacific Rim cuisine. Less formal Terrace dining is no less interesting for breakfast, lunch, or dinner. Both feature as much island-grown food as possible, including venison. Golf clubhouses also serve lunch.

Amenities and services Room service, spa services, concierge, laundry service, fitness center, swimming pool, executive golf course, children's program, high-speed Internet access, valet and self-parking.

ACCOMMODATIONS

Rooms 102, including 14 suites, 2 ADA-approved rooms. The Lodge is a nonsmoking facility.

All rooms Fireplaces, larger space, upgraded amenities, butler service.

Some rooms Fireplaces, larger space, upgraded amenities, butler service.

Comfort and decor Large, immaculate rooms with country chic decor in warm, bright tones feature poster beds, window seats, and oil paintings by local artists. Lighthearted room decor helps offset the dimly lit corridors and other public areas.

RATES, RESERVATIONS, AND RESTRICTIONS

Family plan Children ages 15 and under stay free with parents if using existing bedding. Kids' amenities include child-sized robes, welcome amenity, and special toiletries and furnishings, so be sure to tell the hotel their names and ages in advance. Maximum of 4 guests per room (2 adults and 2 children). $40 charge per extra guest.

Deposit 2-night deposit due within 14 days of booking. Cancellation notice must be given 21 days prior to arrival for refund.

Credit cards All major credit cards accepted except Discover.

Check-in/out 3 p.m./noon. Hospitality rooms available.

kids **Four Seasons Resort Lanai at Manele Bay $$$$$**

OVERALL ★★★★★   ROOM QUALITY ★★★★★   VALUE ★★★★★   LANAI

P.O. Box 631380, Lanai City, HI 96763; ☎ 800-321-4666 or 808-565-2000; fax 808-565-2483; www.fourseasons.com/manelebay

Perched atop windswept cliffs and bright with reflected sparkles from the sea, the Manele overlooks Lanai's magnificent wild coastline and blue Hulopoe Bay. A blend of Mediterranean and Hawaiian design, the hotel is filled with art, including Asian artifacts and grand murals. Lush tropical gardens add color to landscapes, but nothing surpasses the ocean views—more fascinating because chances are good you will see a pod of spinner dolphins cavorting through the bay. It's just a short stroll to Hulopoe Beach, one of the best beaches in Hawaii with excellent water clarity for snorkeling and scuba diving. But if you like, the pool-with-a-view is even closer. Great golf awaits you at The Challenge at Manele. Like the Lodge at Koele, the Manele delivers a memorable experience.

SETTING AND FACILITIES

Location At Hulopoe Bay, a short walk up from the beach.

Dining Hulopoe Court serves breakfast and dinner, with Pacific Rim and refined Hawaiian cuisine. Ihilani serves contemporary Italian cuisine. Fresh local seafood tops the bill at outdoor, oceanfront Ocean Grill for lunch and dinner by the pool. Golf clubhouses serve lunch.

Amenities and services Room service, high-speed Internet access, valet and self-parking, spa with Hawaiian treatments and ingredients, fitness facilities, golf, tennis, business services, babysitting service, concierge service, children's program; separate conference center provides meeting space.

ACCOMMODATIONS

Rooms 236, including 13 suites, 6 ADA-approved rooms. Nonsmoking rooms available.

All rooms Twice-daily housekeeping, A/C, 40-inch flat-screen cable TV, iPod dock, CD and DVD player, phones, radio, safe, lanai, small refrigerator, hair dryer, sitting area, tub and shower, iron and board, robes and slippers.

Some rooms Butler service, extra rooms, dining area, additional lanai furnishings.

Comfort and decor Spacious (average 700 square feet) rooms have refined and comfortable tropical-Asian furnishings, warm neutrals or blue-and-yellow schemes, with eclectic accessories collected from around the world.

Family plan Children ages 15 and under stay free with parents if using existing bedding. Kids get their own amenities, including welcome milk and cookies, robes, etc., so be sure to let the hotel know their ages in advance. Surf Shack Teen Center offers PlayStation 2 games, a pool table, a special sound-and-entertainment system, beach parties, and fishing trips. Maximum of 4 guests per room (2 adults and 2 children).

Deposit 2-night deposit due within 14 days of booking. Cancellation notice must be given 21 days prior to arrival for refund.

Credit cards All major credit cards accepted except Discover.

Check-in/out 3 p.m./noon. Hospitality rooms available.

PART FOUR

GOING HOLOHOLO:
Getting around and Getting to Know Maui

◼ WHEN *you* ARRIVE

IN HAWAIIAN, GOING *holoholo* means traveling around, a perfect way to get to know the three main islands of Maui County. But first you've got to get on the ground. It's likely you'll pass through Honolulu International Airport, one of the busiest in the United States, before flying on to your Maui County destination: Kahului Airport, Hana Airport, or Kapalua Airport on Maui; Hoolehua Airport on Molokai; and Lanai Airport on Lanai. The airports are simple to navigate, particularly the smaller local ones. Gates have numbers; just follow the signs. Baggage claims are designated by letters of the alphabet in the primary Mainland arrival terminals and by numbers in the interisland terminal. Note, however, that West Coast flights by Hawaiian Airlines use the interisland terminal for ticketing and baggage. Latest arrival and departure times appear on the usual video monitors. Baggage claim is on the street level. The wait only seems longer because you're anxious to hit the beach.

Arriving on Maui is a sensual experience. You smell flowers, sometimes hear people playing ukulele and singing Hawaiian music, and feel the tropical warmth and tradewinds. Outside the baggage claim, you will find car-rental agencies, shuttles, and courtesy phones, taxis, buses, shuttles, and private or hotel limousines. If you arrive in Honolulu on an international flight, the first to wish you *aloha* in their fashion are U.S. Customs and Immigration agents. Honolulu is today a far better staffed and more efficient port of entry than it was in the past.

We've noticed that interisland airlines and airports tend to be much more efficient at handling the constant loads of passengers and bags than their Mainland counterparts. For people who live on islands, these flights are essential public transit, and islanders are *akamai* (smart) and quick to deplane.

Of Maui's three airports, Kahului Airport, at the island center, is the main terminal for interisland and Mainland flights. Car-rental desks and taxi service are available outside the baggage claim. Most people take a shuttle to the car compound a few minutes away. Kapalua/West Maui Airport serves only interisland flights on smaller aircrafts but is handy to area resorts and towns. Car rentals are available nearby, and resort shuttles serve the airport. Tiny Hana Airport serves small plane traffic. Molokai's airport is an older, Island-style, open-air facility located mid-island near Kaunakakai. Lanai's airport is a new, modern facility below Lanai City. Arriving guests are met by resort staff and transported to hotels by resort bus.

GROUND TRANSPORTATION AT AIRPORTS

FOR DETAILED INFORMATION ON CAR RENTALS, including contact numbers, see Part Two, Planning Your Visit. Although you can generally rent a car on arrival, it's a better idea to book one in advance; you're guaranteed a car and often a better rate. You don't have to rent a car to reach your hotel, as many offer shuttle service (ask when you book) and there are independent shuttle operators and taxis available at the airports. Nevertheless, a vehicle greatly expands your touring options, particularly on Maui. We recommend securing one at some point during your visit.

Maui: Kahului Airport

RENTAL CARS Alamo, Avis, Budget, Dollar, Hertz, and National are just outside the main terminal (turn right as you leave the baggage area). Thrifty, Enterprise, and others have courtesy phones at the airport information board inside the baggage-claim area.

TAXIS Maui Airport Taxi has a dispatcher inside the baggage claim. Or you can just walk directly across the street and hail a cab at the curb.

SHUTTLES Use the courtesy phone to contact a shuttle service, or make advance reservations by phone or Internet. Costs vary depending on the carrier, number of passengers, destination, excess baggage, and so on. Maui Executive Transportation (☎ 800-833-2303; **www.mauishuttle.com**) charges $33 for two to Wailea and $42 for two to Kaanapali in cash (credit cards incur additional airport fees). Speedi Shuttle (☎ 877-242-5777; **www.speedishuttle.com**) charges around $36 for two passengers bound for Wailea and $52 to Kaanapali.

Maui: Kapalua-West Maui Airport

RENTAL CARS Use the courtesy phone at the baggage-claim area for a free shuttle van to car-rental offices. Taxis are curbside outside baggage claim.

MAUI COUNTY TAXI OPERATORS

MAUI

AB Taxi ☎ 808-667-7575

Alii Cab ☎ 808-661-3688

Central Maui Taxi ☎ 808-244-7278

Classy Taxi ☎ 808-665-0003

Kihei Taxi ☎ 808-879-3000

La Bella Taxi ☎ 808-242-8011

Royal Sedan and Taxi Service ☎ 808-874-6900

Wailea Taxi and Tours ☎ 808-874-5000

MOLOKAI

Molokai Off-Road Tours and Taxi ☎ 808-553-3369

LANAI

No full-time taxi companies serve Lanai. Dollar Rent-A-Car provides taxi service on a driver-available basis. Call ☎ 808-565-7227.

Molokai: Molokai Airport

RENTAL CARS Budget and Dollar are the only car rental agencies at the Molokai Airport. Their service desks are located by the baggage-claim area.

TAXIS One company serves the airport on Molokai but offers no white courtesy phone (remember why you came to Molokai: to escape modern life). If you don't spot a taxi outside the open-air baggage-claim area, call Molokai Off-Road Tours and Taxi (see above for number).

Lanai: Lanai Airport

RENTAL CARS Dollar Rent-A-Car is the only car rental agency on Lanai. On arrival, walk to the reception desk and use the red courtesy phone. A van will pick you up and transport you to Dollar's pickup location, about three miles away.

SHUTTLE A convenient way to get around is Lanai Resort's shuttles. The $30-per-person charge includes round-trip airport transportation and all shuttles between the two Four Seasons Lanai resorts, The Lodge at Koele and Manele Bay hotel. The shuttle vans are located right outside the airport baggage-claim area.

▐ MAUI DRIVING TOURS

RENT A CAR OR A GUIDE AND GET OUT INTO EXOTIC MAUI. You'll see intriguing natural sights, glimpse a different way of life,

MAUI DRIVE TIMES

FROM KAHULUI AIRPORT TO:	TIME TO TRAVEL
Haleakala National Park	1 hour, 45 minutes
Hana	2 hours, 30 minutes
Kaanapali	50 minutes
Kapalua	1 hour
Kihei	25 minutes
Lahaina	45 minutes
Makena	40 minutes
Wailea	35 minutes
Wailuku	10 minutes

and take a few photos—or if you're an active explorer, burn a lot of calories, and if you're a shopper, a dollar or two. You probably won't burn a lot of gas, because these islands are not very big and the roads are not very fast or far.

The following Maui driving tours highlight both the island's natural and man-made attractions, including the elaborate resorts, which we strongly recommend touring. All are open to the public (especially those with shopping centers). And that goes for beaches, too, which are public. We provide basic driving directions, sticking to the main roads. Purchasing a detailed map of the island is a must if you plan to venture off the main arteries. Depending on where you're staying, you may opt to augment these tour routes (especially if your hotel is in the middle of a route), and backtracking is sometimes a necessity, as roads do not circumnavigate the islands of Lanai and Molokai.

WEST MAUI

IT'S A PLEASANT DRIVE FROM CENTRAL MAUI to the island's western shore, where old **Lahaina** town and **Kaanapali** are the main attractions. Two-lane Highway 30 passes through a tunnel on the coastal route; there's a free whale-watch turnout at **McGregor Point,** little tree-shaded beach parks, old Japanese graveyards, and channel views of Lanai and Molokai.

Hot and dry Lahaina (it means "the heat"), with its historic district and harbor, is a popular hangout day or night. There is a great sense of history here—in fact, the entire town is designated a National Historic Landmark—and Lahaina's storied past lives on in its restored relic structures that cluster around a mammoth banyan tree in the town square.

Lahaina was the focal point of the Pacific whaling industry in the mid–19th century; at the height of the whaling era, more than 100 whaling ships anchored offshore in Lahaina Roads, the naturally protected mooring. Along with the whaling ships came hundreds of pleasure-seeking sailors who turned Lahaina upside down with their wild cavorting. A town prison was built in 1852 to contain the worst offenders.

The sailors were frequent antagonists to the disapproving Christian missionaries who lived in Lahaina. It was a constant battle between the two factions. Once, in 1825, a mob of British sailors threatened to kill William Richards, one of the first missionaries to settle on Maui, and to set his house on fire unless a law forbidding prostitution and the sale of alcohol was repealed. Two years later, a cannon from a visiting whaler struck Richards's home. One missionary wrote in 1837, "As a mass, the seamen are sunk in vice."

Today, a stroll through Lahaina includes many historical points of interest (see our walking tour map on page 237). At the **Baldwin Home Museum,** for example, take a guided tour of the fully restored home of the Reverend Dwight Baldwin, a prominent Protestant missionary in the 19th century, and gain insights into the triumphs and tribulations of Hawaii's missionaries. Nearby is **Hale Paahao,** the old prison itself (appropriately enough, on Prison Street), where hundreds of whaling-era sailors took "shelter" for the night, mostly for public drunkenness, still an all-too-common condition after sundown in Lahaina today.

Front Street is the site of **Friday Night Is Art Night,** a weekly celebration of Maui art featuring street entertainment and art demonstrations at participating galleries. Each Halloween night, Front Street hosts Maui's biggest costume parade, Hawaii's version of Mardi Gras with hundreds of scantily clad revelers.

A short drive up from Lahaina is **Kaanapali** ("cliffs of Kaana"), where sugar barons Samuel Alexander and Henry Baldwin converted cane fields into the island's first master-planned resort on a four-mile gold-sand beach. Today it includes two championship golf courses and an open-air mall with shops and restaurants.

The nearly half-century-old resort is touristy but enduring, a popular family resort on a good beach. The shopping center, **Whalers Village,** is home to the **Whale Center of the Pacific**—dedicated to the life and history of the state mammal, the 40-ton Pacific humpback whale (*Megaptera novaeangliae*), which migrates to Maui waters from Alaska every year. Whale-watch boats depart daily from Lahaina Harbor when the whales are in the Islands.

You can ride from Kaanapali to Lahaina via the **Lahaina-Kaanapali & Pacific Railroad,** better known as the "Sugar Cane Train." In the heyday of Maui's sugar era, plantations used privately owned railroad lines to haul cane from fields to sugar mills. The Sugar Cane Train represents the last of these railroads. It's a plodding but scenic half-hour round-trip—popular with children—and the conductor provides narration and entertainment on the way.

Maui Driving Tours

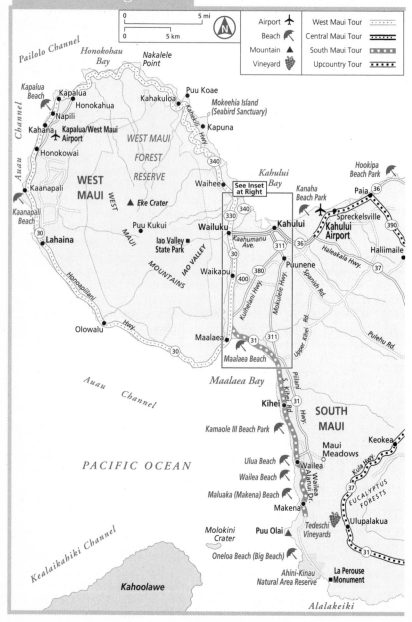

Airport ✈		West Maui Tour	
Beach 🏖		Central Maui Tour	
Mountain ▲		South Maui Tour	
Vineyard 🍇		Upcountry Tour	

Pailolo Channel

Honokohau Bay

Nakalele Point

Puu Koae

Kahakuloa

Mokeehia Island (Seabird Sanctuary)

Kapalua Beach

Kapalua

Honokahua

Kahekili Hwy.

Kapuna

Napili

Kahana

Kapalua/West Maui Airport ✈

WEST MAUI FOREST RESERVE

Honokowai

Auau Channel

WEST MAUI

▲ Eke Crater

Hookipa Beach Park

340

Kahului Bay

See Inset at Right

Kanaha Beach Park

Paia 36

Waihee

WEST MAUI MOUNTAINS

Puu Kukui ▲

330 340

Wailuku

Kahului

Kahului Airport ✈

Spreckelsville

390

Kaanapali

30

Kaanapali Beach

Lahaina

30

Iao Valley State Park ▪

IAO VALLEY

Kaahumanu Ave.

311 36

Haliimaile

Haleakala Hwy.

37

Honoapiilani Hwy.

30

Waikapu

400 380

Puunene

Spanish Rd.

Olowalu

Maalaea

31 311

Maalaea Beach

Kuihelani Hwy.

Mokulele Hwy.

Upper Kihei Rd.

Pulehu Rd.

Auau Channel

Maalaea Bay

Kihei 31

S. Kihei Rd.

SOUTH MAUI

PACIFIC OCEAN

Kamaole III Beach Park 🏖

Maui Meadows

Keokea

Ulua Beach 🏖

Wailea 🏖

Piilani Hwy.

Kula Hwy.

37

Wailea Beach 🏖

Maluaka (Makena) Beach 🏖

Wailea Alanui Dr.

EUCALYPTUS FORESTS

Makena

Molokini Crater

Puu Olai ▲

Tedeschi Vineyards 🍇

Ulupalakua

31

Oneloa Beach (Big Beach) 🏖

Kealaikahiki Channel

Ahini-Kinau Natural Area Reserve

La Perouse ▪ Monument

Kahoolawe

Alalakeiki

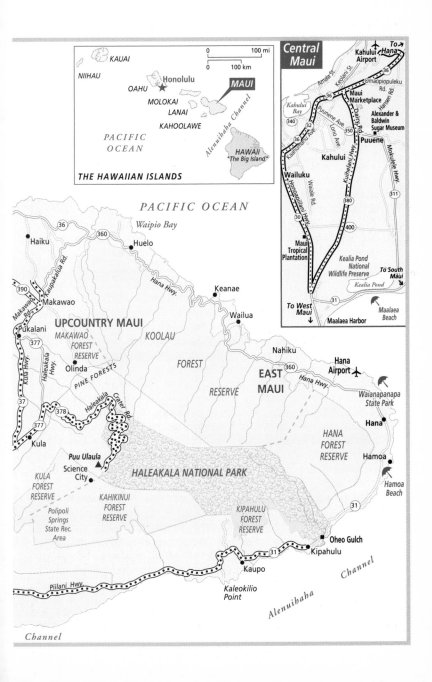

THE HAWAIIAN ISLANDS

KAUAI

NIIHAU

OAHU

Honolulu

MOLOKAI

LANAI

KAHOOLAWE

MAUI

Alenuihaha Channel

HAWAII
"The Big Island"

PACIFIC OCEAN

0   100 mi

0   100 km

Central Maui

To Hana

Kahului Airport

Amala St.

Keolani St.

36

Omaopiopuleku Rd.

Maui Marketplace

Alexander & Baldwin Sugar Museum

Puuene

Kahului

32

350

Kuihelani Hwy.

Dairy Rd.

Hansen Rd.

Mokulele Hwy.

340

Kahului Bay

36

Puunene Ave.

Lono Ave.

Waiehu Ave.

Kaahumanu Ave.

Wailuku

Honoapiilani Hwy.

Waiale Rd.

380

30

311

400

Maui Tropical Plantation

Kealia Pond National Wildlife Preserve

Kealia Pond

To South Maui

To West Maui

31

Maalaea Harbor

Maalaea Beach

PACIFIC OCEAN

Waipio Bay

Haiku

36

360

Huelo

Kaupakalua Rd.

Hana Hwy.

Keanae

Wailua

390

Makawao

Makawao Rd.

Pukalani

377

UPCOUNTRY MAUI

MAKAWAO FOREST RESERVE

Olinda

PINE FORESTS

KOOLAU

FOREST

Nahiku

Hana Airport

360

Hana Hwy.

EAST MAUI

Waianapanapa State Park

RESERVE

Hana

37

Kula Hwy.

Haleakala Hwy.

378

Haleakala

Crater Rd.

377

Kula

Puu Ulaula

Science City

HALEAKALA NATIONAL PARK

HANA FOREST RESERVE

Hamoa

Hamoa Beach

KULA FOREST RESERVE

KAHIKINUI FOREST RESERVE

Polipoli Springs State Rec. Area

KIPAHULU FOREST RESERVE

31

Oheo Gulch

Kipahulu

Piilani Hwy.

Kaupo

Kaleokilio Point

Alenuihaha

Channel

Channel

THE OO BIRD

We love provenance—the lives objects have lived. Which is why we like to haunt small, out-of-the-way museums like the **Bailey House** in Wailuku on Maui. Every time we come, we see and learn about something new. Last time, it was a Maui Oo, an extinct bird last seen on Molokai in 1904, which we had somehow overlooked before. Yet here it was, in a glass case, a black bird with bright yellow wing feathers, its little feet crossed as if it had just dropped out of the sky, not endured a century of extinction. The Kauai Oo (*Moho braccatus*), a related species, was last seen in the Alakai Swamp in 1986. The Oo trophy is now so rare that the Bishop Museum in Honolulu keeps a solitary taxidermy specimen in a dark safe.

If you happen to be in England, you may see a cape once worn by Hawaiian kings made of 20,000 bright yellow Oo thigh feathers at the Pitt-Rivers Museum at the University of Oxford. It's not the same as seeing an Oo on the wing, but Simon Winchester of the *Manchester Guardian* called the Oo cape "certainly one of the most remarkably lovely things in any museum in England." Where, Hawaii folks believe, it has no business being.

In the late 18th century, King Kamehameha declared Lahaina capital of the kingdom. The city was favored for its weather, lush thickets of banana and breadfruit trees, and prime location, tucked comfortably between the West Maui Mountains and the Pacific Ocean. And so it remained for 50 years, until another king moved the political center of Hawaii to Honolulu.

Before establishing Lahaina as capital, Kamehameha secured Maui from the control of its most notorious high chief, the ferocious Kahekili, who built houses out of the skulls of defeated warriors. Kahekili gives his name to a nearby beach and Kahekili's Leap, where he made a daring dive off a cliff. The royal plunge is reenacted nightly at sundown by professional divers at **Puu Kekaa (Black Rock)** on Kaanapali Beach. Despite a lifetime of war, Kahekili survived into his 80s; he died at Waikiki Beach.

Beyond Kaanapali, at Maui's northwest end, lies **Kapalua Resort,** a picturesque resort on former pineapple plantation land with a string of exquisite bays. (Although Kapalua literally translates to "two borders," the preferred interpretation is the more poetic "arms embracing the sea.") A luxury hotel anchors the resort, which includes condominiums, timeshares, three championship golf courses, two tennis complexes, and a cluster of shops, restaurants, and a grocery store.

For hiking enthusiasts, the **Kapalua Nature Society** (☎ 808-669-0244) offers guests hikes in the West Maui Mountains, including one of the world's most expensive walks—a $500 trek into the Puu Kukui rain forest for 12 hikers who win the opportunity by an annual lottery. **Puu Kukui,** the 5,788-foot peak of the West Maui mountains,

On every island, we suppose, there's got to be a practical place where you can commit retail—you know, get gas, find film, eat pizza by the slice, sip lattes, shop for zoris, get fast cash at the ATM, and otherwise hang out at the mall. Until recently, there was little of this Mainland stuff on Maui. Perhaps it all surfaced overnight while everybody was snorkeling. Now, Kahului looks like the place you went to Maui to get away from. It's got a big new mall, streets lined with used car lots, fast food joints, pizza parlors, and blocks of traffic lights and traffic jams. What used to be a wide spot in the road is now an excellent example of bad urban planning—there's a Costco next to a bird preserve, with Maui's three main roads ending in a killer intersection that puts lost, deplaning tourists at direct odds with homebound locals. Unless you're a serious mall rat on holiday, or need to fill up your rental car on the way out of town, you may opt to avoid this least Hawaiian place. But if you need to restock, you might be grateful to patronize Kahului's shops. Open market days at Queen Kaahumanu mall will introduce you to local fruits, vegetables, and arts and crafts.

is the second-wettest spot on earth (after Mount Waialeale on Kauai). Its summit hides a boggy rain forest filled with rare native species of birds and stunted trees. The lucky hikers are flown by helicopter up and over Iao Needle and 4,751-foot Eke Crater, which early Hawaiians believed was heaven's gate.

Down on the shore below, beyond Kapalua, the **Northwest Coast** turns rugged and rocky as the highway winds past Honolua Bay, Nakalele Bay, and the fishing and farming village of **Kahakuloa,** where drivers stop for shaved ice and a break from the tightly curving, often one-lane road.

Just beyond the village up at the top of a cliff, look for **Kaukini Gallery,** featuring 100 local artists' works. Drivers with off-road vehicles and others willing to brave a trip on the unpaved Kahekeli Highway can complete a loop by returning to Highway 330 via Highway 340. The cautious can backtrack around the West Maui Mountains.

CENTRAL MAUI

STARTING IN THE NORTH, from Kahului Airport en route to Kahului, you pass **Kanaha Pond** on the right, a bird preserve in the middle of a congested commercial district complete with Costco, K-Mart, and a Borders bookstore. Once a Hawaiian fishpond, the sanctuary is now Maui's prime waterfowl preserve and home of the endangered Hawaiian stilt. You can see the birds pecking the mudflats—from your car or from a viewing area at preserve's entry at the junction of Highway 36 and Highway 396.

Wailuku is the gateway to **Iao Valley** and a good stop for lunch or to stroll and shop. Maui's historic clapboard county seat, Wailuku is a shopper's haven with art galleries, antiques stores, jewelers, gold-smiths, gift shops, and a farmers' market, which is worth a visit if you've never seen or sampled such tropical fruits as durian, starfruit, and lychee. Fruits and vegetables are tree-ripe from the backyards of Maui residents.

The **Bailey House Museum,** run by the Maui Historical Society, is a relic missionary house full of artifacts dating to 1833, with gardens, early artwork, and a gift shop stuffed with made-on-Maui arts and crafts.

Most travelers pass through Wailuku on the way to **Iao Valley State Park,** the most photogenic valley easily visited in the West Maui Mountains. The centerpiece of the 6.2-acre park is **Iao Needle,** a 1,200-foot volcanic spire sculpted by eons of erosion. Also in Iao Valley is **Kepaniwai Park,** an outdoor museum highlighting Maui's cultural heritage, and the **Hawaii Nature Center**, with guided hikes designed for children. The center also has 30 hands-on exhibits focusing on Hawaii's natural history.

Farther west, **Maui Tropical Plantation** is a roadside attraction and garden of tropical delights, where admission is free but a 40-minute narrated tram ride for two through remnant fields of pineapple, sugar, and other tropical crops is $11 for adults and $4 for kids ages 3 to 12.

An architectural surprise appears at **Waikapu Golf and Country Club,** intended as a private Japanese golf club, on the way west from Wailuku. The curvilinear clubhouse is based on plans designed—but never built—by Frank Lloyd Wright as a house for playwright Arthur Miller and his wife, Marilyn Monroe. You can gaze at the design, but the course is now closed. To return north, take Kuihelani Highway (Highway 380). Riding through the cane fields, you will pass the **Baldwin Sugar Museum** and the **Puunene Sugar Mill,** a short side trip down Puunene Avenue. Take Highway 30 to reach West Maui or Highway 31 to South Maui.

SOUTH MAUI

AT MAUI'S "CHIN" is **Maalaea Bay,** a cluster of aquatic commerce around a boat harbor (a key embarkation for Molokini-bound snor-kel boats) and surfing area. There you'll find **Maui Ocean Center,** a 600,000-gallon aquarium with hundreds of ocean creatures, includ-ing rays, sea turtles, reef fish, and a tiger shark. A transparent walk-through tunnel at the center of the tank provides a 240-degree view as schools of fish glide overhead.

Driving south along Maalaea Bay, you pass **Kealia Pond National Wildlife Preserve,** home to the endangered green sea turtle. Heed the yellow-and-black Turtle Crossing signs and the fences along the beach; those are measures to keep the turtles from crossing the busy highway. Maalaea Beach is good for surfing but not for sunning in the afternoon, when the hard isthmus wind that rises will kick gritty sand in your face and dust your sunscreened bod.

Beyond Maalaea is **Kihei,** a beach resort town with three road-side beach parks, **Kamaole I, II, and III** (III is most popular), some 50 condominium complexes, shops, restaurants, businesses, and a rarity: nightlife, including dancing spots, nightclubs, sports bars, and karaoke bars. If you need a mall to feel at home, the newest is **Piilani Village Shopping Center,** complete with Roy's Kihei Restaurant and Outback Steakhouse, out on Piilani Highway on the way to Wailea. The Safeway store offers Maui-grown delights and foods from home.

South of Kihei is the master-planned resort of **Wailea** ("water of Lea," goddess of canoes), a 1,500-acre oasis of luxury hotels and condos, set on five gold-sand crescent beaches. Wailea is fine dining, boutique shopping, and 54 holes of championship golf. It is the prime luxury resort destination on Maui.

In ancient lore, a mysterious birdman named Manupae arrived at Paeahu, where Wailea is today, in search of a mate. He met and fell in love with a lovely young woman named Kahaea o Kamaole. Kahaea's father, a wealthy and powerful man on the island, did not approve of Manupae and banished him and Kahaea from the area. The young lovers fled to the high slopes of Haleakala Volcano, near a cinder cone called Puu Makua, and had a daughter. They named her Lelehune ("fine rain" or "spray"), after the refreshing mountain mists that breathed life to Maui's dry, thirsty lowlands. Today, the lelehune mists still kiss the shores of Wailea, a gentle reminder of enduring love in the Islands.

If you go hotel hopping (and you should to experience the delights of tropical architecture), start with the Disneyesque **Grand Wailea Resort Hotel and Spa,** the elegant **Four Seasons Maui Resort,** and the Arabian fantasy **Fairmont Kea Lani Hotel Maui.** The Hawaii-style **Wailea Marriott Beach Resort** is the best bargain on this luxury coast. It is exactly what you expect a Hawaii resort to be: open, airy, full of sea breezes, tropical flowers, and gracious staff, with the best location for shopping. Next door are **The Shops at Wailea,** Maui's version of Rodeo Drive, a two-story, $70-million mall of boutiques, including Tiffany, Prada, Mont Blanc, Banana Republic, and Florida import Tommy Bahama's, a combination lifestyle emporium–ocean-view café. Lappert's Ice Cream, home of the $3.50 single scoop of ice cream, is another one of several food outlets, including Ruth's Chris Steakhouse, Longhi's, and Honolulu Coffee Co., where you can get an early-morning latte.

Three miles offshore is the islet of **Molokini,** a natural attraction for fish and folks alike. The 165-foot-high tip of a submerged tuff cone draws fish, and consequently divers, like a magic lure. Fish go to Molokini because it's there. Snorkelers follow the bright tropical fish for a dip and a peek, while experienced scuba divers explore the sheer, convex side of the volcanic tuff cone where big, pelagic fish, including sharks, top the food chain. Molokini is a Marine Life Conservation District, which means all you can take away are pictures or memories of the fish. Feeding them is *kapu* ("taboo" or "forbidden"), too. Out to sea beyond Molokini, you can spot the red-dirt island of **Kahoolawe,** the so-called "target" island used for a half century by the U.S. Navy for aerial bombing runs. When the bombs were stopped by presidential order, the island was returned to native Hawaiians for the creation of a cultural preserve. You can go there only by special invitation, unless you want to help clear the island of unexploded ordnance.

Up on the hill above Wailea is **The Diamond Resort,** a unique Japanese retreat with condos, *onsen* spa bathhouses, sushi bar, and teppanyaki restaurant, created as a private enclave for Tokyo millionaires; it's now open to all and worth a visit, if only for the udon noodles.

Along the Wailea Coast are million-dollar condos and private estates of the rich and famous (Clint Eastwood bought a $7.5-million Wailea oceanfront lot for his wife's birthday present). After Wailea, the paved road dead-ends at the isolated resort of **Makena,** where the restrained, elegant **Maui Prince Hotel** sits in the lee of 360-foot Puu Olai cinder cone, amid 1,800 acres of mostly rugged, natural beauty graced by two championship golf courses. Better hurry, though, because the coconut wireless is buzzing with rumors of tear-down and expansion. The hotel's beach is bordered by a big, sandy dune that is such a favorite haul-out for green sea turtles that snorkel tours dub it **Turtle Town.** Should you happen upon a turtle, remember, they are an endangered species and federally protected.

Makena is a historic embarkation, or landing, where Ulupalakua Ranch cowboys once loaded cattle onto barges bound for market. Locals still say their prayers at the 1832 lava-rock **Keawalai Congregational Church,** where Sunday services are said in Hawaiian.

A seaside graveyard with lei-draped tombstones crawls with feral cats. Dare not take a lei from a tombstone; it's bad luck.

On the other side of Puu Olai stands Oneloa, the Hawaiian word for aptly named **Big Beach;** it's a 3,000-foot-long strand, 100 feet wide, and good for swimming, snorkeling, or tanning. Ahead, the road narrows and the terrain looks terrible, with the sharp, black lava of a 210-year-old flow masked only with sparse vegetation before the road ends. **Ahihi-Kinau Natural Reserve** and **La Perouse Bay** show off Maui's still primitive, natural side. That's it; time to turn around and go back.

UPCOUNTRY MAUI

HEADING IN THE NORTHEAST DIRECTION from Kahului Airport on Highway 36 takes you to **Paia,** a breezy former plantation town now famous for its shopping, art galleries, and crafts shops, like Maui Crafts Guild, a collective of 25 local artists; Natural Impressions, a shop that makes Gyotaku impressions of fish on rice paper in the ancient Japanese style; Moana Bakery and Cafe, famed for Thai curries and upside-down pineapple muffins; and Jacque's North-shore Restaurant Bistro, where you can dine on fresh seafood under a giant monkeypod tree or at a sushi bar that's the local evening surfer hangout.

Strong year-round winds and ideal wave conditions at nearby **Hookipa Beach Park** draw the world's top windsurfers, dubbed the "Maui air force" for their aerial antics. It is a sight to see these daredevils hit waves head-on and gain hang time up in the air before splashing down in the sea. Nearby, Haiku has inexpensive lodging in B&Bs and vacation rentals.

From Paia, head inland (or, as locals say, Upcountry) to the cooler heights of Maui. The drive up the foothills of **Haleakala,** a dormant volcano and the island's top attraction, takes you to **Makawao.** This *paniolo* (cowboy) village has avoided becoming a ghost town by becoming a rustic art and boutique center, somewhat eclipsed these days by Paia down the road. A cappuccino at Casanova's, an open-air roadside bistro, is one good reason to stop, and the local bakery offers gooey cream puffs. Then browse David Warren Gallery, Gallery Maui, and Kirstin Bunney for local art. Monsoon and Tropo are chic shops with jazz, books, and ubiquitous Tommy Bahama's togs.

On the way up or down to Makawao, browse the **Hui Noeau Visual Arts Center** in a Charles Dickey–designed 1917 Mediterranean-style villa on a ten-acre estate that once belonged to Maui sugar baron Harry Baldwin. Hui Noeau is Hawaiian for "society of artists," and you may meet a few in the workshops. And do, like all who love good food, stop for lunch or dinner (reservations required) at Bev Gannon's **Haliimaile General Store.** A meal in this old plantation store full of tasty island treats and local art is on the top-ten checklist for the perfect Maui visit.

Farther upcountry is **Kula,** a scenic community that clings to Haleakala's shoulder at 3,000 feet. Kula is known for its cool climate, perfect for growing varieties of flowers and vegetables (including the sweet Kula onion) that don't always thrive at tropical temperatures. Among the strangest blooms are the South African imports called protea, a large family of bushes and plants painted from Mother Nature's other canvas, with flowers in black and pink or neon-orange or yellow; weird, spiky edges; and stiff, dark-maroon leaves. You can see some of the 700 varieties of protea and other blooms at **Kula Botanical Gardens** on the way to **Ulupalakua Ranch,** where the road leads off into the hinterlands behind Haleakala. The 20,000-acre ranch, a nearly vertical spread where the volcano last erupted around 1790, raises cattle and elk and grows wine grapes. Drop by the tasting room at **Tedeschi Vineyards** to sample their premium wine. Better yet, bring a picnic basket, pair it with a Maui vintage (forget the pineapple wine, created as a novelty), and enjoy the afternoon in the cool uplands.

Beyond Tedeschi, the road runs through eucalyptus groves at the 2,000-foot-elevation, then drops down along a raw and majestic sea coast few ever see. You can reach Hana via **Kaupo** (where there's a store) and **Kipahulu** on little-celebrated Piilani Highway (named for the first great chief of Maui), but plan on a trip of two hours or more to get there on a road that is slow, partly paved, and prone to washouts in bad weather.

From Kula, you can take a mountain road to rival any in the world and wind up to **Haleakala National Park,** the island's greatest natural spectacle. Haleakala, the name of a dormant volcano rising more than 10,000 feet above sea level, translates to "House of the Sun."

> Soon after noon we began to descend; and in a hollow of the mountain, not far from the ragged edge of the crater, then filled up with billows of cloud, we came upon what we were searching for; not, however, one or two, but thousands of silverswords; their cold, frosted silver gleam making the hillside look like winter or moonlight. One thinks of them rather as . . . a prize at Ascot . . . than anything organic.
>
> —Isabella L. Bird, *Six Weeks in the Sandwich Islands*

What really sets Maui apart from all the other islands in Hawaii and the rest of the Pacific is the sleepy volcano that last erupted more than 200 years ago. One of the world's great natural wonders, Haleakala Crater is a red, orange, and black bowl so big and so deep that it makes its own weather, has its own mountain range, and could swallow the island of Manhattan whole. When people say they want to see the real Hawaii, we always steer them away from the coco palm beaches and swanky coastal resorts and send them up 38 steep miles to the hard edge of the cold summit to peer down into the very heart of the matter.

According to Hawaiian legend, the demigod Maui captured the sun with his magic lasso on Haleakala. He convinced the sun to slow down in its travels, effectively lengthening the days and giving his mother, Hina, more time to dry her tapa cloths.

It's cold and windy up there, but blanket-wrapped sun worshipers who witness a Haleakala sunrise are seldom disappointed. Mark Twain called it "the sublimest spectacle" he'd ever seen.

Haleakala is one of only two places in the world (the Big Island is the other) where you may see the exotic silversword, an odd-looking plant with silvery leaves and yellow and violet flowers. Once in its 15-year life it blooms, from June through October, then it dies. Park rangers offer free hiking excursions and informative lectures on topics ranging from Haleakala's geological history to Hawaiian culture.

You'll have to backtrack down Haleakala Crater Road to Kula Highway (Highway 37) to either return to West, Central, and South Maui via Paia the way you came, or head on to Hana on Piilani Highway.

HANA

TAKING A DIFFERENT ROUTE FROM PAIA starts you on the long road to **Hana,** a three-hour drive that crosses 56 one-lane bridges and takes 617 twists and turns (about 12 curves a mile). The rental-car parade goes slow so everyone can ogle Maui's natural beauty: crashing surf, steep green hills, gushing waterfalls, and flowers.

Must stops along the way include **Puohokamoa Stream** (mile marker 11), with two pools and picnic tables, and the palmy **Keanae Peninsula** (just past mile marker 16), a relic taro-pond village with the 1856 Congregational Missionary Church and a few homes. Those who get car sick or impatient with traffic usually turn back here, content to sample this segment of the Hana Highway, while the hardy press on to Halfway to Hana Fruit Stand for a fresh papaya or mango, and stop at **Puaa Kaa State Wayside Park** (mile marker 22) for a memorable tropical picnic beside waterfall pools.

Blink and you might miss **Hana;** it's a small community of about 1,000 residents. The lifestyle here is slow and unpretentious, and the locals wouldn't want it any other way. Highlights include the **Hana Cultural Center,** which recounts area history, **Hana Coast Gallery** in the **Hotel Hana-Maui, Hana Gardenland,** and **Hasegawa General Store,** celebrated in a local pop tune.

A small, elite resort hotel, Hotel Hana-Maui (now owned by the Californians who developed Big Sur's famed Post Ranch and the new Cavallo Point on the Marin headlands of San Francisco's Golden Gate), plus a few condos and bed-and-breakfasts (such as

The Road to Hana

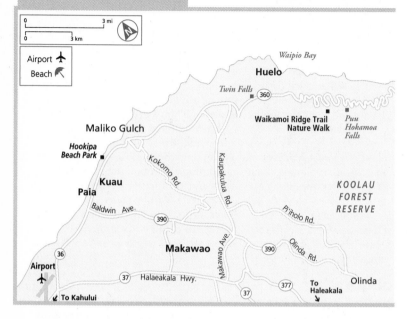

0 ——————— 3 mi
0 ——————— 3 km

Airport ✈
Beach ⚐

Waipio Bay

Huelo

Twin Falls ■ (360)

Maliko Gulch

Waikamoi Ridge Trail
Nature Walk

Puu Hokamoa Falls ■

Hookipa Beach Park ■

Kuau

Paia

Kokomo Rd.

Kaupakulua Rd.

KOOLAU FOREST RESERVE

Baldwin Ave.

(390)

Pi'iholo Rd.

Makawao

Makawao Ave.

(390)

Olinda Rd.

(36)

Airport ✈

(37) Halaeakala Hwy.

(377)

To Haleakala ↓

Olinda

↙ **To Kahului**

(37)

Aloha Cottages) provide lodging.

Ten miles south of Hana is **Kipahulu,** where Charles Lindbergh is buried in the backyard of a cliffside church. The famed American aviator—the first person to fly solo across the Atlantic Ocean, in 1927—first visited Kipahulu in the 1950s. "I love Maui so much, I would rather live one day in Maui than one month in New York," a cancer-stricken Lindbergh told his doctor. The "Lone Eagle" spent the final eight days of his life in a guest cottage near Hana. He died on August 26, 1974, at 72. No signs point to the site, but Lindbergh's grave lies near **Palapala Hoomau Congregational Church.**

The grave, built according to Lindbergh's sketches, is 8 feet square, 12 feet deep, with walls of lava rock. A large piece of Vermont granite is covered with loose, smooth, round ili ili stones, in the Hawaiian tradition. He was placed unembalmed in a casket made of eucalyptus and lined with a Hudson's Bay blanket that Lindbergh received from his mother; a cushion from his plane, *The Spirit of St. Louis,* was placed under his body; and a Hawaiian tapa cloth covered his body. His wife, Anne, added three white flowers before the casket was nailed shut. He was buried barefoot in khakis. His grave notes that Charles Lindbergh died on Maui in 1974 and is inscribed with verse 9 of Psalms 139: "If I take the wings of the morning and dwell in the uttermost part of the sea." Thousands of curious visit

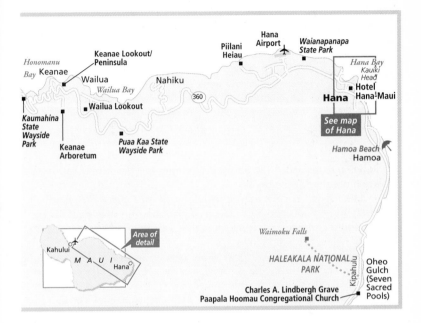

his grave each year. Some bring him hibiscus and plumeria blossoms; others take stones from Lindbergh's grave as souvenirs—and often return them later by mail, citing bad luck that followed the misdeed.

Seven waterfall pools cascade down Haleakala to the deep blue Pacific at Kipahulu and comprise one of Maui's top ten natural wonders. The pools of Oheo Gulch also rank high among Hawaii's fatal attractions, claiming more lives each year than sharks.

Thousands come daily year-round to splash in all seven pools, a local rite of passage, or only to soak up their spectacular beauty. And they are often unaware of the danger this almost paradisiacal place poses. Without warning, a sudden unseen cloud burst high on the cloud-catching slope of 10,000-foot Haleakala can unleash a wall of water that sweeps Pipiwai stream and the waterfall pools, sending the unwary to sure death in a ten-foot crashing surf. The deluge can and often does sweep across the narrow coastal road with enough force to wash Jeeps and rental cars out to sea.

If you take the plunge in the pools, keep an eye on the clouds. Be careful going to and from pool to pool; a slip and fall on slippery rocks can be fatal. Heed all park and ranger warnings for rain, high surf, falling rock, and tsunami.

Often mistakenly called "sacred," no evidence exists that early

Hawaiians regarded the pools as anything but beautiful. And there are more than seven pools.

Hikers will delight in a four-mile walk on Pipiwai Trail, which visits upper pools and meanders past giant banyan trees and into the Kipahulu bamboo forest, which makes a drumming kind of natural music when the wind blows.

Beyond Kipahulu, the two-lane asphalt winnows down to an often rutty trail over the serrated, nearly vertical southeast side of Haleakala that in big storms sometimes washes out and slides into the sea. Off to the south, across the **Alenuihaha Channel,** you can see the more than 14,000-foot summits of Mauna Loa and Mauna Kea, two of the five volcanoes of the Big Island.

At **Kaupo,** a country store sells cold drinks and century-old photos of the coast that, except for the old folks in vintage clothing, look like they were taken yesterday. Along the coast, the main road turns northwest across the **Kaupo Ranch** and four-wheel-drive dirt roads run down to the sea, where surfcasting, *opihi* hunting, and beach-combing are popular local pursuits. At **Pakowai Point,** look for the **Natural Arch,** a coastal landmark that means you soon will leave the splendid isolation of this seldom-seen part of Maui.

Always check weather and road conditions before you set off around the back side of Maui, and don't go there when flash-flood warnings or days of rainy storms might turn the unpaved portions of road into a threat. Wherever the road crosses a stream, federal bridge funds have dictated a few hundred feet of standard road with pavement, yellow line and all, but it soon reverts to slowgoing over gravel and dirt. Further on toward **Ulupalakua,** the road begins to rise, paved, into big views of open land and sea, with rolling terrain and curves you can handle. It's a driver's pleasure against the ever-present majestic backdrop of the huge volcano. Few vehicles use this road except to go between ranches and fishing spots and on backroads tours. The flora, climate, and general countryside change dramatically moment to moment, a trick of Haleakala's weather control, and it's as open and sweeping a panorama as the first part of

Old Bones

We sat at Orchids at Halekulani one golden Waikiki afternoon, talking about old Hawaiian bones that surfaced in sand dunes of Kapalua, Maui, when the Ritz-Carlton Hotel was built a decade ago. It was an odd encounter—two gently militant Hawaiian men, Clifford Naeole and Lopaka, and Yvonne Landavazzo Biegel, then public relations counsel for the Ritz-Carlton. It was her idea to get us together. "Every day more and more bones surfaced," Lopaka said. "It got to the point where it was too much. Enough was enough."

"How many burials?"

"About 1,200. Nobody knew it was that extensive. They just had a few when they started taking them out." The unearthing of ancestral Hawaiian bones happened in 1990, but Lopaka was still angry, a sullen Hawaiian not yet at peace. "All over the state it's been done," he continued, "but this time, we protested, we stopped the construction, we forced the hotel to move away from the graveyard."

"I did the reburial work personally," Lopaka said. "It was spiritual, real spooky, handling the bones of my ancestors." We shivered a little in the tropical sun. "It was hard for me to go to the hotel, even be there," he said. "They didn't move out of the kindness of their hearts; they were forced to, I mean it was like they fought it all the way, they were forced, but they had no choice. If they had their way, they would have put the hotel on the coast."

The public relations counsel for the Ritz-Carlton at Kapalua looked nervous, but also saddened. "Don't you think anyone was sensitive to the issue?"

"Well, personally, no," Lopaka said, and Clifford Naeole agreed. Everyone laughed nervously. "It was an outrageous act, but something good came out in the end, though," Naeole said.

"It was really hard to deal with the hotel," he said. "I never wanted to go there, never wanted to be associated with them until I saw some of the programs that they sponsored, and I felt they really cared about the place."

"You know," he said, "it took a while, but finally I decided these people are good people and should be forgiven." The public relations counsel for the Ritz-Carlton gave a faint smile that flashed bright as the glare off the waves at Waikiki. The sensitive subject was breached, but proved surmountable.

Today, the sand dune area at Kapalua, where 1,200 Hawaiian graves were unearthed, is now held in perpetual trust, surrounded by signs that say "Kapu"—no trespassing—where the hotel was originally to be built. Occasionally, unknowing tourists pay no heed to the kapu signs; they walk across the old Hawaiian graveyard as if it were a golf course.

Strange things, restless things, happen at the Ritz-Carlton at Kapalua. Doors open and close, there are odd shadows in the halls on moonlit nights, and sometimes the elevators seem to have a mind all their own. It's enough to make you wonder if everyone, living or dead, is at peace.

the drive past Kipahulu was cloistered by vegetation and sharp bends in the road. It's a fitting conclusion to a tour of East Maui, and here you are at Tedeschi Vineyards waiting for the tasting room to open.

MOLOKAI DRIVING TOUR

MOLOKAI, LEAST-DEVELOPED OF HAWAII'S MAIN ISLANDS, is a visual reminder of old Hawaii. Some of it is lush, fern-forested wilderness valley, and some, hot, dry, and dusty, so unappealing that Captain James Cook sailed by on his "discovery" voyage in the late 1700s, choosing not to drop anchor.

Although much improved, Molokai even today appeals only to a few visitors who prefer the peace and quiet of a simple, rural island virtually untouched by the veneer of commercial tourism. Of the nearly 7 million people who visit the Hawaiian Islands each year, according to state data, only about 66,000, a little more than 1 percent, make it to Molokai.

Centuries ago, Molokai was a more vibrant place. It is, after all, where hula was born and where, at one of the largest *heiau* in the Pacific, a four-tier stack of sacred rocks, longer than a football field, ancient wizards called kahuna taught the dark art of human sacrifice and established *kapu* (taboo) that still send shivers down the spines of those who believe in ways of the old. But today, with no industry save farming and tourism, Molokai is peaceful and quiet, the ideal place to do nothing but take in fresh air, listen to the silence, and stare out to sea in what Robert Louis Stevenson called "a fine state of haze." Here, each day under the tropic sun passes much like the one before . . .

In Cook's time, Molokai was known as Molokai Pule Oo, or "Molokai of the Potent Prayers." The island was home to priests known as kahuna, who were revered for their *mana*, or spiritual power. Since they could "pray" someone to death, and others knew it, their presence spared Molokai from bloody battles waged by chiefs on other islands.

Inhabitants of Molokai today appear to use other powers to thwart change on this island, which is best described by what it doesn't have: stoplights, shopping malls, a nightclub, or a building taller than a palm tree. For better or worse, Molokai has been spared "progress," and the island's 7,000 residents lead a near-subsistence lifestyle enhanced by a little tourism and a welfare check.

Formed by two volcanoes—1,381-foot-high **Mauna Loa** on the west and 4,961-foot-high **Kamakou** on the east—the long, slender island appears like a big wedge in the sea, rising from rock-rimmed fishponds on the south shore to 3,000-foot-high cliffs on the north.

You arrive at **Hoolehua Airport,** the small, open-air lava-rock terminal in the middle of cornfields, after a short hop from busy Honolulu. The first thing you notice is the silence, then the

Molokai Driving Tour

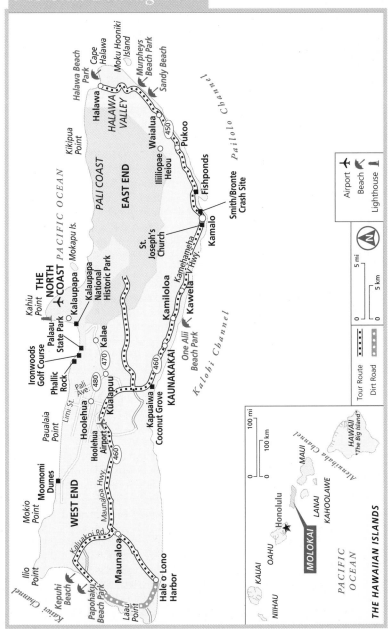

Airport ✈
Beach ⬟
Lighthouse �᫙

N

Tour Route ▪▪▪▪▪
Dirt Road ●●●●●

0   5 mi
0   5 km

THE HAWAIIAN ISLANDS

KAUAI
NIIHAU
OAHU
Honolulu
MOLOKAI
LANAI
KAHOOLAWE
MAUI
Atenuihaha Channel
HAWAII
"The Big Island"

PACIFIC
OCEAN

0   100 mi
0   100 km

MOLOKAI DRIVE TIMES

FROM MOLOKAI AIRPORT TO:	TIME TO TRAVEL
Halawa Valley	2 hours
Kaunakakai	15 minutes
Kepuhi Beach	25 minutes
Mapulehu	35 minutes
Maunaloa	15 minutes
Papohaku Beach	30 minutes

soft patois of others, then smiling, friendly faces. "Welcome to Molokai," a sign says. "Go Slow. You're on Molokai now."

After Honolulu International and Kahului Airport on Maui, Hoolehua Airport looks abandoned, and it often is between flights—although there are rental-car windows and a lunch counter serving the local favorites of chili rice and Spam *musubi* (a favorite island treat made of molded rice with a piece of Spam on top, wrapped together with a piece of *nori* or papery dried seaweed, served room temp) and cold drinks.

On Molokai, there are two main directions, east and west, and two main regions, the **West End** and the **East End.** Those who live in **Kaluapapa,** on the peninsula 3,000 feet below the sea cliffs of the North Shore, call the rest of the island **Topside.**

Which way you head depends on whether you like it hot and dry or lush and tropical, because the 38-mile-long island divides at **Kaunakakai,** the funky island capital, into two different climate zones. The West End looks like Mexico, the East End, like Tahiti. The West End has a defunct resort and golf course; the East End has a condo hotel, plus a collection of small, coastal condos, vacation rentals and bed-and-breakfasts. We'll start by heading west from the island's center, then loop back and head east.

A sun-faded, three-block town with harbor and pier, **Kaunakakai** looks more like an Old West movie set than a tropical village. It is the island's center of commerce, politics, and social affairs. **Maunaloa Highway,** the main approach into town, is lined with spires of churches and the spiky palm trees of **Kapuaiwa Coconut Grove,** planted in 1860 for King Kamehameha V, who was known as Kapuaiwa.

The royal garden originally was planted with 1,000 trees; today only a remnant grove stands. Venture here to collect an authentic souvenir only when there is no wind; a falling coconut can brain you. At the shore, you may spot the spring of fresh water that pours into the sea.

Molokai's chief settlement includes a bank, post office (where you can mail a coconut home), drug store, and grocery, all on **Ala Malama,** the town's main street. Nearby are the medical center and family-run

In 1934, the late R. Alex Anderson, one of Hawaii's most prolific song composers, wrote "The Cockeyed Mayor of Kaunakakai," which Hilo Hattie made famous in the 1940s. Anderson used the term *cockeyed* "mainly because it combined nicely with the last two syllables of the word Kaunakakai," according to *Hawaiian Music and Musicians*. Anderson, who composed nearly 200 songs, including "Lovely Hula Hands," "I Will Remember You," and "I Had to Lova and Leva on the Lava," died in 1995. He was 101 years old. Incidentally, since Molokai is part of Maui County, there is no mayor in Kaunakakai.

businesses: the **Friendly Market, Molokai Drive-Inn, Oviedo's Filipino Restaurant, Outpost Natural Foods,** and **Kanemitsu Bakery,** where 19 different types of bread are baked fresh daily.

At night, you may find a few open shops, but the brightest lights in town shine on **Mitchell Pauole Center,** site of softball games, "huli-huli" chicken roasts, carnivals, and community events.

Unless you brought your own food and drink, you will, like everyone else on Molokai, make the obligatory stop at **Misaki's Market,** a third-generation store where antlered deer-head trophies guard aisles of canned goods. Once a week, when Sause Bros. sends its lifeline barges from Honolulu across the **Kaiwi Channel,** the market is replenished with fresh food and milk. When seas are high, the island's food supply dries up and you will be eating at **Molokai Pizza Cafe,** the only pizza parlor on the island. The only other vital establishment is **Rawlins Chevron Station,** one of two gas stations on the island.

Above Kaunakakai looms defunct **Kamakou Volcano,** the island's tallest mountain and home to a virgin forest of native trees, including rare sandalwood, which was harvested for the China trade.

Up here, 2,774-acre **Kamakou Preserve** is home to native Hawaiian birds and 219 plants that exist nowhere else; you can see them with **Nature Conservancy** permission. Another protected wilderness is **Moomomi Dunes,** where Smithsonian Institute scientists unearthed skeletons of flightless birds like the long-extinct dodo.

Leaving Kaunakakai, the road leads to the **West End,** where the now defunct **Molokai Ranch** once dominated red-dirt rolling hills covered by kiawe, brush, and cactus. But there is a lot to see en route, and Molokai's **North Coast** merits a side-trip, too. At mid-island, you can see, crack open, and taste a macadamia nut at **Purdy's Macadamia Nut Farm** in **Hoolehua** before heading up to **Coffees of Hawaii Plantation Store** in **Kualapuu,** where the island's best fresh coffee is served from field to roaster to your cup in espressos and lattes.

Highway 470 leads from Kualapuu to the **North Shore Lookout** in **Palaau State Park,** a cool, upland forest with the island's best campsite, and **Phallic Rock,** a famous fertility stone that many claim

Margaret (Peggy) Keahi-Leary, the postmaster at Hoolehua's post office on the Island of Molokai, has a lovely bunch of coconuts. She gives them away to tourists. "I provide coconuts free of charge at the post office," Keahi-Leary said. "All the tourists have to do is write or draw or do anything they want on the coconut and then I ship them by priority mail anywhere in the U.S.A." She calls her service Post-a-Nut. The Hawaiian coconut, according to the U.S. Postal Service, is a perfectly acceptable shipping container. "It can go right out in the mail," Keahi-Leary said. "No wrapper, no nothing, just $3 in postage for up to two pounds. As the weight goes up, the postage cost rises accordingly. The coconut is like the spirit of Hawaii. It's a good positive image for Molokai, too," said Keahi-Leary, born and raised on the island, and proud of her small role in Hawaii tourism. "When I came up with the idea I was asking myself, 'If I were a tourist, what would I like?' I'd want something that was authentic and genuine Hawaii. And so the coconut idea came about." She began the Post-a-Nut program in 1992 but lost track of how many coconuts she's shipped. "Some days it's three bags full, other days only two or three coconuts," she said. "The thing is, not every place has access to coconuts. On Molokai, over here, we got a whole coconut grove."

works too well. You can stand on the edge of the lookout and take in the majesty of Molokai's North Shore, but the best way to experience the sea cliffs is the **Molokai Mule Ride,** which takes you on a heart-pounding traverse down the 26-switchback trail to **Kalaupapa,** the former leper colony, now a national historical park. You can also hike down the trail or fly in from Hoolehua Airport via **Damien Tours.** The ground tour includes a visit to **Saint Philomena Church,** built in 1872, and the graveyard where Father Damien de Veuster, a Belgian priest, was buried (after nomination for sainthood, his body was reinterred in his native Belgium).

He did what we have never dreamed of daring . . .

—Robert Louis Stevenson
on Father Damien, the leper priest of Molokai

Hawaiians stricken with leprosy were banished to Kalaupapa beginning in 1860. (They were literally pushed from a boat into the waters off the peninsula and had to swim to shore.) Father de Veuster arrived in 1873 and embraced the outcasts. "The sick are arriving by the boatloads," he wrote to his superiors. "They die in droves." Father Damien spent 16 years caring for his congregation. It was an exhausting labor of love, and he was mostly alone in his efforts. Any contributions by visiting doctors were left on a fence post to avoid physical contact with patients. By the end of the 1870s, approximately 1,000 people were exiled to Kalaupapa.

On April 15, 1889, Father Damien himself succumbed to the disease at age 49.

On the way to or from the edge, you pass coffee plantations, the nine-hole **Ironwood Golf Course,** which was built in 1920 by sugar planters, and **Molokai Museum and Cultural Center,** housed in the restored **Meyer Sugar Mill.** The mill's namesake, German professor Rudolph W. Meyer, came to Molokai in 1849, married a Hawaiian chieftess, and started a steam-engine sugar mill in 1878.

Returning via Kualupuu to Highway 460, you can head east to the 54,000-acre spread of the former **Molokai Ranch** (covering a third of the island), headquartered at **Maunaloa,** a plantation town torn down and rebuilt a few years ago, where retro sugar shacks (made of steel to discourage termites) cost $250,000 or more. Molokai's ranch headquarters, luxury lodge, movie theater, and other amenities are closed following a bankruptcy. You'll still find Daphne Socher's **Kite Factory,** featuring handmade tropical kites. The favorite is a red-and-green hula girl with a skirt that swishes in the wind.

For many years, most Molokai visitors stayed at **Kaluakoi Resort**—long the island's only resort area—but it is closed pending renovation. The 103-room **Kaluakoi Hotel and Golf Club,** an airy structure of lava rock and ohia logs, overlooks Kupuhi Beach and adjoins three-mile-long **Papohaku Beach,** Molokai's biggest. The island's only 18-hole golf course also is closed.

On a nearby plateau is **Kaana,** where tradition holds that Laka, the goddess of the hula, created the native Hawaiian dance. Molokai celebrates the birth of the hula at the annual **Molokai Ka Hula Piko,** held each May at **Papohaku Beach Park,** in a shady seaside grove. The day-long festival features performances, Hawaiian music, food, and local arts and crafts.

From this point, circle south past Laau point to the hamlet of **Hale o Lono** before returning to Maunaloa and then Kaunakakai via Highway 460. From there, it's on to the East End. The trip from Kaunakakai to Puu o Hoku Ranch is only 25 miles, but it seems farther on two-lane King Kamehameha V Highway, because the coast is lush, green, and tropical and there is much to enjoy.

As you head to the East End, you will see some of the most distinguished man-made features of Molokai—**ancient fishponds.** Built of stone and big as lakes, they were built by early Hawaiians who caught fish on the incoming tide and blocked their escape with gates. The first and best of 25 restored fishponds, **Kalokoeli,** appears on the outskirts of Kaunakakai just beyond the **Kaunakakai Harbor.** Many fishponds are still in use today.

Just past **Saint Joseph Church,** about 10 miles out of town, on the *makai* (ocean) side of the highway, look for a hand-painted sign in kiawe brush that says **Smith and Bronte Crash Site.** This is not a memorial to an auto fatality. The sign marks the historic end to the first civilian transpacific flight by Ernie Smith and Emory Bronte in

1927. Bound for Maui from Oakland, California, they flew 25 hours and two minutes at 6,000 feet in a single-engine Travelaire monoplane, but ran out of gas and safely crash-landed on Molokai.

Our Lady of Sorrows Church, one of five built by Father Damien on the island, stands by tombstones draped with lei. The cemetery often crawls with orange tabby feral cats, which you should avoid petting; they are wild and may bite.

On **King Kamehameha V Highway,** you discover affordable seaside condos, like **Wavecrest Resort,** and perfectly sited vacation rentals like **Dunbar Beachfront Cottages** and the **Country Cottage** at **Puu O Hoku Ranch.** The only major retail outlet along the way is **Pukoo Neighbor Store n' Counter,** which sells cold drinks, ice, and plate lunches. It's just beyond **Mapulehu Mango Grove,** a botanical wonder where 2,000 mango trees of various species flourish in a verdant grove perfumed by their blossoms.

At Mapulehu, you can hitch a ride on the **Molokai Horse and Wagon Ride** to one of the spookiest places in Hawaii: **Iliiliopae Heiau,** a school of sacrifice where more than 700 years ago, *kahuna* (priests) taught final rites in a massive temple of doom, three stories high and bigger than a football field. The heiau, legend has it, was built in one night of car-sized boulders passed hand-to-hand by a human chain of 10,000 men, over the spine of the nearly mile-high island from **Wailau Valley,** ten miles away. Each man received one shrimp (*opae*) in exchange for the stone (*iliili*).

If you're ready for a swim, now's the best time, because you're at one of Molokai's best beaches—Waialua Beach at mile marker 19. If it's too crowded, head down to Sandy Beach, a small pocket roadside beach at mile marker 20.

Now King Kamehahema V Highway begins to climb toward **Puu O Hoku Ranch,** where a few lucky folks can bunk for the night in a cabin. The highway turns to hairpins on the very East End and, after scenic vistas of pocket beaches, offshore islets, and dense jungles, dead-ends at **Halawa Valley,** once a major taro-growing valley that rivaled the Big Island's Waipio Valley for production.

Inundated by a 30-foot tsunami in 1946, and by a second in 1957, **Halawa Valley**—a Hawaiian settlement since the seventh century—was abandoned. Now privately owned, the 9,000-acre valley is closed, and the trailhead to 250-foot **Moaula Falls,** once the most accessible waterfall on the island, is posted with "no trespassing" signs. Private treks into the valley are periodically possible. Contact the Molokai Visitors Association for details at ☎ 800-800-6367 or 808-553-3876.

King Kamehameha V Highway winds and narrows and doubles back on itself. Offshore you will see the islet of **Hooniki,** a World War II bombing target of the U.S. Navy (bombing practice was halted in 1958 just before Hawaii became a state), now a seabird sanctuary. At several scenic turnouts you can see, across the **Pailolo Channel,** the north shore of **Maui** and **Kapalua Resort** and the ridges of the **West Maui Moun-**

tains, whose green peaks rise above the cobalt sea. King Kamehameha V Highway comes to a dead-end at **Halawa Beach,** a black-sand beach with two bays and the island's only decent surf break. **Halawa Beach County Park** includes a restroom, barbecue grills, and a parking area, but no lifeguard or other facilities. The water can be murky at Halawa due to runoff from the waterfalls at the head of the valley—which means it's not safe for swimming, since murky water is the favored haunt of reef sharks, especially at sundown. Halawa is as far as you can go by car, but those of you with a kayak may press on around **Cape Halawa** (only in summer when the sea is calm) to discover the raw North Coast, one of Hawaii's natural wonders.

LANAI DRIVING TOUR

LONG AGO, EARLY HAWAIIANS BELIEVED LANAI (the Hawaiian word for "hump" or "swelling") was haunted by spirits so wily and vicious that no human being who went there could survive. Today, nearly everyone who goes there not only gets a good night's sleep, but always leaves refreshed, if reluctantly. Spirits still haunt the island—it is said that the legendary Madame Pele often visits—but mostly Lanai is a high-end retreat for urban souls.

Once home to the largest pineapple plantation in the world, Lanai

LANAI DRIVE TIMES

FROM THE LANAI AIRPORT TO:	TIME TO TRAVEL
Garden of the Gods	45 minutes
Hulopoe and Manele Bays	25 minutes
Lanai City	5 minutes
Munro Trail	15 minutes
Shipwreck Beach	35 minutes

Lanai Driving Tour

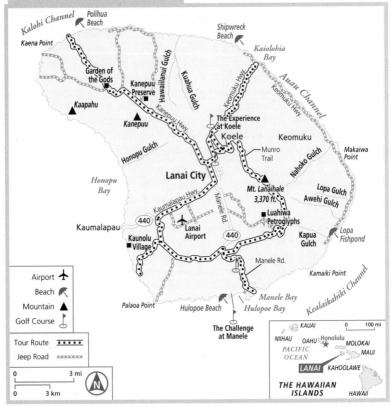

survives now by cultivating well-heeled visitors seeking peaceful surroundings, luxurious resorts, outstanding golf, and one of the best spots for diving in the entire Pacific Ocean.

The sweet and juicy fruit that once covered more than 19,000 acres of the island's red-dirt Palawai Basin is virtually gone (cheaper labor in the developing world hastened the end of Hawaii's plantation era); all that remains is a relic field at the gateway to Lanai Airport, where the gray-green, spiky-leafed plants sport football-sized golden fruit.

In 1987, a California tycoon named David Murdock acquired a controlling interest in Castle & Cooke, one of the Islands' oldest companies. He found in his new portfolio the deed to the Island of Lanai, a place he'd never seen. Since Hawaii's plantation era was ending and plans were already forming to welcome

The anxious faces of first-time Lanai visitors make us smile—chic, over-dressed women in white linen, boldly jacketed men in tasseled loafers—as they look about the Magritte-like landscape for palm trees, tropical flowers, or any of the usual island icons. Instead they see pine trees, mud-spattered pickup trucks, and cute Filipino girls in blue jeans, sweatshirts, and cowboy boots. We once arrived in hunting season to see a trophy deer, its red tongue hanging, splayed over a rusty Jeep hood. Gradually, tourists notice the soft, almost code-like speech of local people (their pidgin patois sounds like an exotic foreign language), catch the scent of tangy salt air mingled with pine trees, and even shiver a little in the cool tropical air. All the incongruities only add to the mysterious attraction of this odd little island.

Lanai sits in the middle of the inhabited Hawaiian chain, in plain sight of every island except Kauai, yet feels removed in time and place. Like the Heartland: Iowa of the Pacific. Sometimes we think it feels like the late 1930s on Lanai, or what we imagine the 1930s were like in America: agrarian and uncertain, with a great gap between rich and poor. In the back of your mind, it is easy to hear distant echoes of Benny Goodman tunes. When people leave Lanai after spending only a few days, they say it seems like they have been gone for weeks. The time-expanding nature of Lanai may be its most compelling virtue, the reason it is such a great island escape. You don't just go there, you return to a place almost lost in memory.

tourists to Lanai, he envisioned an island resort like no other. His vision became reality in the early 1990s when the first of two luxury hotels, the **Lodge at Koele,** opened its doors. A year later, the **Manele Bay** resort made its debut. The resorts, now operated by Four Seasons Resort Lanai, are as distinct in appearance as in location: The Lodge at Koele, reminiscent of an English manor, stands miles from the beach on a hill in the center of the island on an old ranch site amid tall Norfolk Island pine trees, while the Manele Bay overlooks **Hulopoe Bay** and was designed with Mediterranean influences amid elaborate gardens. Snorkelers love to take the plunge at Hulopoe Bay, a marine-life preserve with a postcard-worthy beach. The two palatial properties are a stark contrast to the venerable 1920s-era lodge **Hotel Lanai,** a ten-room inn located just above Lanai City that is a kind of crossroads, with locals and guests chatting it up and sipping drinks as they wait for a table at **Lanai City Grille.**

Lanai City is the old plantation town, a collection of small, brightly painted tin-roof houses in a hillside grove of pine trees. The town includes the island post office, high school, small hospital, even smaller library, one-prisoner jail, and shops, like **Akamai Trading** and **Local Gentry,** and cafés, like **Blue Ginger Cafe** for plate lunch

Supernatural Hawaii

The supernatural world so easily embraced by Polynesians affects visitors in different ways. Hawaiians do not concern themselves with solving riddles. They accept the insolvable. While most tourists want supernatural things to make sense, locals are content not to understand. They know if you solve a puzzle, it is broken.

Consider our recent trip to see Iliiliopae, the great Molokai heiau, where Hawaiian kahuna practiced rites of human sacrifice only 150 years ago. We hired a car at Hoolehua Airport and drove to Kaunakakai, once the summer place of King Kamehameha V, now only a sun-bleached cluster of clapboard stores covered by fine, red dust. It was around Christmas, so icicle lights twinkled in 82°F heat, and shops displayed cheery Santa masks.

At Misaki's Market, where antlered deer-head trophies guard aisles of rusty canned goods, we found shelves stripped bare by a run on fresh goods. A clerk said seas in Kaiwi Channel were so high that supply ships couldn't reach Molokai.

We grabbed the last six-pack of Hinano and local venison jerky and headed down two-lane King Kamehameha V Highway past tranquil fish-ponds, big as lakes and trapped from the sea by coral-stone walls.

We passed a white clapboard church bathed in a bold ray of light. In its graveyard cats prowled among tombstones draped with dead flower lei. We then drove by a roadside sign commemorating a 1927 plane crash. We added the church and crash site to our list of unusual attractions on Molokai, which already included the flirty *mahu* at Pau Hana Inn, a huge penis-shaped boulder known as the Phallic Stone, and the mule ride down the world's steepest sea cliffs to see the old leper colony at Kalaupapa.

Where the island became lush, green, and tropical, we turned makai, down an unmarked red dirt road, and entered the cool, shady oasis of Mapulehu, one of Hawaii's botanical wonders.

Someone long ago had planted a specimen grove of mango trees by the sea, and the many varieties—Atkins, Haden, Ataulfo, Keitts, and Cebu, to name but a few—flourished to create a dreamy Green Mansions–like orchard steeped in perfume so strong it stung our eyes.

Under the sheltering mango trees, we stood in half-light, blinking, just as two galloping horses rounded a corner pulling a wagonful of screaming children, who at first looked terrified, then delighted. The wagon disappeared in a cloud of fine red dust that settled on the green mango trees, and all over us, as a smiling woman appeared to welcome us with a warm aloha.

We've forgotten her name, but not what she told us: **Mapulehu,** where we stood, once was a *puuhonua,* or place of refuge. In ancient days, an errant subject could avoid death by seeking sanctuary here. The location was appropriate; a short hike up the hill, Iliiliopae, the biggest, oldest, most famous heiau on Molokai, served as a school of sorcery.

We had missed the wagon to the heiau, the Hawaiian woman said, but we could go on foot if we liked. She pointed mauka (mountainside) toward cloud-spiked Mount Kaunolu, the 4,970-foot island summit, and issued a caveat: "If you see a rainbow over the valley, look out for the *waikoloa*," she said.

"What's the waikoloa?"

"A hard, wet wind that comes suddenly down the valley," she said, and disappeared, like that, into the mango grove.

We set out on the upland trail through a hale koa thicket spiked by Java plum trees and, after passing an abandoned house, arrived hot, sweaty, and light-headed at the heiau just as the children were hiking back to the wagon. The heiau would be ours alone to explore.

Having read *Molokai: A Site Survey*, by Catherine C. Summers, the definitive work on the island's archaeology, we knew the stone altar was 22 feet high, but no words can prepare visitors for its bulky reality.

Long as a football field, nearly three stories high, Iliiliopae looks more like an early Roman fortification than a Hawaiian temple of doom. It rises in four tiers on the hill overlooking the green mango grove and four fishponds on the south shore of the island. What we found most amazing is that boulders big as Volkswagens had been fitted together so tightly that the temple had been held together for centuries not by mortar, but by its own mass.

Originally, the heiau was three times larger, according to Ohulenui, who grew up in the shadow of the temple and was 96 years old in 1909, when he was interviewed by archaeologist John F. G. Stokes, then director of the Bishop Museum. The heiau once stretched 920 feet across both east and west arms of Mapulehu Stream.

Temple rocks were swept away in legendary storms, or were taken to bolster fishpond walls and build the coast highway, which may account for roadside sightings of the legendary squid woman, who was a woman by day, squid by night, and in old days crept into pens to eat pigs.

Legend says Iliiliopae was built in one night by a human chain of 10,000 men who passed rocks hand over hand up and over the spine of the long, narrow island from Wailau Valley, ten miles away via a precipitous mile-high trail. Each received one shrimp (*opae*) in exchange for the rock (iliili), hence the name.

Even under the glaring tropical sun in full daylight, the heiau is a very eerie place. Heat waves shimmer off the flat surface rocks. The walls vibrate with *mana* (spiritual energy) strong enough to lean on. We felt like someone was watching us.

Having read accounts of what transpired here centuries before no doubt intensified our sense of the mystic aura of the heiau. People were summoned by the beating of drums and loud shouting on the 24th to the 27th days of the moon, when the sacrificial victim was carried into the temple tied to a scaffold. Victims were always men, not young virgins, and they

Supernatural Hawaii (continued)

were strangled while priests sat on lauhala mats watching silently. Victims never were buried, always burned; there was no boneyard, only ashes.

Against all advice, we stepped out on the heiau, walked right out on the flat table-sized rocks to gain a sense of the whole, meaning no disrespect, only wanting to get closer. To what? The primal past, the secrets of the heiau. It's hard to say what compelled us to commit this minor trespass. We knew better, and yet kept walking out farther on the heiau, drawn by something larger than curiosity.

Midway across the heiau, we grew dizzy in the hot sun. It beat down and radiated up from the rocks. Deciding to turn back, we stumbled, slipped ankle-deep between the rocks and fell to the stone. It was as though the altar, having drawn us in, now refused our departure.

For a moment, we both felt as if the heiau had reached out to grab us. We panicked and scrambled along the rocks. Clambering from the heiau, we touched down on terra firma to catch our breath. Looking back, there were no spirits, no ghosts; only a misstep on a wobbly rock.

We cautiously continued up the steep mauka ridge, attempting to get a picture, but the heiau proved too big for our simple lenses. Only an aerial shot would capture the full image in proper context.

I looked up toward the mountain and saw a rainbow beginning to appear and remembered what the Hawaiian woman said. "It's the waikoloa," I nearly shouted, as the rainbow grew bigger and brighter. We decided to hurry back down the dry streambed and reached the sheltering mango grove just as hard rain came pelting down.

That afternoon on Molokai, a flash flood sent water coursing once again through Mapulehu's dry streambed, and rain pounded the hot rocks of the ancient sacrificial heiau, sending up clouds of steam, and the fresh water seeped around old, smooth stones and trickled down to the soul of the temple, where relic ashes repose.

Water ran through the rocks and across the highway, into the mango grove and over the beach, turning the fishponds and the sea blood-red with the island's soil. From our flight back to Honolulu the next morning, we saw that the entire south coast of Molokai was stained red.

Did one thing have to do with the other? Surely it was all coincidence. We never understood what happened that day and probably never will. But, like the Islanders, we are content not to understand.

and **Canoes** for cheeseburgers, set around piney Dole Park at the center of town. The **Lanai Arts and Culture Center** displays art by local residents and details island history.

Golf is the sport of choice on Lanai. Two 18-hole championship courses are available here: **The Experience at Koele,** designed by golf superstar Greg Norman and architect Ted Robinson, and the **Chal-**

lenge at Manele, designed by Jack Nicklaus. Other popular activities on Lanai include swimming, snorkeling, horseback riding, whale-watching, fishing, archery, lawn bowling, croquet, clay shooting, and deer, sheep, and wild-turkey hunting (in season). It's easy to get around Lanai on foot or using the island's shuttle van, a golf cart, or a four-wheel-drive vehicle. The sights may be few, but they are naturally appealing, not man-made. The chief landmark is 3,366-foot **Lanaihale,** the highest point on the island. A hike or drive up **Munro Trail** to the summit on a clear day will afford a sweeping view of most of the major islands. Historians believe Lanaihale served as vantage point for high-ranking chiefs who could keep an eye on canoe traffic in the king-dom's sea lanes. Offshore, along the southwest coast, the sea channel is known as **Kealakahiki,** (or "the way to Tahiti," because that's where it goes). It runs nearly 2,000 miles like a river to the ancestral islands from which archaeologists believe the first voyagers departed for Hawaii in AD 650. The first settlers on this island called it Nanai and lived around the coast in small clusters of thatch and stone.

Early artifacts—knives, awls, scrapers, files, fish sinkers, and pounders and pestles collected by archaeologist Kenneth Emory of Honolulu's **Bishop Museum**—are displayed at **Lanai Conference Center** next to Manele Bay hotel. Emory's 1920 field survey of Lanai found scores of burial sites, 11 large temples or heiau, the largest at **Kaunolu** on the island's west bank, and more than 300 petroglyphs, an early Hawaiian art form. The pecked or incised stone etchings on

---

A PARADE OF PETROGLYPHS

We sat in full sun on the steep hillside overlooking the broad caldera known as Palawai Basin, studying petroglyphs one afternoon on Lanai. That's the best time of day to see the Stone Age art, because the sun lights up the indented stick figures.

It's an amazing cast of characters unlike any on Lanai, or any other island, for that matter. The first time we visited Luahiwa Petroglyphs it was raining so hard we couldn't even see the 20 boulders bearing the artwork. So we returned the following year on a hot August day, climbed up the hillside through bone-dry brush, and, a little out of breath, sat down amid the petro-glyph boulders. Maybe it was the heat, or just imagination, but the figures came alive and seemed to move as if in an ancient cartoon. A sailing canoe cruised across the face of a gigantic red boulder, a curly-tailed dog barked at a centipede, and a horseman with a hat rode a thin horse while two V-chested men walked down a trail. A pair of turtles even seemed to inch across the rock. That's when we felt an icy wind, despite the hot afternoon, and decided to leave. Back at the lodge, when the young Hawaiian woman who serves as concierge asked about our visit with the petroglyphs, we smiled and said it was wonderful. We even suggested that she should go see them herself someday, but she winced and shivered and said, "Too spooky, yeah?"

Living Large on Little Lanai

If we have but one night to spend like royalty, please, please let it be in a butlered suite at the Manele Bay Hotel on secluded, exclusive Lanai. We did it once and would sure like to do it again.

The Lanai experience begins at the state's newest small-island airport when your Aloha Airlines jet lands after a short hop from Honolulu, a form of time travel back to simpler days.

Uniformed staff, who seem to know who to expect on this real-life Fantasy Island, call you by name on arrival, whisk away your bag, and point toward a big, cushy bus, already running and air-conditioned.

It ferries new arrivals on the short ride down to the sea and the Manele Bay Hotel or up to the pine-forested Lodge at Koele, the island's other upscale jewel. The route, one of three paved roads, leads through miles of neglected former pineapple fields, red dirt still littered with fluttering bits of black plastic, once used to keep down the weeds that now thrust up defiantly. It's been more than a decade since Lanai gave up its status as the world's biggest pineapple plantation. The new crop is well-heeled tourists.

En route, passengers chatter with anticipation. One family of five—parents, teens, and a grade-schooler—has been several times before for a week or two at one hotel or the other, sometimes both. No one is sulking, no whining about what's to be done for amusement on this remote islet. Instead, they debate the relative merits of the two golf courses, where all plan to play daily. They recall four-wheeling over dusty, rutted dirt tracks to remote beaches and horseback rides in the shady, cool uplands near the Lodge. They talk about old croquet games on the Lodge lawns. Discussion ensues about kayaking and snorkeling. There's a lot to do on Lanai.

But then the chariot pulls into a grand porte cochère entry with a wall-to-wall view of the surrounding sea beyond, and guests are swept away to registration and glasses of pineapple cider.

A tall, dark, and mysterious fellow in a suit approaches. "I am Enrique, your butler. If you'll follow me upstairs, we can complete registration in your suite." A lady's gentleman, he is charming, not at all intimidating, newly arrived from Italy and willing to unpack your suitcase.

He shows you around Suite No. 2, larger than some apartments and centered thoughtfully over the pool and lobby with a smashing view. The room, with walls of light peach and rugs of green, boasts light-spirited antiques and tasteful art, and a sumptuous bath.

Your butler points out the fresh pineapple and flowers. He brings ice and tea. He leads you on a tour of the gardens and grounds.

Want something special? A wake-up double tall latte with 2-percent milk and raw sugar, fixed Italian style. He beams. You'll have another butler tomorrow, but he can make sure you get the latte from her.

It can be hard to tear yourself away from the lavish surroundings and head for the pool, to splash around with a familiar-faced couple and infant. You might recognize Mom as a television star. She carries the baby off to a sunchair to apply a diaper; nanny must be on break.

Then it's time for dinner up at the Lodge, a half-hour shuttle ride away, with a stop first at "Downtown Lanai City," a tiny village of timeworn old plantation stores around a square filled with towering Island pines. For guests sated with hotel haute cuisine, Lanai City offers something else to explore for dinner: a pizza place and the popular lanai City Grille at quaint Hotel Lanai, an historic 10-room hotel overlooking the village.

But if you're living it up, Koele's Dining Room is more than able to provide five-star fare. Well fed, you may be too languid to get off the return bus for a nightcap at the Hotel Lanai. Besides, your palace awaits, with turndown pillow treats and cool evening breezes billowing through lanai doors.

Most hotel turndown maids are taught steadfastly to shut and lock the doors, even if guests leave them open in lieu of air-conditioning, and to turn on all the lights and perhaps some awful radio station so that bright blare will greet you when you return to go to sleep. Ah, but not on Lanai. Peace reigns, and guests dream of spinner dolphins in a sparkly sea.

The next sunny morning goes far too quickly—that precious latte, breakfast on the open air terrace, personal greeting from the attentive hotel general manager, messages from your new butler, more disappearing luggage, and the inevitable airport shuttle, coda on your Lanai sojourn.

Visitors scan the horizon anxiously for storms, fog—anything to delay the departure. Although it's rare, sometimes Lanai guests do get lucky and find themselves weathered in for an unexpected addendum to their vacation plan. No worries: Most of them can afford it, and there's always plenty more to do on Lanai.

20 boulders in **Luahiwa Petroglyph Field** above **Pulawai Basin** depict a running dog, a turtle, a bird, lizards, and human figures. Kaunolu is the most significant historic site and was the island's first resort of sorts, built by ancient Hawaiians on 1,025-foot-high sea cliffs. A national historic landmark, the royal fishing village overlooking **Kaunolu Bay** once included 86 house sites, 35 stone shelters, 30 garden patches, and nine piles of stones marking graves. King Kamehameha I, who visited Lanai between 1778 and 1810, worshiped in a massive pyramid-shaped temple, **Halulu Heiau,** now a jumbled ruins of uncut stone and boulders. His Majesty also tried his hand at fishing with the blessing of **Kunihi,** a three-foot stone fish god, filled with *mana* (power). The idol is believed to still exist somewhere on Lanai. If you see it, do not touch it. The last person to touch the idol died.

At the cliff edge is **Kahekili's Leap** where Hawaiians practiced the sport of *lelekawa,* or cliff jumping. The king punished his soldiers, according to Emory, by forcing them to "jump 62 feet into 12 feet of water, clearing a 15-foot shelf at the base of the cliff."

To learn more about Lanai's early days, ask for the free interpretive guide to Kaunolu at the hotels or check out *Lanai: A Survey of Native Culture* by Kenneth P. Emory (Bishop Museum Press) at the Lodge library.

Other sites worth exploring include Lanai's version of Stonehenge, set on **Kanepuu,** a mountain ridge near the center of the island. This mysterious collection of strewn boulders and red lava cliffs is the **Garden of the Gods,** which some claim is the dwelling place for spirits of ancient Hawaiian warriors. Go during sunrise or sunset, when the low light casts eerie shadows in the area, and judge for yourself.

Slightly further inland (east), you can take a self-guided tour of a rare dryland native forest at **Kanepuu Preserve.** You'll see 48 plants found only on Lanai, including native olive trees, ebony, and rare sandalwood. The forest, about five miles from the Lodge at Koele, is operated by the Nature Conservancy of Hawaii.

Nature lovers should also consider **Polihua Beach,** on the northwest shore. A favorite green sea turtle nesting site, the remote, nearly two-mile-long golden beach, the island's largest, is accessible only by boat or four-wheel-drive vehicle. The beach is blasted by wind and the water is too roiled for swimming, so few go to Polihua except to see the turtles, or to comb the wide beach for Japanese glass fishing floats, paper nautilus shells, and other flotsam that washes ashore.

So many ships have run aground the shallow reef off northeastern Lanai since 1820 that this eight-mile stretch is known as **Shipwreck Beach.** Two early groundings were the British ship *Alderman Wood* and the American *London,* followed by interisland steamers, pineapple barges, U.S. Navy landing craft, World War II vessels, and pleasure boats. The reef holds a World War II Liberty Ship, and the beach is strewn with debris from the breakup a half century ago of four-masted schooner *Helene Port Townsend,* out of Seattle's Puget Sound.

KAHOOLAWE: *The Target Island*

FROM MAUI OR LANAI, the Island of Kahoolawe appears forbidding and bleak, lost in time. Although the island is only 15 miles across the sea channel from Lanai, its huge red scars were the work of U.S. Navy pilots who for nearly a half century dropped tons of bombs during practice air raids.

The bombing was halted in 1990, by President George H. W. Bush, who claimed he was shocked to learn the U.S. Navy was still bombing a Pacific island—one of the Hawaiian Islands, at that— nearly 50 years after the end of World War II. The 45-square-mile island, about the size of San Francisco, was returned to native Hawaiians in 1993, and the navy was ordered to spend $400 million over the next ten years to sweep the island of unexploded bombs.

Now undergoing a slow, costly cleanup, the uninhabited island served as a penal colony in the monarchy period, a cattle ranch during territory days, and, during World War II, the staging zone for U.S. forces preparing for the invasion of Okinawa. In 1965, the

SHOOTING AXIS DEER

Out on the western plains of Lanai, bumping along in a GeoTracker with the wife of the local butcher (who can fill a freezer with a few well-placed rounds), we watch, fascinated, as a herd of axis deer leaps together in a grand ballet. It's as if the whole Earth moves at once, a phenomenon we've seen often underwater while snorkeling, when thousands of fish move as one. The herds on Lanai, many of them imported species, are so great that deer—and pheasants, wild turkeys, quail, and francolins—outnumber people, some say 100 to 1. Press on to the interior and you'll also see biblical-looking mouflon rams posing stoically in deep ravines that crease the island.

Hunting season is weeks away, and the deer know it; we see them readily and plentiful. They appear at sundown, stepping out of the forest in the open savannas and sometimes may be seen grazing on the lawn at the Lodge, like the statues people put on country estates. Come season—nine weekends from April to June—the deer vanish in canyons to dodge birch arrows and silver bullets.

Deer hunting is a survival skill on an island like Lanai; it keeps the deer from gnawing the island clean to the surf. On certain weekends, you often hear distant gunfire and see critters draped over truck fenders. We never fail to notice on Lanai City houses deer antlers and ram horns, small, important triumphs of man over nature.

navy dropped a 500-ton bomb on Kahoolawe to simulate an atomic explosion; the impact cracked a submarine's water lens and turned the island's fresh water brackish.

Permission is needed to visit Kahoolawe. For information on three- or five-day visits to the island, call Protect Kahoolawe Ohana at ☎ 808-956-7068 or visit **www.kahoolawe.org.**

REMEMBERING BOMBS . . .

We remember bombs falling on Kahoolawe in the summer of 1976. We could see them every night from Ben Keau's green plantation-style house on the slope of Haleakala. The air raids lit up the night like the Fourth of July. Keau was the first person to tell us that the U.S. Navy—our navy—was bombing one of the Hawaiian Islands. We didn't believe him at first. "It's true," he said. "Look tonight." And we did, and there it was—a time-warp rerun of a World War II air battle. Only 12 miles away from where we sat, drinking cold beer on the lanai of his house in Kula, navy planes dive-bombed the neighboring island. You could feel the vibrations across the sea channel. Other U.S. bombs were falling that summer on Vietnam and Cambodia, and what fell on Hawaii was of little concern. Nobody voiced frustration about the bombing practice air raids, even after an errant, unexploded 500-pound navy bomb was discovered in a West Maui sugarcane field. Kahoolawe had been in navy hands since World War II, but local discontent was swelling.

In the summer of 1976, nine native Hawaiians, led by Dr. Emmit Aluli, a Molokai physician, made the first of many risky and unauthorized landings on Kahoolawe to protest the navy's use of the island. They filed a federal lawsuit charging violations of laws pertaining to the environment, historic preservation, and religious freedom. The bombing was finally halted in 1990. Three years later, it was returned to Hawaiians "to be used solely and exclusively for the preservation and practice of all rights customarily and traditionally exercised by native Hawaiians for cultural, spiritual, and subsistence purposes." The official document returning Kahoolawe to Hawaiian sovereignty was written in the Hawaiian language—and English.

PART FIVE

ATTRACTIONS

CHOOSING WHICH ATTRACTIONS to visit during your Maui vacation can be daunting. So much to see and do and so little time! Many of Maui's top visitor attractions, from museums and gardens to historic sites, have a nominal fee, but others are free. Reference the maps in the introduction to locate the attractions.

> *In Hawaii, a man neither rises to heights nor sinks to real depths. He develops acute Polynesia which is related to the Mexican mañana . . . a realization that tomorrow will be very like today, that nothing is of colossal importance beyond the moment. The days slip away uncounted, a month, a year, a lifetime passes with nothing to mark its passing except a blur of happiness, tainted only by a vague feeling that he "should do something about something."*
>
> —Don Blanding, *Hula Moons,* 1930

The following profiles provide basic information on the attractions, such as location, hours of operation, and cost. Each also features a rating for five age groups and a brief description. Given on a five-star scale, the ratings don't guarantee that a certain segment of visitors will love or hate the attraction, but they do provide a reliable evaluation of each group's typical reaction. For example, some teenagers want to visit historical sights, but more want to go to the beach. Together, the information, ratings, and descriptions will help you plan an itinerary pleasing to all members of your family or group.

Maui County Attractions

ATTRACTION NAME	TYPE OF ATTRACTION	AUTHORS' RATING	REGION
Alexander and Baldwin Sugar Museum	Museum	★★★	Central Maui
Alii Lavender Farm	Farm and Store	★★★	Upcountry Maui
Bailey House Museum	Museum	★★★	Central Maui
Baldwin Home Museum	Museum	★★★	West Maui
Haleakala National Park	National Park	★★★★	Upcountry Maui
Hana Cultural Center	Museum	★★★	Hana
Hawaii Experience Domed Theater	Theater	★★★½	West Maui
Hawaii Nature Center	Museum	★★★★	Central Maui
Hui Noeau Visual Arts Center	Gallery	★★★★	Upcountry Maui
Kepaniwai Cultural Park	Gardens	★★★	Central Maui
Kula Botanical Garden	Gardens	★★★	Upcountry Maui
Lahaina-Kaanapali and Pacific Railroad	Hawaiian Railway	★★★	West Maui
Maui Ocean Center	Aquarium	★★★★	South Maui
Maui Tropical Plantation and Country Store	Historic Home and Store	★★★	Central Maui
Molokai Museum and Cultural Center	Museum	★★★	Molokai
Surfing Goat Dairy	Working Farm	★★★	Upcountry Maui
Tedeschi Vineyards	Winery	★★★	Upcountry Maui
Whalers Village Museum	Museum	★★½	West Maui
Wo Hing Temple Museum	Museum	★★½	West Maui

Maui County Attractions by Type

ATTRACTION NAME	AUTHORS' RATING	REGION
AQUARIUM		
Maui Ocean Center	★★★★	South Maui
FARM		
Alii Lavender Farm	★★★	Upcountry Maui
Surfing Goat Daily	★★★	Upcountry Maui
GALLERY		
Hui Noeau Visual Arts Center	★★★★	Upcountry Maui
GARDENS		
Kepaniwai Cultural Park	★★★	Central Maui
Kula Botanical Garden	★★★	Upcountry Maui
HISTORIC HOME		
Maui Tropical Plantation and Country Store	★★★	Central Maui
MUSEUM		
Alexander and Baldwin Sugar Museum	★★★	Central Maui
Bailey House Museum	★★★	Central Maui
Baldwin Home Museum	★★★	West Maui
Hana Cultural Center	★★★	Hana
Hawaii Nature Center	★★★★	Central Maui
Molokai Museum and Cultural Center	★★★	Molokai
Whalers Village Museum	★★½	West Maui
Wo Hing Temple Museum	★★½	West Maui
NATIONAL PARKS		
Haleakala National Park	★★★★	Upcountry Maui
THEATER		
Hawaii Experience Domed Theater	★★★½	West Maui
TRAIN RIDE		
Lahaina-Kaanapali and Pacific Railroad	★★★	West Maui
WINERY		
Tedeschi Vineyards	★★★	Upcountry Maui

MAUI'S ATTRACTIONS:
Rated and Ranked

Alexander and Baldwin Sugar Museum ★★★

APPEAL BY AGE	PRESCHOOL ★½	GRADE SCHOOL ★★	TEENS ★★½
YOUNG ADULTS ★★★	OVER 30 ★★★½		SENIORS ★★★½

3957 Hansen Road, Puunene, Central Maui; ☎ 808-871-8058; www.sugarmuseum.com

Hours Monday–Saturday, 9:30 a.m.–4:30 p.m. **Admission** $5 adults, $2 children ages 6–18. **When to go** Anytime. **How much time to allow** 45 minutes. **Authors' rating** ★★★; a look at Maui's sugar plantation history.

DESCRIPTION AND COMMENTS In a converted 1902 superintendent's six-room home, visitors gain a sense of plantation life from the viewpoint of a sugar planter who controlled the Island economy. The museum features artifacts, photographs, tools (including a red Cleveland Model 336 trench digger), and other relics of an era gone by.

Bailey House Museum ★★★

APPEAL BY AGE	PRESCHOOL ★½	GRADE SCHOOL ★★	TEENS ★★½
YOUNG ADULTS ★★★	OVER 30 ★★★½		SENIORS ★★★½

2375-A Main Street, Wailuku, Central Maui; ☎ 808-244-3326; www.mauimuseum.org

Hours Monday–Saturday, 10 a.m.–4 p.m. **Admission** $4 adults, $1 children ages 7–12. **When to go** Anytime. **How much time to allow** 1 hour. **Authors' rating** ★★★; worth a stop for history buffs.

DESCRIPTION AND COMMENTS The missionary-era Bailey House, built in 1833 of lava rock and native woods, sits on land given to the missionaries by Hawaiian chiefs. Hawaiians attended reading and writing classes here, using Hawaiian-language books printed on Maui. Today, the Bailey House displays Hawaiian artifacts, including tapa, weaving, featherwork, and tools made out of stones, shells, and bones. A gallery of paintings—all from the late 1800s—portrays the beauty of the Valley Isle, and a stroll through the outside gardens reveals rare native plants, a koa-wood canoe, and a surfboard once used by legendary surfer/swimming champion Duke Kahanamoku. A gift shop offers crafts, apparel, Hawaiian music, and books.

OTHER THINGS TO DO NEARBY The Hawaii Nature Center and Kepaniwai Park are a short drive away.

Alii Lavender Farm ★★★

APPEAL BY AGE	PRESCHOOL ★★	GRADE SCHOOL ★★	TEENS ★★
YOUNG ADULTS ★★★	OVER 30 ★★★½		SENIORS ★★★½

1100 Waipolo Road, Kula, Upcountry Maui; ☎ 808-878-3004; www.aliikulalavender.com

Hours Daily, 9 a.m.–4 p.m. (studio gift shop); tours are by reservation. **Admission** Free; guided tea tours, $35. **When to go** Anytime. **How much time to allow** 1 hour. **Authors' rating** ★★★; a spatial, sensual experience in another Eden.

DESCRIPTION AND COMMENTS   Fellas may balk at visiting a lavender farm on Maui—they'd rather drink, smoke a cigar, or golf. But botanists, herbalists, and ordinary dirt gardeners will delight in the sea of lavender that spills down Haleakala like a French impressionist painting by Monet. The site and its scents alone are worth a visit to the greatest concentration of the fragrant, medicinal, edible herb in the tropical Pacific. Alii Kula, a third-generation Hawaiian green thumb, grows more than 30 different varieties on his nearly vertical three-acre farm and explains that lavender can be used to garnish pork, repel mosquitoes, sweeten tea, and massage sore muscles. The guided Lavender Garden Tea Tour includes tea and scones, lasts from 10 a.m. to 12:30 p.m. daily, and costs $35. For reservations, call ☎ 808-878-8090.

OTHER THINGS TO DO NEARBY   Surfing Goat Dairy, Tedeschi Vineyards.

Baldwin Home Museum ★★★

| APPEAL BY AGE | PRESCHOOL ★½ | GRADE SCHOOL ★★ | TEENS ★★★ |
| YOUNG ADULTS ★★★ | OVER 30 ★★★½ | | SENIORS ★★★½ |

120 Dickenson Street, Lahaina, West Maui;
☎ 808-661-3362 or 808-661-3262

Hours Daily, 10 a.m.–4 p.m. **Admission** $5 for families, $3 for individuals, $2 for senior citizens. **When to go** Anytime. **How much time to allow** 1 hour. **Authors' rating** ★★★; a peek into Hawaii's missionary era.

DESCRIPTION AND COMMENTS   This two-story structure was the home of Reverend Dwight Baldwin, a Protestant medical missionary from 1838 to 1871. Today, the home and its grounds, lovingly restored by the Lahaina Restoration Foundation, give visitors a glimpse of what life was like for 19th-century missionary families in Lahaina. On display are various household items and furniture, photographs, and other historic artifacts. Ask for a free self-guided tour map of Lahaina's other restored treasures.

OTHER THINGS TO DO NEARBY   Located at Dickenson and Front streets, the Baldwin Home is one of several historic sights in Lahaina.

Haleakala National Park ★★★★

| APPEAL BY AGE | PRESCHOOL ★★ | GRADE SCHOOL ★★★ | TEENS ★★★½ |
| YOUNG ADULTS ★★★★ | OVER 30 ★★★★ | | SENIORS ★★★★ |

The park extends from the 10,023-foot summit of Haleakala down the southeast flank of the mountain to the Kipahulu coastline near Hana. The summit area is accessible from Kahului via Routes 37, 377, and 378. The park's Kipahulu area, at the east end of the island between Hana and Kaupo, can be reached via Highway 36. Driving time is about 3–4 hours each way. Upcountry Maui; ☎ 808-572-4400; www.nps.gov/hale

Hours Park Ranger Headquarters is open daily, 8 a.m.–4 p.m. The visitor center is open daily, sunrise–3 p.m. (Overnight camping is permissible. The Hosmer Grove Campground in the summit area, located just inside the park's entrance, can be used without a permit; all other camping areas require permits.) **Admission** $10 per vehicle. The entrance fee is good for 7 days. **When to go** Anytime. Haleakala is renowned as a setting for dramatic sunrises and sunsets, although most people come for the sunrise. Be sure to arrive at least 30 minutes before either event. **How much time to allow** Half a day or more, depending on whether you plan to spend time hiking or taking part in one of the park's programs. **Authors' rating** ★★★★; one of the great natural wonders of the world.

DESCRIPTION AND COMMENTS Haleakala ("House of the Sun"), a dormant volcano that last spilled lava a bit more than 200 years ago, was designated as a national park in 1961. The park consists of nearly 29,000 acres, most of it wilderness. In the summit area, see the park headquarters and Haleakala Visitor Center, which houses a variety of cultural and natural history exhibits. Rangers are on duty and can be a tremendous help in making the most out of your visit. In the Kipahulu area, see the Kipahulu Ranger Station/Visitor Center. Each facility has a selection of books, maps, postcards, and other souvenirs for sale.

TOURING TIPS Check the park's bulletin board for a schedule of daily programs and guided hikes. Obey all posted warning signs. It can be cold at the summit, so be prepared. Due to the high elevation (nearly 2 miles high) and reduced oxygen at the park, anyone with a heart or respiratory condition is advised to check with a doctor before visiting.

Hana Cultural Center ★★★

APPEAL BY AGE	PRESCHOOL ★★	GRADE SCHOOL ★★½	TEENS ★★½
YOUNG ADULTS ★★★	OVER 30 ★★★		SENIORS ★★★

**4974 Uakea Road, Hana; ☎ 808-248-8622;
www.planet-hawaii.com/hana**

Hours Daily, 10 a.m.–4 p.m. **Admission** Donations accepted. **When to go** Anytime. **How much time to allow** 1 hour. **Authors' rating** ★★★; a reward after the long journey to Hana.

DESCRIPTION AND COMMENTS This cultural center is home to more than 500 artifacts, 600 books, 680 Hawaiian bottles, and 5,000 historic photographs of the Hana district. Opened in 1983, the nonprofit museum houses Hawaiian quilts, poi boards, stones, *kapa*, ancient tools, fishhooks, gourd bowls, stone lamps, and a century-old fishing net. Also featured are tributes to some of Hana's most notable citizens. The cultural center includes a series of old Hawaiian *hale* (houses), the historic Hana courthouse, and a jailhouse.

Hawaii Experience Domed Theater ★★★½

APPEAL BY AGE	PRESCHOOL ★★★	GRADE SCHOOL ★★★½	TEENS ★★★½
YOUNG ADULTS ★★★½	OVER 30 ★★★½		SENIORS ★★★½

824 Front Street, Lahaina, West Maui; no phone

Hours Daily, 9 a.m.–11 p.m. **Admission** $7 adults, $4 children ages 4–12. If you purchase $25 worth of merchandise at the gift shop, you receive a free ticket to the show. **When to go** Anytime. **How much time to allow** 50 minutes. **Authors' rating** ★★★½; a pleasant diversion in the heart of Lahaina.

DESCRIPTION AND COMMENTS A planetarium-like theater with a domed screen more than three stories high, this attraction features a spectacular 40-minute film shown every hour.

OTHER THINGS TO DO NEARBY Historical attractions in downtown Lahaina, including the Wo Hing Temple and Baldwin Home Museum, are within easy walking distance.

Hawaii Nature Center ★★★★

APPEAL BY AGE	PRESCHOOL ★★★	GRADE SCHOOL ★★★★	TEENS ★★★★
YOUNG ADULTS ★★★★		OVER 30 ★★★★	SENIORS ★★★★

875 Iao Valley Road, Wailuku, Central Maui; ☎ 808-244-6500; www.hawaiinaturecenter.org

Hours Daily, 10 a.m.–4 p.m. **Admission** $6 adults, $4 children ages 4–12. **When to go** Anytime. **How much time to allow** 1 hour. **Authors' rating** ★★★★; good hands-on learning experience.

DESCRIPTION AND COMMENTS The Nature Center's Interactive Science Arcade features more than 30 interactive exhibits celebrating Maui's natural environment. The main exhibit hall features an amazing 10-foot-high, 30-foot-long, three-dimensional replication of four streams that feed into the Iao Stream. Aquariums, rain-forest explorations, arcade games, telescopes, and live insect and animal exhibits are among the other highlights. The gift shop features an extensive selection of nature-themed merchandise. All proceeds go to environmental education programs for Maui elementary-school children.

TOURING TIPS The best is Rainforest Walk, a guided tour into the wet, wonderful world of Maui, where you meet carnivorous creatures and exotic plants under the rainbow. Tickets are $30 adults, $20 children ages 5 and older.

OTHER THINGS TO DO NEARBY Kepaniwai Cultural Park and the Bailey House Museum.

Hui Noeau Visual Arts Center ★★★★

APPEAL BY AGE	PRESCHOOL ★★	GRADE SCHOOL ★★½	TEENS ★★★
YOUNG ADULTS ★★★		OVER 30 ★★★½	SENIORS ★★★½

2841 Baldwin Avenue, Makawao; 1 mile below Makawao town, Upcountry Maui; ☎ 808-572-6560; www.maui.net/~hui

Hours Monday–Friday, 8:30 a.m.–5 p.m. Gallery Hours are Saturday, 10 a.m.–4 p.m. **Admission** Donations accepted. **When to go** Anytime. **How much time to allow** 1 hour. **Authors' rating** ★★★★; a haven for art lovers.

DESCRIPTION AND COMMENTS Occupying a beautiful nine-acre estate in Makawao, this nonprofit art center features works by both local and international artists. The Mediterranean-style estate is a historic landmark (built in 1917 by architect Charles W. Dickey for Harry and Ethel Baldwin) dotted with pine, camphor, and lemon gum trees and adorned with an immaculate formal garden and reflecting pool. The arts center features classes and workshops for aspiring artisans, painters, and potters, and exhibits are open to the public on Saturdays. The gift shop offers a selection of original artworks, note cards, books, and other gift items.

Kepaniwai Cultural Park ★★★

| APPEAL BY AGE | PRESCHOOL ★★ | GRADE SCHOOL ★★½ | TEENS ★★★ |
| YOUNG ADULTS ★★★ | | OVER 30 ★★★½ | SENIORS ★★★½ |

Iao Valley Road, Central Maui; no phone

Hours Daily, 7 a.m.–7 p.m. **Admission** Free, self-guided tour. **When to go** Anytime. **How much time to allow** 1 hour. **Authors' rating** ★★★; a pleasant stop if you're in the area.

DESCRIPTION AND COMMENTS Picturesque gardens and architectural pavilions representing Hawaii's ethnic groups.

OTHER THINGS TO DO NEARBY The Hawaii Nature Center and Bailey House Museum are nearby.

Kula Botanical Garden ★★★

| APPEAL BY AGE | PRESCHOOL ★★ | GRADE SCHOOL ★★½ | TEENS ★★½ |
| YOUNG ADULTS ★★½ | | OVER 30 ★★★ | SENIORS ★★★½ |

0.7 miles from Kula Highway, on Kekaulike Avenue (Highway 377) in Kula, Upcountry Maui; ☎ 808-878-1715

Hours Daily, 9 a.m.–4 p.m. **Admission** $5 adults, $1 children ages 6–12. **When to go** Anytime. **How much time to allow** 90 minutes. **Authors' rating** ★★★; a botanist's dream come true.

DESCRIPTION AND COMMENTS Kula, blessed with a mild, cool climate and fertile soil, is the home of this five-acre wonderland originally owned by Princess Kekaulike. Opened in 1969, the garden today features more than 1,700 tropical plants, including exotic flora such as proteas, heliconias, orchids, anthurium, and gingers.

Lahaina-Kaanapali and Pacific Railroad ★★★

| APPEAL BY AGE | PRESCHOOL ★★½ | GRADE SCHOOL ★★★ | TEENS ★★ |
| YOUNG ADULTS ★★ | | OVER 30 ★★ | SENIORS ★★½ |

975 Limahana Place, Suite 203, Lahaina, West Maui; ☎ 808-667-6851 or 808-499-2307

Hours 12 rides scheduled daily, beginning at 10 a.m. **Admission** $16 adults, $10 children ages 3–12 (round-trip). **When to go** Anytime. **How much time to allow** 90 minutes. **Authors' rating** ★★★; a short train ride offering views of the West Maui coastline.

DESCRIPTION AND COMMENTS The "Sugar Cane Train," with its 1890s locomotive and distinctive whistle, was used by the Pioneer Mill to transport sugar crops until the early 1950s. Today, the train shuttles visitors between Lahaina and the resort area of Kaanapali. The six-mile route through a cane field lasts about 40 minutes each way. A friendly conductor shares the history of Maui's sugar industry.

Maui Ocean Center ★★★★

APPEAL BY AGE	PRESCHOOL ★★★★½	GRADE SCHOOL ★★★★	TEENS ★★★★
YOUNG ADULTS ★★★★★		OVER 30 ★★★★★	SENIORS ★★★★½

**Maalaea Harbor Village, 192 Maalaea Road, South Maui;
☎ 808-270-7000; www.mauioceancenter.com**

Hours Daily, 9 a.m.–5 p.m. Admission $20 adults, $13 children ages 3–12, children under age 3 are free. Senior citizens and military personnel, 10 percent discount. When to go Anytime. How much time to allow 2 Hours. Authors' rating ★★★★; a must-see for anyone interested in understanding Island marine life.

DESCRIPTION AND COMMENTS The star attraction is a 750,000-gallon ocean aquarium tank with a walk-through acrylic tunnel that lets you get a good view of the more than 2,000 inhabitants, including a six-foot tiger shark, four black-tip reef sharks, eight sandbar sharks, spotted eagle rays, mahimahi, triggerfish, sea turtles, eels, and a dazzling array of colorful reef fish.

Descend if you dare (and are a certified diver age 15 and older) into the Open Ocean tank to swim with more than 60 species of tropical fish. Once the exclusive domain of staff divers, aquarium dives are a relatively new feature, offered on Maui and in Monterey and Florida. Dives are offered year-round on Monday, Wednesday, and Friday at 8:15 a.m. They last two and a half hours, cost $199, and include one guest, weight belt, air tank, and an underwater guide. Reservations are required.

Other exhibits include a supervised touch pool for kids, allowing them to hold sea critters; interactive displays about the humpback whale; and smaller aquariums that afford a close look at eels, shrimp, coral, and other sea life. The Reef Cafe and Seascape Cafe and Bar provide food and drinks, and the large gift shop carries logo and ocean-themed goods.

OTHER THINGS TO DO NEARBY The Ocean Center overlooks busy Maalaea Harbor, where cruise boats come and go. Try combining a trip to the aquarium with a snorkeling tour to look at the sea creatures in the wilds. Lunch and dinner available at nearby restaurants, where the catch of the day, of course, appears on the menu.

Maui Tropical Plantation and Country Store ★★★

APPEAL BY AGE	PRESCHOOL ★★	GRADE SCHOOL ★★½	TEENS ★★★
YOUNG ADULTS ★★★½		OVER 30 ★★★★	SENIORS ★★★★

1670 Honoapiilani Highway, Central Maui; ☎ 808-244-7643

Hours Daily, 9 a.m.–5 p.m. **Admission** Free. Tram tours cost $10 adults and $4 children ages 5–12 (plus tax). **When to go** Anytime. **How much time to allow** 75 minutes. **Authors' rating** ★★★; when you want to know more about tropical crops, this is the place. Pick up fresh fruits at the country store.

DESCRIPTION AND COMMENTS From the visitor center, head out to the plantation's 50-acre garden, which is filled with tropical plants, including pineapple, sugarcane, papaya, guava, star fruit, anthuriums, and protea. A restaurant and plant nursery are also available.

TOURING TIPS Narrated 45-minute tram tours of the garden are available. The first train leaves at 10 a.m.; the last train leaves at 3:15 p.m.

OTHER THINGS TO DO NEARBY The Bailey House Museum is a mile or so to the north.

Molokai Museum and Cultural Center ★★★

APPEAL BY AGE	PRESCHOOL ★½	GRADE SCHOOL ★★	TEENS ★★½
YOUNG ADULTS ★★★	OVER 30 ★★★		SENIORS ★★★½

On Kalae Highway, just west of Kaunakakai, Molokai; ☎ 808-567-6436

Hours Monday–Saturday, 10 a.m.–2 p.m. **Admission** $3 adults, $1 students ages 5–18. **When to go** Anytime. **How much time to allow** 1 hour. **Authors' rating** ★★★; not terribly exciting, but filled with history.

DESCRIPTION AND COMMENTS The museum is located in a converted sugar mill that was established in 1878 by Rudolph Wilhelm Meyer, an engineer and surveyor who arrived on Molokai in 1851 and married a Hawaiian princess. Now listed on the National Register of Historic Places, the mill houses original machinery and other artifacts from the island's sugar plantation days. Guided tours and Hawaiian cultural programs are offered.

Surfing Goat Dairy ★★★

APPEAL BY AGE	PRESCHOOL ★★★	GRADE SCHOOL ★★★	TEENS ★★
YOUNG ADULTS ★★★	OVER 30 ★★★½		SENIORS ★★★½

3651 Omaopio Road, Kula, Upcountry Maui; ☎ 808-878-2870; www.surfinggoatdairy.com

Hours Monday–Saturday, 10 a.m.–5 p.m.; Sunday, 10 a.m.–2 p.m. **Admission** $5 families, $3 individuals, $2 senior citizens. **When to go** Anytime. **How much time to allow** 1 hour. **Authors' rating** ★★★; family fun on the farm.

DESCRIPTION AND COMMENTS While kids milk goats at Surfing Goat Dairy, Mom and Dad taste fresh, Hawaiian goat cheese laced with local pineapple, kiawe ash, or Maui lavender. On the alpine-like slopes of Haleakala, a German couple, Eva and Kafsak, create the Island's first and only award-winning goat cheese.

OTHER THINGS TO DO NEARBY Alii Lavender Farm, Tedeschi Vineyards.

Tedeschi Vineyards ★★★

APPEAL BY AGE	PRESCHOOL ★½	GRADE SCHOOL ★★	TEENS ★★½
YOUNG ADULTS ★★★	OVER 30 ★★★		SENIORS ★★★

Ulupalakua Ranch, about 10 miles past the junction of Highways 377 and 37 in Kula, Upcountry Maui; ☎ 808-878-6058; www.mauiwine.com

Hours Daily, 9 a.m.–5 p.m. Guided tours are held daily, 9:30 a.m.–2:30 p.m. **Admission** Free. **When to go** Anytime. **How much time to allow** 1 hour. **Authors' rating** ★★★; worth a taste for wine lovers.

DESCRIPTION AND COMMENTS Tedeschi Vineyards is known for its Island-style wine, including Maui Blanc Pineapple Wine, a popular fruit-forward novelty souvenir. Wines are available for tasting and purchase at the tasting room in the King's Cottage, once used as a retreat by King Kalakaua. Hawaii-made specialty goods, books, and gifts are also on sale.

TOURING TIPS The tour explains how the wines are processed and bottled. But it's not necessary to take a tour to enjoy sampling the wines and walking through the shady lawns and gardens. Bring a picnic, sip Maui wine, and enjoy the cool upland setting.

Whalers Village Museum ★★½

APPEAL BY AGE	PRESCHOOL ★★	GRADE SCHOOL ★★½	TEENS ★★½
YOUNG ADULTS ★★½		OVER 30 ★★½	SENIORS ★★½

Whalers Village (3rd floor), 2435 Kaanapali Parkway, Kaanapali Beach Resort, West Maui; ☎ 808-661-5992; www.whalersvillage.com

Hours Daily, 9:30 a.m.–10 p.m. **Admission** Free. **When to go** Anytime. **How much time to allow** 1 hour. **Authors' rating** ★★½; displays and historic artifacts about whaling, entertainment for the family if they get restless shopping.

DESCRIPTION AND COMMENTS This museum traces the history of Lahaina's colorful whaling era, roughly from 1825 to 1860. Among more than 100 items on exhibit are a six-foot model of a whaling ship, harpoons, maps, logbooks, and an extensive collection of scrimshaw.

Wo Hing Temple Museum ★★½

APPEAL BY AGE	PRESCHOOL ★	GRADE SCHOOL ★★	TEENS ★★
YOUNG ADULTS ★★½		OVER 30 ★★½	SENIORS ★★★

Front Street, Lahaina (between Papalaua and Lahainaluna streets), West Maui; ☎ 808-661-3262

Hours Daily, 10 a.m.–4 p.m. **Admission** Donations accepted. **When to go** Anytime. **How much time to allow** 30 minutes. **Authors' rating** ★★½; good for historians; young kids will be bored.

DESCRIPTION AND COMMENTS A Buddhist shrine is the centerpiece of this restored 1912 Chinese temple, which provides a revealing look at how early Chinese settlers lived in Lahaina. Old photographs and artifacts are also on exhibit. A cookhouse (built separately from the main building to reduce the risk of a house fire) sits just to the right of the building. Two Hawaii films shot in 1898 and 1906 by Thomas Edison are among the highlights. The temple is affiliated with Chee Kung Tong, a Chinese fraternal society with branches throughout the world.

OTHER THINGS TO DO NEARBY The Baldwin Home Museum.

PART SIX

OUTDOOR ADVENTURES

The **TRUE NATURE** *of* **MAUI**

IF YOU THINK MAUI IS ONLY FOR HONEYMOONERS, game-show prize winners, or the rich and famous, take another look. If you have never heard of Molokai or Lanai, better keep reading.

These islands are more than just a collection of fancy resorts and shops. Maui is the land of adventures, and you have so many choices. It's the nature of the place: reliable tradewinds, beaches, lagoons, waterfalls, the biggest dormant volcano in the world, the second-wettest spot on earth, and neighboring islands that beg to be explored. Each element provides an entry to adventure unlike what you know back home.

You can snorkel in the clear waters of the crescent islet of Molokini (a sunken crater between South Maui and the Island of Kahoolawe), splash in waterfall pools all the way to Hana, soar through challenging waves on high-tech windsurfing boards on the North Shore, four-wheel or mountain-bike through the red-dirt Lanai backcountry, kayak the Molokai wilderness coast, or lounge on a booze-cruise sailing deck and watch the sun set over your mai tai. Don't forget hiking the moonscape inside Haleakala Crater or coasting down the volcano, 38 miles from summit to sea, on a specially equipped bicycle. Of course, you could do nothing more

TWAIN IN HAWAII

During his 19th-century Hawaiian sojourn, a young Mark Twain dropped his pen for six weeks. "In explanation and excuse, I offer the fact that I spent that time on the Island of Maui," wrote Twain. "I never spent so pleasant a month before, or bade any place goodbye so regretfully." When he got back home, Twain went on to become one of America's best-loved and most successful writers.

than commute from your vacation digs to the nearest beach cabana. Then again, if fabulous golf courses are your dream, you're going to be busy. Maui's storied links, crafted by world-class designers in world-famous settings, are too numerous to play on one trip. Watch for unusual natural hazards, such as the sight of a whale leaping from the sea just when you've planned your shot.

WILDLIFE WATCHING

WILDLIFE, TOO, IS DIFFERENT ON MAUI'S ISLANDS. No snakes or alligators, only curious critters that resemble escapees of Alice's Wonderland. In fact, the allure of exotic fauna is as much a reason to explore Maui's outdoors as extreme sports or the promise of a great tan. For example, Maui is home to the mongoose, the low-slung creature of Rudyard Kipling's *Rikki Tikki Tavi,* thanks to a failed sugar baron's rat-control experiment; the diurnal mongoose was introduced to thwart nocturnal rats in the cane fields, but the twain never met. Then there are the endangered nene geese, birds whose ancestors blew in from Canada on a tailwind and stayed, but over time transformed their tender webbed feet into claws to walk on lava; the little Happy Face spiders (*Theridion grallator*), so called because a pattern resembling a smiling clown face appears on the thorax; and Pacific humpback whales, who prefer Maui's waters to any others for the world's largest annual meeting of the migrating giants. They quit Alaska's chilly waters each winter in favor of Maui's tepid Maalaea Bay.

Out There, in the Water

If you go to Maui in winter and don't see a whale, you've missed the really big show. Actually, it's difficult to go to Maui in winter and not see a whale. They're everywhere offshore: look for the telltale spouts and belly-flop splashes. Whale-watching in winter is the Islands' major spectator sport. Boat tours will take you close enough to get a good look, but not too close, for the whales' sake. The best free spot on Maui to whale-watch is **McGregor Point,** a scenic turnout on the road to Lahaina. Bring your binoculars to see leviathans at play.

Spinner dolphins frolic year-round on Maui's southwest and northwest shores at Nakalele Bay and often flash across **Lanai's Hulopoe Bay;** they are an unforgettable sight, from the shore and from the sea, where they sometimes perform elaborate ballets for boat passengers. Manta rays "fly" through these tropical waters. Huge turtles play in the surf, then clamber ashore to make nests and lay eggs. Maui's effort to keep them safe is evident in the beach fence that now lines the shore by the busy highway between Maalaea and Kihei.

Other, more menacing denizens of the deep include moray eels and sharks, particularly tiger sharks that patrol the coast in search of food and sometimes mistake board surfers or swimmers for tasty turtles or seals. A surfer's silhouette—squat body, little flippers—is

BLACKBIRD, BYE-BYE

Everywhere else the crow is a pest. In Hawaii, *Corvus hawaiiensess* is nearly extinct. Hunters shot them; developers spoiled their habitat; the birds were plagued by disease and reproductive disorder.

Hawaiians, who considered the crow an *aumakua,* or family guardian, denied Captain James Cook a specimen. After the last flock began to go extinct on Maui in the 1980s, the captive birds were taken to the Big Island's Endangered Species Facility, where a few cling to existence.

the same to a shark, who is always looking for something to eat. Sharks may be considered friendly by local custom—they are venerated as sacred *aumakua*, or family guardians—but nonetheless, they bite, so beware. Attacks have occurred in recent years off Maui shores at places such as **Olowalu Reef,** a popular snorkeling spot along the West Maui highway outside Lahaina, prompting the placement of seven permanent shark warning signs (written by lawyers to avoid civil liability) along the shore. If you see such a sign, don't go in the water there. There are other common sense ways to avoid sharks: Never swim at sunset, when sharks like to eat. Avoid murky water; what you can't see can hurt you. Always swim with a buddy. If a shark attacks you, punch it on its sensitive nose or eye, then swim for shore. Fortunately, most folks only see sharks close-up at Maui Ocean Center.

Up There, on the Land

On land, Maui is home to some distinctive flora as well as fauna. The rare silversword plant clings to the lava cinders of Haleakala and blooms but once before it dies, spouting a hundred purplish daisylike buds at once on a tall, slim stalk above feathery silver leaves, like some kind of mutant delphinium. Lanai's most common tree isn't the ubiquitous palm, but the towering Cook and Norfolk pines of its uplands, planted years ago by a wise rancher. The thick ridgetop groves snag rain clouds and milk their moisture onto the dry land. The island teems with axis deer (imported from China as a gift to an ancient king), mouflon rams with curved biblical horns, wild turkeys, and game birds called chukars that call out like lost souls. Molokai is famous for its mules that daily traverse the world's steepest sea cliffs carrying riders, but cows and horses outnumber people. Molokai also has herds of diminutive deer.

ELEVEN NATURAL WONDERS OF MAUI

SOME PEOPLE COME TO MAUI ONLY TO SIT on the beach, and there's nothing wrong with that. But if you like active sports, the great outdoors is just too good to miss, from climbing Puu Olai on the southern end of Maui, to plunging in Kipahulu's waterfall pools, to snorkeling and diving off Lanai in pursuit of the sunshine-yellow long-nosed butterfly fish, the most common in a rainbow collection of tropical fish. Many adventures and guided tours can be arranged by a concierge or hotel activity desk. You can do many on your own. Below, we highlight some favorites for your must-see list.

Haleakala Crater

Known as the "House of the Sun," this crater is reputed to be the biggest hole on earth, big enough to hold the Big Apple. It is 10,023 feet above sea level, 33 miles wide, and 2,000 feet deep. With its own weird weather, a nine-peaked mountain range, and strange inhabitants such as a bird that barks like a dog, it is like no place on earth. This primal Hawaii has virgin fern forests, scorched badlands, cinder cones, bubble caves, lava tubes, boiling pots, and here and there, the burial sites of ancient Hawaiians, which are best left untouched. You reach the peak on the only road in the world that goes from sea level to 10,023 feet in 38 miles, switching back 33 times through 12 climate zones past endangered Hawaiian Nene geese and rare Silversword plants that bloom once and die. It's the ultimate drive. For more information, see the profile of Haleakala National Park that follows in the "National and State Parks" section.

Molokini Crater

Hawaii's most popular dive site, Molokini, is a sunken C-shaped crater with one edge 165 feet above water off the coast of South Maui. It is a natural habitat for fish large and small. Bright little tropical reef fish thrive inside the crescent's concave embrace while big, pelagic fish roam the outer depths. Snorkelers and divers can choose one of the fast charter boats that leave Maalaea Harbor, then spend the day with Maui's tropical schools.

Puu Kukui Forest

Puu Kukui, the summit of the West Maui Mountains, is a great, green place best seen by helicopter. The second-wettest spot on earth (with 340 inches of rain a year), Puu Kukui includes the Wall of Tears, a weepy vertical massif; a dwarf forest of native plants; and Eke Crater, which early Hawaiians considered to be Heaven's gate, the doorway from this world to the next. Each year 12 lucky hikers who win the Kapalua Nature Society's lottery can enter the otherwise *kapu* (forbidden) native forest with a guide to see rare native plants and birds. For information, contact the Kapalua Nature Society at ☎ 808-669-0244. To arrange a flyover, call Sunshine Helicopters at ☎ 808-871-0722 or 800-469-3000 or visit **www.sunshinehelicopters.com**.

Seven Pools of Kipahulu

Nearly an hour's drive beyond Hana, 24 pools cascade down Oheo Gulch to the Pacific—but only seven get all the attention. Sometimes

The big 6.7 earthquake that rattled Hawaii early on Sunday, October 15, 2006, collapsed the concrete 1912 bridge to Kipahulu; blocked Hana Highway with boulders, isolating Hana; caused cliffs to shear at Waianapanapa; jolted Kula houses off foundations; cracked cornices in Wailuku; and statewide caused an estimated $200 million in damage. A disaster, in other words, but nobody died.

While repairs are now complete, always be on guard for falling rocks, crumbling cliffs, landslides due to torrential rain, aerial erosion (everpresent tradewinds cause mischief), or the infrequent earthquake on any Hawaii visit. Kick back, but stay alert.

called "sacred," the seven pools on the coast inspire legend and bravado. Some folks try to swim in each pool; others are content to gaze at the watery spectacle from the bridge over Pipiwai Stream. The pools naturally attract a crowd, so go early or stay late, and remember, get out of the steep waterway canyon immediately if it starts to rain. You could get washed out to sea. Rangers are posted in the area, which is part of Haleakala National Park.

Kaihalulu Beach

Glowing like embers in azure breakers, Maui's red-sand beach is the bright spot on Hana's emerald coast, and one of only two red-sand beaches in the world (the other is in Iceland). Hike a thin coastal trail past tipping tombstones to the remains of a cinder cone that long ago surrendered its seawall to perpetual waves and spilled vermillion clinkers to create this believe-it-or-not red beach.

Jaws

A dozen times a year in what passes for winter here, big waves from Alaska race down the Pacific to Maui's north shore, strike an underwater ridge, and rise up as Jaws—the biggest wave on Earth. The surf often hits 70 feet and more, according to National Geographic, and attracts fearless surfers and spectators, alike. Forget about catching the monster wave, it's for hardcore surfers only, but you can watch, safe on shore, when Jaws roars.

Silversword

Spiky, silver Jack-in-the-Box-like plants (they look like an artichoke on LSD), the rare and endangered Silversword is a true botanical wonder of the world. It clings to the windswept, sun-struck talus slopes of Haleakala with a solitary taproot and shoots up sometimes eight feet tall. Once in a blue moon, it blooms at night, then dies like a droopy giant. Ancestral windborne descendant of California's tarweed, relative of the ubiquitous Sunflower, distant cousin of the Yucca, the Silversword is its own adapted Hawaiian self.

Five Needles

On Lanai's little-seen coast a cluster of sea stacks (one is 110 feet high) attracts every tropical variety of fish known in Hawaii's waters. Tangs, wrasses, and other tropicals light up the ultra-clear cobalt blue water swept daily by the Kalakahiki current on its trans-Pacific race to Tahiti. This marine landmark called Five Needles is accessible by tour and fishing boat from Maui across nine-mile Au'au Channel, a little sea adventure on choppy days.

Ahihi-Kinau Natural Area Reserve

Where Haleakala lava last ran into the sea in about 1790, the stark, black coast at Maui's southern tip ends is one of Maui's best snorkel sites: Ahihi-Kinau Natural Area Reserve. The 2,000-acre preserve includes the barren shoreline and its black lava pools filled with turquoise water and tropical fish. All sea life is protected here, so leave your speargun at the bar. Only looking is permitted. Call Snorkel Bob's for more information on diving safely here. ☎ 808-879-7449.

Sea Cliffs of Molokai

The highest sea cliffs in the world (according to *The Guinness Book of Records*) form the north shore of Molokai, a sheer precipice that stretches 14 miles and drops 3,500 feet to the crashing surf. One misstep and you're *limu* (seaweed). You can see the cliffs from above by small plane or from below by kayak in the summer when the Pacific is calm. Some hike or ride a mule down to Kalaupapa National Historic Park to look back at the monumental cliffs. Contact the Molokai Ranch Outfitters Center at ☎ 808-552-2791 for details. Or, you can stand in awe at the edge of Palaau State Park and soak up the grandeur. It's the best scenic outlook in Hawaii. For more information, see the park's profile in the "National and State Parks" section that follows.

Garden of the Gods, Lanai

On this island that once was the world's largest pineapple patch, you will find what appears to be a vestige of Arizona, a geologic badlands so ethereal that it's dubbed the Garden of the Gods. This boulder-strewn gulch looks so eerie that some believe it to be the work of aliens. Geologists say Lanai's rock garden is just an "ongoing post-erosional event" not unlike the Painted Desert of the American Southwest. This badlands, accessible from the roadside, is worth exploring, especially at sunset when sun rays turn the stones into red, yellow, orange, and ochre gems.

The **BEACH EXPERIENCE**

WITH APPROXIMATELY 33 MILES OF SANDY SHORELINE, Maui has more than 80 beaches—too many to explore in a single visit.

TAKE THE PLUNGE

Hawaii's waterfall pools are idyllic, but freshwater lakes, ponds, or marshes are rare, curious delights if you can find them. And we have—in a Maui cloud forest.

Lake Violet is a deep-blue puddle dotted by red dragonflies in a jade-green cloud forest. Anywhere else this dollop of a pond wouldn't rate a second look, but up on the boggy slopes of 5,871-foot-high Puu Kukui in the West Maui Mountains, it's a rare find. Only a few hikers can visit Lake Violet on this still-forbidden mountain, which, according to legend, marked the intersection of heaven and earth. Now part of Kapalua Nature Preserve (see page 234), Puu Kukui is one of the last unspoiled upland forests and the second wettest spot on the planet. It rained 654.83 inches in 1982—that's 54 feet! You would think Lake Violet would be bigger.

Maui's best beaches are mostly pocket beaches tucked between sheltering reefs, safe for swimming, snorkeling, bodysurfing, and splashing in the waves. So that you won't waste a minute, we selected our favorites, based on safety, access, scenic qualities, and swimmability. State law provides that all beaches in the Islands are open to the public, and public accessways, parking, and facilities such as restrooms and outdoor showers are provided free even within private resorts and residential areas. In return, the public is expected to respect neighbors and their property.

LANAI AND MOLOKAI

EACH OF THESE ISLANDS HAS PLENTY OF BEACHES, but only one on each island is nearly perfect—a relative paucity compared to Maui, but it's one more perfect beach than most places. Lanai has 18 miles of sandy shoreline, including long, empty beaches like **Shipwreck Beach,** an ideal spot for beachcombing with a real ship wrecked just offshore, and **Polihua,** where green sea turtles cavort. But Lanai's jewel is the accessible, golden crescent beach called Hulopoe, best all around for swimming, snorkeling, and watching spinner dolphins play. This is the beach just below the Manele Bay Hotel.

With 23 miles of shoreline, Molokai has long, lonesome gold beaches on its West End and a nearly beachless collection of fishponds on its East End. The most outstanding beach is **Papohaku,** a three-mile stretch of sand so golden that it has been exported to replenish Waikiki Beach. The water is usually too rough for safe swimming, but this beach is good for sunning, picnics, sunset barbecues (bonfires are allowed), and long walks under a full moon.

WEST MAUI

Kaanapali Beach

LOCATION Honoapiilani Highway, fronting Kaanapali Beach Resort.

Maui Outdoor Pursuits

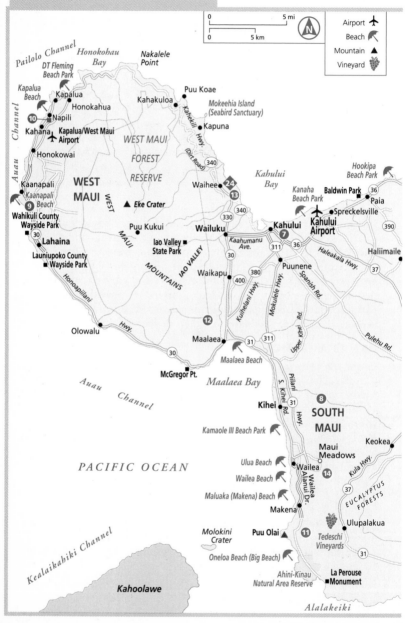

0   5 mi
0   5 km

N

Airport ✈
Beach ☂
Mountain ▲
Vineyard 🍇

Pailolo Channel
Honokohau Bay
Nakalele Point
Auau Channel
DT Fleming Beach Park
Puu Koae
Kapalua Beach
Kapalua
Kahakuloa
Mokeehia Island (Seabird Sanctuary)
Honokahua
10
Napili
Kapuna
Kahana
Kapalua/West Maui Airport
WEST MAUI FOREST RESERVE
340
Kahului Bay
Hookipa Beach Park
Honokowai
Waihee
24
Kanaha Beach Park
Baldwin Park
36
Kaanapali
13
Paia
Kaanapali Beach
9
▲ Eke Crater
340
330
340
Kahului
Spreckelsville
390
Wahikuli County Wayside Park
Puu Kukui
Wailuku
7
Kahului Airport
30
Lahaina
WEST
Iao Valley State Park
Kaahumanu Ave.
311
36
Haliimaile
Launiupoko County Wayside Park
MAUI
IAO VALLEY
Waikapu
400
380
Puunene
Haleakala Hwy.
37
Honoapiilani Hwy.
MOUNTAINS
12
Kuihelani Hwy.
Mokulele Hwy.
Spanish Rd.
Olowalu
Maalaea
31
311
Pulehu Rd.
Auau Channel
McGregor Pt.
Maalaea Beach
30
Pilani Hwy.
Upper Kihei Rd.
Maalaea Bay
Kihei
31
8
SOUTH MAUI
Keokea
PACIFIC OCEAN
Kamaole III Beach Park
Maui Meadows
S. Kihei Rd.
Ulua Beach
Wailea
14
Kula Hwy.
Wailea Beach
Wailea Alanui Dr.
Maluaka (Makena) Beach
EUCALYPTUS FORESTS
Makena
37
Ulupalakua
Molokini Crater
Puu Olai ▲
11
Tedeschi Vineyards
31
Kealaikahiki Channel
Oneloa Beach (Big Beach)
Ahini-Kinau Natural Area Reserve
La Perouse Monument
Kahoolawe
Alalakeiki

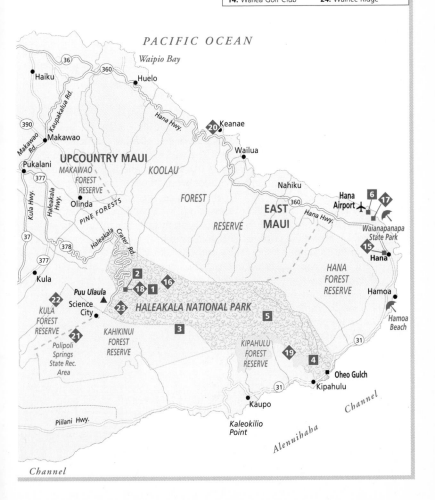

**■ CABINS AND
   CAMPGROUNDS**
1. Holua Cabin
2. Hosmer Grove
3. Kapalaoa Cabin
4. Kipahulu Campground
5. Paliku Cabin
6. Waianapanapa
   Campground

● GOLF COURSES
7. The Dunes at Maui
   Lani
8. Elleair Maui Golf
   Club
9. Kaanapali Golf
   Course
10. Kapalua Golf Club
11. Makena Courses
12. Sandalwood Golf
    Course
13. Waiehu Golf Course
14. Wailea Golf Club

◆ HIKES
15. Fagan's Cross
16. Halemauu Trail
17. Hana-Waianapanapa
    Coast Trail
18. Hosmer Grove
    Nature Trail
19. Kaupo Gap
20. Keanae Arboretum
21. Polipoli Loop
22. Skyline Trail
23. Sliding Sands Trail
24. Waihee Ridge

Activities Bodysurfing, bodyboarding, snorkeling, scuba diving, windsurfing, kayaking, sailing, fishing. **Special appeal** Places to hang for students and other young people, coastal walkway, boats that cruise from beach landings.

COMMENTS Swimming conditions are good when the surf is flat; this is subject, however, to strong currents and surf. The base of Black Rock, a volcanic cinder cone jutting up at the center of the four-mile beach, is excellent for snorkeling and diving. A lifeguard is on duty at the Lahaina end. Beach concessions and outdoor showers are available all along the walkway that links Kaanapali's neighboring hotels and condos.

Every afternoon a spanking breeze comes up and sends sailboats streaking out in the channel. If you're too comfortable to go over to Lahaina harbor to catch a cruise, some launch from the beach to enjoy a sunset sail or snorkel tour.

Kapalua Beach
LOCATION **Lower Honoapiilani Highway, Kapalua Resort.**

Activities Swimming, snorkeling, scuba diving, sailing, kayaking. **Special appeal** Quiet atmosphere, good swimming and snorkeling, safe for kids, vivid scenery.

COMMENTS This secluded strand in front of Kapalua Bay Hotel, the best of several spectacular strands in the area, is one of Maui's most beautiful and most swimmable beaches. The water is so clear that it's easy to see where the gold of the sand turns to green and then blue as the water gets deeper. Lava promontories protect both sides of the beach from rough seas. Public facilities are available, and a resort service desk rents equipment and makes reservations for adventure activities, but no lifeguards are posted. The sunset is often spectacular, spotlighting Molokai across the channel. This gold-sand beach and its see-through water lure swimmers, snorkelers, and kayakers, who can test their skill here before paddling down the coast to Honolua Bay to snorkel. Go in the morning when the wind is light and the sea calm.

Fish hang out by the rocks, as if they know this is a marine preserve. The beach is not so wide that you burn your feet getting in or out of the water. It's bordered inland by a shady path and cool lawns with outdoor showers at both ends. Public access and parking are located nearby, at the southern end of the resort.

SOUTH MAUI

Big Beach, Makena State Park
LOCATION **Makena Alanui, Makena.**

Activities Swimming, surfing, snorkeling, bodysurfing, bodyboarding, fishing.
Special appeal Scenic beauty, undeveloped nature, good for walking.

COMMENTS Makena State Park at Maui's southern end has two scenic golden-sand beaches, known as Big Beach and Little Beach. Big Beach, 3,300 feet long, is Maui's longest and a favorite spot for experienced bodyboarders and bodysurfers. Little Beach, meanwhile, is a small cove with gentler ocean conditions, a good prospect for novice wave riders. No lifeguards are on duty, nor are there public restrooms or showers. Secluded Little Beach is a popular "unofficial" nude beach, although public nudity is prohibited by law.

On the southern end of the Maui resort coast, development dwindles and succumbs to a wild, dry countryside covered with thorny, green kiawe trees. The Maui Prince Hotel sits grandly by itself, the only hotel on 1,800 acres of Makena Resort, shared with some condos and homes, a couple of first-rate golf courses, and a necklace of perfect beaches. The strand nearest the hotel is Maluaka Beach, noted for its beauty, good swimming conditions, frequent turtle sightings, and view of Molokini crater and Kahoolawe.

Under the sea, at the 80-foot depth, sits a World War II–vintage U.S. Army tank that serves as a fish magnet. Every sea denizen seeking shade goes to the tank, and so should you. The South Maui coast offers Maui's best scuba diving for easy viewing and diversity of underwater life.

Kamaole Beach III
LOCATION **On South Kihei Road in Kihei town.**

Activities Swimming, bodysurfing, picnicking. **Special appeal** Easy access, wide, sandy beach, grassy knoll.

COMMENTS Sunbathers like Kamaole Beach Parks I, II, and III, the top draw of Kihei town. If every small town in America had a beach like Kihei's, nobody would ever leave home. This long, wide golden strand in the heart of town has a shaded grassy knoll with picnic facilities for families, a lifeguard, views of the West Maui Mountains and the islands of Lanai and Kahoolawe, and plenty of inexpensive beachfront condos nearby that make Kihei Maui's best beach bargain. Bars, restaurants, and shopping plazas line the busy main drag for lots of accessible action. Popular with early Hawaiians, who lived in thatched huts along the shore, this beach area was "discovered" in the 1970s by Canadian snowbirds looking for an affordable warm place to dodge winter. However, even the waters off these fine beaches require vigilance by surfers and swimmers: sharks, too, live here, and most shark attacks off Maui have occurred off Kihei and Olowalu beaches, mainly in murky depths or at sunset.

Wailea Beach
LOCATION **Wailea Alanui, Wailea Resort.**

Activities Swimming, bodysurfing, bodyboarding, snorkeling, scuba diving, windsurfing, kayaking, fishing. **Special appeal** Scenic beauty, gentle waves, luxury resort surroundings.

COMMENTS Wailea Resort has five golden-sand beaches: Polo, Wailea, Ulua, Mokapu, and Keawakapu. Of all the beaches on Maui's sun-baked Gold Coast, none is finer for swimming than Wailea, the mile-long, gold-sand beach named for Lea, the Hawaiian goddess of canoe makers. Beachgoers can enjoy the gorgeous view of Molokini crater and the island of Kahoolawe on one side of an ocean channel and Lanai and West Maui on the other. The clear waters tumble to shore in waves just the right size for riding, with or without a boogie board. Wailea Beach is protected on both sides by lava reef points. It's the front yard of the Four Seasons Wailea and Grand Wailea Resort Hotel and Spa, two of Maui's most elegant and spectacular beach hotels. The Four Seasons beach boys run a dripper hose down the sandy slope so that beachgoers can get across the hot sand between the water and a paved coastal path without scalding their feet.

Ulua is the centermost beach, 1,000 feet long and 200 feet wide, between the Renaissance Wailea and Marriott Wailea Beach. Locals regard the offshore reef here as one of Maui's best snorkeling spots. A deeper reef, excellent for scuba diving, is about 100 yards out from shore.

A 1.5-mile coastal trail throughout Wailea Resort links several public accessways to all beaches and hotel and condo properties. The popular trail features native plants (each with a name tag), an old village site, and various architectural styles from ancient *heiau* to Kea Lani's Arabian fantasy. Panoramic views take in neighbor islands, unreal sunsets, and Pacific humpback whales in season.

Public facilities include parking, restrooms, and showers. Resort beach concessions offer board rentals and instruction. No lifeguards are posted.

CENTRAL MAUI

Hookipa Beach
LOCATION Paia town, off Hana Highway.

Activities Windsurfing and watching windsurfing. **Special appeal** Constant strong wind, big waves.

COMMENTS Skilled windsurfers head directly for world-famous Hookipa Beach on the North Shore to join the "Maui air force," daredevils who sail into waves and go airborne. They now attach kites to their rigs to increase hang time and allow them to hop over the waves. Home of the annual Aloha Classic windsurfing meet, Hookipa is the proving ground for gutsy experts who challenge each other to fly higher, farther, faster; it's the sailboarders' Bonneville and, for the rest of us, a must-see photo-op stop just past Paia, on the way to Hana.

HANA

Hamoa Beach
LOCATION Adjacent to the Hana Pier.

Activities Swimming, bodyboarding, surfing. **Special appeal** Little visited, scenic beach with good bodysurf waves.

COMMENTS Half moon–shaped Hamoa Beach is a gray-sand beach (a salt-and-pepper mix of coral and lava sands) in a truly tropical setting.

- Beaches on Maui, Molokai, and Lanai are composed of coral, lava rock, erosional runoff, and shell sands, which cause them to be golden, black, red, gray, and black and white.

- Beaches change. They may be big in winter and small in summer, or vice versa. Strong Pacific surf can rearrange a flat, hard beach into one with a steep slope of loose sand. Strong storms also rearrange beaches.

- Lucky beachcombers can find treasures like shells and glass fishing floats on certain beaches, including those on Maui's north and east shores. We have also found shells on Kihei beaches. People-watchers are endlessly entertained at more crowded beaches, such as Kaanapali. Seekers of solitude can easily find remote strands where the only footprints are their own, right along the highway in West Maui.

- Wailea and Kaanapali resorts have inviting coastal paths to walk or jog that lead by all the hotels and public accessways. The resorts also maintain historic sites for public view, such as those at Kapalua fronting the Ritz-Carlton and on the Wailea trail between Four Seasons and Kea Lani. The public is welcome in hotel restaurants, spas, stores, and bars, although the hotels restrict use of their pools to guests.

It's a favorite of VIP sunbathers who seek rest and refuge at the Hotel Hana-Maui, side by side with neighborhood kids who demonstrate by example how best to enjoy the water conditions of the day—boogieboarding, for instance, or riding waves in a plastic kayak, or windsurfing. The 100-foot-wide beach, 300 yards long, is bordered by 30-foot sea cliffs, traversed by stone steps. Surf breaks offshore and rolls up on the beach. Its stunning beauty inspired author James Michener to remark, "Paradoxically, the only beach I have ever seen that looks like the South Pacific was in the North Pacific—Hamoa Beach, on Maui Island in Hawaii, a beach so perfectly formed that I wonder at its comparative obscurity."

Kaihalulu Beach (Red-Sand Beach)
LOCATION **On the ocean side of Kauiki Head crater.**

Activities Hiking, swimming. **Special appeal** Rare red-sand beach, semiprotected in-shore pool, scenic beauty.

COMMENTS Hana sightseers visit Hasegawa's General Store but often miss the most unusual natural attraction nearby—a red-sand beach. It's officially known as Kaihalulu Beach, which means "roaring sea," but everyone here calls it "Red-Sand Beach." It's easy to see why. The beach is a strand of dark-red cinnabar sands, lining an exotic cove reached by a sometimes daunting and precipitous dirt path along the steep hillside.

Kauiki, a 390-foot-high volcanic cinder cone, lost its seaward wall to erosion and spilled red cinders everywhere to create the building blocks of the red-sand beach. The redness is the result of volcanic iron deposits; the only other known red-sand beach in the world is in Iceland. Maui's is warmer.

Waianapanapa Beach
LOCATION **Waianapanapa State Park, off Hana Highway, north of the city of Hana.**

Activities Tent and cabin camping. **Special appeal** Dreamlike tropical pocket beach with black sand edged by palms, clouds of sea mist.

COMMENTS Shiny, black-sand Waianapanapa Beach features bright-green jungle foliage on three sides and cobalt blue water lapping at its feet. *Waianapanapa* is Hawaiian for "glistening water," which you can see for yourself on a day trip to this unusual beach park near Hana. Surf is rough at times, with a rugged shore break and dangerous rip currents offshore.

The park features tent sites and a dozen rustic beach cabins with ocean views, the cheapest beachfront retreat on Maui at a mere $45 a night for four. The cabins sleep six and are minimally equipped with kitchens, utensils, and linens. It's such a deal that reservations are booked a year in advance. Call ☎ 808-984-8109 to secure yours.

MOLOKAI
Papohaku Beach
LOCATION **Kaluakoi Road, just beyond Kaluakoi Resort.**

Activities Surfing, bodyboarding, bodysurfing, snorkeling. **Special appeal** Broad strand, wild beauty, shady picnics, excellent sunset views of Oahu.

COMMENTS Three miles long and 400 feet wide, Papohaku Beach is the biggest beach on Molokai and one of the only sandy Molokai beaches that is easily accessible for families. This isn't a swimming beach, but board riders like it. It has a wilderness atmosphere, thanks to a shoreline kiawe forest, but with good paved-road access and public-beach park facilities—restrooms, showers, parking, and sheltered camping sites under the trees. Dangerous swimming conditions exist because no reefs offer protection from the full force of sea and surf, which pounds the sands impressively. High-surf conditions can occur any time of year. No lifeguards are on duty.

Sandy Beach
LOCATION **Kamehameha V Highway, seven miles past Wave Crest Resort, near Kaunakakai and mile marker 21 on the East End.**

Activities Swimming, bodysurfing. **Special appeal** Good swimming, beautiful views of Maui.

COMMENTS It's not easy to find a swimming beach on Molokai, with its rough open seas, sheer cliffs, and muddy fishponds. This small, reef-sheltered pocket beach is the rare exception. Soft, golden sands and gentle waters make it safe for kids. Don't stub your toes on the rocky bottom while admiring the West Maui Mountains across the channel. Restrooms are available, but not lifeguards. Good swimming conditions also prevail at nearby Waialua Beach, just before mile marker 19.

LANAI

Hulopoe Beach Park
LOCATION **Manele Road, near Manele Bay Hotel.**

Activities Swimming, surfing, bodyboarding, bodysurfing, snorkeling, fishing, picnicking, camping. **Special appeal** Kids' tide pool, shade, scenery.

COMMENTS This is the only beach park on Lanai. But it's a fine one, much prized by island residents who play and camp there, along with the Manele Bay patrons who walk down a trail shaded by a kiawe grove to reach it.

Hulopoe features a large tide pool carved into a lava cliff with all-season swimming for children. Palms dot the golden beach, which is 1,500 feet long and 200 feet wide. Beach swimming is subject to wave action, but it's usually calm enough inshore. Snorkeling is rewarding along the sheltering lava headland, which also provides a place to hike and explore on shore. Public restrooms, showers, picnic areas, and campsites are provided.

MAUI WATERS: WHAT YOU SHOULD KNOW

THOUGH THE BEACHES ARE GRAND, the water is even better. The seawater is clear, ideal in temperature, and salty enough to keep you afloat. To swim easily in the ocean or play in the waves is one of the most special aspects of a trip to Maui.

The same mid-Pacific location that keeps Island waters clean and warm demands attentive respect for the seas and their hazards. The biggest dangers are seasonal surf and currents, posted on most park beaches. Heed warning signs and never turn your back on the ocean. Many beaches are sheltered by reefs, but those that are not get pounded by relentless waves that slap the shore with such force that they can knock the unwary off their feet and send them out to sea.

You can see and hear rising surf; it's an awesome phenomenon, best observed safely from shore. When the surf comes up, surfers head out to meet the challenge. But novices and swimmers are wise to head out of the water and stay ashore to watch.

Currents are insidious, because you can't always tell when and where they are. The Hawaiian Islands are sunken mountains with steep sides that result in strong, swirling ocean currents. Kealaikahiki Channel, off the south coast of Lanai, is famous for a powerful current that leads to Tahiti, 1,500 miles away. Should you get carried out by a rip current, don't panic. Conserve your strength, determine which direction is perpendicular to the current and also leads toward shore, and swim across the current toward safety.

You might meet the mild Hawaiian version of Portuguese man-o-war jellyfish, known as blue bottles, which float in from time to time. On the water's surface, this jellyfish appears as an innocent floating bubble, but a nearly invisible blue tendril trailing behind it leaves a searing burn and may take a while to go away. Our hint for a quick antidote is the blue-colored aloe vera gel widely sold in Hawaii as a sunburn soother. A dab on a blue bottle sting will usually extinguish the fire, but more extreme allergic reactions may need medical care.

Swimmers and snorkelers sometimes run into sharp pieces of coral and get cut or scraped. Coral cuts tend to infect quickly, so keep a bottle of inexpensive hydrogen peroxide handy to flush and treat them.

Obviously, an important protective item is sunscreen. This close to the equator, the tropical sun is especially strong, the air is clear, and burns happen very quickly, particularly on children's tender skin. Sunscreen is essential. Apply it before you go outside; reapply it after swimming, snorkeling, or sweating a lot; and try to avoid mid-day exposure. You can still get a head-turning tan at 9 a.m. or after 4 p.m., even with SPF 15 sunscreen.

One other precaution: Leave your most valuable belongings in your room safe when you head for the beach. If you carry a good camera or money, don't leave it unattended. You wouldn't tempt fate at home; don't do it in the Islands.

The authoritative beach book is *The Best Beaches of Maui County* (revised and updated), by John R. K. Clark. The 156-page book, published by the University of Hawaii Press, includes details on Molokai, Lanai, Kahoolawe, and Molokini. Or try Dr. Stephen Leatherman's "Dr. Beach" Web site, **www.topbeaches.com.**

DIFFERENT STROKES:
Paddling Maui

TO SEE MAUI THE WAY EARLY HAWAIIANS DID, go down to the sea and paddle. Since the first voyagers landed from the South Pacific, paddling boats in the seas has been a way of life. Outrigger canoe paddling is a fiercely competitive local sport. You'll often see teams of paddlers practicing in the waters off Kihei.

Kayaking is the way to go if your interest in paddling is strictly recreational, although it can be competitive as well. The biggest kayak contest, the annual World Championship Kayak Race, takes off from Kepuhi Beach on Molokai each May, when solo paddlers run across the dunes and beach carrying their kayaks, jump in the sea, and paddle to Oahu 32 miles away. Expert kayakers take on wilderness trips, such as a summertime paddle around Molokai's back side, where wild valleys pierce the wall of tall sea cliffs that plunge down to the coast. Just for the fun of it, you can rent a kayak or, better yet, go on a guided kayak trek with a local paddler.

Maui Eco-Tours guides kayak–snorkel trips along the Makena coast in South Maui. Tours depart daily at 7:15 a.m. for intermediate-level activities and kids over age 11, and 7:45 a.m. for beginners and kids ages 5 and under, to see turtles and spinner dolphins—and have lunch on the beach. Call ☎ 808-891-2223 or visit **www.mauiecotours.com** for details.

Kayaks are available for rent at Kaanapali, Kapalua, and Wailea resorts and cost about $40 for a single-person kayak for a full day and $50 per day for tandem kayaks. A short lesson is usually included in the price. Two of the best kayak adventures are found at opposite ends of Maui.

Kayak to Ahihi-Kinau

Take a kayak down Maui's rugged Makena coast with local water-man Dino Ventura to see a natural shoreline—jagged black lava fingers, emerald lagoons, and gold-sand beaches often tracked by green sea turtles. You may meet dolphins out there, or even a whale.

Embark from historic Makena Landing, where cowboys once herded cattle into the sea so the herd could be hoisted onto ships bound for market. It's a brisk five-mile paddle south past Turtle Town (so dubbed because turtles haul out of the sea there) and around Puu Olai, the distinctive cinder cone overlooking Makena Beach that punctuates the southwest end of the island.

Paddlers anchor at Ahihi-Kinau Natural Area Reserve, a 2,000-acre marine-life sanctuary that offers Maui's finest snorkeling. Then it's just you and about a million fish who thrive in black lava tide pools. Call **Makena Kayak** at ☎ 808-879-8426 or visit **www. makenakayaks.com.**

Kayak to Honolua Bay

From Fleming Beach by the Ritz-Carlton, Kapalua, head out and turn starboard—that's right for you landlubbers. You are bound for

Honolua Bay. High surf in winter turns this picturesque bay into a surfers' paradise (it's regarded as the best break on Maui) but summer belongs to the kayakers. The bay's calm, clear water is full of tropical fish—it's a marine conservation district—and sometimes boils with schools of akule, a big-eyed small fish that likes glassy water. Honolua (Hawaiian for "two harbors") won a footnote in nautical history on May 1, 1976, when *Hokulea*, the first modern-day replica of a twin-hulled Polynesian voyaging canoe, set sail here on the first 20th-century Pacific crossing from Hawaii to Tahiti. The 34-day sea voyage revived interest in Pacific voyaging and helped spark a renaissance in Hawaiian culture.

Call **Maui Eco Tours** at ☎ 808-891-2223 or 866-891-2223, or visit **www.mauiecotours.com.**

DIVE, DIVE, DIVE

MAUI'S UNDERWATER TREASURES—lava caverns, reefs filled with tropical fish, and marine preserves filled with wintering humpback whales, corals, and other sea life—lure divers to Maui, Molokai, and Lanai. *Skin Diver* magazine rates Lanai one of the top-ten snorkel and scuba sites in the world. Its waters, exceptionally clear since little runoff clouds the edges of this dry island, include some 20 different dive sites with intriguing submarine lava formations and large schools of brightly colored fish among the attractions. Spinner dolphins live along its coast year-round.

Most divers arrive for dive tours already certified, but certification courses are offered at local dive shops. Rates range from $60 for a beachside lesson to $300 or more for full open-water instruction and certification. You pay an additional fee for a scuba certification card. Equipment is provided.

Most dive tours require participants to be certified by a scuba training organization, such as the Professional Association of Diving Instructors (PADI), National Association of Underwater Instructors (NAUI), National Association of Scuba Diving Schools (NASDS), or World Association of Scuba Instructors (WASI). Specialized dives—including explorations of wrecks or caves and night diving—require more advanced training.

Introductory dives, often conducted in a swimming pool, give would-be divers a chance to experience diving. Participants receive basic instruction, get fitted for scuba gear, and dive with the instructors. The entire experience lasts two to four hours, with rates ranging from $100 to $150.

Snuba is another option for uncertified divers who want to explore the Islands underwater. It's a hybrid of snorkel and diving that takes place at dive sites, but anyone can do it. Just breathe through a 20-foot hose linked to a floating oxygen tank. Jump in the

A Few Tips for Divers

- In choosing a dive operator, ask about their dive experience, their safety expertise, the type of boat, the dive destination, and other details to make sure the guides meet your expectations.

- Be careful where you put your hands and feet underwater. Some marine life—such as eels, jellyfish, and scorpionfish—can bite or sting. Do not touch any animal you don't recognize. Try to avoid touching or crushing coral, which leaves a permanent dent in the underwater environment and puts you at risk for coral cuts.

- Never dive alone.

- If you're attempting underwater photography for the first time, shoot from within four feet. For best results, use an underwater camera with a 15 mm or 20 mm lens.

water and take a deep breath, towing your tank behind you. Several snorkel cruises offer snuba.

Rates for certified dive tours are $120 and up, depending on the size of the boat, equipment, and number of dives included on the trip. Booking deposits are usually required, refundable if you cancel in advance. Expect to spend at least half a day on a guided scuba adventure. The actual time you spend in the water will vary—the deeper the water, the faster you use your air supply—but usually it's 90 minutes to two hours. The diver-to-guide ratio has a legal maximum of six to one.

MAUI'S TOP DIVE SITES

THE MOST POPULAR AND ONE OF THE BEST Maui dive sites is **Molokini,** the sunken cinder cone about three miles off the coast of South Maui, near Kahoolawe. Molokini, a Marine Life Conservation District, has high visibility and thriving ocean life, including reef fish, sea turtles, and manta rays. But it gets congested with snorkelers and tour boats as the day goes on, so it's best to book an early boat.

RECOMMENDED DIVE COMPANIES

Ed Robinson's Diving Adventures: ☎ 808-879-3584 or 800-635-1273, **www.maui-scuba.com**

Lahaina Divers: ☎ 808-667-7496 or 800-998-3483, **www.lahainadivers.com**

Maui Dive Shop: ☎ 800-542-3483, **www.mauidiveshop.com**

Mike Severns Diving, Kihei: ☎ 808-879-6596, **www.mikesevernsdiving.com**

A favorite South Maui dive site is **La Perouse Pinnacle,** in the middle of picturesque La Perouse Bay beyond Makena. The pinnacle rises 60 feet from the sea floor to about 10 feet below the ocean's surface and is exceptional for snorkeling as well as shallow dives. Look for brilliant damselfish, triggerfish, puffers, and wrasses.

Divers of all skill levels probe **Five Caves** in Makena, South Maui. Lava ridges and small pinnacles provide food and shelter for anglerfish, sea turtles, eels, and white-tipped sharks. The depth here is 30–40 feet, and the waters can be accessed from shore as well as from boat.

At **Cathedrals,** off the south shore of Lanai, a stained-glass effect occurs when sunlight pours through the holes in twin underwater caves. This dive site is for experienced divers.

If diving with giant wintering whales is your dream, sign up with Captain Ed Robinson on Maui, a veteran dive captain who knows how to find them (contact information below).

SNORKELING:
Discover the Undersea World

SNORKELING ADDS AN UNDERSEA DIMENSION to your Island adventures, even if you don't dive as deep as scuba tanks allow. You can go to many of the same sites and see the fish and sealife below you from near the surface of the water. It's not difficult or scary. Just jump off the boat stern, paddle your flippers, look through your face mask, and breathe through your tube.

MAUI'S TOP SNORKELING BEACHES

Ahihi-Kinau Preserve, South Maui
LOCATION **On the remote south shore of Maui, beyond Makena, at the end of a dirt road.**

Activities Snorkeling.

COMMENTS Black, barren lava reefs reach into aquamarine pools full of tropical fish. The best snorkeling on Maui is in this scenic 2,000-acre nature preserve on the rugged south coast, where Haleakala last spilled red-hot lava into the sea in 1790. It's difficult to reach but easy to enjoy. No facilities.

Five Needles, Lanai
LOCATION **Off the remote south shore of Lanai.**

Activities Snorkeling, swimming.

COMMENTS Spiky sea stacks dominate an almost-secret snorkel spot on Lanai's rugged south side. Go there only by kayak, sailboat, or launch,

Snorkeling Tips

- Know how to swim, to ensure your own safety in the water, even if you're snorkeling close to shore or a boat.
- Novices should practice in shallow water.
- Always snorkel with a buddy or in groups.
- Don't stray too far from shore or the boat.
- Check your snorkel gear carefully before entering the water. Popular wisdom suggests you spit on your mask's eyepiece and rub the lens before dunking it in saltwater and then putting it on. Make sure it fits, airtight, to your face.

mostly by tours departing from Maui. Take Trilogy Excursions for this unforgettable outing (see information on guided tours below). Water clarity and abundant sea life make this an outstanding snorkel site. No facilities.

Kaupoa Beach, Molokai

LOCATION **West End, on Molokai Ranch property (access is limited to ranch guests, unless you can navigate a boat there).**

Activities Summer snorkeling, swimming, beachcombing, sunbathing.

COMMENTS Head for Kaupoa Beach by ranch bus or on horseback, swap boots for flippers, and take a plunge in the warm saltwater, soothing after a morning in the saddle on Molokai Ranch. Horses graze under coco palms while you snorkel with triggerfish. The trail boss grills rib-eye steaks. Way out west on Molokai, this is what surf and turf is all about. Facilities include a beachside bar and dining pavilion, a restaurant, showers, and bathrooms.

GUIDED SNORKEL TOURS

GUIDED SNORKELING ADVENTURES are available from an abundance of tour boats for rates mostly $50 and up for adults. In addition, many shops rent snorkeling fins, masks, snorkels, and gear bags. Guided snorkel tours take half a day or more. Instruction for beginners is available. Snorkel outings are weather-dependent. The following are our favorite guided snorkel tours.

Maui

Trilogy Excursions, the oldest and best snorkel and scuba operator on Maui, sails a fleet of sailing catamarans on snorkel and scuba dives to Molokini, an area off Kaanapali Beach, and its best-known tour, Lanai, combined with a land tour of the island. Its six-hour excursions include barbecue lunch and continental breakfast. Trilogy Excursions, owned and operated by brothers Jim and

Rand Coon and their families, has a well-deserved reputation for delivering a superior experience. Call ☎ 888-MAUI-800 or visit **www.sailtrilogy.com.**

Navatek II is a special high-tech boat, an 82-foot, 149-passenger SWATH vessel designed to ease queasy stomachs, which sails from Maalaea Harbor to Lanai's south shore on a "Voyage of Discovery," as well as sunset dinner cruises and whale-watching trips in season. The vessel, also available for weddings and private functions, is fast and fully equipped, and the tours include gear, hamburgers to order for lunch, and cold drinks. The boat is easy to get on and off of in deep water. *Navatek II* and several other snorkel sail cruises are operated by **Royal Hawaiian Cruises.** Call ☎ 800-852-4183 or visit **www.royalhawaiiancruises.com.**

Molokai

Walter Naki of **Molokai Action Adventures** takes four snorkelers on four- or six-hour dives in seldom-explored territory aboard his 21-foot Boston whaler and also leads fishing and diving tours. Call ☎ 808-558-8184.

Molokai Fish and Dive, activity providers for the very active Molokai Ranch crowd, lead one- or two-tank dives for experienced divers to explore a reef wall and blue holes along Hawaii's longest barrier reef—the south side of Molokai. Night dives and charters can be arranged. Call ☎ 808-553-5926 or visit **www.molokaifishanddive.com.**

Lanai

Trilogy Ocean Sports operates a concierge desk at Manele Bay Hotel to book Lanai guests on tours and act as an arrival point for day-trippers from Maui. Snorkel adventures, introductory dives on Hulopoe Beach, sunrise scuba tours to the Cathedrals, marine-mammal watches, guided kayak rides, and private charters are available. Trilogy cautions scuba divers that because of the upland elevation of the Lodge at Koele, divers must spend 24 hours at sea level before returning to that hotel. Fortunately, they can easily arrange a stay at the Manele Bay Hotel.

CATCH *a* WAVE

HAWAII'S OWN KINGS PERFECTED *hee nalu*—that's wave sliding in Hawaiian—and the rest of the world soon discovered the joy of surfing. No place does it better or offers more consistent surf, bigger waves, or deeper tubes.

On Maui, the best surf spots are Honolua Bay in winter, Lahaina Harbor in summer, Maalaea (beyond the breakwater), and Hookipa Beach in the morning, before the wind comes up and the windsurfers take over the waves.

No one knows exactly when surfing originated, but many historians believe Polynesians were already well versed in the sport when they migrated to the Hawaiian Islands nearly 2,000 years ago. Only the high chiefs enjoyed access to the best surf spots. King Kamehameha I was said to be an avid surfer.

Today, waves are shared according to skill. Beginning surfers can get quick lessons on Maui by signing up for formal training with an expert instructor, like Nancy Emerson, a champion surfer and stuntwoman since 1961, who claims she can get you up and surfing with one lesson. Surfing instruction is available year-round. Equipment is provided. Buzzy Kerbox, one of Maui's top surfers, also gives personal and group instructions and specializes in teaching beginners.

I saw it coming, turned my back on it, and paddled for dear life. Faster and faster my board went, till it seemed my arms would drop off. What was happening behind me I could not tell. One cannot look behind and paddle the windmill stroke. I heard the crest of the wave hissing and churning, and then my board was lifted and flung forward. I scarcely knew what happened the first half-minute. Though I kept my eyes open, I could not see anything, for I was buried in the rushing white of the crest. But I did not mind. I was chiefly conscious of ecstatic bliss at having caught the wave. At the end of the half-minute, however, I began to see things, and to breathe. I saw that three feet of the nose of my board was clear out of water and riding in the air. I shifted my weight forward and made the nose come down. Then I lay, quite at rest in the midst of the wild movement, and watched the shore and the bathers on the beach grow distinct.

—Jack London, "A Royal Sport: Surfing at Waikiki,"
from A. Grove Day's *Hawaii and Points South,*
True Island Tales

RECOMMENDED SURFING RESOURCES

SCHOOLS

Buzzy Kerbox: ☎ 808-573-5728, **www.buzzykerboxsurf.com**

Goofy Foot Surf School, Lahaina: ☎ 808-244-9283,
www.goofyfootsurfschool.com

Nancy Emerson School of Surfing, Lahaina: ☎ 808-244-7873,
www.surfclinics.com

Check out **www.mauisurf.com,** which lists a group of independent surfing instructors on Maui.

RENTALS

Local Motion, Kihei: ☎ 808-879-7873

Local Motion, Lahaina: ☎ 808-661-7873

Surfing Safety and Etiquette Tips

- Check with lifeguards first. They can point out the hazardous rip currents, jagged reefs, and tricky waves to avoid. Obey posted warnings.
- Never surf alone, and make sure someone on shore knows where you are.
- Be considerate of other surfers. Do not drop in on someone else's wave.
- Don't surf after dark.
- Use leg ropes to control your board, for your safety and the safety of fellow surfers.
- If you get in trouble, don't panic. Signal for help by raising one arm vertically.

Activities desks and concierges at hotels know where to get good rental surfboards.

Lessons for one or two students or groups of up to five per instructor are conducted in areas where waves are small and the beach uncrowded. Students learn the basics on the beach, including ocean safety, how to paddle a surfboard, how to get up and stand on the board, proper foot placement, and where to shift body weight. Then they get in the water to do it again, and then catch a real wave and ride it. Once you get the hang of it, you'll learn other basic maneuvers, such as turning your board to move in a certain direction.

Surfers come in all shapes, sizes, and ages. You should know how to swim and expect to do a lot of paddling and kicking in the water. Most schools have a minimum age of 5 to 7 years for surfing lessons.

Group rates generally start at $60 for one-hour lessons to $250 for all-day lessons. Private lessons are about $100–$175 for two-hour lessons and $400 for all-day lessons. Multiday and weeklong rates are also available. Book at least a day in advance, although most surf schools will try to accommodate last-minute students.

The Surfer's Guide to Hawaii, by Greg Ambrose (published by Bess Press, **www.besspress.com**), is the best local surf book with tips, descriptions, and maps.

RIDE THE WIND

A WHOLE DIFFERENT SPORT SEEKS TO CHALLENGE THE WIND as well as the waves—windsurfing or boardsailing, the combination of sailing and surfing. A day of brisk tradewinds prompts a hatchout of colorful, butterfly-like sails as windsurfers zip here and there across the water, enjoying the pure sensation of natural speed. In the

RECOMMENDED WINDSURF OUTFITTERS AND SCHOOLS

Hawaiian Island Surf and Sport, Kahului: ☎ 808-871-4981 or 800-231-6958, **www.hawaiianisland.com**

Hawaiian Sailboarding Techniques (champion windsurfer Alan Cadiz shares his world-class techniques with beginners), Kahului: ☎ 800-968-5423 or 808-871-5423, **www.hstwindsurfing.com**

Maui Windsurf Company, Kahului: ☎ 808-877-4816 or 800-872-0999, **www.maui-windsurf.com**

Islands, where water sports are a way of life, ocean devotees surf when the waves are right, windsurf when the winds are right, and kayak when it's calm.

But Maui's North Shore is famous for its superb combination of tricky strong winds and robust waves. Expert windsurfers will want to try their hand or just watch the pros at Kanaha Beach and Hookipa Beach on this stretch of coast, known as the Aspen of windsurfing, where the world's top wave riders gather.

All the action is centered around Kahului and Paia, the best places to find gear, rentals, and lessons. Some windsurfers travel to Maui to buy state-of-the-art gear as well as rent it.

GO FISH

WITH ALL THAT OCEAN, IT'S NO SURPRISE that saltwater fishing, by shorecasting and trolling, is a popular pastime and also a major commercial activity, which provides local tables with a rich bounty. Saltwater fishing in Hawaii does not require a permit, and many species are not subject to seasons or catch limits, except in waters protected by state or federal law.

Shorefishing from the beach or low reefs is popular on all islands, primarily in pursuit of feisty bonefish and tasty papio, the juvenile stage of jack trevally, known as ulua when it grows up. But the rough seas, four to eight feet on normal good-weather days, and dangerous channels rule out barebones (no crew) boat rentals and instead require a powerboat and experienced captain, so charter sportfishing is the way to pursue your dream fish. The boats are expensive but can be shared or chartered for less than a full day.

Marine research suggests the major game fish tend to hang out 2 to 30 miles offshore along two undersea ledges that surround the Islands, one at 240 feet and another at 600, vestiges of past ice ages when the sea level was lower. Some species choose the warm surface waters, such as marlin, ahi, and mahimahi, while others go for the cold bottom environment, notably prized snappers like onaga and opakapaka.

RECOMMENDED FISHING CHARTERS

MAUI

Aerial Sportfishing Charters: ☎ 808-667-9089,
www.aerialsportfishingcharters.com

Fish Maui: ☎ 808-879-3789, **www.fishmaui.com**

Lahaina Charter Boats: ☎ 866-888-6784 or 808-667-6672

Luckey Strike Charters: ☎ 808-661-4606, **www.luckeystrike.com**

MOLOKAI

Alyce C Sportfishing: ☎ 808-558-8377, **www.alycecsportfishing.com**

Fun Hogs Hawaii: ☎ 808-567-6789, **www.molokaifishing.com**

LANAI

Spinning Dolphin Charters: ☎ 808-565-6613

If you've dreamed of hooking a 1,000-pound "grander" Pacific blue marlin, your dreams may come true off Maui. The Big Island's Kona Coast is considered the big-game fishing capital of the world because of its history of record catches, but you never know what you may hook off Maui, Molokai, or Lanai, which are, after all, just up the channel from Kona. World-record fish—marlin, ono, ahi, and mahimahi—have been hooked off Maui. The best local fishing occurs around Lanai and Kahoolawe, islands easily reached aboard a charter boat out of Lahaina or Maalaea harbors on Maui, as well as Molokai and Lanai harbors. Below are some charter options; note that Lanai hotel concierges will arrange fishing charters on request.

OFF-ROAD SHOREFISHING EXPEDITIONS

SERIOUS FISHERMEN, HERE'S THE BEST BET in the Maui Islands. For eight years, David Bloch has led hard-core anglers in pursuit of giant ulua on his private shorefishing expeditions. You take a four-wheel-drive to a secluded off-road site, then camp overnight to be in the right place at the right time and tide to nail Hawaii's fabled fish from the shore. Around the campfire, you likely will hear true fish tales, like how a 563-pound *hapuu* (sea bass) caught from shore on Maui still holds the shorefishing record.

Call **Off-Road Shorefishing Expeditions** at ☎ 808-878-8582 for over-night camping/fishing treks and shore at four-wheel-drive only sites.

WATCH *the* WHALES

MOST OF THE PACIFIC HUMPBACK WHALE POPULATION migrates to warm Hawaiian waters each winter to breed, give birth, and nurse their young. Right behind them come the whale-watchers, in pursuit

WHALE WATCHING: HAWAIIAN PASTIME

You must be careful driving on Maui in whale season, especially along Olowalu, the flat coastal plain between McGregor Point and Lahaina. Motorists often jam on the brakes and leap out of their cars, abandoning them right on Honoapialani Highway at the sight of a distant spout.

The most whales we've ever seen in one place at one time in Hawaiian waters wasn't anywhere near Maui. It was late April one year on the forbidden island of Niihau. We spent the day snorkeling the crystal clear lagoons of Keamanu Bay in search of lobster with chopper pilot Tom Mishler. Suddenly, the blue water began to boil. Scores of whales began spy-hopping, chin-slapping, tail-slapping and fluking, and jumping straight out of the water. To our delight, this great performance lasted more than an hour. We applauded when it ended. It was a whale of a party.

of the spectacle of a whale leaping out of the sea and crashing back with a huge splash, obviously having a great time. You can see such whale behavior from your hotel lanai or from the roads of any of the islands in winter. But it is off Maui's shores that the giants seem to congregate, and you'll get the best view from a boat in the whale season, between mid-December and mid-April. Whale-watching excursions are concentrated off the south and west coasts of Maui, the heart of the whale migration and, coincidentally, of the visiting humans as well.

Luck plays a big role in observing interesting actions by large, live creatures on the move, but some tours are staffed by naturalists who offer substantial expertise and are equipped with state-of-the-art gear, such as hydrophones that let you hear whale songs. Some tours support nonprofit marine conservation and research groups like Pacific Whale Foundation and Whales Alive. The boat captains are required by federal law to keep a distance of at least 100 yards between their vessels and the whales. Some cruises guarantee sightings by giving you a rain check if you don't actually see a whale, and some do tours year-round, watching for other marine mammals when the humpbacks go north for the summer. Five other whale species can be viewed throughout the year—sperm whales, pilot whales, melon-headed whales, false killer whales, and beaked whales. Spinner dolphins live year-round in the waters around Maui, Molokai, and Lanai.

Watching for whales is much like watching for a lover. There is much expectation, and there is much time spent where there are no whales to see. I have always seen whales when I was not looking for them but was looking out, my eyes open for an instant.

—Joana McIntyre Varawa,
The Delicate Art of Whale Watching

If you want to see spinner dolphins from land, drive Maui's northwest coast to Nakalele Bay overlook. One early morning, bound for Kahakuloa, several of us talked about Hawaii's wonderfully elusive sights—the green flash, moonlight rainbows, and spinners in motion. We confessed that after 15 years in Hawaii, we had never seen dolphins spinning. We rounded a curve and stopped to look at Nakalele Bay. Suddenly they came, hundreds of shiny gray chorus girls in a follies revue, twirling and dancing on wave tops, splashing and spinning clockwise and counter-clockwise and end to end, flipping for sheer joy. We screamed with delight. They danced all the more.

Whale-watching boats come in all sizes, from rigid-hulled rubber rafts that bounce through the surf to large, motorized catamarans and sleek sailing sloops, and offer a wide range of comforts, such as shaded decks and bathrooms on board.

The cost of daily whale-watching cruises ranges $20–$60 for adults and $10–$30 for children ages 11 and under. Book your tour several days in advance during holiday periods. Most tours last two to three hours and provide snacks and juice. Some tours offer hotel transportation. Wear swimsuits or casual attire, and bring binoculars and cameras. Here is a list of some good whale-watching tour operators.

Tip: To see whales best from shore, get to an elevated viewing post that gives you a better perspective. Look for spouts, geysers of sea spray that shine in the sun and seem to disappear into thin air, to alert you that whales are cruising by. Look for large black bodies

WHALE-WATCHING CRUISES

MAUI

Hawaii Ocean Rafting (rafts departing Lahaina): ☎ 808-661-RAFT, **www.hawaiioceanrafting.com**

Maui Princess (yacht departs Lahaina): ☎ 808-667-6165, **www.mauiprincess.com**

Pacific Whale Foundation (from Lahaina and Maalaea): ☎ 808-879-8860, **www.pacificwhale.org**

Trilogy Expeditions (sails from Kaanapali Beach twice daily in season): ☎ 888- 225-MAUI, **www.sailtrilogy.com**

MOLOKAI

Molokai Charters: ☎ 808-553-5852

LANAI

Spinning Dolphin Charters: ☎ 808-565-6613

Trilogy Expeditions: ☎ 888- 225-MAUI, **www.sailtrilogy.com**

poking their noses above water as they "spy-hop," possibly to get a better look at you. There's no best time of day for whale-watching, but we've noticed that when the sea is glassy and there is no wind, we always see more. A Scripps Institute marine biologist told us that's because whales are the only mammals without hair and they don't like wind on their bodies when they leap out of the water.

If you're in the resort area of Wailea, Maui, check the telescope in front of the Marriott Wailea Beach Resort. The first person to report a whale sighting to the cafe each day gets free breakfast.

Informative Web sites on humpback whales include **www.pacific whale.org** and **www.ilovewhales.com.** Every cruise and sailboat that runs tours goes whale-watching in winter, and you can charter private whale-watching excursions on most.

YACHTING: *Over the Ocean Blue*

LOOKING AT ALL THAT OCEAN, ONE WOULD THINK MAUI, Molokai, and Lanai would be overrun with yachts and sailboats. Plenty of watercraft fill the infrequent harbors, but not as many tourists as you would think actually go sailing—most of the cruise boats are motorized. Actually, there's too much ocean for all but expert blue-water sailors, and the seas are filled with deep-running channels and tricky currents, tossed about by strong winds and big waves and edged by boat-eating reefs. However, the intrepid seafarer thirsting for world-class sailing in the middle of the ocean will find several yachting options in Maui.

America II is a genuine America's Cup 12-meter racing yacht that makes three two-hour trips a day from Slip 5, Lahaina Harbor, between late morning and late afternoon, plus morning whale-watching in winter. Private charters are available. Call ☎ 808-667-2195 for details. *Paragon* offers sailing tours from Lahaina and Maalaea aboard high-performance sailing catamarans that also use America's Cup technology to fly like the wind in comfort. Call ☎ 800-441-2087 or 808-244-2087, or e-mail paragon@ maui.net for details.

Island Star, a 57-foot charter yacht that comfortably sleeps ten, will take you wherever you want to go around the Islands with a crew that includes a chef, a naturalist, and a scuba instructor. Call ☎ 888-677-7238 or 808-669-STAR, or go to **www.islandstarsailing.com** for information.

Kapalua Kai, a 53-foot catamaran, sails from Kaanapali Beach to Honolua Bay north of Kapalua for snorkeling and sunset sails. Call ☎ 888-667-5980 or 808-665-0344, or visit **www.sailingmaui.com** for details. The sister ship, *Shangri La,* is available for luxury charters. For information, try the Web site or phone ☎ 888-855-9977 or 808-665-0077.

TAKE *to the* TRAILS

IF YOU'VE FINALLY EXHAUSTED THE MYRIAD WATERSPORTS Maui offers, or if you're just a landlubber by nature, there's plenty of adventure inland. Why not start out on foot? Maui is laced by trails leading along the coastal cliffs, up into woods and along ridges, down among the cinders inside Haleakala Crater, and on the ancient lava-stone path known as the King's Trail. You can hike to waterfalls, through bamboo forests, and into valleys, to scenic points with views you'll never forget. You can go with a guide or just follow your feet along a marked trail. Conditions are generally fine for meeting the natural environment face to face, and the natural environment is extraordinary, presenting few dangers to detract from the rewards. You won't be risking a rash or a snake attack—there are no snakes and no wild plant leaves that are noxious to the touch (except, for some people, mango, which is a relative of poison ivy). Mosquitoes may find you irresistible in the damp, green jungles, but generally the hiking climate is benign. These are some of the reasons why hiking is one of the most popular off-beach outdoor activities in the Islands.

Some trails are historic, smoothed by generations of ancient feet long before other means of overland travel were available. Some are fantasies-come-true, forested paths edged with leaves bigger than your head and tropical fruit like mountain apple, guava, wild mango, and avocado waiting to be plucked; waterfall streams with pools make ideal spots to cool off after a tropical trek. Maui boasts trails in Haleakala National Park and adjacent Polipoli Springs State Recreation Area. Plus, there are six forest reserves in Upcountry Maui: Makawao, Koolau, Hana, Kipahulu, Kahikinui, and Kula. The West Maui Forest Reserve and Iao Valley State Park await to the west. Molokai has a choice of wilderness trails, guided hikes, and one memorable tilt down a vertical cliff. The Nature Conservancy offers guided treks through its preserves in the high-country—boggy home of rare, native species—at Kamakou and on the shore at Moo-momi sand dunes, where skeletons of extinct birds have been found (call the Conservancy at ☎ 808-553-5236 or e-mail hike_molokai@tnc.org). Lanai has guided hikes in the Uplands' cool forest and on the sunbaked cliffs near Hulopoe Beach by the sea, but one you can find yourself leads to a spectacular viewpoint.

GUIDED HIKES

GUIDED HIKING TOURS BRING THE COUNTRYSIDE to life as only touching and walking through it can, in the company of expertise. This is the best way to get out into otherwise private and inaccessible country, discover shy indigenous creatures you might otherwise never see, and understand more about Maui. The best hiking guide operation on Maui is Ken Schmitt's **Hike Maui.** Schmitt, an Island

Maui Hiking Tips

- Rain forest means slippery, muddy trails and mosquitoes.

- Waterfall valleys are steep and narrow and are sometimes inundated by flash floods after cloudburst deluges upstream, with frightening and even fatal results.

- Dry hikes on lumpy lava and steep, crumbly dirt trails require close attention to your footing and drinking lots of water. No matter what the locals do, avoid hiking in rubber slippers (beach thongs) in favor of supportive footwear, but not your favorite snowy white sneakers, which won't fare well after a Hawaiian red-dirt trek, muddy forest jaunt, or a rough lava trail.

- Don't let the views keep you from watching where you put your feet. Yes, it is *Green Mansions* and *Blue Lagoon* and *Castaway* all rolled into one, but stand still while you admire the scenery.

- Stick to the trails. Rain-forested mountains swallow up injured or missing hikers from sight almost instantly. If possible, carry a charged cell phone on remote ventures.

- Inviting and wild though the streams may be, don't drink the water or swim with open cuts, as you risk getting leptospirosis, a wild pig–related bacterial fever that can turn into meningitis.

naturalist since 1983 who has hiked every trail on the island, and his crew weave together bits of geology, botany, culture, history, myth, and legend out there on the trail. Hike Maui, the oldest, largest hiking company, brings water, lunch, and insect repellent on hikes that range from a few hours to all day.

Contact Hike Maui at P.O. Box 330969, Kahului; ☎ 808-879-5270; or visit **www.hikemaui.com.**

Molokai Outdoor Adventures guides hikers with snacks and a day-pack to the heights of the island to find waterfalls and rain forest. They also rent equipment and offer a range of tours to the heart of the most natural island. Call ☎ 808-553-4477 or visit **www.molokai outdoors.com** for details.

THREE SHORT MAUI HIKES, TWO LONGER ONES

MOST FOLKS DON'T LIKE TO TREK VERY FAR, especially in the tropics, where the hot and humid climate slows down even the most avid hiker. So you don't miss a thing, here are a few short hikes with really big payoffs. They take you into Haleakala Crater, to a waterfall on the Hana coast, and into a valley once inhabited by ancient people. One of these treks, to Kahakuloa Valley, requires a guide. The last two hikes are more difficult but arguably more rewarding: the switchback trail taken by the Molokai Mule Ride and the trek up Lanai's Mount Lanaihale. If you're looking for a more relaxing route, see "A Good Walk" on page 234.

Each hike definitely will give you a memorable look at Maui's great outdoors.

Inside Haleakala

Sliding Sands Trail takes you down into the biggest hole on earth for a glimpse into a surreal landscape. And the trail lives up to its name. Your feet slip and slide on lava cinders, making crunchy noises as you go. The two-hour, two-mile hike sounds easy until you step off the edge of the crater rim, elevation 9,800 feet, and onto a switchback trail. (Did you remember to check in first at the Summit Visitors Center?)

Your toes begin to squinch and complain as you descend a few thousand feet down to the crater floor, 6,600 feet above sea level. If you start to tire, turn back; remember, it's all uphill on the way back. Expect to be breathless at this altitude, and dizzy. The scenery, too, will leave you a little light-headed; it's like a backdrop from an alien planet.

Hikers with stamina to press on will find 27 miles of trails inside the crater that can occupy you for a few hours or several days. (Did you bring the map?)

To the Falls

The best short hike on the Hana coast ends with a splash in a waterfall pool. Start at Pipiwai Stream from Oheo Gulch through a bamboo forest to 400-foot Waimoku Falls. The two-mile hike over a boardwalk leads through a noisy, rattling forest of green and yellow bamboo, a treat in itself. What makes this hike worthwhile is the waterfall pool at the end. Other hikes and a tour of the Hana Cultural Center are available free by contacting Haleakala National Park. Call ☎ 808-248-7375 for a schedule or visit Kipahulu Visitors Center.

Into the Valley of Ancients

Get a glimpse of Island life as it used to be, or as close as modern-day Hawaiians can get to it, in a remote stream valley on Maui's little-known northwest coast. Kahakuloa Valley was once off-limits to outsiders, but now visitors can experience it with a guide. In our opinion, this tour is the best we've taken on Maui, because it puts tourists in touch with Hawaiians and their efforts to resurrect some nearly lost cultural skills. Any tour that starts with fording a stream rock to rock and then taking off your shoes to sink over your ankles in the silky mud of a taro patch has to be different.

What you will experience in this Valley of Ancients is a Maui seldom seen: tales and trails of night marchers; relics like early C-shaped rock shelters, native plants, and sometimes endangered birds; and a well-tended taro patch fed by waterfalls. You'll meet caretakers eager to talk story about their experiences of trying to live Hawaiian in modern times and about the days of old, when Chief Piilani ruled and Maui thrived on fish and poi.

To arrange a trip, contact **Ekahi Tours,** in Kahului. Call ☎ 808-877-9775 or 888-292-2422, or visit **www.ekahi.com.**

Or, in Lahaina, contact **Maui Eco-Adventures** at ☎ 808-661-7720 or 877-661-7720, or visit **www.ecomaui.com.**

Two Legs on a Mule Trail

You can ride a mule down Molokai's steep sea cliffs, or you can take a hike. Many do walk the thin trail, sidestepping mules, and claim it is the most challenging and rewarding hike in all the Islands. The trail is only 2 miles long, but it's got 26 hairpin turns within a drop of 1,600 feet and a panoramic view that will leave you breathless. At the bottom, you can join the bused tour of the Kalaupapa National Historic Park to see the settlement where victims of leprosy were once banished and also the haunting view of Molokai's wilderness coast. Call ahead to get a tour or at least a permit to enter the restricted peninsula park, where some former leprosy victims still live. When it's time to go back, you'll discover that while the downhill trip tested your balance, the uphill hike will test your legs. Someone should hand out medals to all who accomplish this hike, one of the most unusual in all the tropical Pacific.

For guide information, contact **Damien Tours** at ☎ 808-567-6171.

Lanai Lookout

Get up early on a clear, dry morning on Lanai and set off in pursuit of a very special phenomenon: the chance to see five major Hawaiian islands from one perch. To get there, hike the eight-mile Munro Trail, the red-dirt jeep road that runs over the razorback ridge of Mount Lanaihale, the 3,366-foot peak of Lanai. Lanai sits in the middle of the major islands, a geographic fact not lost on ancient Hawaiian chiefs, who could observe interisland canoe traffic from its strategic peak and tell who was coming for dinner or to violate the peace.

Up at the summit on a clear day, Maui, Molokai, Kahoolawe, Oahu, and the Big Island are all visible at spots along this trail. That's all the major islands except northernmost Kauai and Niihau. And you see most of Lanai getting there.

The abundant Cook pine trees are the legacy of George Campbell Munro, a rancher who planted them in the 1920s in a natural rain-making scheme. The trees snag clouds in their branches to water dry Lanai, situated in the rain-shadow of Haleakala. When it rains, get a good book or find another adventure, because the Munro Trail becomes slick and boggy.

Clubs such as Hawaiian Trail and Mountain and student groups from local colleges post helpful information and maps for Maui hiking on the Web (visit **www.traildatabase.org** for links).

A Pueo Tale

People in Hawaii say owls are sacred. They are considered guardian angels. Hawaiians call them *aumaku;* it means family spirit.

We know people who claim owls have kept them from harm, warned them of danger, shown them the way home. Until one day in early September on Lanai, that sort of superstition struck us merely as quaint, if silly.

Overnight, a tropical rainstorm had battered the tin-roof houses, disturbing the peace of Lanai City. It was a restless night, and we rose before dawn, leaving the empty lodge in search of coffee.

As the sun rose, we could see it would be a good day to seek the 3,379-foot summit of Mount Lanaihale, the island's peak. Up there on a clear day, so longtime Island residents say, you can see six islands in a single glance: Maui, Molokai, the Big Island of Hawaii, Oahu, Kahoolawe, and Molokini. It's one of the eight natural wonders of Hawaii. The spectacle is possible because Lanai sits smack dab in the middle of the inhabited island chain. Only Kauai and Niihau are too far to the northwest to be seen.

In 20 years in the Islands, we had tried often but never managed to top the summit on a clear day. Clouds always obscured the view. Now, the morning after a storm, the clear blue sky held promise and we had a gassed-up Jeep.

A lone owl swooped low over abandoned pineapple fields of Puuwai Basin as we turned left off the two-lane blacktop and followed a red-dirt deer trail toward Lanaihale. Having never seen the Hawaiian *pueo* on the wing, we braked to watch the endangered bird glide across the fields, swooping low in search of prey, finding only little black, flapping scraps of plastic. The owl was the first rare sight that day.

In golden sunlight, we headed up the old shield volcano on the Munro Trail, the narrow, winding razorback ridge road that runs to Lanai's peak.

No road sign shows the way to the summit. No sign tells that you've arrived. A local man in Lanai City had instructed us, "Just go down the road, turn left, go up the hill. No need sign."

The Hawaiian pueo appeared now and again just ahead of the Jeep, obviously pointing the way. It disappeared behind bushes and trees but always reappeared ahead, leading us on.

At the summit, the owl landed on a wind-bent ohia tree and shut its eyes. Our eyes opened to see Maui, Hawaii, Kahoolawe, and Molokini, all laid out on a blue sea chart like a real-life topographic map. We looked for Molokai and Oahu, but trees stood in the way, something of a disappointment.

The owl took wing again. It flew beyond the trees around a bend in the road. We followed to find a clear view of Molokai, more than 30 miles away, and in the distance on the horizon, the thin outline of Oahu.

A rare bird of prey and six Hawaiian islands visible from one peak. Some things must be seen to be believed.

HIKING KAHAKULOA

Standing barefoot in a taro patch, wiggling our toes in the silky mud—it was an odd beginning for a most unusual hike into Kahakuloa Valley, a cleft on Maui's northwest coast where old Hawaii exists as if in a dream.

"Feel how smooth it is," said Oliver Dukelow, the Hawaiian caretaker who tends this taro patch in the valley, just as the first settlers did centuries ago.

The valley, long off-limits to visitors, lies beyond a locked gate like a Polynesian version of Camelot. It's an almost mythic place lost in the mists of time. You may go there now, but only with a guide like Dukelow, who will take you deep into the valley, carved by a stream that's the tag of a silvery waterfall.

Simple, tidy little houses with bright colorful Polynesian *pareau* (sarongs) in the windows stand amid banana and papaya trees and flowers galore on the wide western banks of Kahakuloa Stream, which runs big enough at times to be called a river.

The stream is diverted here and there into *loi,* or taro patches, the cornerstone of Hawaii's early agriculture.

Here, ankle deep in primal mud, Hawaiians share their cultural roots, let you touch hard evidence of early inhabitants—remnants of shrines, platforms, terraces, and heiau. Here, you can see a house that stands in the path of the ghosts called night marchers and hear skin-crawling stories about spirits of ancient alii who stroll with alacrity through the valley, revisiting lifetime haunts.

There in Kahakuloa Valley, by the babbling stream that irrigates the taro, we sat in the sun, talking story, savoring the moment, wishing all Hawaii could be like this. When we had to go it was hard to leave this place, and we suddenly understood the dilemma of the departed and why they return.

For free trail maps, call the State Department of Forestry and Wildlife at ☎ 808-587-0166 or go to **www.hawaiitrails.org.**

More Information

Island bookstores and the Internet offer a wealth of information about Island hikes. Here are a few books for those hoping to discover more of Maui, Molokai, and Lanai on foot:

Hawaiian Hiking Trails, by Craig Chisolm, published by Fernglen Press, 1999. A detailed look at 50 of the best hiking trails on the six major islands.

Great Outdoor Adventures of Hawaii, by Rick Carroll, published by Foghorn Press, San Francisco, 1991. The first ecoguide to Hawaii's best outdoor activities.

Hawaiian Heritage Plants, by Angela Kay Kepler, published by Fernglen Press, 1998. A thorough presentation of native plants, with color photos.

A RARE HIKE BETWEEN HEAVEN AND EARTH

The helicopter drops us on a wilderness ridge, the start of a rare adventure high in the West Maui Mountains. There are a dozen of us, winners of an annual lottery; the prize is a once-in-a-lifetime guided six-mile hike through a virgin cloud forest on 5,871-foot-high Puu Kukui. Off-limits except to scientists, Hawaii's largest private nature preserve is an 8,661-acre, 10-million-year-old enclave of rare native plants, birds, and snails.

Spiky silverswords and unassuming sedges, rare daisies, wild orchids, and giant ferns flourish in a soggy sanctuary traversed by a narrow boardwalk. We stand in total silence amid a hundred shades of green. Nearly everything in the bog is only ankle high, stunted by nature's own high-altitude pruning. It is as if we've suddenly grown 20 feet tall. Venturing out on the boardwalk, one cautious step at a time, guide Randy Bartlett warns that each foot of bog depth represents 10,000 years. A hiker's foot slips off the boardwalk and sinks an inch or so, back to about AD 650. Having gently pried the shoe from the viscous muck, the phrase "bogged down" takes on new meaning.

As we hike on, the almost surreal beauty of the setting emerges in tiny details. Little damsel flies dart across Lake Violet, so small and hopelessly blue it looks like a broken mirror that fell from the sky. Miniature Hawaiian land snails ease across the moss. Puffy clouds scud over Eke Crater, a lofty plateau amid spiky peaks. Survivors of "the great flood at the beginning of time" landed their canoe on Eke, according to Hawaiian legend. New Age disciples claim Eke is the landing zone of extraterrestrials. Neither canoe nor spacecraft is in evidence this day; we are the only strangers here.

Take your chances with Kapalua Nature Center, Kapalua Resort's eco-tourism arm, which holds the Puu Kukui lottery and also conducts guided hiking tours in Kapalua's 17,000 acres of Upcountry watershed and pineapple plantation lands. Call Kapalua Nature Society at ☎ 808-669-0244.

Trees of Hawaii, by Angela Kay Kepler, published by University of Hawaii Press, 1990. A colorful and informative look at native and introduced trees.

Hawaii's Birds, published by the Hawaii Audubon Society, 1993. A full-color guide to native and introduced birds in the Islands.

A GOOD WALK

MAUI HAS SEVERAL GOOD WALKS TO ENJOY, including the following favorites. One goes to an ethereal state park, one strolls through a nearby turn-of-the-20th-century plantation town, and yet another takes a look at Lahaina's rich past.

Find the Needle

For a quick and cooling jungle fix, leave the toasty beaches behind, bring a picnic, and head up beyond Wailuku to Iao Valley, a misty state park filled with tropical plants, rainbows, waterfalls, swimming holes, and hiking trails, all rimmed by green mountains. It was the scene of a fierce battle in 1790, when King Kamehameha fought to gain control of Maui. When the fighting ended, so many bodies blocked Iao Stream that the battle site was named Kepaniwai, "damming of the waters."

Now the area has been transformed into a plantation heritage architectural park, with examples of cottages in Hawaiian, Japanese, Chinese, Filipino, and New England styles. Nearby is the Maui Nature Center, offering guided hikes, rain-forest displays, and nature interpretive programs for children and others who like to learn.

Iao Valley Road ends at a parking lot for people stopping to view the landmark Iao Needle, a finger of basalt pointing skyward. The natural stone monument is a requisite photo-op stop that draws bus tours, but its singular beauty cannot be denied.

A Walk Through Wailuku

Wailuku, the 19th-century hillside plantation town overlooking Maui's north shore and central valley, was made for walking. The county seat of Maui since 1905, Wailuku is not all government business. It's slowly becoming a charming collection of funky shops, antiques stores, art galleries, and bistros. A federally funded Main Street restoration program helped put a spit shine on the old brown shoe, but Wailuku and its tin-roof clapboard structures still have the flavor of early Maui and the days of sugar rule.

Several interesting shops are clustered along Market Street. After sipping what may be Maui's best lattes at **Cafe Marc Aurel,** check out the art galleries, antiques stores, goldsmiths, and jewelry shops, where black pearls gleam in the windows. Handsome Chinese and Japanese antiques dominate the collection at **Gottling Ltd.,** oldest of the Antique Row shops of Wailuku. Worth a look: **Sig Zane's** original bold and graphic aloha shirts and muumuu at 53 Market Street, and next door, **Gallerie Ha,** where local artist Pat Matsumoto paints papayas, pineapples, and various close-ups of female body parts. Browse through the Farmer's Market next door, where apple bananas, fresh pineapple, and exotic Asian veggies can be bought at bargain prices.

Bird of Paradise is a most unusual shop at 56 North Market Street. Joe R. Myhand has gathered an amazing array of Hawaii antiques, collectibles, and artifacts that range from poi pounders to Hawaii license plates.

Get the local "scoops" at *Maui Time Weekly,* the free newspaper published every Friday in a second-story loft on Market Street, or visit **www.mauitimeweekly.com.**

Don't leave town without visiting **Bailey House Museum,** an 1833 missionary home that houses the Maui Historical Society and a good selection of made-in-Hawaii arts and crafts in the gift shop. The Bailey House Museum is at 2375-A Main Street; call ☎ 808-244-3920 for details.

Hungry for lunch? Do what Wailukuans do: go to **Sam Sato's** at 1750 Wili Pa Loop (☎ 808-244-7124) for the town's best Japanese/Hawaiian saimin noodle soup laced with your choice of chicken, fish, or pork. Or try **A Saigon Café** at 1792 Main Street (☎ 808-243-9560).

Historic Lahaina

Lahaina's reputation as a party town goes way back. Blessed with a sheltered harbor, Lahaina was once the hub of the Hawaiian kingdom and also a rowdy winter R&R stop for the whalers and sailors who roamed the Pacific more than a century ago.

When New England whalers hit Lahaina in the 1800s, they found strong drink, sweet-smelling girls, and the tattoo parlor. You may still find them all in Lahaina, including Skin Deep, the Front Street tattoo parlor. The last time we stopped by, a Kona boat captain was having a shark etched on his ankle and an ex–fighter pilot from the Netherlands was getting a sea chart of the seven inhabited Hawaiian Islands tattooed in four colors on his left shoulder. Good thing he liked Hawaii better than the Philippines—it's got 7,108 islands. Best-selling tattoos at Skin Deep seem to be Japanese and Chinese ideograms, and those wraparound Polynesian bands of black-and-white triangles for biceps and ankles. Sailors don't get "Mom" or "Remember Pearl Harbor" tattooed on their forearms anymore.

The missionaries left their tempering influence, too. There's so much to see in the relatively compact town of Lahaina that we've included a walking-tour map to help make sure you don't miss the sights. Free maps and information are available from the Maui Visitors Bureau and at key locations in Lahaina town.

History is found on every corner in the bustling town, now crowded with tourists from around the world. You can thank members of the Lahaina Restoration Foundation, who work tirelessly to keep Lahaina's history alive in its original buildings. Arrange a special group guided tour or take the self-guided walk back in time past Government House, Lahaina Prison, U.S. Seamen's Hospital and Seamen's Cemetery, the Hale Pai print shop, Wo Hing Temple, and the Pioneer Inn, circa 1901, at the corner of Hotel and Wharf streets. Teachers, take note: One of the first things the missionaries established was Lahaina Luna High School, the oldest operating public school in the West, still housing students up the hill from the town center.

Begin at a former Master's Reading Room for sea captains, the mariners' haunt for a time after the missionaries shut down Lahaina's grog shops and banned prostitution. The oldest building on Maui, it is now the coral-block headquarters of **Lahaina Restoration Foundation.** Next door is the **Baldwin Home** at Dickenson and Front streets, which once was home to the family of Reverend Dwight

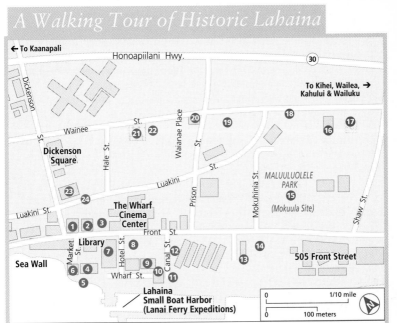

A Walking Tour of Historic Lahaina

← To Kaanapali

Honoapiilani Hwy.

30

To Kihei, Wailea, →
Kahului & Wailuku

Dickenson

Wainee   St.

21 22

20   19   18

16   17

Waianae Place

St.

Dickenson Square

Hale St.

Luakini   St.

MALUULUOLELE PARK

15

(Mokuula Site)

Mokuhinia St.

Shaw St.

23

24

Luakini St.

The Wharf Cinema Center

Prison

Front St.

Library

Market St.

Hotel St.

7   8

Canal St.

12

14

13

505 Front Street

Sea Wall

6   4

9

10 11

5

Wharf St.

Lahaina
Small Boat Harbor
(Lanai Ferry Expeditions)

0   1/10 mile
0   100 meters

● ATTRACTIONS
1. Masters' Reading Room
2. Baldwin Home
3. Richards House
4. Taro Patch
5. Hauola Stone
6. Brick Palace
7. Pioneer Inn
8. Banyan Tree

9. Courthouse
10. Fort
11. Canal
12. Government Market
13. Holy Innocents
        Episcopal Church
14. Hale Piula
15. Maluuluolele Park
        (Mokuula Site)

16. Wainee Church
17. Waihee Cemetery
18. Hongwanji Mission
19. David Malo's Home
20. Old Prison
21. Episcopal Cemetery
22. Hale Aloha
23. Buddhist Church
24. Luakini Street

Baldwin, a missionary doctor who built it in 1834. After nearly 20 years' service, he was granted 2,600 acres of land at Kapalua and began experimenting with the golden fruit Hawaiians called *hala kahiki*—pineapple. The Baldwins remain one of Maui's most prominent families, and pineapple is still a significant cash crop, now spreading over thousands of acres at Kapalua.

Don't miss the ancient giant banyan tree whose wandering aerial roots take up a whole block. For a historic brew, stop at the **Pioneer Inn.** Browse the art galleries, but brace yourself for some high-pressure salesmen peddling whale art.

Someday Lahaina's treasures will expand with a truly important addition—Mokuula, the first native Hawaiian historic jewel to join the ranks of Lahaina's restored heritage sites. Across the street from the **505 Front Street** complex, underneath tons of sand and dirt in a softball park, is the sacred site of the royal home of Prince Kauikeaolui, who became King Kamehameha III in 1825 at the age of

10. The palace, built on an island in a small lake, was also the setting for a very sad love story. The king lived there with his sister, Princess Nahienaena. The relationship was viewed by Hawaiian nobility as appropriate royal behavior in order to protect royal bloodlines, but the just-arrived missionaries saw this incestuous marriage as the horrifying work of the devil. The princess, torn between her love for her brother and the newly imposed Western morality, grew despondent and died at the age of 21. Kamehameha III lived on to preside over 29 eventful years in the Islands, a time when the kingdom became a constitutional monarchy and power and land began shifting into the hands of the opportunistic Westerners—missionaries, sugar planters, and merchants. The palace was plowed under in 1918, but a fundraising campaign is under way to bring it back to life.

Award-winning tours by **Maui Nei Native Expeditions** led by certified *kumu* and chanters offer a unique, accurate cultural experience. A two-hour walking tour of Lahaina is the most popular; other guided tours go to Haleki'i and Pihana Heiau, Iao Valley, Bailey House Museum, and Haleakala. For more information, visit **www .mokuula.com.**

NATIONAL *and* STATE PARKS

BESIDES NUMEROUS FOREST RESERVES, PRIVATE LAND sanctuaries, and county and city parks, Maui County is home to a major national park, three state parks, and a state recreation area. The crown jewel of Maui's public lands is Haleakala National Park, the celebrated House of the Sun, which encompasses the dormant volcano from its 10,023-foot alpine summit to the sea on its southeastern, tropical-wilderness side, at Kipahulu near Hana. Of its 28,655 acres, 19,270 are wilderness. Haleakala National Park was designated an International Biosphere Reserve in 1980. Its heights, above the vast caldera, house an Air Force Super Computer telescope that peers into near-space, searching out satellites that might be spying on the United States. Its depths are a world away, a rain forest where waterfall pools plunge into the sea. In between are a dizzying array of microclimates, from high lava desert to cloud forest and fertile uplands to coastal tropics, with rare plants and endangered birds.

Altogether, Haleakala is a singular ecological wonder that should not be missed, especially since it's easy to see. So set aside at least a day for Haleakala, if not a sunrise. Sunrise over the crater is a mystical experience that few viewers find disappointing, even though they arose in the middle of the night to drive up to see it. Maui's most famous ride is the guided bike tour on specially equipped cycles down the entire mountain (see the section "Bicycling: Pedal Power").

Haleakala National Park, Upcountry Maui

LOCATION The summit area is accessible by way of Roads 37, 377, and 378 up the mountain through Kula, a community at the 3,000-foot level. The park entrance is above Kula. The drive to the top takes at least three hours round-trip from the Kahului area below. Add more time to get to and from resort areas. Kipahulu, at the island's East End, between Hana and Kaupo, can be reached via Hana Highway. Driving time is about three hours between Kahului and Kipahulu.

Phone ☎ 808-572-4400

Web site **www.nps.gov/hale**

Hours Park Ranger headquarters open daily, 7:30 a.m.–4 p.m.; Visitor Center open daily, sunrise–3 p.m.

Admission $10 per vehicle, good for a week; $5 per person without a vehicle.

WHEN TO GO Anytime. Haleakala is renowned for dramatic sunsets and sunrises. Be sure to arrive at least 30 minutes early. It's also well worth the drive at other times of day—including evenings after dark, when it is a fabulous place for stargazing.

HOW MUCH TIME TO ALLOW Up to half a day, depending on whether you take part in park programs. Rangers offer guided hikes on all Haleakala's trails, at the cindery summit, in the cloud forest, or down below in the lush tropical forests of Kipahulu. These are a good option for exploring the park. Take your pick of environments.

COMMENTS At the summit, the park headquarters and visitor center house cultural and natural history exhibits. Haleakala, originally part of Hawaii Volcanoes National Park, was designated as an individual park in July 1961.

In the Kipahulu area, all trails begin at the ranger station/visitor center. The Kuloa Point Trail is an easy half-mile loop toward the ocean that affords a look at the pools and waterfalls, as well as the sea and the Big Island, but go early or late if you want to avoid crowds. Enjoy a picnic on the grass next to the remnants of an ancient fishing shrine and house site.

Check the park bulletin board for a schedule of daily programs and guided hikes. Obey posted warnings. Because the weather at the summit is unpredictable—temperatures range from 40°F to 65°F, but with wind chill factored in, can dip below freezing—wear lightweight, layered clothing and comfortable, sturdy shoes. No restaurants or gas stations are available in the park. People with heart or breathing problems should use caution because of the high elevation and thin air.

Limited drive-in and wilderness overnight camping is permitted in the crater and below at Kipahulu. The Hosmer Grove Campground in the summit area is located just inside the park entrance (see the "Camping in the Wilds" section for details).

Haleakala National Park

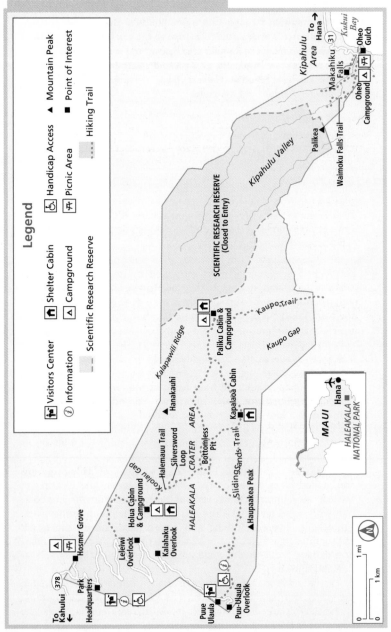

STATE PARKS

FOR INFORMATION ON HAWAII'S EXTENSIVE SYSTEM of state parks, recreation areas, beach parks, historic sites, and other points of interest, write to the Division of State Parks, 1151 Punchbowl Street, Room 310, Honolulu, HI 96813, or call ☎ 808-587-0300. The State Parks Office on Maui is located in Wailuku (☎ 808-984-8109).

For a free Maui recreation map detailing hiking trails and other points of interest, contact the State Department of Land and Natural Resources office on Maui, 54 South High Street, Room 101, Wailuku, HI 96793, or call ☎ 808-873-3506.

In addition to Waianapanapa State Park near Hana (described under Beaches) and Iao Valley State Park (described under Hiking), another standout is found in the cloud-forest high country, for dedicated hikers and drivers willing to take on a challenging mountain road off Highway 377 above Kula.

Polipoli Spring State Recreation Area, Central Maui
LOCATION **Waipoli Road, 10.5 miles above Highway 377.**

COMMENTS Way off the beaten path at the 6,000-foot level of Haleakala in the Kula Forest Reserve, surprises await the intrepid few who make it past the narrow, bumpy, switchback road that climbs 3,000 feet in the first six miles. This is a "good weather" expedition, more treacherous than fun in wet weather. Once in the ten-acre park, hikers will find themselves surrounded by towering redwoods. Hardy trekkers can climb another 1,000 feet to the top of a cinder cone with an amazing view of neighboring islands in the blue sea. Below Polipoli, connecting trails (Redwood, Plum, Haleakala Ridge, and Polipoli) form a satisfying 3.5-mile loop. Other trails of varying difficulty offer great views. One cabin is available through reservation with the State Parks Office in Wailuku, ☎ 808-984-8109.

Palaau State Park, Molokai
LOCATION **End of Kalae Highway in Palaau.**

COMMENTS This leafy 230-acre park overlooks historic Kalaupapa, the peninsula where people stricken with Hansen's disease (leprosy) were once banished. Picnicking and camping areas are available. A short trail leads to a monolithic stone aptly named Phallic Rock, reputed to enhance fertility in women who sleep beside it overnight. Take a short walk to the very edge for an awesome view of the island's north shore.

CAMPING *in the* WILDS

CAMPSITES ON MAUI, MOLOKAI, AND LANAI, while limited in number and sometimes tough to reserve, come in a royal choice of setting—beachside, hunkered under sheltering groves of trees or out in a meadow beside waterfall pools; and upland, surrounded by open mountain terrain or lush (wet) rain forests. Nearly all require camping permits. Book as far ahead as possible, and be prepared to compete with residents in a lottery to get the permits. Camping is the affordable way to vacation in the Islands.

For gear, you'll need a tent with a rain flap or tarp to ward off overnight showers, a ground pad, and lightweight sleeping bags (to sleep on more often than in, unless you're headed for cool higher altitudes). You'll need bug repellent and drinking water, a water purifier, or a container to boil water until it's safe. Don't drink wild, untreated water.

The Islands have some bugs of tropical proportions, capable of nasty stings—giant centipedes, five inches or longer; small, delicate scorpions in rocky areas; and black widow and brown recluse spiders under damp wood. Shake out your shoes and bed gear before using them, and wear shoes or use a flashlight to watch your step, even in soft grass at night. Other than tropical creepy crawlies, the only animals there to encounter in the wild are escaped pets, chickens or turkeys, and the occasional feral pig or goat. You can scare them away by making lots of noise or sudden movements. Otherwise, leave them alone and they'll extend the same courtesy. Some plants are poisonous to eat, so consume nothing you're not entirely familiar with.

If you want to camp without lugging all the gear from home, rent equipment from suppliers such as those listed below, most of which also rent kayaks, mountain bikes, and other outdoor equipment.

WHERE TO CAMP

HERE ARE OUR SUGGESTED CAMPSITES. You may also wish to contact the state parks mentioned previously to inquire about sites and availability. Not all campgrounds require or grant reservations, but we strongly recommend making them whenever possible. Remember to get groceries and gas before you head to Haleakala National Park, home to our three Maui Island picks. A good resource to learn more is *Camping Hawaii*, written by resident camping expert Richard McMahon and published by the University of Hawaii Press.

Holua Wilderness Campground, Upcountry Maui
LOCATION Inside Haleakala Crater, 4 miles down the Halemauu Trail.

Type of camping Tent and cabin camping.

Permit Tent permits are issued at the park headquarters on a first-come, first-serve basis on the day of use. The campground is limited to 25 people, with no more than 12 in a single group. Reservations for wilderness cabins at Holua (and those at Paliku and Kapalaoa) must be made 3 months in advance. Be sure to include alternate dates. Write to Haleakala National Park, P.O. Box 369, Makawao, HI 96768; call ☎ 808-572-4400 or go to **www.nps.gov/hale.**

Stay limit 3 nights.

Park Safety and Rules

- Guard against tropical sunburn in high, thin air.
- Never leave your valuables unattended in a car at a scenic lookout.
- Drinking or possession of alcoholic beverages is prohibited in parks.
- Build fires only in fireplaces and grills. Portable stoves and other warming devices may be used in designated picnicking and camping areas.
- Do not disturb any plants or geological, historical, or archaeological features.

Cost Free for tent campers. The 3 cabins are $40 (accommodates 1–6 people) and $80 (7–12 people) per night.

COMMENTS Awe-inspiring views of Haleakala Crater, big enough to contain Manhattan with room to spare, are among the highlights here at the near-7,000-foot elevation. You are likely to meet the endangered nene goose, the state bird, and see the rare native silversword plants that bloom only once in 15 years, then die. Facilities for tent camping are sparse, and the campground is rocky. Cabins contain bunks with mattresses (but no bed linens), table, chairs, cooking utensils, and a wood-burning stove with firewood.

Hosmer Grove, Upcountry Maui

LOCATION At the 6,800-foot level, just off Haleakala Crater Road. Watch for the sign for Hosmer Grove, which is almost 10 miles from the Crater Road turnoff.

Type of camping Tent and vehicle camping. Vehicles must stay in the parking lot.

Permits None required; first come, first served. The campground is limited to 25 people, with no more than 12 in a single group.

Stay limit 3 nights.

Cost Free.

COMMENTS The campground, a grassy clearing surrounded by trees, has a covered pavilion with 2 picnic tables and 2 grills, restrooms, and drinkable water. Hiking is the activity of choice. A half-mile loop nature trail begins at one end of the parking lot. Pick up hiking trail information at the park headquarters. Bring extra blankets—it can get cold at night.

. . . and why are we the only ones enjoying this incomparable grandeur? Why aren't there thousands of people climbing over one another to hang all around the rim of 'the greatest extinct crater in the world?' Such reputation ought to be irresistible. Why, there's nothing on earth so wonderful as this!"

—Jack London, quoted in
Our Hawaii Islands and Islanders by Charmian K. London

Kipahulu Campground, Upcountry Maui
LOCATION **Hana Highway, about 10 miles past Hana.**

Type of camping Tent and vehicle camping.

Permits None required. Space is limited to 100 people on a first-come, first-serve basis. On busy holiday weekends, arrive early to get your space.

Stay limit 3 nights.

Cost Free.

COMMENTS Camping in this extraordinary spot, a grassy area overlooking the sea and the Oheo Gulch pools and waterfalls, is so memorable that even noncampers ought to get a tent and give it a try. Facilities include restrooms, picnic tables, and grills, plus the showers and pools provided by nature. Bring drinking water. No food or gas is available. Swimming and jungle hiking are right at hand.

Exploring the infamous curvy road to Hana and its old-time villages, swimmable waterfall pools, and botanical gardens can be one of Maui's finest experiences when you combine the long drive with an overnight stay in the Hana area. Lodging is limited in Hana, and camping at Kipahulu is a fun alternative. Also nearby is Waianapanapa State Park (at the end of Waianapanapa Road off the Hana Highway; ☎ 808-984-8109).

Papohaku Beach Park, Molokai
LOCATION **Just off Kaluakoi Road, western shore. Head west on Highway 460 to the turnoff to the Kaluakoi Resort; continue past the hotel along Kaluakoi Road.**

Type of camping Tent and vehicle camping.

Permits Available at the Pauole Center Multipurpose Building in Kaunakakai. For advance reservations and more information, write to the Maui County Parks Department at P.O. Box 526, Kaunakakai, HI 96748, or call ☎ 808-553-3204.

Stay limit 3 nights.

Cost $3 per person per night.

COMMENTS This site is both easily accessible and fairly isolated. Facilities include restrooms, showers, picnic tables, grills, and drinking water. One drawback is that the water is too rough for swimming.

Hulopoe Beach Park, Lanai
LOCATION **At the end of the road in Manele Harbor.**

Type of camping Tent camping at 3 sites, limited to 6 people each.

Permits Camping on this privately owned island requires a permit. Write to Lanai Company, Attn: Camping Permits, P.O. Box 310, Lanai City, HI 96763; or call ☎ 808-565-8206.

Stay limit 1 week.

Cost $5 per person per night.

COMMENTS Right up the hill, high-rollers are paying the price of your plane ticket per night to stay at the elegant Four Seasons Resort Lanai at Manele Bay. The next morning, you're already at the beach. You can thank island residents who fought to save their right to use this picturesque beach when the island owner considered making it off-limits to all but his guests. Park facilities include restrooms, showers, picnic tables, grills, and drinking water.

▌▌ BICYCLING: *Pedal Power*

EXPLORING THE ISLANDS BY BIKE puts you in touch with your surroundings at your own speed. The Islands have mountains in the middle, which adds a challenging element. The most popular cycle adventure on Maui is cruising down the steep and scenic slopes of Haleakala Crater. Several tour companies will put you on special downhill-cruising bikes with heavy-duty brakes to keep you under control on the 38-mile descent down a serpentine road. From the summit to the seashore, you streak past pasturelands, farms, and forests. Some companies also provide hotel transportation and a snack; others offer unguided tours, letting you set your own pace. Be forewarned: Some deceptive grades and curves coming down the mountain have launched even experienced bikers over the side. Take the curves more slowly than you normally would. Dress in layers; the top third of the ride is alpine, while the bottom is tropical.

It's not even close to dawn, but here you are, rubbing your eyes awake, on the top of Maui's sleeping volcano. It's colder than you ever thought possible for a tropical island. The air is thin. Your shoes grind in the clinkers, crunch crunch, as you stomp your chilly feet while you wait, sipping some hot brew. Then comes the sun, exploding over the yawning Haleakala Crater. A mystic moment you won't soon forget, imprinted on a palette of dawn colors. Now you know why Hawaiians named it the House of the Sun. But there's no time to linger. Decked out in your screaming yellow parka, you mount your special steed and test its most important feature—the brakes. You are awake enough now to hear the instructions, the safety cautions, the itinerary. And off you go through the colorful early morning,

- Wear a helmet and comfortable shoes.
- If possible, carry a first-aid kit and cell phone in case of emergency.
- Familiarize yourself with your rental bike and the tropical heat and humidity before riding off.
- Ride with a partner or a group.
- Bring drinking water, sunscreen, and sunglasses.
- If traveling in a group, keep at least five lengths between riders.
- Don't use headphones while riding or get distracted by views.
- Novice mountain bikers should avoid narrow, single-track trails, which sometimes skirt the edge of dangerous cliffs. Instead, ride on the dirt roads.

a line of downhill cruisers, wobbly at first until you get the knack. You're about to see Maui top to bottom, a 38-mile coast down a 10,000-foot volcano. In a few hours. On a bike!

In the past millennia, Haleakala erupted every 200 years or so. It last erupted in 1790, which means it could be overdue right now. Hold that thought as you scan the black-and-brown cindery landscape for a glimpse of Hawaii's endangered bird, the nene goose, which has adapted claw feet for walking on sharp lava. Or a spiky silversword plant, growing determinedly in the scorched earth. This is quite a landscape, but it's just the beginning. You've got a lot more to see. Besides, if it erupted, you could probably outrun the flow on your cruiser bike.

Maui's single greatest physical feature is Haleakala, a mountain so big many people don't see it. By midday, the summit and the white knobs of observatories are often lost above a wreath of clouds. But your morning ride is sunny and crystal clear, as grass and trees begin to cover the lumpy volcanic terrain. By the time you get to Kula, it's an over-the-rainbow experience. Tall, fragrant eucalyptus forests. Blooming blue jacaranda. Flower farms and emerald pastures. Pleasantly cool temperatures, sweet country smells, a horsey idyll from a romance novel. There should be a yellow brick road for your bikes.

Down below, past the cane fields and commuter communities, you cruise to your objective—the sea-level floor of Maui—and return to the tropical breezes and warm seas, just the way you left them. This swim will be the best ever.

Multiple biking tours are available. **Backroads**, the well-known bike vacation agency in Berkeley (call ☎ 800-462-2848 or visit **www. backroads.com**), has multisport adventures on Maui and Lanai.

Maui has bike-friendly lanes on some roads, with stunning views of neighboring Molokai, Lanai, and Kahoolawe. One road-biking candidate is the one-lane road around Maui's northwest end between Kahului and Kapalua. The scenery and the winding road slow

BIKE RENTAL SHOPS

MAUI

Haleakala Bike Co.: Haiku Marketplace, Haiku; ☎ 808-575-9575;
www.bikemaui.com

Island Biker: 415 Dairy Road, Kahului; ☎ 808-877-7744;
www.islandbikermaui.com

South Maui Bicycles: 1993 South Kihei Road # 5, Kihei; ☎ 808-874-0068

West Maui Bicycles: 840 Wainee Street, C-5, Lahaina; ☎ 808-661-9005;
www.westmauicycles.com

MOLOKAI

Molokai Bicycle: 80 Mohala Street, Kaunakakai; ☎ 808-553-3931;
www.bikehawaii.com/molokaibicycle

everyone down. Stop and get a refreshing shaved ice at Kahakuloa. Or drive up to Kula, on the 3,000-foot shoulder of Haleakala, park the car, and cruise by bike along the hilly country road to Ulupalakua Ranch and back, through flower farms, blue jacaranda trees, botanical gardens, and pastures. If you want to do it with special equipment and a tour with an expert, **Aloha Bicycle Tours,** run by a former state bicycling champion, cruises Upcountry Maui, starting after breakfast from a point just inside the Haleakala National Park entrance rather than the top of the summit. Bikers go at their own pace down 21 switchback turns through Haleakala Ranch and stop when they like, en route to the Tedeschi Winery at Ulupalakua Ranch for picnic lunch and wine tasting. For information, call ☎ 800-749-1564 or 808-249-0911, or visit **www.mauibike.com.**

Maui, Lanai, and Molokai are terrific places for mountain biking, with a wide range of terrain, scenic sites, and trails. The favorite Maui venue for mountain bikers is Polipoli Spring State Park, where you'll find more than ten miles of single-track that winds through thick forests of eucalyptus and redwood trees. Molokai, with 125 miles of trails, is a favorite playground for mountain bikers. For off-road bike adventures on Molokai, go to Molokai Ranch, where you can stay in a plush tent cabin, eat communally in camp pavilions, and do your pedaling thing on the 52,000-acre ranch's superb single-track. Mountain biking is one of several activities included in the price of your stay. Here and elsewhere, the rugged trails provide optimal riding conditions, from dusty coastlines to lush forests. Plenty of dirt roads on Lanai call to mountain bikers, as well as the challenging climb to the 3,370-foot summit of Lanaihale, the island's highest point. Several of Lanai's destinations make appealing day trips by bike. You can ride the Expeditions ferry from Lahaina to Lanai for $25 per person plus $10 for the bike. Get ready for an exceptional workout. **Hawaii Bicycling League** (☎ 808-735-5756 or 877-682-7433; **www.hbl.org**)

offers bike-route maps and rides to remote places like sacred Kaaawa Valley on Oahu's windward side. They also issue a newsletter for local biking enthusiasts. John Alford's *Mountain Biking the Hawaiian Islands* features maps and photos as well as detailed descriptions of best biking trails. You can order it through **www.bikehawaii.com**.

Daily rentals run roughly $20–$35 for a mountain bike and $20 for a road bike.

HORSEBACK RIDING:
Back in the Saddle

YOU MAY NOT OFTEN THINK OF MAUI as part of the Wild West, but it's really way out there.

Horses were brought to the Islands more than a century ago, and a grateful populace, who had either walked or sailed everywhere before that, eagerly took to riding when they got the chance. Big ranch spreads blossomed across the open volcanic slopes. Horseback riding is the best way to get off the roads and into the countryside of those vast ranches that invite visitors to come for tropical trail rides. In the Islands, the wide-open spaces lead between volcanoes, along beaches and sea cliffs, and into jungled valleys with waterfalls. The horses are well trained and know their trails, leaving you free to enjoy the views. Riding adventures abound on Maui, Molokai, and Lanai, with colorful and personable guides to share local lore. Rates range from $35 per person for a one-hour ride to $60–$100 for a two-hour trek. A three-hour ride, with lunch, runs $130.

Call for age, height, and weight restrictions if you're concerned: the minimum age for riders is usually 8 years old but may be higher, and the maximum weight ranges up to 275 pounds. Book your reservation at least a day in advance, or a week ahead if you have a group. Most rides are limited to 12 people. You can secure a reservation with a credit card, and most operators also accept traveler's checks or cash. Call on the morning of your ride (or leave a phone number where you can be reached) to check weather conditions. All riders must sign liability waivers.

Prior riding experience is not a requirement; first-time riders are common. Operators will ask your experience level and match you to an appropriate horse. The group goes at the pace of the least-experienced rider. An orientation on horsemanship and safety precautions for the island's conditions precedes the tour. Some ranches offer intermediate- and advanced-level rides. Most stables use thoroughbreds and quarterhorses. Rides often include stops for a picnic lunch or barbecue, a sampling of local fruit, or a cooling-off swim. Full-cover shoes or boots are mandatory, long pants are suggested, and sun protection such as a hat and long-sleeved shirt are strongly recommended.

Ride to the Source

The horses' forelocks are wrapped in cowhide to guard against the razor's edge of lava. Slowly, our train of riders picks its way around jagged shards of lava. A fall in this *terra terribilis* could slash a person to shreds.

Riders lean far forward in the saddle as we head from Makena up the south side of Haleakala on Maui's Ulupalakua Ranch, a vertical spread on a nearly two-mile-high volcano that's not done yet. This old volcano is officially classified as dormant, meaning it could go off at any moment. Not today, we hope.

We are riding to Puu Mahoe, origin of lava that spilled from Haleakala Crater around 1790, the last time Maui experienced a volcanic eruption.

In the deep time of geology, that's only yesterday. Admiral Jean-Francois Galoup, Compte de la Perouse, the first white man to set foot on Maui on May 29, 1786, described "a shore made hideous by an ancient lava flow," and sailed on after meeting friendly coastal villagers, never to be seen again, yet another mystery of the Pacific.

The old, black lava reflects the sun's heat deep into your bones. A wide-brimmed hat and water in your saddlebag are must-haves.

The thought of eruption is very much on our minds as we ride to Maui's youngest crater. We ride by kiawe with stiletto thorns that can pierce a leather boot, past old, sun-bleached bones (human or animal, no one knows), across wide stretches of nothing but lava—lava that once was molten hot and dribbling down to the shore.

Nothing stirs in this dead zone except fine clouds of suffocating red dust kicked up by our horses. Riders wipe their sweating faces—another must-have is a bandanna—as we ride on deeper into the land of Pele, Hawaii's fire goddess.

We rein in at the source: a classic cone crater with a telltale tongue of pahoehoe sticking out its downhill lip.

Walk to the edge, look down the throat of this old crater's hellhole, and you see only dead ashes. Way down there somewhere the pot still boils.

From there to the sea, Maui looks like an 18th-century engraving of itself, an island frozen in time, smothered by miles of lava in every direction as far as the eye can see, a black and silent place—Pele's world.

Out of the sun-struck sea a whale leaps. In that moment, on the dormant crater, Maui seems to have returned to a primeval state. We saddle up, glad to head down Haleakala and return to the present.

MAUI'S BEST HORSEBACK-RIDING ADVENTURES

Just Say Giddyup

If you wonder how to talk to a horse and make sense, or make a horse do what you want without a struggle, sign up for an **Adventure on Horseback** with wrangler Frank Levinson, also known as "the horse whisperer," on his 55-acre ranch in Haiku, on the way to Hana. He teaches you how to use the techniques made famous in Robert Redford's 1997 film, *The Horse Whisperer,* to train horses with respect and understanding instead of fear and punishment. If you learn improved motivational skills or something else pertinent to your personal life as well as equine psychology, so much the better. In Levinson's The Maui Horse Whisperer Experience program, you don't even have to ride but can elect simply to learn more about horses and spend a day or half a day in the tropical ranch country. Naturally, participants can elect to ride and put their skills to use. He offers a range of trail rides and a special program for families with teenagers, Horse Sense for Humans. You can talk, walk, and ride with horses, and private guided trail rides can be arranged. After you learn how to talk to your horse, go on a trail ride along the coast or through rain forest to a tropical waterfall pool for lunch. Something to whisper about back home.

For details, contact **Adventures on Horseback** at P.O. Box 1419, Makawao; ☎ 808-572-6211; or visit **www.mauihorses.com.**

Riding Ulupalakua Ranch

Trail riding on historic Ulupalakua Ranch affords a view of Maui you never suspected and can't get any other way. On Maui's largest ranch, a 20,000-acre spread that extends across the southwestern flanks of Haleakala, horses nimbly pick their way through razor-sharp lava on a trail to the last volcanic eruption site on Maui. Sometime around 1790, at about 2,000 feet, a crater belched fire and smoke and sent red-hot lava spilling into the sea five miles away.

The ribbons of black lava fanned out to create hundreds of acres of badlands in this dry territory, dotted by native ohia trees and thorny kiawe brush.

The black lunar-like landscape is a stark contrast to the sights below—the green waters of Ahihi-Kinau, a marine sanctuary of tropical fish; the deep, blue Pacific; and in the distance across the ocean channel, the Island of Kahoolawe, former military bombing-practice target now being rescued by Hawaiians. If you go at sunset, look for the fabled green flash. The green flash is a fleeting spot of intense stoplight green that occurs on the horizon for a split second just after the sun sets, or as it is rising. It's best seen when the horizon is cloud-free, especially in winter.

Contact **Makena Stables** in South Maui, ☎ 808-879-0244 or **www.makenastables.com**, for information about guided two- and three-hour rides up the moody mountain.

Inside the Crater

When the **Pony Express** trail boss saddles up his tour on the south rim of Haleakala Crater, it's all downhill at first. He takes you down, down,

down inside Haleakala on a unique trail ride only possible on Maui. The trail begins at Sliding Sands Trailhead (elevation 9,800 feet) and ends 2,500 feet below the rim, 3.8 miles later at Ka Moa O Pele Junction, where you dismount, often bowlegged, for a picnic lunch in a lunar setting. You may ride in and out of fog, brilliant sunshine, sometimes rain, and even snow; weather in the crater is unpredictable and changes fast. You may spot wild nene geese, Hawaii's endangered state bird, and the rare silversword plant Hawaiians call *ahinahina*. Experienced riders take the 12-mile round-trip to the Bottomless Pit, where volcano goddess Pele once lived. Then it's up, up, up all the way back.

Contact **Pony Express Tours** at P.O. Box 535, Kula; ☎ 808-667-2200 or visit **www.ponyexpresstours.com.**

Mauka to Makai

The Mendes Ranch is a 300-acre working cattle ranch with all the essential elements of earthly paradise—rainbows, waterfalls, palm trees, coral sand beaches, lagoons, tide pools, and a mountain rain forest. You see it all on horseback on a ride that runs mauka to makai (mountain to the sea). The trail takes you past longhorn steers, Brahma bulls, and wild horses. If you know how to ride, the trail boss will match you to a great steed and let you go for a gallop, rare for any trail ride. The two-hour morning ride on Maui's wild northeast coast ends at the corral with a Maui-style cowboy barbecue with steak and beans.

Contact **Mendes Ranch and Trail Rides** at 3530 Kahekili Highway (four miles beyond Wailuku); ☎ 808-244-7320 or visit **www.mendes ranch.com.**

Molokai Mule Ride

The sea cliffs are a gasp. Almost vertical, they rise 3,000 feet out of the Pacific. You descend on a zigzag trail of 26 hairpin turns carved out of the rock in 1887. You can hike down and back (and save $150), but most prefer to ride a nimble mule. "We've never lost a rider yet," says trail boss Buzzy Sproat, whose trusted mule train daily traverses the breathtaking three-mile trail. A surefooted mule is the steed you want on this trail ride down the world's steepest sea cliffs. The ride's a thriller, but the destination's chilling—Kalaupapa Peninsula, a place of haunting beauty and sad history. Here, 11,000 banished victims of leprosy lived in exile in the late 19th century, below the cliffs, which separated them from the rest of the island. Today, the peninsula is a national historic place where the few remaining residents are former patients, now cured, who choose to continue a life of near seclusion rather than coping with the rest of the world.

On the ground, visitors board a yellow school bus bound for the grave of Father Damien de Veuster, the Belgian priest who cared for the ill until 1889, when he too fell victim to the awful disease

Hawaiians call the "separating sickness." Father Damien's tomb, next to Molokai's St. Philomena Church, is empty; his body was disinterred and reburied in his native Belgium. Only his hand, a relic of his martyrdom, remains in Kalaupapa.

In the 1940s, sulfa drugs were found to cure leprosy. You try to count tombstones of hundreds who died of the disease now readily controlled. The slow, plodding climb back up Molokai's steep cliffs delivers sobered riders back to the 20th century as Kalaupapa, never lost in memory, recedes in the sea mist.

For details, contact **Molokai Mule Ride** at ☎ 808-567-6088 or 800-567-7550, or visit **www.muleride.com.**

Lanai

To see this nearly roadless island the way its earlier residents did, take a horse. You can ride the upland wilderness trails with a wrangler from the **Lodge at Koele Stables** to awesome view points notable for a plenitude of open land and sea and the absence of buildings. Call ☎ 808-565-4424 or visit **www.lanai-resorts.com** for more information.

HANG GLIDING AND ZIPLINES:
The Bird's-eye View

THOSE OF YOU WHO WANT TO SPREAD your kite and fly high can do it above Maui's most famous landmark: Haleakala Crater. You can sign up for an instruction course followed by a memorable tandem flight with your instructor, using a traditional glider or a motor-powered glider. Veteran pilot Armin Engert of **Hang Gliding Maui** offers a four-hour adventure from the top of Haleakala, with shorter excursions using a motorized glider. Call ☎ 808-572-6557 or visit **www.hangglidingmaui.com** for more information.

Hooked in a harness to a high wire you leap off a platform and go zipping on an aerial runway over canyons like a bird—top speed 40 mph, from 40 to 200 feet off the ground. Not for everyone (afraid of heights? bad back? beware), but the new thrill on the hill on Maui puts you in virgin turf without leaving a footprint. **Skyline Eco Adventure** operates two lines: one on 10,000-foot Haleakala; the other in the West Maui Mountains above Kaanapali. Each offers spectacular Island views. Five lines (each named for a different native Hawaiian bird) skim over cliffs and valleys. Each zip is longer and faster than the one before; the last is 750 feet across a 125-foot-deep canyon. The two-hour adventure ends too soon. Safer (and swifter) than driving Kihei, each harness is tested to 6,000 pounds; cables are rated at 14.5 pounds. Guides double-check your harness at each station. Zippers must be over age 10 and weigh between 80 and 260 pounds. Wear long pants, closed-toe shoes, and, if you go in the morning, layer up—it's chilly on Haleakala at 4,000 feet. Call ☎ 808-878-8400 or visit **www.zipline.com** for details.

SPAS

WHILE NOT NECESSARILY AN OUTDOOR ACTIVITY, spa treatments in Hawaii often take advantage of the Islands' natural beauty and incorporate the age-old remedy of fresh air. Plus, if you've spent hours on a surfboard, on a mountain bike, or in the saddle, a massage might be the perfect ending to your active Maui vacation day.

Just as East meets West on the Island dining table, the methods and traditions of Pacific Rim spas meet on the massage table and in the imaginative treatments and aromatic ingredients that make up the modern spa treatment. Ancient Hawaiians, who knew how to take good care of themselves, had a word for the process of safeguarding and restoring good health: *hooponopono*, or making things right. Our word for sinking into a tub filled with exotic scents, submitting to the heritage massage called *lomilomi* in a tent by the sea, feeling the water in a many-jetted shower zing your stress away, zoning out under the influence of hot lava rocks? Fantastic.

Hawaii is a healthy place by nature and tradition. If nothing else, get a lomilomi massage, a cultural experience. The therapist uses forearms as well as hands in a smoothing, stretching technique that is relaxing to the point of being hypnotic. So splurge: You owe it to yourself to do this. You can request a male or a female massage therapist, as you prefer. Be sure to tell your therapist about any particular sensitivities, medical conditions, injuries, or allergies, and your preference for gentle or rigorous treatment. One spa in West Maui publishes a card titled "How to Receive a Massage" that encourages new massage patrons to shut their eyes and relax, focus on deep breathing, go limp like a rag doll and let the therapist move their arms or legs, avoid unnecessary talk, and even doze off if they want during the soothing treatment. It's normal.

One note of warning: Don't skip out on your spa appointment. All the spas have cancellation policies that include forfeiting part or all of the prepaid fee.

The following are some of Maui's top spa choices:

Grand Wailea Resort Hotel and Spa, South Maui

LOCATION Wailea Resort

Phone ☎ 808-875-1234

Hours Daily, 8 a.m.–7 p.m.; fitness/workout rooms 6 a.m.–8 p.m.; beauty salon 9 a.m.–7 p.m.

Lying in a white caravan tent on the black lava coast of the Big Island of Hawaii, women we just met introduced us to lomilomi, the classic Hawaii massage. Tradewinds ruffled the palm trees. Waves lapped the shore. Now and then from a distance whale-watchers cried in delight as the aquatic behemoths leapt out of the blue Pacific.

Another blissful outdoor Hawaiian experience added to our list. After more than two decades in the Islands, only a few goals still elude us—such as Mauna Loa's 13,679-foot summit on the Big Island and the 80-foot dive at Cathedrals off the south coast of Lanai. Although some such excursions border on the extreme, almost anyone can enjoy the real Hawaii. The choices are staggering.

You can kayak out for a sea-level encounter with humpback whales or dive among white-tipped sharks; visit the Puu Oo rain forest with a naturalist; explore coral reefs with marine experts, or volunteer to tag Hawaiian Monk seals on Kure Atoll in the seldom-seen northwest Hawaiian Islands; or hunt wild pigs with dogs on the slopes of Haleakala (and do Hawaii an eco-favor by eliminating descendants of the European boar introduced by Captain James Cook).

Save the Islands: hunt pig. Since Captain Cook introduced the European boar (Sus scrofa) in 1776, the pig has served as the main entree in local luau. But the porkers are also a public nuisance. They root around in the rain forest, gnawing rare Silversword plants and other endangered tropical flora. Left unchecked, they would eat the island right down to the waterline.

You can help save the Islands by joining a fair chase pig hunt on more than 100,000 acres of private ranchland in the remote Maui Uplands above Haiku. The hunt goes on year-round from sunrise to sunset. Everything

COMMENTS The Grand Wailea's Spa Grande is the island's largest, at 50,000 square feet, and a favorite with the spa-going world. The Spa Grande mixes traditional Hawaiian healing techniques and ingredients with European, American, Indian, and Asian therapies. You can purchase massage treatments, aromatherapy, body treatments, facials, hair care, manicures, pedicures, and waxings; participate in yoga and meditation instruction; and play racquetball or basketball. Hawaiian therapies and ingredients are used liberally, from the seashell massage to the volcanic ash facial. Most soothing is the spa's Termé Wailea Hydrotherapy Circuit, a refreshing hour-long treatment that begins with a quick shower and includes some quality time in a Roman bath, the steam room, and sauna before a personalized loofah scrub, a cleansing treatment that exfoliates surface skin cells and produces healthier-looking skin. The treatment continues with a soak in specialty baths—Moor mud, limu/seaweed, aromatherapy, tropical enzyme, and mineral salt—followed by a Swiss jet shower. Sounds invigorating? If your little ones are chafing because Mom is going to the spa, consider taking them along for a *keiki* (child) spa package—chocolate/coconut is provided—a four-wheel-drive, guns and ammo, meat storage, packing for shipping, and even taxidermy service if you bag a trophy. For more information contact Bobby Caires of Hunting Adventures of Maui at (808) 572-8214 or 645-B Kaupakalua Road, Haiku, Maui 96708.

Many resorts now offer ecological tours. Some of the best are found at Maui's Kapalua Bay Resort, which sits between a marine preserve and the West Maui rain forest. Guests can explore Kahakuloa Valley, in the almost always off-limits Puu Kukui rain forest, and snorkel Honokohau Bay, which teems with tropical fish and occasionally spinner dolphins.

Or take a Nature Conservancy hike through Molokai's eerie Moomomi Dunes, where shifting sand yields skeletons of flightless dodo-like birds found nowhere else on the planet. You can ride from *mauka* to *makai* (mountain to sea) out in West Maui on the 300-acre Mendes Ranch owned for three generations by a proud Portuguese-Hawaiian family.

Stargazing is an old Island pastime. You can search for the Southern Cross, low on the horizon; or find Hokulea, Hawaii's own star that long ago led Polynesian voyagers in seagoing canoes to discover these islands between AD 300 and 500. For wilder nightlife, some visitors, no longer content with trying hula as a joke, now learn from real *kumu hula* (hula teacher).

Many of these adventures—and many more—are described in this chapter. If you want to arrange an authentic Hawaiian experience, your hotel concierge is likely in the know. The truth about Hawaii is this: despite more than a century of American veneer, the Hawaiian Islands continue to offer travelers an authentic, natural, almost foreign experience. All you have to do is look beyond the big hotels.

massage, manicure or pedicure, braids, and one small henna tattoo to bliss them out.

Non-hotel guests pay a surcharge added to the first spa treatment (salon and wellness services not included). The surcharge is waived if you book two or more spa treatments on the same day. Non-hotel guests need a major credit card to reserve an appointment. All spa and salon services are subject to an additional 15 percent service charge plus tax. Use of the cardiovascular gym, weight-training gym, and all fitness classes is free for hotel guests, or available for a daily fee for nonguests. Call the resort for more information or visit **www .grandwailea.com**.

The Health Centre, Four Seasons Resort Maui, South Maui
LOCATION Wailea Resort

Phone ☎ 808-874-8000

Hours Daily, 6 a.m.–9 p.m.

COMMENTS Here's the best headache relief prescription anyone has yet invented: Go down to the sea in front of your hotel early in the day and float in the womblike waters while a masseuse smooths the crimps and pains from your head, shoulders, and neck. It's one of the new treatments at Four Seasons' Health Centre, the hotel's expanding fitness and spa facilities, which have undergone a $3 million update. The unique aqua cranial treatment, a type of cranial-sacral massage developed by Rebecca Goff, is administered in the clear, warm sea off Wailea Beach. Therapist and client don wet suits and head into the water. The guest lolls easily on the surface as the sun is coming up over Haleakala, while the therapist massages head, neck, and shoulders. Oh, what a beautiful morning. The spa also offers a variety of other massages, including a Thai technique that involves stretching and movement, without oil, performed in a tent outdoors or in your room. Couples can relax together with massage for two in a private outdoor cabana. Deep-tissue massages with neuromuscular and acupressure techniques get at the heart of sports injuries. Tennis and fitness services are also operated from the Health Centre. Visit **www .fourseasons.com**/maui for more details.

Hyatt Regency Maui Resort and Spa, West Maui
LOCATION Kaanapali Beach Resort

Phone ☎ 808-661-1234

Hours Daily, 7 a.m.–8 p.m.

COMMENTS Besides a full range of massages and facials, the Hyatt Regency Maui Moana Spa offers workout classes so you can balance exertion and relaxation. The spa's newest fitness class, Beach Boot Camp, offers a workout with Mother Nature. No indoor weight bench, no treadmill, and no step machine here. Instead, you tackle the real thing—a three-mile stretch of beach, coconut weights, and the sparkling blue ocean, with a regimen of high-impact aerobics. The resistance provided by soft sand and ocean currents helps build muscle strength and endurance. Classes begin with beach stretches and go on to sprints along the sand, lunges through the water, and abdominal crunches along a hilly incline. The one-hour class is offered at 8 a.m. every Wednesday, Friday, and Sunday for a nominal fee.

Spa Kea Lani, Fairmont Kea Lani Maui, South Maui
LOCATION Wailea Resort

Phone ☎ 808-875-4100

Hours Daily, 7:30 a.m.–8 p.m. for treatments, 24 hours for fitness facilities

COMMENTS Here's a way to deal with that pesky cellulite: a dose of natural black Moor mud and thermal mineral water. It rejuvenates tired muscles and dull skin as well. Cellulite activating gel is applied to tone and firm your skin while you get an acupressure facial massage.

Kea Lani also offers a glycolic facial peel aimed at removing fine lines, wrinkles, and age spots, and an anti-free-radical face mask containing concentrated vitamins—a treatment that begins with a skin analysis and cleanings and concludes with a facial massage.

The Spa offers body wraps and polishes, a range of massage techniques, personal fitness training sessions, and spa lunches. For more information, visit **www.kealani.com.**

The Spa at Four Seasons Resort Lanai at Manele Bay
LOCATION Manele Bay, south Lanai

Phone ☎ 808-565-2088

Hours Daily, 8:30 a.m.–7 p.m.

COMMENTS Pineapple polishes and banana-coconut scrubs are among the luscious-sounding treatments available at the Manele Bay spa, just redesigned in a $1-million redo. If you're rarely kind to your feet, make up for it with the "hehi lani," or "step into heaven," foot treatment, which consists of a foot-wrap in hot eucalyptus-scented towels followed by an aromatic scrub, a foot massage with rich lotion, and a finishing spritz of cooling oils, 50 minutes of pedal bliss. New treatments include hot-rock massages and hot-rock facials. Massage facilities come in indoor or outdoor environments, and massages in all varieties of technique, some intended to ease sports-aches and golf-aches. Separate rooms are set aside for hair, nail, and facial work. Guests can choose fitness activities such as aquatics and coastal trail hikes to tone those muscles. For more information, visit **www.fourseasons.com/manelebay/spa.**

Third Heaven Spa and Massage, West Maui
LOCATION Napili Plaza Shopping Center, Suite 112-B

Phone ☎ 808-665-0087 or 808-665-1112

Hours On call daily, 9 a.m.–6 p.m.

COMMENTS This is a storefront day spa in the Napili-Kapalua area of West Maui, one of dozens of independent spas and therapists operating on Maui. Third Heaven's therapist will travel to you in Lahaina, Kihei, or Napili to perform a variety of massage therapy techniques, facials, hand, foot, and scalp treaments with local ingredients—kukui-nut face therapy and seaweed hand mask, for instance—or a sea kelp facial, Maui sugar scrub, sea-salt body scrub, an eye-lift treatment with collagen mask, and others. Make a double booking and save $20. Other services include acupuncture, yoga, and hot-stone therapy.

OTHER HEALTH AND FITNESS SERVICES ON MAUI

MOST MAUI RESORT HOTELS OFFER EXTENSIVE FITNESS facilities so you can keep up your workout regimens. If you want to make certain you have access to a particular piece of workout equipment, ask your hotel before you book. If you're staying in a condo or B&B,

> **MAUI HEALTH AND FITNESS ALTERNATIVES**
>
> Aloha Spa: Islandwide, on-call licensed massage therapists will come to your room or unit for lomilomi, sports, dual massages for two, or Swedish massage therapies. Call ☎ 808-573-2323 or 800-730-9774, or visit **www.alohaspamaui.com.**
>
> Gold's Gym: ☎ 808-874-2844 in Kihei; ☎ 808-242-6851 in Wailuku

it's easy to take advantage of local gyms at a day-use rate or local spas (like Third Heaven, profiled above). And yet another option is to have a fitness trainer or massage therapist come to you.

SPECTATOR SPORTS

MAUI HOSTS SEVERAL MAJOR SPORTING EVENTS throughout the course of a year. If you're looking to augment your beach time, here is a game plan:

FOOTBALL

ALTHOUGH THE NATIONAL FOOTBALL LEAGUE'S PRO BOWL, the All-Star end game, is held in Oahu's Aloha Stadium (a week after the Super Bowl), most players head for Maui's high-end resorts to kick back after the final whistle. You are most likely to bump into your favorite NFL player in Wailea or Kapalua on the beach or golf course.

GOLF

THREE MAJOR PROFESSIONAL GOLF EVENTS BRING MAUI into the homes of golf fans via television. If your vacation coincides with one of them, you may be lucky enough to see it in person. In early January, the Mercedes Championships at Kapalua, Maui, launches the PGA tournament season, featuring top players competing for more than $5 million in prize money. Call ☎ 808-669-2440 for details.

One of the final stops on the Senior PGA Tour is the EMC Kaanapali Classic on Maui. Held in October, this event annually draws some of the game's greatest legends and old-time favorites. Call ☎ 808-661-3691.

OCEAN SPORTS

WINDSURF COMPETITIONS ARE HELD ON Maui's north shore at Kanaha and Hookipa beaches, at various times throughout the spring. The Professional Windsurfing Association's World Tour stops at Hookipa in April. Call ☎ 808-244-3530 for information.

A surf meet provides a different kind of experience for sports fans. It's a good chance to see Hawaii's most prized individual sport at its finest while hanging out at the beach. Admission is always free. Competitors take to the water in four-man heats, each lasting 20–30 minutes. The surfers ride as many waves as they can. A panel of five judges uses a point system to name the winners. Criteria include the size of the waves, length of the rides, board control, and creative maneuvers. On Maui, check Kahului and Paia surf shops in winter (when surf's up) for details on local surf meets.

You won't be able to follow all the action of the annual Bankoh Na Wahine O Ke Kai and the Bankoh Mokokai Hoe, two 41-mile outrigger canoe races from Mokokai to Waikiki—unless you're aboard a chase boat. However, the races are videotaped for local television specials, usually aired a week later from Honolulu. (The women's wahine race is held in late September, while the men's race takes place in early October.) But you can watch the exciting start on Molokai at Hale o Lono Beach as the paddlers go down to the sea and launch in the surf. Most spectators line Waikiki Beach (near Duke Kahanamoku Beach) to cheer on the six-member canoe teams paddling to a colorful finale. Both events draw international outrigger canoe teams from Australia, Canada, and Tahiti, as well as Hawaii and other states. For details, contact the Maui Visitors Bureau at ☎ 808-989-4808.

PART SEVEN

GOLF: *Tee Time*

GETTING LINKED *on the* GOLF COAST

MAUI, MOLOKAI, AND LANAI: the golfer's dream trio. That's why we've devoted an entire chapter to Maui County's favorite sport. Sixteen courses on three islands, with exotic names like Kapalua, Pukalani, Wailea, and The Challenge at Manele, are set like jewels by the sea, on turquoise lagoons, on the slopes of old volcanoes, and in lush rain forests. Best of all: you can play under sunny skies virtually 365 days a year. No season, no downtime.

Nowhere else on earth can you tee off to the sight of whale spouts out there in the largest water hazard, putt under rainbows, or play around a dormant volcano or an ancient *heiau* (altar or temple). But be forewarned: these courses are trickier than they look. They feature different grasses (from Bermuda to Kukuya, a thick-bladed African species) and hellish natural hazards, such as razor-sharp lava, gusty trade winds, distracting views, an occasional wild pig, and tropical heat. There's only one major geographic disadvantage: that blue ocean between you and the islands poses a time and distance problem. It's impossible to play all of Maui's courses unless you move here and take up golf full-time (which some do). The only alternative is to choose your preferred courses and catch the next plane to Maui.

Here are helpful resources for planning your Maui golf vacation:

- *Discover Hawaii's Best Golf*, an 86-page book by golf writer George Fuller. This volume provides vivid descriptions and photos of the state's top courses. Check your local bookstore, or call ☎ 808-487-7299.

- *Island Golf*, a free monthly golf guide with reliable and well-researched information. Visit **www.islandgolfreview.net,** or call ☎ 808-874-8300.

When you choose where to stay and play, keep in mind that many resort hotels offer package rates for room, car, and golf that provide guests with lower course fees and more readily available tee times. The busiest times are weekends and winter tourist season. Most courses let you request a tee time a few days in advance. For a last-minute tee time, try **Stand-By Golf,** which gives visitors a discount. The company makes a small margin on each booking, you get discounted rates, and course managers are happy to fill in empty time slots (☎ 888-645-BOOK for details). **Maui Golf Company** also can help you arrange tee times and obtain discounts; ☎ 808-874-8300. Or, ask your hotel front-desk clerk or concierge to help you. Shorts are acceptable golf attire on Hawaiian courses. Denim is *kapu* on some courses; that means no blue jeans. Collared shirts, a necessity to avoid sunburn on the back of your neck, are often required (no T-shirts or tank tops). Soft-spiked shoes are common.

The GOLF COURSES *of* MAUI, MOLOKAI, *and* LANAI

GREENS FEES

BELOW ARE MAUI'S TYPICAL GREENS FEES, based on one 18-hole round, with or without cart. Rates are subject to change.

- Resort courses: $110–$225
- Semiprivate: $20–$135
- Private: $50–$100
- Public: $14–$135
- Municipal courses: $40–$54

MAUI

The Dunes at Maui Lani   CENTRAL MAUI

ESTABLISHED 1999; DESIGNED BY ROBIN NELSON.

LOCATION 1333 Mauilani Parkway, Kahului. (From the Kahului Airport, head toward Lahaina on Dairy Road until you turn right on Kuihelani Highway [380]. The course is 1½ miles off to the right. The entrance is marked by green flags.)

Phone ☎ 808-873-0422.

Web site www.mauilani.com.

Status Public; 18 holes, par 72.

TEES *Championship:* 6,840 yards. *Blue:* 6,413 yards. *White:* 5,833 yards. Red: 4,768 yards.

FEES $99, includes cart. Twilight rate, $75 after 2 p.m. Club rentals, $30. Tee times reserved up to 3 months in advance (with possible cancellation fees). Most major credit cards accepted.

FACILITIES Driving range, 15-acre practice facility, putting greens, clubhouse, pro shop, and restaurant.

COMMENTS Maui's newest and most surprising course is an Irish links–style course incorporating natural sand dunes not on the coast, where Maui has none, but inland, where the sea left them a million or so years ago in a valley. Architect Robin Nelson took advantage of ancient dunes up to 80 feet high to provide drama on several holes. His layout is a true mental challenge. There is a peek of the sea now and then, but it's mostly rolling terrain with a forest of thorny kiawe trees. Instead of the beach, the killer views are of towering Haleakala. The short par-3 third hole is a classic dune hole fashioned after the sixth at Lahinch in Ireland. The course anchors a residential development.

Elleair Maui Golf Course (*formerly Silversword*) SOUTH MAUI

ESTABLISHED 1987; DESIGNED BY BILL NEWIS.

LOCATION **1345 Piilani Highway, Kihei (on the mauka, or uphill, side of Highway 31).**

Phone ☎ 808-874-0777.

Web site **www.elleairmauigolfclub.com.**

Status Public; 18 holes, par 71.

TEES *Championship:* 6,801 yards. *Men's:* 6,404 yards. *Ladies':* 6,003 yards.

FEES $120. $95 after noon. Carts included. Club rentals, 40. Tee times reserved 30 days in advance. Visa, MC accepted.

FACILITIES Driving range, nighttime lighting, pro shop, and restaurant.

COMMENTS Morning and late-afternoon trade winds usually hit the course, and many holes bring the winds into play. Views of the sea are afforded from most of the greens on this public course. The signature ninth hole is a long par 4 with a pond on the right side.

Kaanapali Golf Course WEST MAUI

ESTABLISHED 1962 (NORTH), 1997 (SOUTH); DESIGNED BY ROBERT TRENT JONES JR.

LOCATION **Kaanapali Resort, Lahaina. (Take Highway 30 past Lahaina to Kaanapali Beach Resort. Turn left at the first entrance, then right to the golf course.)**

Phone ☎ 808-661-3691 or 866-454-GOLF.

Web site **www.kaanapaligolf.com.**

Status Resort; 8 holes, par 71 (both courses).

TEES *Men's:* North, 6,994 yards. South, 6,555 yards. *Ladies':* North, 5,417 yards; South, 5,485 yards.

FEES $235. $190 for resort guests. Includes cart. Special $120 twilight rate (South course only), noon–2:30 p.m. Twilight rate on both courses after 2:30 p.m., $77. Repeat rounds, $49. Club rentals, $45; $29 at twilight. Tee times reserved 2 days in advance. Major credit cards, except Discover, accepted.

FACILITIES Driving range, putting green, pro shop, restaurant, and locker room with showers.

COMMENTS Two excellent 18-hole courses. The 18th on the North course is one of Hawaii's toughest finishing holes, with water hazards lined up on the right side and the kidney-shaped green bordered by two treacherous bunkers on the left. The shorter South course, with more forgiving greens and wider fairways, is the likely preference for less experienced golfers. The North hosts the annual Kaanapali Classic, a Senior PGA Tour event.

Kapalua Golf Club   WEST MAUI

ESTABLISHED 1975 (BAY COURSE) AND 1991 (PLANTATION COURSE); DESIGNED BY BILL CRENSHAW AND BILL COORE.

LOCATION **300 Kapalua Drive, Kapalua. (Take Highway 30 past Lahaina and Kaanapali to Kapalua Resort, turn left at Kapalua Drive, then right to clubhouse.)**

Phone Bay, ☎ 808-669-8820; Village, ☎ 808-669-8835; Plantation, ☎ 808-669-8877.

Web site **www.kapaluamaui.com/golf**.

Status Resort. Bay, 18 holes, par 72; Plantation, 18 holes, par 73.

TEES *Men's:* Bay, 6,600 yards; Plantation, 7,263 yards. *Ladies':* Bay, 5,124 yards; Plantation, 5,627 yards.

FEES Bay Course: $215. Plantation Course: $295, twilight $125. Club rentals, $55. Cart rentals, $20. Tee times reserved 4 days in advance. All major credit cards accepted.

FACILITIES Driving range, putting green, pro shop, clubhouse, and restaurants.

COMMENTS Surrounded by a pineapple plantation on Maui's northwest coast, Kapalua Resort's 1,500 tidy acres include two of the world's most beautiful and challenging 18-hole courses: the Bay and Plantation courses. These courses provide drop-dead views at every turn.

   The Bay course's par-3 Hole 5 is one of the world's most dramatic signature holes, requiring a 205-yard-long tee shot over Oneloa Bay. The links-style Plantation course, highly regarded by many pros, is the home of the PGA Tour's Mercedes Championships. No tank tops or cutoffs allowed. The Village course is closed.

Makena Resort Golf Club   SOUTH MAUI

ESTABLISHED 1983 (SPLIT INTO TWO SEPARATE COURSES IN 1994); DESIGNED BY ROBERT TRENT JONES JR.

LOCATION **5415 Makena Alanui, Makena. (From Kahului Airport, take Dairy Road to Piilani Highway, turn right at the end, then left at the stop sign on Wailua Alanui and go south past Wailea. The entrance is on the left.)**

Phone ☎ 808-879-3344.

Web site **www.makenagolf.com.**

Status Resort; 18 holes, par 72 (South Course closed for renovation until 2009).

TEES *Championship:* North, 6,500 yards; *Men's:* North, 6,100 yards. *Ladies':* North, 5,300 yards.

FEES North Course: $135, guest $120; twilight $70, guest $65. Club rentals, $30. Includes cart. Tee times reserved 3 days in advance. Major credit cards, except Discover, accepted.

FACILITIES Practice range, putting green, pro shop, and locker room with showers.

COMMENTS Located by the Maui Prince Hotel. Both courses rate among the state's best, with views of the ocean, Haleakala, Molokai, Lanai, and Kahoolawe. The courses were designed by Robert Trent Jones Jr. Severe slopes and fast greens make for very challenging play. The lack of strong winds at Makena is a big plus. The South Course's 15th and 16th holes are among Hawaii's most picturesque oceanfront holes. The North Course is generally considered the more difficult of the two.

Kahili Golf Course (formerly Sandalwood) SOUTH MAUI

ESTABLISHED 1991; DESIGNED BY ROBIN NELSON AND RODNEY WRIGHT.

LOCATION 2500 Honoapiilani Highway, Wailuku (turn uphill off Highway 30, just south of Wailuku).

Phone ☎ 808-242-4653.

Web site **www.kahiligolf.com.**

Status Resort; 18 holes, par 72.

TEES *Championship:* 6,433 yards. *Men's:* 5,918 yards. *Ladies':* 5,162 yards.

FEES $125. Golf program participants, $100. Includes cart. Twilight rate, $85 after 2 p.m. Club rentals, $40. Tee times may be reserved in advance over the phone or online. Major credit cards, except Discover, accepted.

FACILITIES Driving range, pro shop, banquet facility, locker rooms, clubhouse, putting and chipping greens, and restaurant.

COMMENTS Robin Nelson and Rodney Wright designed this layout among sandalwood trees at Waikapu, nestled into the side of the West Maui Mountains overlooking Maui's isthmus of green cane fields. Sloping fairways and hefty trade winds can make for a challenging day, along with a lot of elevated greens and par 4s that are long, straight, and into the wind.

Waiehu Golf Course CENTRAL MAUI

ESTABLISHED 9-HOLE COURSE OPENED IN 1933; BACK 9 ADDED IN 1966; DESIGNED BY LOCAL CIVIL ENGINEERS.

LOCATION Wailuku. (From Highway 340, turn right just past Waihee Park. The entrance is on the right.)

Phone ☎ 808-244-5934.

Web site **www.mauigolf.org/waiehu.**

Status Municipal; 18 holes, par 72 (par 73 for women).

TEES *Men's:* 6,330 yards. *Ladies':* 5,555 yards.

FEES $38. Cart, $10 per person. Club rentals, $20. Tee times reserved 2 days in advance. Cash.

FACILITIES Driving range, putting green, pro shop, clubhouse, and restaurant.

COMMENTS Maui's only municipal course is off the tourist trail, most affordable, and great fun to play. The front nine are relatively flat; the back nine are hilly in spots. This course features one lake and more than 40 sand bunkers. Three view holes front the ocean. The signature, par-5 Hole 7 plays along the beach.

Wailea Golf Club　SOUTH MAUI

ESTABLISHED 1972 (BLUE), 1993 (GOLD), 1995 (EMERALD); DESIGNED BY ARTHUR JACK SNYDER, CONVERTED BY ROBERT TRENT JONES JR.

LOCATION 100 Wailea Golf Club Drive, Wailea. (From Kahului Airport, take Dairy Road to Piilani Highway, drive to southern end of the road, and turn right. At the stop sign, turn left on Wailea Alanui. Turn left again and drive uphill to the clubhouse and three courses.)

Phone Gold and Emerald courses, ☎ 808-875-7450; Blue course, ☎ 808-875-5155.

Web site **www.waileagolf.com.**

Status Resort; 18 holes, par 72 (all 3 courses).

TEES *Championship:* Gold, 7,078 yards; Emerald, 6,825 yards; Blue, 6,758 yards. *Men's:* Gold, 6,653 yards; Emerald, 6,407 yards; Blue, 6,152 yards. *Ladies':* Gold, 5,442 yards; Emerald, 5,268 yards; Blue, 5,291 yards.

FEES Blue Course: $95; twilight, $70 after 1 p.m. Gold Course: $225. Emerald Course: $225. Club rentals, $50. Tee times reserved 5 days in advance. All major credit cards accepted.

FACILITIES Driving range, putting greens, pro shop, and restaurant.

COMMENTS Three championship courses distinguish Wailea Resort in South Maui: the newer Gold and Emerald courses, as well as the par-72, 18-hole Blue Course, considered the Grand Lady of Wailea. *Golf for Women Magazine* recently named the Wailea Golf Club one of the three most women-friendly golf Facilities in the country. The Gold Course at Wailea gilds the lily on this island already noted for great courses. This Robert Trent Jones Jr. course is a rugged, natural-style 7,070-yard par-72 layout that plays over the foothills of Haleakala.

All three courses have breathtaking ocean and mountain views. The Blue Course, with wide, open fairways, is the easiest, but it does have 74 bunkers and four water hazards. The Gold Course has traditionally been host to the nationally televised Senior PGA Tour's Senior Skins game in January.

The Emerald Course offers stunning views of Haleakala and the Pacific. Considered a friendlier course for high-handicap players, the course's signature hole is the 18th, a 553-yard par-5 challenge with a downhill slope. Collared shirts are required.

LANAI

LANAI MAY HAVE MORE DEER THAN PEOPLE, but it boasts two stunning resort golf courses: **The Experience** at Koele and **The Challenge** at Manele. The Challenge is a target-style course carved from lava cliffs by the sea. The water hazard on the par-3, signature 12th hole at Manele is a wave-lashed coast of jagged lava. This course on the south coast of Lanai will test your patience and increase your impolite vocabulary.

If you're still game, face The Experience's signature hole, which plays into a ravine from a knoll 250 feet above the fairway of this upland course. The layout begins high on the slopes of 3,366-foot Mount Lanaihale, complete with Norfolk pine forest and a gallery of deer, pheasant, and wild turkey. This course features the only bentgrass greens in Hawaii.

The Challenge at Manele

ESTABLISHED 1993; DESIGNED BY JACK NICKLAUS.

LOCATION Manele Bay (transportation via Lanai Resorts shuttle).

Phone ☎ 808-565-2222.

Web site www.manelebayhotel.com.

Status Resort; 18 holes, par 72.

TEES *Championship:* 7,039 yards. *Men's:* 6,684 yards. *Ladies':* 5,024 yards.

FEES $225. $185 for guests staying at The Lodge at Koele, Manele Bay Hotel, or Hotel Lanai. Club rentals, $55 for full round. Tee times reserved 30 days in advance. Major credit cards, except Discover, accepted.

FACILITIES Driving range, putting and chipping greens, locker rooms, pro shop, and restaurant.

COMMENTS This links-style course offers great ocean views from every hole. Fairways are open; greens are small and fast. Built on the side of a hill, the course features several changes of elevation and requires several blind tee and approach shots. Winds often come into play. Bring extra balls for Hole 12, a 202-yard par 3 that includes a tee shot across 200 yards of Pacific Ocean. The tee area on a cliff 150 feet above the crashing surf is the picturesque spot where Bill and Melinda Gates were married in 1994. Archaeological sites are among the course's features. Collared shirts are required; no denim.

The Experience at Koele

ESTABLISHED 1991; DESIGNED BY GREG NORMAN AND TED ROBINSON.

LOCATION Lanai City (transportation via Lanai Resorts shuttle).

Dangerous Development

If you go to Hawaii, you must be careful. They are out there. Watching. You almost always can feel their presence. Sometimes you may even see them. Night marchers still walk ancient paths to conduct rituals and ceremonies. Kahunas (priests) talk to rocks, and the rocks talk back.

More than a century and a half after the demise of idolatry and human sacrifice and despite the work of zealous Christian missionaries, Hawaii is alive with mystery. Some may call it devil's work, but in Hawaii, where people live in both past and present, it's the old Hawaiian way.

The ancient ways are there just beneath the surface of modern Island life. Hawaii is alive with ancestral spirits, animism, primal fears, and both old and new kapu (taboos), around the edges like myth and legend, plus religions introduced from Japan, China, and America.

Some places are still kapu, off-limits. Secret caves contain old canoes and feathered capes of long dead alii (chiefs, nobles). There are signs to heed, rules to obey. Or else . . .

Or else inexplicable things happen. Houses shake. Freeways collapse. And bulldozers fly. It happened on the Big Island, where developers are carving multimillion-dollar beach estates on sacred land, suggesting that angry ancestral Hawaiians haunt the project.

It's enough to give you chicken skin. That's the local pidgin expression for goose bumps. In Hawaii, chicken skin is common as palm trees.

Ghosts of angry ancestral Hawaiians, it seems, regularly halt construction projects, especially golf courses where developers turn Hawaiian temples

Phone ☎ 808-565-4653.

Web site **www.lodgeatkoele.com.**

Status Resort; 18 holes, par 72.

TEES *Tournament:* 7,014 yards. *Resort:* 6,217 yards. *Forward:* 5,424 yards.

FEES $225; $185 ($100 for 9 holes) for guests staying at The Lodge at Koele, Manele Bay Hotel, or Hotel Lanai. Club rentals, $55 for full round. Tee times reserved 30 days in advance. Major credit cards, except Discover, accepted.

FACILITIES Driving range, putting and chipping greens, executive putting course, clubhouse, and snack bar.

COMMENTS A magnificent course designed by Greg Norman and Ted Robinson, the front nine were carved from the side of a mountain, while the back nine are more open and flat. Water features are prominent, with seven lakes, streams, and waterfalls. Hole 8—a 444-yard, par 4—is the signature, featuring a 250-foot drop from tee to fairway, with a lake bordering one side and thick shrubs and trees lining the other. Even Jack Nicklaus needed seven attempts to get the ball in play here. Hole 17 is surrounded by a lake. Collared shirts required; no denim.

into hazards and invite trespass into the supernatural realm. If your shot goes awry, you can always blame ancient spirits.

On Maui, the Ritz-Carlton Kapalua had to move its multimillion-dollar beachfront hotel off the beach when bulldozers uncovered a mass grave in coastal sand dunes. The Ritz avoided the wrath of displaced spirits by dedicating the graveyard as a memorial.

Not so lucky are Kieweit Pacific Co. crews who completed Honolulu's so-called H-3 interstate freeway, a ribbon of concrete snaking through the Halawa Valley in the majestic 3,000-foot-high Koolau mountain range on Oahu. Strange mishaps kept stalling construction of what now is the world's most expensive freeway—a 16.1-mile stretch of road begun in the 1960s with a $1.6-billion price tag.

Hawaiians consider the valley to be sacred, the home of Papahanumoku, a female god of the native religion. In 1993, a curse was placed on the project when construction violated a rare, ancient heiau (altar or temple) where Hawaiian women once observed rites.

On July 27, 1996, the freeway's elevated ramp collapsed for no apparent reason. The incident, in which four 120-foot, 40-ton concrete girders fell, was the latest in a series of mysterious accidents. Two workers died, eight were injured, and many walked off the job.

"Troubles on H-3 Strengthen Beliefs in Power of Supernatural Wrath," said a page-one headline in the Honolulu Advertiser.

MOLOKAI

NOBODY EXPECTS MUCH OF MOLOKAI, so it is a big surprise when you discover one of the oldest golf courses in Hawaii and realize it's still one of the best. That's Ironwood Hills, an Island-style course that is a real delight to play. Once there were two golf courses on Molokai, and there may be again if defunct Kaluakoi Resort reopens on the island's West End. With six holes along the sea, the 18-hole par-72 Kaluakoi Golf Course is reported to be under new ownership, but with the demise of Molokai Ranch, don't hold your breath. Meanwhile, don't miss Ironwood.

Ironwood Hills

ESTABLISHED 1939; DESIGNED BY DEL MONTE PLANTATION EXECUTIVES.

LOCATION Kualapuu, Kalae Highway, just before the Mule Ride Barn on the road to the lookout.

Phone ☎ 808-567-6000.

Status Private; 9 holes, par 35.

TEE 3,088 yards.

FEES $31, includes cart when available. Most major credit cards accepted.

FACILITIES Pro shop.

COMMENTS This historic plantation course, at 1,200 feet in Molokai's cool uplands, is one of the oldest golf courses in Hawaii and now the only golf course on Molokai still in play. Named for the two prominent natural elements—ironwood trees and rolling hills—the course has open fairways, thick foliage, and excellent island views.

PART EIGHT

DINING *and* RESTAURANTS

EVERYONE HAS TO EAT, even on vacation, and dining Island-style is one of the great joys of a trip to Maui County. If yours is a timid palate, you'll be comforted to know that a wide assortment of familiar Mainland fast-food restaurants and other chains can be found on Maui. But if your sense of adventure extends to dining, you have endless choices. You can enjoy the dishes of many cultures, served fast or leisurely, at great or small cost. You'll have to leave the resort environs to find a lot of the good, affordable restaurants, but hotels and resort shopping centers offer excellent prospects, as well. If you're cooking in a condo or vacation rental, the markets and fruit stands are full of intriguing ingredients. If your culinary talents include only cutting a ripe papaya in half and scooping it out with a spoon, you've got a promising start on the day.

HAWAII REGIONAL CUISINE *and* MULTICULTURAL CUISINE

AS LUXURY HOTELS PROLIFERATED DURING THE LATE 1980S, they brought talented young chefs out to the Islands to tackle the food problem: Most of what had been served in Hawaii hotel dining rooms for decades was frozen, or at least made of ingredients from elsewhere, and predictable, if not boring. The Islands, despite their terrific growing weather, imported almost everything in the stores and restaurants. Tropical bugs were a problem for mass-grown produce, and there was little call for gourmet foods in a plantation-based local economy. But things changed. New farmers immigrated, including the Vietnamese, who grow the fresh herbs required for their own dishes. Many of the sugar and pineapple plantations of Maui, Molokai, and Lanai turned to tourism as a cash crop, changing the way local people live, shop, eat, and use the land. The chefs went out to coax farmers and fishermen to provide what was needed in the way of fresh ingredients: prime fish and seafood, flavorful vegetables, exotic fruits. The chefs also talked to local cooks and sampled home cooking and favorite local dishes. Inspired, they began to meld their classic European training and fresh, local ingredients with Asian methods and flavors—as well as the traditions of local tables—and a new cuisine was born. Hawaii Regional Cuisine, or HRC, was early to the fusion movement that subsequently swept the country, and it is still unmatched, in our opinion, since it is based on Island foods and geared to Island tastes.

HRC also raised "hotel food" in the Islands to a whole new standard. The chefs who developed it in hotels have moved on to start their own restaurants, but they left a strong legacy at the hotel kitchens. The Maui resorts continue to attract bright stars, including the Wolfgang Puck restaurant Spago at Four Seasons Maui at Wailea. Today, the HRC celebrity-chef restaurants are often located in unlikely places—an old plantation general store, neighborhood and resort shopping centers—and count on local residents for a great share of their clientele. Their fare is definitely worth seeking out. Universally, hotel food today is at least pretty good in the Islands—but it's also, almost universally, outrageously expensive. If that matters to you, stay in a place where you can easily seek alternatives nearby, or in a unit or suite with a kitchen.

Although HRC and other kinds of fine dining are popular and pervasive, plenty of Maui restaurants feature different cuisines entirely. If you're not a foodie, you can still eat very well, especially if you like Chinese, Californian, Japanese, Korean, French, Mexican, Thai, Filipino, Vietnamese, American, and Italian foods, as well as vegetarian fare, seafood, and oh yes, Hawaiian food.

All kinds of cuisine are available in the Islands, because people of many ethnic and cultural backgrounds live there and love to eat the foods of their own heritage—and everyone else's, too. It's a Hawaiian passion. Island hospitality is based on an ancient tradition, the invitation to share food first with strangers or travelers who appear at the door, and then find out why they stopped by. When it comes to fast food, it's hard to catch up with the Island pace. Plantation people were usually in a hurry to eat, because their lunchtime was short and their appetites sharpened by hard work, and the tradition lives on. In many local and Asian restaurants, patrons order from a to-go deli board or are barely seated with menus before a server appears. An enduring plantation legacy called the Plate Lunch remains a mainstay of local food to take out or eat in—two or three hearty entrees of various ethnic origins (fish tempura, beef stew, and pork adobo, for example), plus the obligatory two scoops of rice and one of macaroni salad. The concept was born of field workers of varied backgrounds sharing lunch as they worked side by side, so that a Japanese man might trade a bit of teriyaki for a Filipino neighbor's pancit noodles and a bit more for his Korean friend's kal bi barbecued ribs, and so on. However, for food on the go, none can beat the *manapua* truck, a mobile wagon whose driver sells food from a makeshift stand in the vehicle. Hot food is already cooked and waiting in steamers for patrons, who line up outside to get manapua, the Hawaiian name for the steamed Chinese dim sum called *char siu bao* (fresh rolls filled with barbecued pork), other handheld snacks, and takeout plate-lunch meals. The lunch wagons, born of plantation days, still pull up in front of office buildings and beach parks. If you prefer a more leisurely meal, restaurants on Maui, Molokai, and Lanai range from old-fashioned 1950s eateries with unremarkable atmosphere and modestly priced favorite local dishes to very sophisticated world-class dining rooms with oceanfront views and prices to match. You can take advantage of the Islands' fine weather to eat in open-air restaurants or outdoors just about anytime, anywhere, and at any price.

GO FISH

HAWAII'S BOUNTY OF OCEAN FISHES is truly exceptional. Most coastal areas have at least a few prized regional fishes and shellfishes, but Hawaii has a whole bucketful of noteworthy species that move through or are native to the mid-Pacific, and more that are imported from around the Pacific Rim. A few basics you should know about fish in Hawaii: The catch of the day on Maui means just that. The fish on your plate was likely in the ocean that morning. When you order fresh seafood from Lahaina to Maunaloa to Hana, it's really fresh. That's in no small part because it is eaten raw in local dishes like Hawaiian *poke*—marinated cubes of fish, mixed with ingredients such as crunchy seaweed, onion, finely ground tropical *kukui* nuts, hot-pepper flakes, sesame seeds and sesame oil, soy sauce or ginger—and sashimi, slices of fresh raw fish served with wasabi (hot, green Japanese horseradish) and soy sauce, garnished with pink slices of pickled ginger. Sushi, generally a molded tidbit of seasoned rice topped or rolled with a slice of raw fish or other seafood and seaweed, can be made with a host of fishes, or no fish, or even Spam (try *musubi*—rice and Spam wrapped in nori—for breakfast). Sometimes it's made vegetarian-style with cucumbers or Japanese vegetable pickles.

> A land with many fishponds was called a "fat" land (aina momona).
>
> —Samuel Kamakau, *The Works of the People of Old*

Fish in Hawaii is seldom frozen or battered and fried, the standard method of delivering seafood on the East Coast and elsewhere, and as a result, it's seldom cheap. Be aware that crabmeat in the Islands is often the imitation variety that features a bit of crab juice flavoring some innocuous whitefish. A few local crabs, Kona and rock crabs, can be found, but there is no continental shelf for other crabs to prowl here. Rock crabs are seasoned as a kind of poke and eaten raw. Always with fish, if you have doubts, ask whether it is fresh or frozen. On Maui, it makes no sense to eat frozen fish, because a new supply of one species or another comes in to the market every morning. Trouble is, most visitors don't know their *opakapaka* from a rainbow trout.

The fish in Hawaii are known by a confusing but colorful jumble of Hawaiian and Japanese words. Since the State of Hawaii began marketing Hawaiian fish to the Mainland some years ago, you may be familiar with fishes that fly well: Ahi, or yellowfin tuna, and mahimahi, or dolphinfish, are both so well known that local tuna and dolphinfish on the Mainland coasts are sometimes identified by their exotic Hawaiian names. You likely know a fish that formerly was only exported, but now shows up on Island menus and in markets: *shutome*, or Pacific swordfish. But when *opah, ono, moi,* and *monchong* appear on the menu, you get caught in a fish trap. Don't let it happen. You can learn to talk fish like a local. Here's a quick guide to the fish of Hawaii most likely to land on your dinner table.

- Ahi, or yellowfin tuna, has red, translucent flesh that turns to a firm light gray when cooked. It's best when only seared on the outside and still rare in the middle, or at least undercooked and still juicy. And by all means, buy ahi steaks at any Maui grocery store, marinate them in soy and fresh ginger, and grill them fast on hot coals for an excellent home dinner.

- Mahimahi, also called dolphinfish or dorado, has firm, light flesh that cooks to white. This is the fish that tastes so good they named it twice. Not to be confused with Flipper, the dolphinfish is a bullheaded fighter with gold colors that flash like neon rainbows when hooked. A good fish to catch, an even better fish to eat, it's the most common fish in Hawaii's restaurants. It's excellent solo when fresh, but it also goes well with trimmings, especially macadamia nuts and lemon-butter sauce.

- Moi, also called threadfish, was popular with early Hawaiians who raised it in captivity. Moi is a traditional favorite of Islanders today. Everyone likes the moist, mild white flesh of this fish steamed and served over rice with bok choi.

- Monchong, or big-scale pomfret, is an Asia-Pacific favorite. A smooth-textured, delicate-flavored fish, monchong cooks to a moist white finish; it's excellent with Chinese vegetables.

- Onaga, the most-prized snapper, is also known as ruby or long-tailed snapper. Its thick, pale-pink flesh cooks to white with a delicate flavor and silky texture when prepared slightly underdone.

- Ono, or wahoo, is a firm-textured, mild-flavored flaky whitefish often served in thick steaks. Once you're hooked on wahoo, you may never eat mahimahi again. Ono, by the way, is Hawaiian for "delicious," and the ono lives up to its name. Most fishermen would rather hook and eat an ono than mahi.

- Opah, or moonfish, is a popular dinner entree around the Pacific. Rich and delicate, this big, round fish cooks to light pink.

- Opakapaka, or crimson snapper, is a favorite Island fish (partly because people like to say its name). This pink-fleshed, delicate fish is often served steamed Chinese-style, or crusted and sautéed.

- Shutome, or broadbill swordfish, is firm, well-textured, and mild-flavored. Pinkish, it cooks to white. Prepare it fast, like ahi, and Hawaiian swordfish will be moist and flavorful, not dry and dull.

GOING SHOPPING

IF YOU DON'T KNOW HOW TO BAIT A HOOK and land a fish, don't worry. You can catch a good-tasting fish at the local market. On Maui, you can find many of the fish listed above in the supermarkets (24 hours a day at the Kahului Safeway) or occasionally, at the weekly produce markets where fish vendors may sell their fresh catch from coolers. In the cornucopia of Maui farmers' markets, you will also find sweet, juicy Maui pineapple; strawberry papayas; cherimoya; small, lemony apple bananas; starfruit; sweet Maui onions; Asian greens; and long Japanese cucumbers and eggplants. Fish vendors sell fresh line-caught Pacific ono, mahi, opakapaka, moonfish, and sometimes live, farmed shrimp.

Look for fresh green or purple *limu* (seaweed) at ethnic groceries or ask at the supermarket fish counters. As you shop, check out the Asian deli sections, complete with a wide choice of chilled specialties like kimchi, fish cake, lomilomi salmon, and vegetables, as well as a bewildering choice of condiments and Asian sauces.

Nagasako, the large Japanese supermarket in Lahaina, sells wasabi, jasmine rice, glass noodles, and red Hawaiian sea salt, known as alae, best for seasoning poke. Look for fresh green or purple limu seaweed at ethnic markets, though even supermarkets carry pickled condiments, pickled ginger, and Asian sauces.

For a treat at home or in your condo or hotel room, slice sashimi and serve it with shredded daikon, soy sauce and wasabi, and pink pickled ginger. It's excellent with ice-cold beer.

TO LUAU OR NOT TO LUAU?

MOST PEOPLE NEVER GET INVITED TO A REAL HAWAIIAN LUAU. So the commercial luau was created in Hawaii in the 1960s to share the centuries-old Polynesian feast with six million dinner guests each year. Many commercial luau (the word is both singular and plural) are a pale imitation of the real thing and should be avoided.

You sit with 500 strangers (mostly couples wearing matching Hilo Hattie aloha garb) and sip too-sweet, watered-down Mai Tais, eat overcooked pork, two-finger poi that makes everybody go yuck, and some weird-looking green stuff that belongs in an aquarium.

Then you are treated to corny lei jokes by wisecracking hosts who introduce cute Filipino girls in coconut bras who fling tennis balls on a cord in the air and big, tattooed fellows in skirts who stick out their tongues at you. You may even be dragged up on stage to shake your booty Tahitian style while everyone howls at your foolishness. All this can run up to $100 per person—and leave you wishing you'd stayed in your room writing postcards home.

On Maui, however, three excellent luau deliver a sophisticated, even authentic, experience with decent food and drink. If you must.

THE FEAST AT LELE Sophisticated and culturally relevant, The Feast at Lele, on the beach in Lahaina, is small, intimate, and serves various Pacific cuisines at separate tables in a bistro setting. Popular with honeymooners. For more information call ☎ 866-244-5353 or visit **www.fesastatlele.com.**

OLD LAHAINA LUAU Since 1987, Old Lahaina Luau has presented a traditional feast in an architecturally keen longhouse by the sea to earn accolades and repeat visits from locals and visitors alike. "Keep It Hawaii" award-winner. For more information call ☎ 800-248-5828 or visit **www.oldlahainaluau.com.**

WAILEA MARRIOTT LUAU On Wailea's coco-palm coast, the roast pig comes out of the pit at sunset as ancient and modern hula dancers sway and three-time world champion fire-knife dancer Ifi So'o stars in a breathtaking finale. Best for families.

The **RESTAURANTS**

OUR FAVORITE ISLAND RESTAURANTS

Explaining the Ratings

We have developed detailed profiles for the best restaurants and for those that offer some special reason to visit, be it decor, ethnic appeal, or bargain prices. Each profile features an easily scanned heading that allows you, in just a second, to check out the restaurant's name, cuisine, overall rating, cost, quality rating, and value rating.

CUISINE In a locale where Hawaii Regional Cuisine has been seeking to define itself only since 1992, categorizing cuisine becomes a challenging endeavor. Hawaii Regional Cuisine itself is a blend of ethnic foods and cooking styles, so we've ended up with dishes that incorporate Asian, Hawaiian, Cajun, Pacific Rim, and Mediterranean flavors, and more. In most cases, we let restaurant owners or chefs name their own categories. Many times, fusion cuisines are called simply "contemporary cuisine." Even restaurants that once served classic French cuisine now prepare sauces with a lighter hand and are innovative with Island ingredients, one of the prerequisites of Hawaii Regional Cuisine. You can get an idea of the type of food served from the heading, then glean a better understanding by reading the detailed descriptions of specialty items and other recommendations.

OVERALL RATING The overall rating encompasses the entire dining experience, including style, service, and ambience, in addition to the taste, presentation, and quality of the food. Five stars is the highest rating possible and connotes the best of everything. Four-star restaurants are exceptional, three-star restaurants are well above average, and two-star restaurants are good. One star indicates an average restaurant that demonstrates an unusual capability in some area of specialization—for example, an otherwise unmemorable place that has great *saimin* (noodle soup).

COST To the right of the cuisine is an expense description that provides a comparative sense of how much dinner entrees will cost. Dinner entrees in Hawaii often include salad or soup and vegetables. Appetizers, desserts, drinks, and tips are excluded. Categories and related prices are listed below:

Inexpensive	$14 and less per person
Moderate	$15–$30
Expensive	More than $30 per person

QUALITY RATING To the right of the cost appear stars that rate food quality on a scale of five stars, where five is the best rating attainable. It is based expressly on the taste, freshness of ingredients, preparation, presentation, and creativity of the food served. Price isn't considered. If you want the best food available, and cost is not an issue, you need look no further than the quality ratings.

VALUE RATING Because hotel restaurants have a reputation for being overpriced, you should check the value rating. Remember, the perception of value can vary from state to state and country to country. Hawaii is a tourist destination, so restaurant prices probably compare favorably with prices in New York, San Francisco, and other major tourist destinations, but not so favorably with smaller, residential towns. Because it is a common perception that hotel restaurants are universally overpriced (where else would you pay $4–$6 for a glass of orange juice?), we have indicated restaurants of this sort with a two-star rating rather than a discouraging one star. The two-star rating is meant to convey that yes, the restaurant charges perhaps more than you would pay for a similar entree somewhere else, but because the setting, service, and preparation are

Maui's Best Restaurants by Cuisine

RESTAURANT/REGION	OVERALL RATING	COST	QUALITY RATING	VALUE RATING
AMERICAN				
Stella Blues Café | **South Maui**	★★★★½	Mod	★★★★	★★★★
Lahaina Grill **West Maui**	★★★★½	Exp	★★★★½	★★★
Lanai City Grille | **Lanai**	★★★★	Mod/Exp	★★★★	★★★★
Kimo's | **West Maui**	★★★	Mod/Exp	★★★	★★★
Maalaea Grill Restaurant **Central Maui**	★★★½	Mod	★★★★	★★★
CONTEMPORARY				
The Dining Room, Four Seasons Lanai, Lodge at Koele | **Lanai**	★★★★★	Exp	★★★★★	★★★★
Mala, an Ocean Tavern **West Maui**	★★★★½	Inexp/Mod	★★★★★	★★★★★★
Seawatch Restaurant **South Maui**	★★★½	Mod/Exp	★★★★	★★★★
Spago at Four Seasons Resort Maui | **South Maui**	★★★★½	Exp	★★★★★	★★★
Plantation House Restaurant **West Maui**	★★★★	Mod	★★★★	★★★
FRENCH				
Chez Paul | **West Maui**	★★★★★	Exp	★★★★★	★★★★
Gerard's | **West Maui**	★★★★½	Exp	★★★★	★★★★
HAWAII REGIONAL				
Haliimaile General Store **Upcountry Maui**	★★★★★	Mod/Exp	★★★★½	★★★★★
IO | **West Maui**	★★★★½	Mod	★★★★★	★★★
PacificO | **West Maui**	★★★★½	Exp	★★★★★	★★★
Hula Grill Kaanapali **West Maui**	★★★★½	Mod/Exp	★★★★	★★★★½
Roy's Kahana Bar & Grill **West Maui**	★★★★★	Mod/Exp	★★★★	★★★
Roy's Kihei Bar & Grill **South Maui**	★★★★★	Mod/Exp	★★★★	★★★
Sea House Restaurant **West Maui**	★★★	Mod/Exp	★★★	★★★

RESTAURANT/REGION	OVERALL RATING	COST	QUALITY RATING	VALUE RATING
ISLAND (TRADITIONAL)				
Aloha Mixed Plate | West Maui	★★★	Inexp	★★★	★★★
Blue Ginger Café | Lanai	★	Inexp	★★★	★★
ITALIAN				
Ihilani, Four Seasons Lanai, Manele Bay Hotel | Lanai	★★★★★	Exp	★★★★★	★★★
Molokai Pizza Café | Molokai	★★★	Inexp	★★★½	★★★★
BJ's Chicago Pizzeria West Maui	★★★	Inexp	★★★	★★★
JAPANESE FUSION				
Sansei Seafood Restaurant and Sushi Bar | West and South Maui	★★★★★	Mod/ Exp	★★★★★	★★★★
MEDITERRANEAN				
Longhi's West and South Maui	★★★	Mod/Exp	★★★	★★★
MEXICAN				
Cilantro Fresh Mexican Grill West Maui	★★★	Inexp	★★★★	★★★
PACIFIC				
The Banyan Tree, Ritz-Carlton, Kapalua | West Maui	★★★★★	Exp	★★★★★	★★★★
SEAFOOD				
Maalaea Waterfront Restaurant | Central Maui	★★★½	Exp	★★★★★	★★★
Mama's Fish House Central Maui	★★★★½	Exp	★★★★★	★★★
VIETNAMESE				
A Saigon Café | Central Maui	★★★	Inexp	★★★★	★★★★★

Maui's Best Restaurants by Region

RESTAURANT	OVERALL RATING	COST	CUISINE
WEST MAUI			
Aloha Mixed Plate	★★★	Inexp	Island
The Banyan Tree, Ritz-Carlton, Kapalua	★★★★	Exp	Pacific Regional
BJ's Chicago Pizzeria	★★★	Inexp	Italian and Pizza
Chez Paul	★★★★★	Exp	French
Cilantro Fresh Mexican Grill	★★★	Inexp	Mexican
Gerard's	★★★★½	Exp	French
Hula Grill Kaanapali	★★★★½	Mod/Exp	Hawaii Regional
IO	★★★★½	Mod	Hawaii Regional
Kimo's	★★★	Mod/Exp	American
Lahaina Grill	★★★★½	Exp	American
Longhi's	★★★	Mod/Exp	Mediterranean
Mala, an Ocean Tavern	★★★★½	Inexp/Mod	Contemporary
PacificO	★★★★½	Exp	Hawaii Regional
Plantation House Restaurant	★★★★	Mod	Contemporary
Roy's Kahana Bar and Grill	★★★★★	Mod/Exp	Hawaiian Fusion
Sansei Seafood Restaurant and Sushi Bar	★★★★★	Mod/Exp	Japanese Fusion
Sea House Restaurant	★★★	Mod/Exp	Pacific Rim
SOUTH MAUI			
Longhi's	★★★	Mod/Exp	Mediterranean

RESTAURANT	OVERALL RATING	COST	CUISINE
SOUTH MAUI (CONTINUED)			
Roy's Kihei Bar and Grill	★★★★★	Mod/Exp	Hawaiian Fusion
Sansei Seafood Restaurant and Sushi Bar	★★★★★	Mod/Exp	Japanese Fusion
Seawatch Restaurant	★★★½	Mod/Exp	Contemporary
Spago at Four Seasons Resort Maui	★★★★½	Exp	Contemporary
Stella Blues Café	★★★★½	Mod	American
CENTRAL MAUI			
Maalaea Grill Restaurant	★★★½	Mod	American
Maalaea Waterfront Restaurant	★★★½	Exp	Seafood
Mama's Fish House	★★★★½	Exp	Seafood
A Saigon Café	★★★	Inexp	Vietnamese
UPCOUNTRY MAUI			
Haliimaile General Store	★★★★★	Mod/Exp	Hawaii Regional
MOLOKAI			
Maunaloa Room	★★★	Exp	Hawaii Regional
Molokai Pizza Café	★★★	Inexp	Pizza
LANAI			
Blue Ginger Café	★	Inexp	Island
The Dining Room, Four Seasons Lanai, The Lodge at Koele	★★★★★	Exp	Contemporary
Lanai City Grille	★★★★	Mod/Exp	American
Ihilani, Four Seasons Lanai, Manele Bay Hotel	★★★★★	Exp	Italian

exceptional, it's still worth the splurge. We wouldn't want to rate the restaurant one star, causing a reader to automatically forgo a special dining experience. The value ratings are defined as follows:

★★★★★	Exceptional value; a real bargain
★★★★	Good value
★★★	Fair value; you get exactly what you pay for
★★	Somewhat overpriced
★	Significantly overpriced

LOCATING THE RESTAURANT On the far right is a designation for the restaurant's region: West, Central, South, or Upcountry Maui, Lanai, or Molokai. This will give you a general idea of where the restaurant described is located. The restaurants are plotted on the maps in the introduction, and their addresses are included to further assist you.

PAYMENT We've listed the type of payment accepted at each restaurant using the following codes:

AE	American Express		DC	Diners Club
CB	Carte Blanche		MC	MasterCard
JCB	Japan Credit Bank		V	Visa
D	Discover			

WHO'S INCLUDED Restaurants open and close frequently in Hawaii, so most of those we've included have a proven track record. However, some of the newest upscale restaurants owned and operated by chefs who have become local celebrities have been included to keep the guide as complete and up-to-date as possible. The list is highly selective. The absence of a particular place does not necessarily indicate that the restaurant is not good, only that it was not ranked among the best in its genre. Detailed profiles of individual restaurants follow in alphabetical order at the end of this chapter. Below you will find our personal favorites for various cuisines. Under "More Recommendations," you'll find a few restaurants that aren't profiled, but for one reason or another have unique appeal to special appetites.

Our personal list of bests (profiles follow):

Best Asian Fusion Sansei Seafood Restaurant and Sushi Bar, Kapalua or Kihei

Best Fish on the Beach Mama's Fish House, Paia

Best French Chez Paul, Olowalu Village, West Maui

Best Hawaii Regional Fare Haliimaile General Store, Upcountry Maui

Best Pizza BJ's Chicago Pizzeria, Lahaina

Best Vegetarian Stella Blues Cafe, Kihei

MORE RECOMMENDATIONS

- **Best Oceanfront Restaurant Hula Grill**, Whalers Village, Kaanapali Beach Resort: ☎ 808-667-6636
- **Best Brew Pub Fish & Game Brewing Co. and Rotisserie,** 4405 Honoapiilani Highway, Kahuna Gateway Shopping Center; ☎ 808-669-3474
- **Best Deli Caffe Ciao** in Fairmont Kea Lani Maui, Wailea; ☎ 808-875-4100
- **Best Late-night-to-Early-morning Restaurant Lahaina Coolers,** 180 Dickenson, Lahaina; ☎ 808-661-7082
- **Best Alfresco Lunch Mala Ocean Tavern,** 1307 Front Street, Lahaina; ☎ 808-667-9394
- **Best Local Plate Lunch Sam Sato's,** Wailuku Millyard complex; ☎ 808-244-7124
- **Best (Fish and Other) Tacos Maui Tacos,** Napili Plaza, Napili; ☎ 808-665-0222

RESTAURANT PROFILES

MAUI

 Aloha Mixed Plate ★★★

ISLAND	INEXPENSIVE	QUALITY ★★★	VALUE ★★★	WEST MAUI ·

Beachfront, 1285 Front Street, Lahaina; ☎ 808-661-3322; www.alohamixedplate.com

Reservations Not accepted.

When to go Sunset or lunch.

Entree range $4–$14.

Payment V, MC, AE, DC, D.

Service rating ★★½

Parking Free, but limited in front.

Bar Full service.

Wine selection Limited.

Dress Casual.

Disabled access Adequate.

Customers Islanders and tourists.

Lunch and dinner Daily, 10:30 a.m.–10 p.m.

SETTING AND ATMOSPHERE Can't beat it—beach- and oceanfront gardens (next to the Old Lahaina Luau gardens), shaded by huge trees. The bar has a shed roof in case of blessings (showers).

HOUSE SPECIALTIES Coconut prawns are the prize-winning pupu (appetizer). The plate lunch, on paper plates, is also popular. If you can't swing the price of a luau, you can get the flavor at least with a Hawaiian plate, featuring such local favorites as *kalua* pig and cabbage, Korean barbe-cued beef and short ribs, *laulau*, *lomilomi* salmon, macaroni salad, and two scoops of rice, followed by *haupia* (coconut pudding) for dessert. Small appetites will be appeased with a miniplate of shoyu chicken or the other plate lunch specials.

The Banyan Tree, Ritz-Carlton, Kapalua ★★★★★

PACIFIC REGIONAL   EXPENSIVE   QUALITY ★★★★★   VALUE ★★★★   WEST MAUI

One Ritz-Carlton Drive, Kapalua; ☎ **808-669-6200**

Reservations Highly recommended.

When to go Sunset.

Entree range $35–$45 (not including market-priced lobster).

Payment V, MC, AE, DC, D.

Service rating ★★★★

Parking Valet or hotel lot.

Bar Full service.

Wine selection Excellent.

Dress Resort attire.

Disabled access Adequate.

Customers Hotel guests, other visitors, and Islanders.

Dinner Tuesday–Saturday, 5:30–9:30 p.m.

SETTING AND ATMOSPHERE Romantic terrace overlooking the sea with extraordinary views; open-beamed ceiling with no walls unless weather demands. Or go for the full outdoor experience on the lanai under the stars.

HOUSE SPECIALTIES Chef Jojo Vasquez defines his approach as "eclectic Pacific," and dishes such as chorizo crusted opah with oyster mush-rooms, cauliflower, and yellow curry or crispy *ehu* (fish) with locally produced goat cheese polenta and beet and watercress salad illustrate his point and his skill. Start with the Maui onion and fennel soup, garnished with peas and tomato, for instance, or miso-braised Manila clams with shiitake mushrooms and edamame. For dessert, in addition to the delectable rich pastries, chocolates, and cheeses, you can opt for ice cream or tropical sorbets and fresh-baked cookies.

OTHER RECOMMENDATIONS For dessert, a chocolate tasting dessert features dark fudge cake, milk chocolate molten cake, and white chocolate sorbet. That's if you can get past apple cider beignets with rum dipping sauce and dulce de leche gelato. Other house-made icy treats include Maui lavender sorbet and macadamia nut spice gelato. A vegetarian menu is available on request. A special sunset three-course menu is available for $55 per person from 5:30 to 6:30 p.m.

SUMMARY AND COMMENTS This Four-Diamond AAA winner has also won honors as Maui's best restaurant.

BJ's Chicago Pizzeria ★★★

730 Front Street, Lahaina; ☎ 808-661-0700

Reservations Suggested.

When to go Sunset, for the oceanfront view.

Entree range $8–$25.

Payment MC, V, AE, D.

Service rating ★★★

Parking Paid; nearby lots.

Bar Full.

Wine selection Limited.

Dress Casual.

Disabled access Fair.

Customers Tourists, Islanders.

Lunch and Dinner Sunday–Thursday, 11 a.m.–11 p.m.; Friday and Saturday, 11 a.m.–midnight.

SETTING AND ATMOSPHERE Second-floor, Lahaina waterfront view.

HOUSE SPECIALTIES Deep-dish, Chicago-style pizza so good that local folks brave the Lahaina traffic to come into town to get it. Pizzas include shrimp thermidor and barbecued chicken as well as cheese and tomato, veggie, and ham with pineapple. Appetizers, such as spinach and artichoke pizzadilla and Charleston-style crab cakes, will get you started.

OTHER RECOMMENDATIONS Pasta dishes, salads, and sandwiches on freshbaked breads are other choices to wash down with a wide choice of microbrewery beers.

SUMMARY AND COMMENTS When you need a pizza fix, come here. It satisfies, with standard and creative choices and a sunset view Lake Michigan just can't match.

Chez Paul ★★★★★

Highway 30 (6 miles south of Lahaina), Olowalu Village; ☎ 808-661-3843; www.chezpaul.net

Reservations Highly recommended.

When to go Dinner seatings.

Entree range $29–$39.

Payment V, MC, AE, D.

Service rating ★★★★★

Parking Free in adjacent lot.

Bar Full service.

Wine selection Good; wine cellar.

Dress Resort attire.

Disabled access Good.

Customers Islanders, a few tourists, celebrities.

Dinner Daily, seatings at 6:30 p.m. and 8:30 p.m.

SETTING AND ATMOSPHERE "Centrally located in the middle of nowhere," proclaims chef/owner Patrick Callerac, and he's right. But it's only about six miles from Lahaina and absolutely worth the drive to savor the cuisine of this bright, personable chef, formerly executive chef at the Ritz-Carlton, Kapalua. His approach is classic Provençal with an Island touch. You might smell the garlic wafting in through your open car window if you drive past this little blink-and-you'll-miss-it roadside restaurant at Olowalu, a wide spot in the road and a most unlikely setting for a great French restaurant.

HOUSE SPECIALTIES Don't miss the homemade duck pâté, a great starter before entrees such as fresh Kona lobster; *escabeche* (a spicy marinated fish) made with ahi tuna, sweet peppers, and onions; fresh fish in champagne sauce; or slow-roasted duck in cassis sauce. The desserts to die for are crème brûlée baked in a Maui pineapple and banana *clafouti* (cobbler) with coconut ice cream. Cheeses, fresh fruits with crème fraîche and Grand Marnier, and hot, runny chocolate cake might also tempt you.

OTHER RECOMMENDATIONS This is the place to satisfy yearnings for classic French dishes—escargots, warm goat-cheese salad, coq au vin, or tournedos with peppercorn brandy cream sauce. Fresh duck fois gras is a delicacy prepared according to the chef's mood. Crêpes suzette are prepared at your table.

SUMMARY AND COMMENTS It's so tempting not to move your car from its Maui resort parking space, but this cozy (14 tables plus banquettes and a private room) restaurant is definitely worth the drive.

Cilantro Fresh Mexican Grill ★★★

CONTEMPORARY MEXICAN	INEXPENSIVE	QUALITY ★★★★	VALUE ★★★
WEST MAUI			

170 Papalaua Avenue, Lahaina; ☎ 808-667-5444; www.cilantrogrill.com

Reservations None.

When to go Anytime.

Entree range Under $10, whole chicken under $14.

Payment V, MC.

Service rating ★★★

Parking Free lot.

Bar None.

Wine selection None.

Dress Casual.

Disabled access Good.

Customers Islanders and tourists.

Lunch and Dinner Monday–Saturday, 11 a.m.–9 p.m.; Sunday, 11 a.m.–8 p.m.

SETTING AND ATMOSPHERE Casual and colorful restaurant in Old Lahaina Center, a block from Front Street. Chef/owner Paris Nabavi left the world of high-toned hotel dining rooms some years back to launch his own creative endeavors—such as this dine-in or take-out Mexican restaurant. "A fresh take on Old Mexico" is the goal, and it is met with fresh, healthy, flavorful dishes with roots not in Tex-Mex but in Mexico's more traditional dishes and delicious handmade street food.

HOUSE SPECIALTIES Lemon-herb-chipotle marinated rotisserie chicken is the signature product—take it home whole or find it tucked into burritos or tacos made to order with fresh corn tortillas. Cilantro pesto and a variety of housemade salsas spice things up. The chunky salsa is called "tom tom"—tomatoes and tomatillos chopped together with avocadoes and onions. For dessert, try *tres leches*—a moist vanilla cream cake with peaches and cinnamon.

OTHER RECOMMENDATIONS Other ingredients for tacos, burritos, salads, and tortas include adobo-roasted pork, margarita shrimp, carne asada (beef), and grilled or battered ono (also known as wahoo)—accompanied by Mexican cheeses, *pepitos* (pumpkin seeds), beans (black, ranchero, or refried), jicama slaw, and pico de gallo.

SUMMARY AND COMMENTS Chef was looking for a challenge when he went to Mexico to find out how cooks there produced the tasty dishes of Jalisco and Yucatan. Then he returned home to Maui and set about making authentic dishes affordable and accessible. Cilantro is the result.

Gerard's ★★★½

CONTEMPORARY/ISLAND/FRENCH EXPENSIVE QUALITY ★★★★ VALUE ★★★★
WEST MAUI

Plantation Inn, 174 Lahainaluna Road, Lahaina; ☎ 808-661-8939; www.gerardsmaui.com

Reservations Recommended.

When to go Dinner.

Entree range $38 and up.

Payment V, MC, AE, DC, D, JCB.

Service rating ★★★★

Parking In nearby lot.

Bar Full service.

Wine selection Excellent, consistent award-winner.

Dress Casual resort attire.

Disabled access Good for garden-level dining, adequate via a back entry for in-house dining.

Customers Tourists and Islanders for special occasions.

Dinner Daily, 6–9 p.m.

SETTING AND ATMOSPHERE Located in a plantation-style inn with a lushly planted lanai, Gerard's has the feel of a gracious home dining room, with flowered wallpaper, stained-glass windows, and candle lamps.

HOUSE SPECIALTIES Diners rave about the tuna and salmon carpaccio with fennel and lemon cream, or the shiitake and oyster mushrooms in puff pastry. Though chef/owner Gerard Reversade changes the menu, some dishes remain constant—for instance, escargots with burgundy butter and wild mushrooms in garlic cream, or roasted snapper with star anise and savory in orange-ginger emulsion with fennel fondue. Homemade tropical sorbets are refreshing, but you can also choose from an assortment of rich desserts as well as a cheese plate, and for the finale, a glass of Ulupalakua raspberry wine.

OTHER RECOMMENDATIONS Start with Kona lobster and avocado salad in herb-curry vinaigrette. Move on to pork tenderloin with rhubarb compote, roasted banana puree, fried sweet potato, and ginger marinade sauce.

SUMMARY AND COMMENTS Since Gerard's opened in 1982, Reversade has incorporated lighter sauces and tropical ingredients into traditional dishes, evolving his own Hawaiian-French blend. He has been featured on PBS's *Country Cooking* and the Discovery Channel's *Great Chefs of America*. The wine list repeatedly receives *Wine Spectator*'s award of excellence.

Haliimaile General Store ★★★★★

**HAWAII REGIONAL   MODERATE/EXPENSIVE   QUALITY ★★★★★   VALUE ★★★★★
UPCOUNTRY MAUI**

**900 Haliimaile Road, Haliimaile; ☎ 808-572-2666;
www.haliimailegeneralstore.com**

Reservations Highly recommended for dinner.

When to go Anytime on weekdays.

Entree range Lunch $7–$22; dinner $22–$39.

Payment V, MC, DC, D, JCB.

Service rating ★★★★½

Parking In adjacent lot.

Bar Full service.

Wine selection Good, many by the glass.

Dress Casual.

Disabled access Adequate, via ramp.

Customers Islanders and tourists.

Lunch Monday–Friday, 11 a.m.–2:30 p.m.; mini-menu, 2:30–5:30 p.m.

Dinner Monday–Friday, 5:30–9:30 p.m.

SETTING AND ATMOSPHERE Chef/owner Bev Gannon's Hawaii Regional Cuisine is famous throughout the Islands, but you'll still feel as if you've made a discovery when you search out the restaurant, located in the middle of vast Upcountry sugarcane and pineapple fields, partway up the slope of Haleakala. Once a plantation general store, the large, airy, casual, and occasionally noisy room is now a creative dining destination.

HOUSE SPECIALTIES The crab boboli is legendary for lunch, but for dinner, check out the fish preparations, as they vary every night. As an appetizer, sashimi Napoleon—a crispy wonton layered with smoked salmon, ahi tartare, and sashimi and served with a spicy wasabi vinaigrette—is always in demand. Rack of lamb Hunan-style keeps diners coming back for more. House-special martinis include the Upcountry, with pineapple juice, triple sec, and coconut rum.

OTHER RECOMMENDATIONS Paniolo ribs done with a secret lime barbecue sauce and coconut seafood curry are also popular. Lemon-rosemary chicken cooked under a brick and Maui-grown rib-eye steaks offer other choices. Individual Maui pineapple upside-down cake tops the dessert choices, if you can get past rhubarb crisp, warm chocolate cake, or lilikoi brûlée with almond brittle and berry compote. Kids will find not only their own menu for food but also a kids' cocktail menu. How about a Green Gecko (kiwi soda) or a Baby Blue Whale (lemonade with blue oranges)?

SUMMARY AND COMMENTS Chef Gannon was one of the two women among the founding members of the Hawaii Regional Cuisine movement. Winner of numerous awards, Gannon has started a cooking school of her own. The Gannons also run a catering service and Joe's Place (named for her husband) at Wailea, a casual restaurant at the tennis complex. Her latest venture was helping launch Lanai City Grille on Lanai.

Hula Grill Kaanapali ★★★★½

HAWAII REGIONAL   MODERATE/EXPENSIVE   QUALITY ★★★★   VALUE ★★★★½
WEST MAUI

Whalers Village, 2435 Kaanapali Parkway, Kaanapali; ☎ 808-667-6636; www.hulagrill.com

Reservations Recommended for dinner.

When to go Anytime, but it's best on the open lanai at sunset.

Entree range Lunch $8.50–$18, dinner $18–$34.

Payment V, MC, AE, D, DC.

Service rating ★★★★

Parking Validated, in shopping-center garage.

Bar Full service.

Wine selection Good, 10 wines by the glass.

Dress Casual.

Disabled access Good.

Customers Tourists and Islanders.

Lunch Daily, 11 a.m.–10:30 p.m. (Pizzas, salads, and sandwiches are served through the day in the casual Bar efoot Bar.)

Dinner Daily, 5–9:30 p.m.

SETTING AND ATMOSPHERE Hula Grill is oceanfront and center at Kaanapali Beach Resort, in the Whalers Village complex. This Hawaiian plantation–style beach-house setting is charming and comfortable, with two distinct dining and cocktail options: the interior dining room, with its nostalgic decor of warm koa-wood paneling and Hawaiiana memorabilia, and the outdoor Barefoot Bar, on a roofed lanai with some umbrella-shaded tables set right in the sand. During the day, you'll see the parade of passing beachgoers walking along Kaanapali's promenade that borders the golden beach; at night, flickering torches light the path.

HOUSE SPECIALTIES With menus crafted by another originator of Hawaii Regional Cuisine, chef Peter Merriman, even the quesadilla is special at Hula Grill (shrimp and goat cheese with macadamia nuts and black bean–Maui onion relish). For starters, try poke tacos or scallop-and-lobster potstickers served in bamboo steamer baskets. The signature item in the dining room is mahimahi crusted with macadamia nuts, among five fresh fishes nightly. Some diners swear by the Steak Kiana, a fillet with shiitake mushroom cream and lilikoi butter.

OTHER RECOMMENDATIONS This is a great place to cool off and enjoy a casual lunch, maybe a warm roasted-vegetable sandwich with grilled eggplant, tomato, Maui onion, mushroom, and cheese on focaccia—one of the best preparations of this Italian sandwich—or a chicken focaccia sandwich with Monterey Jack, roasted poblano pepper, avocado, and tomato-chile aïoli. These and the pizzas topped with Puna goat cheese, fresh spinach, tomato, and mushrooms come crispy hot from the kiawe wood–fired oven.

There's a formidable cheeseburger, fresh-fish sandwich or plate, Hawaiian ceviche (fresh raw fish in lime and coconut with Maui onion and chili), and a fresh Island version of fish and chips. You might want to share Hula Grill's famous dessert—a homemade ice-cream sandwich, made with two chocolate macadamia-nut brownies, vanilla ice cream, raspberry puree, and whipped cream.

ENTERTAINMENT AND AMENITIES It's easy to slip off the beach for a Lava Flow, a piña colada–like drink made with fresh coconut, pineapple juice, and rum, and topped with a strawberry "eruption," during happy hour, when a guitarist and vocalist entertain from 3 to 5 p.m. Hawaiian musicians return during dinner hours from 6:30 to 9 p.m., and hula dancers sway tableside around 7 every night.

SUMMARY AND COMMENTS Chef Merriman was instrumental in founding the Hawaii Regional Cuisine movement, and his expertise is reflected in Hula Grill's fare. The restaurant can accommodate large parties and weddings of up to 350 people.

IO ★★★★½

HAWAII REGIONAL   MODERATE   QUALITY ★★★★★   VALUE ★★★   WEST MAUI

505 Front Street, Lahaina; ☎ 808-661-8422; www.iomaui.com

Reservations Recommended.

When to go Sunset for great views.

Entree range Dinner $30–$39.

Payment V, MC, AE, DC, JCB.

Service rating ★★★★½

Parking Free in lots next door and across the street.

Bar Full service.

Wine selection Extensive; carefully chosen to complement the food; by-the-glass pairings suggested for entrees.

Dress Casual.

Disabled access Adequate.

Customers Tourists and Islanders.

Dinner Daily, 5:30–10 p.m.

SETTING AND ATMOSPHERE Sunset views are exceptional from the outdoor tables set amid tropical plants on a beachfront lanai. But the three-island ocean vista is also fine from the airy, artful interior of this intimate café, where the decor of light woods and stainless steel is like a frame for the decorative glass—two huge see-through murals of aqua-tinted glass etched with underwater scenes to resemble an aquarium and ceiling lights made like bouquets of glass flowers.

HOUSE SPECIALTIES "Fresh new Pacific cuisine" sums up the fare. Several Hawaiian fishes are featured daily in a variety of preparations, including one called "rainbow catch" that dresses roast fish with lemongrass pesto, tomato, truffle oil, and goat cheese fondue sauce crusted with sesame-coconut-lemongrass paste. For a little cultural fusion, try smoked, seared sashimi.

OTHER RECOMMENDATIONS If you're really hungry, consider this Io trio: lobster curry with a petit filet and a petite veal osso buco with mushroom risotto. Vegetarians, consider sesame herb–crusted tofu with polenta, root vegetables, Kabocha pumpkin sauce, and a touch of pesto. Wine pairings are suggested with entrees, and the drink menu is extensive, including choices of sake, martinis, cognacs, scotches, and dessert wines. For dessert, try chocolate pate or *haupia* (coconut custard) cheesecake.

ENTERTAINMENT AND AMENITIES Live jazz is featured at 505 Front Street Thursday through Saturday, 9 p.m. to midnight.

SUMMARY AND COMMENTS Executive chef/owner James McDonald, voted best chef on Maui, also owns and operates PacificO next door, reviewed below, and The Feast at Lele, a sophisticated beachfront sunset luau held next door on the opposite side, with food prepared at IO's kitchen featuring the cuisines of four Polynesian cultures (see Nightlife, page 331). McDonald's eight-acre vegetable farm in Kula, OO Farm, supplies the eateries with some of their fresh ingredients.

Kimo's ★★★

AMERICAN MODERATE/EXPENSIVE QUALITY ★★★★ VALUE ★★★★ WEST MAUI

845 Front Street, Lahaina; ☎ 808-661-4811; www.kimosmaui.com

Reservations Recommended.

When to go Daytime, sunset for the views.

Entree range Lunch $8–$13; dinner $18–$35.

Payment AE, V, MC, DC, D, JCB.

Service rating ★★★

Parking Street.

Bar Full service.

Wine selection Adequate.

Dress Casual.

Disabled access Access to the main dining room is inadequate for wheelchairs, but seating is available downstairs in a secondary area next to the Bar.

Customers Tourists and Islanders.

Lunch Daily, 11 a.m.–3 p.m.

Dinner Daily, 5–10:30 p.m.

SETTING AND ATMOSPHERE Front and center in old Lahaina, on the waterfront with Lanai and Molokai framing the ocean views, Kimo's can fairly call itself a Lahaina landmark. It's been there since 1977, dispensing laid-back ambience and fresh fish and steaks so successfully that it sparked an entire chain (TS Restaurants) in Hawaii and California. Upstairs, you'll find a dining room with koa-wood walls and a decor reflecting early missionaries; downstairs, it's Hawaiian-style for the waterfront lanai and bar.

HOUSE SPECIALTIES Kimo's is the birthplace of hula pie—macadamia-nut ice cream pie with chocolate cookie crust and a topping of fudge, whipped cream, and more mac nuts. It's wise to have something else first, so decide judiciously between four fresh-fish preparations, including one with lobster stuffing, or the famous prime rib or various steaks.

OTHER RECOMMENDATIONS For lunch on the outdoor lanai, the fresh fish comes in tacos, on sandwiches, crusted in coconut with peanut sauce, or raw in sashimi, battered, as fish–chips, or grilled on a Caesar salad. Traditionalists can opt for the Angus cheeseburger while minimalists will find grilled and chilled veggies, substantial salads, shrimp cocktail, and fresh sashimi. Cioppino, pork ribs glazed with plum sauce, teriyaki chicken, and market-priced lobster are among the dinner standards. Kids can choose fish, shrimp, teriyaki chicken, ribs, or steak in addition to the usual small burgers and grilled cheese.

ENTERTAINMENT AND AMENITIES Live Hawaiian music nightly.

SUMMARY AND COMMENTS On a cold gray winter's day at home, Kimo's is the kind of place you dream of, slurping a mai tai and nibbling on fresh sashimi under a deck umbrella by the sea. Perhaps its greatest endorsement is from folks who work in resorts with four-star restaurants—Kimo's has the best fish dishes at the best prices on Maui.

Lahaina Grill ★★★★½

CONTEMPORARY AMERICAN   EXPENSIVE   QUALITY ★★★★½   VALUE ★★★
WEST MAUI

127 Lahainaluna Road, Lahaina; ☎ 808-667-5117; www.lahainagrill.com

Reservations Highly recommended.

When to go Early or late to avoid the 7 p.m. crowd.

Entree range $28–$45.

Payment V, MC, AE, DC.

Service rating ★★★★★

Parking On street or in adjacent lot.

Bar Full service.

Wine selection Extensive, many by the glass.

Dress Resort wear.

Disabled access Good; separate wheelchair access.

Customers Islanders and tourists.

Dinner Daily, 6–10 p.m.

SETTING AND ATMOSPHERE This hopping bistro, a consistent favorite and prize winner in the middle of the Lahaina action, has two dining rooms and a private, intimate room for Chef's Table dinners for up to eight. Diners may also eat at the bar. Soft pastels and flowers, a pressed-tin ceiling, and works by Maui artist Jan Kasprzycki restore a measure of calm to the somewhat hectic atmosphere.

HOUSE SPECIALTIES The signature dishes of tequila shrimp with firecracker rice or appetizer Kona lobster crab cake compete with the macadamia nut–smoked Kurobuta pork chop and kalua duck with reduced plum-wine sauce, seasonal vegetables, and Lundberg rice for top billing on the dinner menu. Kona coffee–roasted rack of lamb boasts a full-flavored Kona coffee–Cabernet demiglaze served with garlic mashed potatoes.

OTHER RECOMMENDATIONS The vegetarian entrees include four-cheese manicotti with fresh pasta and baked artichoke/roasted tomato sauce; and the grilled polenta stack with grilled eggplant, portobello, roasted pepper, tomatoes, and goat cheese, topped with Maui onion sauce. Then there is the Maui onion and sesame–crusted seared ahi with vanilla-bean rice and an apple cider soy-butter vinaigrette–perhaps light enough to add dessert, a luscious pie of raspberries, blueberries, and black currants with whipped cream, or fresh sorbets, or decadent Kauai Pie with Kona coffee ice cream, chocolate fudge, coconut flakes, and macadamia nuts. The dessert menu suggests wine and liqueur pairings. If you just can't decide what to order, try the chef's tasting menu at $76 per person for two or more (reserve it in advance).

ENTERTAINMENT AND AMENITIES Thursday through Saturday evenings, a jazz pianist plays and sings.

SUMMARY AND COMMENTS If you'd like a quiet little table for a romantic dinner, ask for Table #28, #29, or #34. These tables for two are tucked into an out-of-the-way corner of the restaurant, where you can check out the action in the dining room but the action can't check out you. Lahaina Grill's awards include *Honolulu Magazine's* Hale Aina Award, received 15 years in a row for Best Maui Restaurant.

Longhi's ★★★

MEDITERRANEAN/ITALIAN	EXPENSIVE	QUALITY ★★★	VALUE ★★★
WEST MAUI/SOUTH MAUI			

800 Front Street, Lahaina; ☎ 808-667-2288; The Shops at Wailea, Wailea Resort; ☎ 808-891-8883; www.longhi-maui.com

Reservations Recommended for dinner.

When to go Anytime.

Entree range Breakfast $8–$21; lunch $9–$35; dinner $26–$42, except for lobster, $120 for a 3-pounder.

Payment AE, V, MC, DC, D, JCB.

Service rating ★★★

Parking Free valet at dinner in Lahaina; free self-Parking in adjacent lots in Lahaina and Wailea.

Bar Full service.

Wine selection Extensive, many Italian wines and 3 house wines, 20 by the glass.

Dress Casual.

Disabled access Good for downstairs dining.

Customers Tourists and Islanders.

Breakfast Daily, 7:30–11:30 a.m.

Lunch Daily, 11:45 a.m.–4:45 p.m.

Dinner Daily, 5–10 p.m.

SETTING AND ATMOSPHERE Both Longhi's Maui locations have ocean views in open-air settings and casual surroundings. The second floor in Lahaina offers additional tables open to the trade winds.

HOUSE SPECIALTIES Be tempted with appetizers like steamed clams, Penn Cove mussels marinara, chilled marinated scallops, shrimp, and calamari, or Parmesan-fried eggplant and zucchini, with or without melted mozzarella and tomato sauce, not to mention grilled portobello mushrooms with warm goat cheese and pesto. Follow up with entrees such as shrimp Longhi (shrimp sautéed in butter-lemon-wine sauce with fresh Maui basil and tomatoes and served on garlic toast), a classic served since the restaurant opened in 1976. Fresh-fish Véronique is garnished with green grapes, and wild salmon Mediterranean is cooked in a brick oven with tomatoes, olives, and basil. Plenty of steak, chicken, and veal choices await meat-lovers.

OTHER RECOMMENDATIONS The in-house bakery prepares oven-fresh cinnamon buns, macadamia-nut rolls, coffee cakes, quiches, and cheesy jalapeño and pizza bread. Pastas made on the premises and fresh salads are available both at lunch and dinner. Signature desserts include macadamia-nut pie a la mode and the special chocolate soufflé (allow 20 minutes to fix it fresh).

ENTERTAINMENT AND AMENITIES Live bands play dance music upstairs on Friday nights in Lahaina, from 9:30 p.m. to closing.

SUMMARY AND COMMENTS Created by "a man who loves to eat," Bob Longhi, these restaurants are a family affair, with son Peter the general manager and daughter Carol O'Leary as executive chef. The restaurant wine list has repeatedly received *Wine Spectator's* award of excellence. Longhi's waiters recite a verbal menu, which can prove irritating or fun, depending on your mood. Entrees are also spelled out on the Internet site.

Maalaea Grill Restaurant ★★★½

| AMERICAN | MODERATE | QUALITY ★★★★ | VALUE ★★★ | CENTRAL MAUI |

300 Maalaea Road, Maalaea; ☎ 808-243-2206; www.cafeoleirestaurants.com/thegrill

Reservations Recommended.

When to go After the Ocean Center, or sunset.

Entree range $17–$33 (plus fresh fish at market price).

Payment V, MC.

Service rating ★★★½

Parking Free in nearby lot.

Bar Full service.

Wine selection Extensive, 50 by the glass.

Dress Resort attire.

Disabled access Adequate, via elevator.

Customers Islanders and tourists.

Lunch Daily, 10:30 a.m.–3:30 p.m.; café menu 3–5 p.m.; dinner, Tuesday–Saturday, 5:30–9 p.m.

SETTING AND ATMOSPHERE Conveniently situated in the Maui Ocean Center complex and overlooking busy Maalaea Harbor, this open, airy room is simply dressed with teak furniture and bamboo rails, old-fashioned hanging lights and fans from high ceilings, cream walls, and flowers.

HOUSE SPECIALTIES Rotisserie-roasted duck with orange or honey–macadamia nut sauce might tempt you away from the fresh fish, even though you are right there over the harbor and could watch the catch being unloaded. This is a seafood haven, with mahimahi served four ways, four shrimp dishes, fresh-catch specials, seared ahi, lobster, and king crab as well as jumbo scallops. But there are beef, chicken, and pasta choices as well.

OTHER RECOMMENDATIONS Feel like a burger? How 'bout a pound of Bill Eby (Maui-grown) rich beef with cheese, tomato, grilled onions, and shoestring fries? You might feel you have to make do with half-pound burgers of Kobe beef, or chicken or fish burgers at lunch. Lunch also features plate-lunch-of-the-day, sandwiches, fish dishes, and a wide range of salads—Caesar, Asian, curried chicken, seared tuna, and vegetarian quinoa salad with roasted marinated veggies, the grain quinoa, and goat cheese with balsamic vinaigrette. Dessert decisions are almost as complex, but it would be hard to go wrong with lemon-coconut cheesecake or Kona-coffee crème brûlée.

SUMMARY AND COMMENTS Large parties or weddings with seatings of up to 300 people can be accommodated, and the parent Café O'Lei group of Maui restaurants also has a catering arm. Other restaurants in the popular group include Fish and Poi at Napili Beach.

Maalaea Waterfront Restaurant ★★★½

SEAFOOD/CONTINENTAL   EXPENSIVE   QUALITY ★★★★★   VALUE ★★★
CENTRAL MAUI

50 Haouli Street, Maalaea; ☎ 808-244-9028; www.waterfrontrestaurant.com

Reservations Highly recommended.

When to go Sunset.

Entree range $19–$38, plus market prices for fish and lobster.

Payment V, MC, AE, DC, D, JCB.

Service rating ★★★½

Parking Free in upper level of adjacent condominium garage.

Bar Full service.

Wine selection Extensive, many by the glass.

Dress Resort attire.

Disabled access Adequate, via elevator.

Customers Islanders and tourists.

Dinner Daily, 5 p.m.–closing.

SETTING AND ATMOSPHERE Textured pale-green walls, white tablecloths with candles and tropical flowers, and Island paintings on the walls make for a restful interior in this oceanfront restaurant. Outdoor dining on the deck is lovely on a balmy night, but bring a wrap if the trade winds are brisk.

HOUSE SPECIALTIES The emphasis is on fish, fresh from the waters and boats right in front of the restaurant. Depending on what the fishermen bring in each day, five or more different kinds of fish are served in nine preparations. This means there are always 45 or more choices to make while you sip some lobster chowder or nibble on homemade bread slathered with the house's special beer-cheese spread or watch the tableside construction of your Caesar salad.

OTHER RECOMMENDATIONS Besides rack of lamb and prime rib, the menu features game, such as venison, pheasant, or ostrich, as a daily special. For dessert, try the white-chocolate blueberry cheesecake or upside-down apple pie.

SUMMARY AND COMMENTS Maalaea Waterfront Restaurant is a family endeavor, opened in 1990 by the Smiths: Mom; Bob, the chef; Gary, the manager; and Rick, the detail man. Their success is evidenced by the support of local patrons—the restaurant has repeatedly been cited the best in seafood and service.

Mala, an Ocean Tavern ★★★★½

CONTEMPORARY INEXPENSIVE/MODERATE QUALITY ★★★★★ VALUE ★★★★★
WEST MAUI

1307 Front Street, Lahaina; ☎ 808-667-9394; www.malaoceantavern.com

Reservations Suggested.

When to go Anytime.

Entrée range Lunch, $13–$15; dinner, $14–$25.

Payment V, MC, AE, DC, D, JCB.

Service rating ★★★★

Parking Free and ample in adjacent lot or across the street at Lahaina Cannery Mall.

Bar Full service.

Wine selection Good.

Dress Casual.

Disabled access Good.

Customers Locals, visitors.

Brunch Saturday and Sunday, 9 a.m.–3 p.m.; lunch, Monday–Friday, 11 a.m-3 p.m.

Dinner Monday–Saturday, 4:30–10 p.m.; Sunday, 4:30–9 p.m.

SETTING AND ATMOSPHERE Unpretentious, hip little plantation-style waterfront wine bar—tapas eatery celebrates the creative genius of one of the original Hawaii Regional Cuisine chefs, Mark Ellman. He was chef-proprietor of the popular Avalon Restaurant farther down Front Street until he sold it some years ago to launch the successful fast-fusion Maui Tacos chain (blending Mexican and Island flavors) across the Islands and later throughout many Mainland states. Now he's back in town with this wonderful cafe on the quiet edge of Lahaina, so close to the water that you could get splashed on the lanai.

HOUSE SPECIALTIES Many tastes on small plates to be shared: this tapas concept lets you sample lots of the chef's considerable talent. At Mala, tapas are Spanish mostly in name and portion size, although plenty of Latin touches pepper the multicultural fare, such as Spanish Naia Verdejo wine, sangria, and treats such as dry Manchego cheese. The menu leans to organic, healthy dishes. Appetizers, for instance, include a dish of sugar snap peas dressed in a ginger, sambal chili, and sesame sauce, as hot as you choose; Indonesian *gado gado* salad; tomato shiitake flatbread with mozzarella and basil; and a Middle Eastern plate of hummus, raita, olives, baba ghanoush, fried chickpeas, and feta cheese served with pita and lavosh. Look for steamed clams

Avalon, with a ginger-garlic black-bean sauce, or spicy lamb in a pita. Specials change daily. At Mala, even the cheeseburgers are made of Kobe beef. For dessert, hail the return of Avalon's Caramel Miranda, a dessert platter stacked with macadamia-nut ice cream piled with tropical fruit like Carmen Miranda's hat and drizzled with caramel to make it irresistible.

OTHER RECOMMENDATIONS Crunchy calamari with aioli, seared sashimi with shiitake-ginger sauce, and rich tomato soup are among the offerings, along with a variety of flatbreads, one being a thin crust bearing shrimp, cilantro pesto, and grape tomatoes. Sweets include the key lime pie martini. The flan is also highly recommended.

SUMMARY AND COMMENTS Patrons who mourned the loss of Avalon are delighted to have Ellman back in town, where he also runs Penne Pasta, an inexpensive and excellent pasta house that also serves pizza and specials, with dinner nightly and lunch on weekdays, 180 Dickenson Street, ☎ 808-661-6633. Now there's also Mala Wailea at the Wailea Beach Marriott Resort.

Mama's Fish House ★★★★½

SEAFOOD   EXPENSIVE   QUALITY ★★★★★   VALUE ★★★   CENTRAL MAUI

799 Poho Place, Paia; ☎ 808-579-8488; www.mamasfishhouse.com

Reservations Highly recommended.

When to go Anytime, but sunset is most romantic.

Entree range Lunch $25–$44, dinner $31–$50.

Payment V, MC, AE, DC, D, JCB.

Service rating ★★★★

Parking Valet or adjacent lot.

Bar Full service.

Wine selection Excellent, half a dozen by the glass.

Dress Casual resort wear.

Disabled access Good, but it's a distance from the lot.

Customers Tourists and Islanders.

Lunch Daily, 11 a.m.–2 p.m.; **Pupu** Daily, 2:30–3 p.m.

Dinner Daily, 5–9:30 p.m.

SETTING AND ATMOSPHERE You'll find Mama's in a rambling, open-air beach house at the end of a gecko-patterned walkway beside the ocean, with cool, green lawns and shady coconut palms out front. A wooden bar and wooden paneling inside are made of tropical almond, monkeypod, and mango wood. It's a perfect place to while away an afternoon over a Mai Tai Roa Ae—a fresh-fruit-and-rum concoction like that originated by Trader Vic years ago—or to sample other retro drinks: Singapore slings of Raffles hotel fame, zombies, and scorpions.

HOUSE SPECIALTIES Fishermen get credited by name or boat on the menu for catching the fresh fish of the day, and Executive Chef Perry Batemen is himself a free-diving fisherman. So the fish is always top-notch, whether you have ono, ahi, uku, opah, opakapaka, salmon (from New Zealand), or whatever. Preparations include sautéed with garlic, mushrooms, tomato, white wine, and capers; sautéed with Penang curry; topped with Maui onion and avocado; stuffed with lobster and baked in a macadamia nut crust; or sugar-cane grilled with ginger-soy glaze. A signature dish, Pua me hua Hana, features sautéed fish in coconut milk with kalua pig, grilled banana, fresh coconut, fruit, and Molokai sweet potatoes.

OTHER RECOMMENDATIONS To sample Island-style cooking, try a *laulau,* pieces of mahimahi wrapped and baked in ti leaves with mango and coconut milk and served with tender, moist kalua pig and poi. Another imaginative entree with local flair is crispy kalua duck with mango-mui glaze served with baby bok choy and wild rice. The New York steak is Big Island–grown, a local treat for beef lovers.

SUMMARY AND COMMENTS The open-air, Polynesian atmosphere of "Grandma's Living Room" draws residents to hang out, listen to vintage Hawaiian music, and snack on pupu rather than ordering a pricey full meal.

PacificO ★★★★½

HAWAII REGIONAL   MODERATE/EXPENSIVE   QUALITY ★★★★★   VALUE ★★★
WEST MAUI

505 Front Street, Lahaina; ☎ 808-667-4341; www.pacificomaui.com

Reservations Recommended.

When to go Sunset.

Entree range Lunch $12–$15.50; dinner $26–$40.

Payment V, MC, AE, DC, JCB.

Service rating ★★★★

Parking Free in lot across the street.

Bar Full service.

Wine selection Excellent.

Dress Casual.

Disabled access Adequate, but it's a long way from the Parking lot.

Customers Tourists and Islanders.

Lunch Daily, 11 a.m.–4 p.m.

Dinner Daily, 5:30–9 p.m.

SETTING AND ATMOSPHERE The outdoor terrace is hard to resist, with tables and umbrellas set close to the sea. Inside, ceiling fans spin lazily and windows are open wide to the ocean breezes and the three-island view.

HOUSE SPECIALTIES Try the award-winning *yuzu* divers appetizer—a crispy coconut roll with seared scallops, arugula pesto and zesty yuzu lime sauce. The Pan-Pacific menu features one of Maui's best lobster values ($40) for an innovative dish—two tails poached in ginger butter and served with lobster coconut sauce. At lunch, you may be torn between an Angus burger trimmed with blue cheese and grilled mushrooms and the house original sesame fish, seared and served with baby greens and wasabi sesame dressing. When it comes to salad, you'll find some house originals—layers of homemade buttermilk cheese in the stack of tomato slices, basil, crispy artichoke hearts, and curry dressing; or house salad fresh from the house farm.

OTHER RECOMMENDATIONS Fresh catch comes crusted with macadamia nuts and coconut; seared and served over greens with avocado, salsa, goat cheese, and macadamia nuts; seared with Asian spices and tomato-curry vinaigrette; or dusted with Indian spices and topped with a foam of sea urchin and coconut. The melt-in-your-mouth dessert of banana pineapple *lumpia* (spring roll) and macadamia-nut ice cream is a beautiful blend of texture and taste.

ENTERTAINMENT AND AMENITIES Live jazz after dinner, Thursday through Saturday, 9 p.m. to midnight.

SUMMARY AND COMMENTS The same talented chef/owner, James McDonald, also owns IO, the chic little restaurant next door, and The Feast at Lele luau, also a beachfront neighbor. His Oo Farm supplies fresh greens, herbs, and vegetables to all three. (Oo Farm is open to visitors two days a week to tour, pick some produce, and eat it for a gourmet lunch; see **www.oofarm.com.**)

Plantation House Restaurant ★★★★

CONTEMPORARY **MODERATE/EXPENSIVE** **QUALITY ★★★★** **VALUE ★★★**
WEST MAUI

Plantation Course Clubhouse, 2000 Plantation Club Drive, Kapalua Resort; ☎ 808-669-6299; www.theplantationhouse.com

Reservations Recommended for dinner.

When to go Anytime; lunch or sunset for the smashing view.

Entree range Lunch, $8.50–$16; dinner, $27–$42 (plus lobster at market price).

Payment V, AE, MC, DC.

Service rating ★★★

Parking In adjacent lot.

Bar Full service.

Wine selection Extensive.

Dress Casual.

Disabled access Good, drop off at front door.

Customers Golfers, tourists, and Islanders.

Breakfast and lunch Daily, 8 a.m.–3 p.m.; light menu 3–5 p.m.

Dinner Daily, 5:30–9 p.m.

SETTING AND ATMOSPHERE High above the shoreline, diners in this not-your-average-golf-club restaurant can admire sweeping views of moody Molokai, wind-whipped blue ocean, green fairways, and the rest of Kapalua Resort through windows open to cool upland breezes.

The decor is a blend of swanky and casual, as befits the well-heeled golfers, with lots of rattan and tropical woods setting off a large mural of pineapple workers in the Kapalua fields. A double-sided fireplace creates a warm glow to ward off any evening chill up on the slope of Puu Kukui.

HOUSE SPECIALTIES Fresh fish comes dressed for dinner in many styles, including an Oscar with asparagus, crabmeat, and lemon-butter sauce, and a Venetian choice with shrimp, baby fava beans, green beans, and pine nuts. Vegetarians can substitute tofu for fish in any of the featured preparations or request other meatless entrees. A full roster of eggs Benedicts tops the breakfast/lunch menu, including one that could stretch your fusion limits—Cajun-style ahi sashimi Benedict with wasabi hollandaise.

OTHER RECOMMENDATIONS Hungry duffers will find substantial fare like lamb shanks and mashed potatoes, roast duck, lobster, and pork tenderloin.

SUMMARY AND COMMENTS Chef Alex Stanislaw created an inspired and varied menu deserving of the spectacular setting, merging Mediterranean flavors and Island ingredients. It's a refreshing alternative to the other resort restaurants down below.

Roy's Kahana Bar and Grill and Roy's Kihei Bar and Grill ★★★★

HAWAIIAN FUSION   MODERATE/EXPENSIVE   QUALITY ★★★   VALUE ★★★
WEST MAUI/SOUTH MAUI

Kahana Gateway Shopping Center, 4405 Honoapiilani Highway, Kahana; ☎ 808-669-6999; Piilani Village Shopping Center, 303 Piikea Street, Kihei; ☎ 808-891-1120; www.roysrestaurant.com

Reservations Highly recommended.

When to go Anytime.

Entree range $24.50–$35.

Payment V, MC, AE, DC, D, JCB.

Service rating ★★★★★

Parking Free in shopping-center lot.

Bar Full service.

Wine selection Excellent, 10–15 by the glass.

Dress Casual.

Disabled access Good, via elevator to upstairs restaurant in Kahana.

Customers Tourists and Islanders.

Dinner Roy's Kahana: 5:30–10 p.m.; Roy's Kihei: 5:30–9:30 p.m.

SETTING AND ATMOSPHERE The new Kihei eatery in South Maui and the established Kahana Roy's in West Maui offer the same creative fare Roy's lovers expect, with only a few miles between them. Like most Roy's, the Maui restaurants are in small shopping complexes. Both feature 20 to 25 specials nightly, with the distinctive Roy's touch—lots of seafood choices, succulent meats and tender steaks, creative fusion of ingredients, happy (and often noisy) atmosphere, smooth service, and good wines and cocktails. It's a winning combination, in 37 Roy's Restaurants in the United States, Guam, and Japan.

HOUSE SPECIALTIES Newest signature dish on the menu is Roy's Classic Trio, composed of three international favorites, says Chef Roy Yamaguchi: blackened ahi with soy mustard butter sauce, hibachi-grilled salmon with citrus ponzu sauce, and Hawaiian-style misoyaki butterfish with sizzling soy vinaigrette. That makes the menu choice one step simpler, but still sometimes agonizing, since so many things look and taste so good. Specials change often, but everything is made with the freshest local ingredients with Euro-Asian accents in the flavors and preparations. Appetizers like Szechuan baby back ribs and Roy's shrimp-and-pork spring rolls with hot sweet mustard and black-bean sauce set the scene. Lemongrass-crusted *shutome* (swordfish) reflects a touch of Thailand, with sticky rice and basil peanut sauce. Braised and charbroiled short ribs are delectable.

OTHER RECOMMENDATIONS The "poketini"—poke in a martini glass with aïoli and avocado—is a silky, rich appetizer. Or try the appetizer "canoe" for two, a chef's special sampling of pan-Asian treats like dim sum, potstickers, and lumpia, done up with Hawaiian ingredients. For dessert, melting hot chocolate soufflé will please chocolate lovers.

SUMMARY AND COMMENTS You really can't go wrong with Roy's Hawaiian fusion brand of cuisine, dishes that are exciting and rarely disappointing. Yamaguchi is a genius in the kitchen but has an even rarer skill to select and train other chefs to guide his restaurants—7 in Hawaii (where it all began 20 years ago in Hawaii Kai, a Honolulu suburb), plus 28 on the Mainland and one each in Guam and Japan. He has won so many awards that it's difficult to track them. *Gourmet* magazine, the James Beard Foundation, and many others applaud this imaginative and energetic chef, whose television cooking show airs in 60 countries. Tokyo-born, Hawaii-influenced Yamaguchi was introduced to Maui seafood as a child, then went on to the Culinary Institute of America and soon, stardom.

A Saigon Café ★★★

VIETNAMESE INEXPENSIVE QUALITY ★★★★ VALUE ★★★★★ CENTRAL MAUI

1792 Main Street, Wailuku; ☎ 808-243-9560

Reservations Recommended, especially for dinner.

When to go Anytime.

Entree range $7–$20.

Payment V, MC.

Service rating ★★★★

Parking In adjacent lot.

Bar Full service.

Wine selection Limited.

Dress Casual.

Disabled access Good.

Customers Islanders and a few tourists.

Lunch and Dinner Monday–Saturday, 10 a.m.–9:30 p.m.; Sunday, 10 a.m.–8:30 p.m.

SETTING AND ATMOSPHERE Sit at the low wooden bar or choose a Formica table or booth for lunch and dinner in this basic, white-walled restaurant minimally decorated with Vietnamese lacquered art. A gold Buddha greets guests at the door, ceiling fans whir overhead, and the TV might be on at the bar. It's a low-key place that can be difficult to find because there is no sign: Cross the bridge into Wailuku from Kahului, take the first right turn onto Central, and then take the first right turn onto Nani. At the stop sign, look for an "OPEN" sign on a small bungalow with trees in pots by the doorway.

HOUSE SPECIALTIES Fresh herbs, greens, and other vegetables are the hallmark of good Vietnamese food, and that's what you find here. Start with *cha gio* (fried spring rolls)—little deep-fried bundles of ground pork, long rice, carrot, and onion wrapped in rice paper; the waiter will show you how to roll them in romaine lettuce with mint leaves and vermicelli noodles, then dip them in sweet-sour garlic sauce. Or try the Vietnamese classic, ground marinated shrimp grilled on a stick of sugar cane. Popular entrées include stuffed tofu, and fried shrimp served with sautéed ginger and green onions on bean sprouts and lettuce.

OTHER RECOMMENDATIONS With 92 items on the menu, it's hard to choose. Green-papaya salad is a favorite accompaniment. For lunch, the noodle soups—with seafood and chicken, calamari and shrimp, wonton, and other ingredients—provide a big bowl of steaming goodness. The several rice-in-a-clay-pot dishes feature chicken, catfish, shrimp, or pork.

SUMMARY AND COMMENTS Everybody loves A Saigon Café, and regulars admire proprietor Jennifer Nguyen, as well. Nguyen opened the restaurant in January 1996, but its sign is still stored in a box somewhere. The sprightly, hardworking proprietor says, "We've been so busy, we've never gotten around to putting it up!"

Sansei Seafood Restaurant and Sushi Bar ★★★★★

JAPANESE FUSION   MODERATE/EXPENSIVE   QUALITY ★★★★★   VALUE ★★★★
WEST MAUI/SOUTH MAUI

Honolua Village, 600 Office Road, Kapalua; ☎ 808-669-6286
Kihei Town Center 1881 South Kihei Road, Kihei; ☎ 808-879-0004;
www.sanseihawaii.com

Reservations Highly recommended.

When to go Early or late for discounts.

Entree range $16–$43.

Payment V, MC, AE, D, JCB.

Service rating ★★★★

Parking In adjacent lots.

Bar Full service.

Wine selection Extensive, also array of sakes.

Dress Resort attire.

Disabled access Good.

Customers Islanders and tourists; late-night karaoke crowd.

Dinner Daily, 5:30–10 p.m. Late-night laser karaoke Thursday and Friday, 10 p.m.–1 a.m.

SETTING AND ATMOSPHERE Brand-new building on the main entry to Kapalua Resort, between the Village Clubhouse (home of sister restaurant Vino Italian Tapas & Wine Bar, see below) and the Honolua General Store. Booths and tables fill up fast in the intimate, new 120-seat Kapalua restaurant, which includes a sushi bar and cocktail lounge area as well as three dining rooms, one for private parties. The Kihei location, in a shopping complex along Kihei Road, is a hit as well. Restaurant decor blends a bit of Japan with a Maui plantation look, echoing the blend of flavors—Japanese with Pacific Rim influences. Samurai pictures decorate the walls, and the sushi bar, with its scalloped awning, could have come from Tokyo (as some of the sushi chefs did).

HOUSE SPECIALTIES There's no end to Sansei's creativity, matching Eastern ways with Western flavors and vice versa. The dishes are some of Maui's tastiest. Try many dishes and share. With sushi this is easy, and Sansei offers up delicious tidbits, from crab and mango salad hand rolls to spider rolls with soft-shell crab to bagel rolls with smoked salmon, Maui onion, and cream cheese. The family-style concept applies to entrées as well. Pass around the house special: Peking duck breast with shiitake potato risotto. Other favorites: Asian rock-shrimp cake, Japanese calamari salad with greens in a crispy won ton basket, and nori ravioli of shrimp and lobster.

OTHER RECOMMENDATIONS Come early (before 6 p.m.) and get a 25 percent break on the tab for food and sushi. Come late (after 10 p.m.) and enjoy half-priced appetizer specials along with laser karaoke. Pay attention when the waiter describes nightly specials like asparagus tempura, or try shrimp tempura fried in a light-as-air batter, or grilled fresh mahi-mahi on Kula greens. The Granny Smith apple tart is a pure American finish to any meal.

ENTERTAINMENT AND AMENITIES Sansei's karaoke after 10 p.m. on Thursday and Friday draws a happy crowd at both restaurants.

SUMMARY AND COMMENTS Most Hawaii cuisine is at least good, fresh, and pleasing. Sansei is also fun, and that makes it hard to beat. The Kihei restaurant is good news for South Maui patrons who used to have to drive an hour each way to indulge in Sansei Kapalua treats. Chef/owner D. K. Kodama, who has also opened Sansei and Vino restaurants in Honolulu, says his menu reflects the way he likes to eat, with playful flavors and bits of this and that.

Sea House Restaurant ★★★

PACIFIC RIM   MODERATE/EXPENSIVE   QUALITY ★★★   VALUE ★★★   WEST MAUI

5900 Honoapiilani Highway, Napili; ☎ 808-669-1500; www.napilikai.com

Reservations Recommended.

When to go Anytime you can see the view.

Entree range Breakfast, under $13; lunch, $9–$13; dinner, $24–$34.

Payment AE, V, MC, DC, D, JCB.

Service rating ★★★★★

Parking Free but limited in adjacent lots.

Bar Full service.

Wine selection Good.

Dress Casual resort attire.

Disabled access Not easy.

Customers Hotel guests, other tourists.

Breakfast Daily, 7–11 a.m.

Lunch Daily, 11 a.m.–2 p.m.

Dinner Daily, 5:30–9 p.m.

SETTING AND ATMOSPHERE Beachfront, down a winding path from the parking areas through low-rise, lushly landscaped Napili Kai Resort, the Sea House is built on a slight rise over Napili Bay Beach. It has an awesome island-and-sea view.

HOUSE SPECIALTIES Appetizers such as stacked seared ahi Napoleon with avocado, tomato, onion salsa, and wasabi-soy vinaigrette or California roll in a crispy macadamia-nut crust with red Thai curry sauce will get you started. Then consider tucking into Ono Margarita style, with a tequila-chili citrus glaze, or award-winning *hulihuli* (turned on a spit) lamb chops with a pepper/garlic/ginger crust and mango garnish, green papaya salad, and Poha berry sauce, in two portion sizes.

OTHER RECOMMENDATIONS Many guests here stay awhile, so the Sea House keeps interest up with nightly specials—prime rib on Monday and Wednesday, Alaskan king crab on Tuesday and Friday, cold-water lobster on Thursday and surf–turf on weekend nights. Children's menu includes pizza, pastas, burgers, and chicken nuggets.

SUMMARY AND COMMENTS Neither trendy nor hip, the Sea House gets the job done in a beautiful setting.

 Seawatch Restaurant ★★★½

CONTEMPORARY   MODERATE/EXPENSIVE   QUALITY ★★★★   VALUE ★★★★
SOUTH MAUI

**100 Wailea Golf Club Drive, Wailea; ☎ 808-875-8080;
www.seawatchrestaurant.com**

Reservations Recommended.

When to go Anytime you can see the view, but aim for sunset.

Entree range Breakfast/lunch, $8.50–$15; dinner, $26–40 (except lobster and fish entrees, which are market priced).

Payment AE, V, MC, DC, D, JCB.

Service rating ★★★★★

Parking Free in adjacent lots.

Bar Full service

Wine selection Good.

Dress Casual resort attire.

Disabled access Good, via elevator.

Customers Hotel guests, other tourists, and Islanders.

Breakfast/Lunch Daily, 8 a.m.–3 p.m.

Dinner Daily, 6–9 p.m., Bar open 6–11 p.m.

SETTING AND ATMOSPHERE Another of Maui's classy golf-club restaurants, Seawatch is true to its name: From this lofty perch on the lower slope of Haleakala, the island-studded ocean view is extraordinary, especially on the outdoor lanai, where diners and cocktail sippers can watch humpback whales spouting far below. Indoors, Jan Kasprzycki's vivid paintings adorn the walls and large, glass doors admit the trade winds and the view.

HOUSE SPECIALTIES Chef Todd Carlos's five inspired fish preparations compete for attention with weekly specials and an array of grilled meats and poultry. Osso buco is worth a splurge, as are Alaskan scallops (appetizers) or fresh Hawaiian fish (entree) seared with a crust of tea, lemongrass, and citrus. For appetizers, if you can resist the seafood, try macadamia nut–crusted brie with pineapple chutney and crostini.

OTHER RECOMMENDATIONS Dinner's fine, but breakfast is a find—not only in terms of spectacular setting, but also imaginative and well-priced entrees compared to hotel food. If you're golfing early or getting up late, call it brunch or lunch—you can order Molokai sweet-bread French toast, crab-cake Benedict with red-pepper hollandaise, loco moco (grilled burger with eggs, rice, and gravy), kalua pork and scrambled eggs, or stir-fried fresh veggies with black bean sauce, among other options. Save some room for Kona pie (Kona-coffee ice cream in an Oreo crust) for dessert, or other dessert choices from light (tropical sorbets and fruit) to decadent (brownie with ice cream and hot fudge). The children's menu (for kids 12 and under) includes a dessert sundae with dinner entrees, ranging from salad, grilled cheese, or burgers to fish, steak, or chicken with mashed potatoes and vegetables.

SUMMARY AND COMMENTS This is a satisfying alternative dining spot for Wailea and Makena guests, a special-occasion choice for area residents, and a great site for parties and weddings. Seawatch and Plantation House at Kapalua share ownership, situation (golf clubhouses with fabulous views), and approach (golfers deserve good food, too, especially considering today's green fees).

kids Spago at Four Seasons Resort Maui ★★★★½

CONTEMPORARY   EXPENSIVE   QUALITY ★★★★★   VALUE ★★★   SOUTH MAUI

Four Seasons Resort Maui, 3900 Wailea Alanui, Wailea; ☎ 808-874-8000; www.fourseasons.com or www.wolfgangpuck.com

Reservations Highly recommended.

When to go Sunset is spectacular.

Entree range $31–$48.

Payment AE, V, MC, DC, D, JCB.

Service rating ★★★★★

Parking Complimentary valet or self-Parking in covered hotel lot.

Bar Full service.

Wine selection Extensive and international, prices vary.

Dress Resort attire.

Disabled access Good, via elevator.

Customers Hotel guests, other tourists, and Islanders for special occasions.

Dinner Daily, 6–9 p.m.

SETTING AND ATMOSPHERE Spago's interiors set a scene of relaxed elegance with contemporary Asian design, featuring stone, wood, and art, and—of course—big ocean vistas of beaches, offshore islands, and the Maui coastline. It's very romantic, but this is also an example of the refined Hawaii restaurants that have gone to some effort to accommodate families, too.

HOUSE SPECIALTIES Chef Cameron Lewark's own style of Hawaii/California fusion menu features dishes such as pan-roasted *uku* (snapper) with lobster sauce and caramelized pork chop with lomilomi tomatoes, polenta, braised greens, and fried garlic. Wolfgang Puck classics appear among the choices, including grilled Chinois-style lamb chops with Hunan eggplant and chili-mint vinaigrette; and whole steamed *moi* (threadfish) Thai–style, with ginger, chili, garlic, baby bok choy, and rice. Desserts with Island flair include tropical sorbets and mango upside-down cake with lilikoi sorbet.

OTHER RECOMMENDATIONS Starters with a bow to local ingredients include tomato salad with Maui goat feta, basil, and shaved Maui onion, and spicy ahi poke served in sesame-miso cones. Hawaiian-style ceviche features *opakapaka* with lemon-soy and tomato-onion relish. Sweet Upcountry corn is featured in a risotto.

SUMMARY AND COMMENTS Four Seasons and the Wolfgang Puck Fine Dining Group formed a new kind of partnership in Spago at the Four Seasons Resort Maui, with others to follow in Mainland Four Seasons hotels. Southern Californians who frequent this hotel and any diners who love stylish food will be at home at Spago, where chef talent meets Island ingredients and multicultural traditions. Puck created his first children's menu here (chicken fingers, pasta with butter and cheese or "volcano" tomato sauce, cheese pizza, or grilled cheese).

Stella Blues Café ★★★★½

AMERICAN   MODERATE   QUALITY ★★★★   VALUE ★★★★   SOUTH MAUI

Azeka II Mall, 1279 Kihei Road; ☎ 808-874-3779; www.stellablues.com

Reservations Recommended.

When to go Anytime.

Entree range Lunch $6–$13; dinner $16–$28 (fresh fish is market price).

Payment Cash only.

Service rating ★★★

Parking Free, shopping-center lot.

Bar Full service.

Wine selection Good, bottled and by the glass.

Dress Casual.

Disabled access Good.

Customers Residents, visitors.

Breakfast Daily, 7:30–11 a.m. (until 2 p.m. Sunday).

Lunch Daily, 11 a.m.–5 p.m.

Dinner Daily, 5–10 p.m., plus late-night light menu and drinks until 11 p.m.

SETTING AND ATMOSPHERE Stella Blues, once a little vegetarian lunchroom, has moved up and out, taking over a large, modernistic place just up the street and expanding its daily menu to three meals of "New American comfort food." With curving walls and warm Mediterranean colors, the new site has an exhibition kitchen surrounded by a bar where diners can watch chefs at work, as well as an outdoor lanai.

HOUSE SPECIALTIES The menu takes a something-for-everyone approach with an extensive list of "small plates" ranging from hummus to crab cakes, served from 5 to 11 p.m.; plus pastas, pizzas, fresh fish, and something special to try: Maui-grown beef, in burgers, steak sandwiches, and steak-and-eggs. Vegetarian roots are still evident in dishes like vegetarian shepherd's pie and tofu curry. For dessert, go light with tropical sorbets or rich with *lilikoi* (passion fruit) cheesecake or brownie à la mode.

OTHER RECOMMENDATIONS If you're pining for breakfast that doesn't cost $20 or more and isn't the same old buffet, drive in for smoothies and espresso drinks, lox and bagels, or the choice of hungry dawn-patrol surfers, loco moco (hamburger patty with two eggs, rice, and gravy over all). You can build your own omelet or savory tofu scramble, not to mention eggs with cheese and jalapeños. Takeout and catering are also available.

SUMMARY AND COMMENTS Some things actually change for the better, and

Stella Blues' popular lunch formula shows every sign of success on a much broader scale. If you've wondered how the average Maui resident manages to survive in a world of resort prices, this is how: good grinds, good wines, plenty of choices, and affordable prices.

LANAI

Blue Ginger Café ★

ISLAND ECLECTIC   INEXPENSIVE   QUALITY ★★★   VALUE ★★   LANAI

409 Seventh Avenue, Lanai City; ☎ 808-565-6363

Reservations Large parties.

When to go Anytime.

Entree range $6.50–$14.95.

Payment Cash only.

Service rating Self-serve.

Parking Street.

Bar Full service.

Wine selection Limited.

Dress Casual.

Disabled access Good.

Customers Islanders, travelers.

Breakfast Daily, 6–11 a.m.

Lunch and Dinner Daily, 11 a.m.–9 p.m.

SETTING AND ATMOSPHERE Set in a little wooden plantation building in Lanai City's main square. Diners pick up their orders from a counter and eat at tables with plastic cloths in this plain and simple local-style alternative to Lanai's fancy hotel restaurants.

HOUSE SPECIALTIES Try the tasty vegetarian breakfast omelet that comes with rice, or order fresh-baked apple turnovers or cinnamon rolls. For lunch, the bacon-cheddar cheeseburgers are better than Big Macs, but you might want to try the Island soup called *saimin,* a generous steaming bowl of noodle soup garnished with sliced fish cake, green onions, and shredded egg. At dinner, sautéed mahimahi with capers, onions, and mushrooms is the signature dish. Top it off with an ice-cream dessert. Blue Ginger serves Dave's ice cream, made in the Islands with local ingredients.

OTHER RECOMMENDATIONS Banana or blueberry pancakes accompanied by cappuccino are great for breakfast. For dinner, try a local plate with a choice of teriyaki beef, *katsu* chicken, or hamburger with gravy, plus rice and macaroni salad. The stir-fried veggies are plentiful and cooked just right.

SUMMARY AND COMMENTS This has been a Lanai hangout owned by the same family for years. Blue Ginger and Pele's Other Garden, located across the park, are the best independent restaurants around the square in Lanai City.

The Dining Room, Four Seasons Resort Lanai/ The Lodge at Koele ★★★★★

CONTEMPORARY   EXPENSIVE   QUALITY ★★★★★   VALUE ★★★★   LANAI

Four Seasons Lanai/The Lodge at Koele, Keomuku Drive, Lanai City;
☎ **808-565-4580; www.fourseasons.com/koele**

Reservations Highly recommended.

When to go Anytime for dinner.

Entree range $32–$75.

Payment V, MC, AE, DC, JCB.

Service rating ★★★★★

Parking Valet, hotel lot.

Bar Full service.

Wine selection Excellent.

Dress Resort casual (collared shirts, long pants, and closed footwear for men.)

Disabled access Adequate.

Customers Hotel guests and other visitors.

Dinner Daily, 6–9:30 p.m.

SETTING AND ATMOSPHERE The mood is relaxed and refined in this room, which looks out onto the lodge's huge backyard—reflecting pool; wide, green lawns; and forested slope beyond. A fire in the fireplace lends a romantic touch. But the emphasis is on enjoying a truly fine dinner.

HOUSE SPECIALTIES Imaginative use of fresh, local ingredients is the signature approach in heartier fare that befits cool Upcountry evenings. For starters, it's hard to top the quail prepared two ways, seared breast with raisins and fava beans and a leg confit with artichoke puree and orange-balsamic glaze, or island venison seared on lava rock, prepared tableside with apple, celery, and candied nut salad and cranberry relish. Fresh catch and shellfish enrich the bouillabaisse, while duck breast roasted with honey and Maui lavender and presented with savory bread pudding and cranberry cassis sauce reflects the woodland setting.

OTHER RECOMMENDATIONS If you're a fan of lobster, the Maine lobster with roast salsify, Hollandaise, and caviar might fill the bill. Vegetarians will find a chef's-choice plate of four seasonal vegetables prepared in different ways. But keep dessert in mind—roasted pineapple with coconut-rum ice cream, for instance, or warm bittersweet chocolate cake with roasted banana and Kona coffee ice cream.

ENTERTAINMENT AND AMENITIES Dinner music, often traditional Hawaiian songs or classical musical scores, drifts in from the adjoining lobby. You can extend what is sure to be an expensive evening by relaxing in the lobby after dinner with a snifter of brandy in front of a crackling fire. Just be careful not to spill the Rémy Martin Louis VIII, which tops a list of after-dinner drinks that includes sweet wines, brandies, ports, madeira, and sherries rivaling the selection in some French airport duty-free shops.

SUMMARY AND COMMENTS This intimate atmosphere could be the perfect place to pop the question. No wonder The Dining Room keeps winning high praise.

Ihilani, Four Seasons Resort Lanai at Manele Bay ★★★★★

CONTEMPORARY ITALIAN   EXPENSIVE   QUALITY ★★★★★   VALUE ★★★   LANAI

**Four Seasons Resort Lanai at Manele Bay, 1 Manele Road, Lanai City;
☎ 808-565-7700; www.fourseasons.com/manelebay/**

Reservations Recommended.

When to go Anytime.

Entree range $50–$75; vegetarian menu, $28–$32.

Payment V, MC, AE, DC, JCB.

Service rating ★★★★★

Parking Valet.

Bar Full service.

Wine selection Extensive.

Dress Resort wear.

Disabled access Good.

Customers Tourists and visitors from the neighbor islands.

Dinner Tuesday–Saturday, 6–9:30 p.m.

SETTING AND ATMOSPHERE Fine china, silver, and lace-clothed tables under hand-blown Italian crystal chandeliers set the elegant mood in this formal room, with views of pool and sea.

HOUSE SPECIALTIES Italian flavors with a flair, using fresh seafood and Island fruits and vegetables, dominate the menu in this hotel restaurant perched on a seaside cliff. Choices range from light to rich (Caprese salad of tomatoes, mozzarella, basil, and olive oil, or baked scallops with Muscato zabaglione sauce, for instance) to inventive (seared ahi wrapped in phyllo and served with tomato compote and cucumber sorbet). Diners rave about the truffled cauliflower soup with lobster medallions and homemade spinach gnocchi in marinara sauce. And that's just for starters: creative and enticing desserts include zucotto— a praline and chocolate mousse with caramelized local bananas and hazelnut sponge cake—and housemade gelatos such as Meyer lemon and olive oil, almond, Waialua coffee, and raspberry.

OTHER RECOMMENDATIONS A nightly set menu of six or seven courses can be ordered paired with wines if you choose. Prices may change according to what is featured. You might begin with oysters, then sample Maine lobster with shiitake mushrooms, proceed to pan-fried ahi, and savor a main course of roasted duck breast in red wine port sauce with Molokai sweet-potato puree and sautéed endive. Next, a selection of cheeses and walnut bread is served, plus a dessert selection, followed by other sweets.

SUMMARY AND COMMENTS This is the kind of dining experience that may take several leisurely hours to do all the courses justice. A more casual new favorite at Manele is the Ocean Grill by the pool, featuring seafood with an Asian accent for lunch and dinner.

Lanai City Grille ★★★★

AMERICAN COUNTRY   MODERATE/EXPENSIVE   QUALITY ★★★★   VALUE ★★★★
LANAI

Hotel Lanai & Cottages 828 Lanai Avenue, Lanai City; ☎ 808-565-7211; www.hotellanai.com

Reservations Highly recommended.

When to go Anytime for dinner.

Entree range $12–$28.

Payment V, MC.

Service rating ★★★★

Parking Hotel lot; many people ride a shuttle from the 2 Four Seasons hotels.

Bar Full service.

Wine selection Good, especially California wines, many available by the glass.

Dress Casual.

Disabled access Adequate.

Customers Tourists and Islanders.

Dinner Wednesday–Sunday, 5–9 p.m.

SETTING AND ATMOSPHERE Two white-coral fireplaces create a warm glow, along with cream walls, golden-wood floors, and a friendly tropical wood bar. Island scenes by Lanai artists add to the old-Hawaii country charm.

HOUSE SPECIALTIES When new owners bought the property in 2007, they enlisted the help of an old friend, Maui celebrity chef Bev Gannon, to help recast the restaurant. She designed the menu and keeps a hand in, with signature items from her Maui restaurants such as Joe's famous meat loaf and barbecued baby-back ribs, described as "stolen from Haliimaile General Store." Executive Chef Mike Davis, who came to the operation from Four Seasons Lanai, adds his own creative expertise in dishes such as seared venison over mushroom risotto with port wine reduction and pecan-crusted fresh catch with chipotle-honey butter. Rotisserie chicken is a signature dish.

OTHER RECOMMENDATIONS Indulge in some Maryland crab cakes or tuna tartar with avocado in a tortilla shell to get appetites going.

SUMMARY AND COMMENTS This is the best dinner value on the island, considering the cost comparison with the luxury hotel restaurants. The tent room out back provides space for music and fun on Friday nights.

MOLOKAI

kids Molokai Pizza Café ★★★

PIZZA AND SANDWICHES   INEXPENSIVE   QUALITY ★★★½   VALUE ★★★★
MOLOKAI

15 Kaunakakai Place, on Wharf Road; ☎ 808-553-3288

Reservations Not accepted.

When to go Anytime.

Entree range $14–$24.

Payment Cash only.

Service rating ★★

Parking Adjacent lot.

Bar None.

Wine selection None.

Dress Casual.

Disabled access Good.

Customers Locals and tourists.

Lunch and Dinner Monday–Thursday, 10 a.m.–10 p.m.; Friday and Saturday, 10 a.m.–11 p.m.; Sunday, 11 a.m.–10 p.m.

SETTING AND ATMOSPHERE This clean, air-conditioned café with booths and tables is a Molokai family kind of place, often decorated with artwork and thank-you cards by schoolkids. Some of the Formica-topped tables are set in a quieter area at the front of the restaurant, and guests are welcome to bring their own wine or beer to enjoy with dinner on the outside lanai.

HOUSE SPECIALTIES Fresh fish is served at market price when available, and the barbecued baby back rib plate is a hit. Wednesday nights, a Mexican menu features burritos, fajitas, tacos, and nachos, and Thursday is Hawaiian night. On Sunday nights, prime rib is the draw.

OTHER RECOMMENDATIONS You can order pizza by the slice, order a Molokini pizza for a single person, or get a big one to go or to share in the café. Chicken dinners come with rice or fries and veggies. Sandwiches, pasta, salads, and frozen yogurt are also served.

ENTERTAINMENT AND AMENITIES Strolling musicians perform for big private parties and sometimes for special holidays.

SUMMARY AND COMMENTS Eventually everyone stops by the Pizza Café, one of the most appealing among Molokai's baker's dozen of restaurants. Kids hang out here after school, and tourists stop by for a slice of pizza, as it's one of the few places that serve food as late as 10 p.m. on weeknights, 11 p.m. on weekends.

PART NINE

SHOPPING

MADE-ON-MAUI *with* ALOHA, *and* OTHER TROPICAL SHOPPING

MADE ON MAUI? Or Bali, or in Laguna Beach, Paris, or China. You'll find goods from all over the world for sale in Maui's wide-ranging retail markets and the shopping centers that spring up everywhere. Who buys all these wares? Retailers hope you will, along with free-spending young Asians and other visiting shoppers throughout the spending ranks from budget to profligate, as well as the folks who live here.

Gone are the days when Mauians could buy only what the plantation company store had not yet sold, at whatever price the proprietor wanted to charge. Direct-mail catalogs were more than a burden in the mailbox then. As tourism replaced the plantations, retailers slowly realized that visitors want to shop when on vacation—and not just for T-shirts and gimcracks but for finely made Island arts and crafts. Shopping on Maui soared from dismal to extraordinary as the island attracted an increasingly well-heeled crowd, especially the Japanese, who are bound by tradition to bring home *omiyagi* (gifts) and who prize the famous brands of European and American designer boutiques. Smart-shopping Americans have found there's no better place to buy cool resort wear than at a cool resort destination. The people of Maui benefit from the bigger retail market tourists help create—more goods are available at better prices nowadays, and more residents are able to buy them. The retail boom on Maui rests partly on the advent of Mainland chains and discount stores that never bothered with the Islands until waves of Japanese visitors proved to be a lucrative market.

The best reason to shop on your Maui vacation, even if you are not a recreational shopper, is to find goods that just aren't readily available elsewhere. The Aloha State is known for high costs, understandable since most of the goods—and the buildings that contain them—are imported. But its low sales tax of 4.16 percent makes purchases more palatable. Besides, there's no going home empty-handed after an enviable trip to Hawaii, and you can't stay in the tropical sun all day every day. So get ready to shop.

RULE #1: When you're after something widely available—plumeria jewelry, aloha shirts by your favorite purveyor, retro hula-girl lamps, or something as basic as half a papaya for breakfast—comparison shopping will pay off. That papaya? The price of half a papaya with a piece of lime one summer morning, surveying Kaanapali Beach Resort restaurants along the promenade, doubled from one spot to another in just a quarter of a mile. That purveyor? The price of Tommy Bahama's silky resort togs, never low, varies according to whether the shop you're in has them on sale, often up to 50 percent off. The Tommy Bahama store at Shops at Wailea is not the place to find a bargain, although it has a better selection.

RULE #2: When you fall in love with something unique—antiques, art, or a must-have collectible—get it, even if you have to arrange to get it home. That's not difficult in a place with lots of pack-and-ship stores, catering to lots of people in the same dilemma. Many stores will ship it for you and pack it correctly, whether it's a live flower lei or a lava-rock sculpture.

BUYIN' HAWAIIAN

LOCAL ARTS AND CRAFTS ARE FLOURISHING. Finding them is much easier than it once was, but the search is still fun. Local wares sold by their makers dominate the frequent crafts fairs held throughout the Islands. Hawaiian product stores have proliferated (some are listed below). Occasionally, you'll find local things among the cheap imports in tourist-zone kiosks and souvenir stores. You can find local books, music, clothing, jewelry, and other goods at favorable prices in Hawaiian and Pacific Island shops, in the national chain stores such as Costco, Longs, Sears, and Borders, as well as the local resort sundries chains, such as ABC stores.

Hawaii's indigenous products range from inexpensive to astronomical in price. They include foods like macadamia nuts, coffees, teas, wines, tropical jams, syrups and honeys, candies, and real Maui potato chips; soaps and cosmetics with tropical ingredients and fragrances; fiber arts made of coconut leaves, lauhala, pandanus, and other natural materials; wearable art such as hand-painted silks, swimwear, aloha-print shirts, baby clothes, totes, bag tags, dresses, glasses cases, even golf-ball bags; Hawaiian books and music; warm-weather designer clothing; high-tech windsurfing gear and surfboards and equipment; furniture, bowls, and boxes handmade from tropical woods; artful creations from mother-of-pearl, abalone, and other shells; one-of-a-kind Hawaiian appliquéd quilts, sewn only with permission of the family that created the design; and jewelry, including Hawaiian symbols like flowers, fish hooks, petroglyphs, palm trees, or even slippers (flipflops) rendered in gold and diamonds, Niihau shell lei, koa wood, coral of various colors and quality, and the South Pacific pearls—black, blue, and now also chocolate hued—that dominate Lahaina shops.

One solution to the nice-but-not-too-nice gift dilemma is packaging. Buy some affordable soaps or foods and bed them in a colorful piece of aloha fabric or natural fiber inside a lidded *lauhala* (woven-fiber) box. Then tie it with fiber ribbon and decorate it with a shell. Gifts are sold prepackaged this way, too.

Hawaiian heirloom gold jewelry, Victorian name bracelets, and other pieces in an arcane style created for 19th-century royals are among the precious gifts of choice for special occasions in the Islands. Heirloom jewelry pieces include medallions, pendants, watchbands, link bracelets, rings, and earrings for men as well as women. They are sold at jewelry shops and at jewelry counters in other stores. Prices vary by gold weight and creative design. Most women in the Islands wear at least one oval gold bangle bracelet ornately patterned and bearing their Hawaiian name, or their Western name translated into Hawaiian, in black enameled script. Mothers may wear their daughters' bracelets until the girls are older; many women wear them by the armload. Many bracelets never come off. A bracelet at 2008 gold prices might cost anywhere from $600 for a simple pattern on a narrow 8 mm band to $3,000 or more for a complex design on a wider, bigger band. This is a subjective purchase based on design, but do shop around enough to satisfy yourself that the price is fair for what you want. Shop for a bracelet early in your trip, to allow time for sizing and name engraving. The case samples are inscribed "Kuuipo," meaning "my sweetheart."

Hot trends in Hawaiian jewelry right now: Guaranteed to delight your Kuuipo is jewelry made of rose gold and/or chocolate Tahitian pearls. Neither is cheap, but both are beautifully different.

Island goods are widely available on the Internet. Here are a few sites worth bookmarking:

- **Flowers and lei: www.hanaflowers.com** (☎ 800-952-4262) grows the proteas, gingers, anthuriums, and orchids of their bouquets, lei, and flowering plants (pesticide-free) at an upcountry farm in Hana, picks the flowers to order, washes and packs them for FedEx delivery in the United States and Canada within two days, then tracks them to make sure they get where you send them. The site includes informative tips on handling tropical flowers when you receive the exotic wonders. These products are not cheap, but they are guaranteed fresh when picked and shipped and, barring incorrect addresses, delivered.

- **Island-style treats: www.cybersnacks.net** by Wholesale Unlimited, Inc. (☎ 800-820-7629) sells crack seed, mochi crunch, wasabi peas, cookies, and other Broke Da Mouth Hawaiian kine foods. (Coconut syrup for your mac nut or banana pancakes? Shredded dried cuttlefish? Beef jerky? It's here.) Homesick Islanders and newly addicted visitors can find the stuff they crave. The firm has five express outlets around Oahu.

- **Aloha fabrics: www.hawaiianfabricshop.com** (☎ 877-391-3300) offers many choices of material for make-your-own luau wear, as well as some bargain apparel, craft supplies, calendars and gifts, squares of fabric for wrapping gifts, and other items. Like many Hawaii sites, it also offers Island information snippets you might enjoy (brief history of hula, luau, lei, outrigger canoe racing, and so on).

- **Car seat covers and surfer décor: www.surferbedding.com** (☎ 866-515-5560) is actually based in Florida, but it has a wealth of aloha-print accessories for home and car (infant to adult seat covers). You'll find everything from luau supplies and tiki torches to tropical wallpapers, grass (raffia) bed skirts, and scenic bamboo curtains.

WHERE *to* SHOP

IT'S HARD TO AVOID SHOPS, BEGINNING WITH THE LOBBY stores in resort hotels, where stylish, high-quality resort clothing, swimsuits, spa cosmetics, and shoes can often be found, and ending at the airports, where gift shops actually carry local gifts, foods, and fresh tropical flowers.

Maui has become a favorite place to buy art while on vacation, and the galleries are numerous and exceptional. South Maui has acquired its own branches of favorite stores, galleries, and restaurants popular in West Maui, a long 45-minute drive away from Wailea. Even without billboards (not a Hawaii species), we know you can find local versions of national chain stores on your own, so we've mentioned only the larger shopping complexes and some independent stores worth attention. Expect slightly higher prices on some items, even at Wal-Mart. Hilo Hattie's stores, crammed with matching bold-print aloha wear, are everywhere. Their filing for bankruptcy late in 2008 is indicative of the suddenly shaky retail climate in Hawaii, captive of worldwide economic changes.

Below are some notable places to find local arts and crafts and other goods. The first group features specialty storefronts, galleries, and the like; the second includes shopping complexes with multiple stores, independents and national and international chains alike. All are subject to changing economic realities, so call before you go in search of a specific shop. To make the shopping easier, Kaanapali resort and Lahaina town are linked by frequent $1 shuttle buses run by Maui Public Transit. Wailea resort has a private shuttle that links its hotels and the Shops at Wailea.

SPECIALTY SHOPS

West Maui

Gold Fantasy

Location 3350 Lower Honoapiilani Road (Kahana area).

Contact ☎ 808-661-6288, **www.goldfantasy.com.**

Hours Monday–Saturday, 9 a.m.–5:30 p.m.

DESCRIPTION Master goldsmith and platinumsmith Robert Cohn does custom orders and displays his own works. If you have a pearl in your pocket, see what he can do with it.

Honolua Store

Location Office Road, Kapalua Resort.

Contact ☎ 808-669-6128, **www.kapalua.com.**

Hours Daily, 6 a.m.–9 p.m.

DESCRIPTION Historic plantation grocery store features books, gifts, and clothing, along with fresh plantation pineapples, groceries and beverages, hot breakfasts, deli and plate lunches and dinner specials.

Honolulu Cookie Company

Locations Whalers Village, Kaanapali (and many other locations throughout the islands)

Contact ☎ 808-661-8248, **www.honolulucookie.com.**

Hours Daily, 9 a.m.–10 p.m.

DESCRIPTION Luscious Hawaiian shortbread cookies in a dozen tropical flavors, some dipped in chocolate or enriched with macadamia nuts or bits of dried fruit. They are shaped into pineapples, individually wrapped, and gift boxed, tinned or packed into lauhala baskets for easy transport home. If they make it home. Free samples are available to whet cookie monsters' appetites, which makes for a very popular store.

Lahaina Mail Depot

Location 658 Front St., Lahaina Wharf Cinema Center.

Contact ☎ 808-667-2000.

Hours Monday–Friday, 10 a.m.–4:30 p.m.; Saturday, 10 a.m.–1 p.m.

DESCRIPTION Send those purchases packing here—shipping, materials, FedEx, UPS, and mail-a-coconut services.

Lahaina Printsellers

Location Whalers Village, Kaanapali.

Contact ☎ 800-669-7843 or 808-667-7617, **www.printsellers.com.**

Hours Daily, 9:30 a.m.–10 p.m.

DESCRIPTION Premier vendor of vintage prints and etchings, antique maps of locations around the world, sea charts, and early Hawaii maps. Second gallery features Giclee and other artwork, also at Whaler's Village.

Maui Rainbows

Location Whalers Village, Kaanapali

Contact ☎ 808-661-9010.

Hours Daily 9:30 a.m.–10 p.m.

DESCRIPTION Island jewelry store with better prices than most for popular treasures such as rose gold, pearls, heirloom bracelets and the like.

Mr. Wine

Location 808 Wainee Street, Lahaina.

Contact ☎ 808-661-5551.

Hours Monday–Saturday, 11 a.m.–7 p.m.

DESCRIPTION More than 600 boutique wines, Champagnes, and sparkling wines, including premiums kept in the 55°F wine cellar. Hawaiian microbrews and cigars are also available, along with Hawaiian music CDs and cassettes.

Pacific Treasures Gift Boutique

Location Whalers Village, Kaanapali

Contact ☎ 808-667-0919.

Hours Daily 9:30 a.m.–10 p.m.

DESCRIPTION Truly unusual and well priced jewelry, apparel, tropical handicrafts, and gifts from the Pacific, including jewel boxes made of whole mother-of-pearl shells, occasional dishes of coconut, shell and tropical woods, unique earrings and bracelets designed by owner Blandine Willis and crafted in Bali.

Sandal Tree

Locations Whalers Village and Hyatt Regency Maui shops, Kaanapali; and Grand Wailea Shops in South Maui.

Contact Whalers Village, ☎ 808-667-5330; Hyatt Regency, ☎ 808-661-3495; Grand Wailea, ☎ 808-874-9006.

Hours Daily, 9 a.m.–10 p.m.

DESCRIPTION Best collection we know of sandals for women and men, from fancy rubber beach slippers to strappy dancing shoes, manly topsiders and strapped sports sandals. Plus: kids' wear, socks, handbags, backpacks, and even a hat or two.

Totally Hawaiian Gift Gallery

Location Whalers Village and Marriott Ocean Club, Kaanapali

Contact ☎ 808-667-4070 or ☎ 808-667-2171, **www.totallyhawaiian.com.**

Hours Daily, 9:30 a.m.–10 p.m.

DESCRIPTION Hawaiian-made gifts and goods, from Christmas tree ornaments to expensive wood bowls turned so thin you can see through them; also Niihau shell lei and other jewelry, hand-sewn Hawaiian quilts and pillowcases, toys and dolls, ceramic koi fish for your pond, bowls from the stems of proteas and pottery. Purchases may be shipped.

Central Maui

Kaukini Gallery

Location Kahakuloa Head, northwest coast.

Contact ☎ 808-244-3371, **www.kaukinigallery.com.**

Hours Daily, 10 a.m.–5 p.m.

DESCRIPTION One of Maui's best, and certainly the most interesting to find in its serendipitous setting, this gallery is a delight. More than 100 local artists' paintings, prints, jewelry, ceramics, fabric arts, and woodworks are displayed and sold in a modern, plantation-style yellow house, part of a small cluster of buildings by the road in an incredibly scenic remote setting. They are the only buildings at the top of the hill over tiny Kahakuloa village, almost midway along the narrow (one-lane at times) country road that hugs Maui's wild northwest seaside cliffs between Wailuku and Kapalua. Huge wood sculptures welcome you in the gardens, while affordable-to-pricey Maui creations compete for your attention inside. Look for bracelets of woven gold-and-silver wire intricately worked in mariners' knots designs, linens, art works, and jewelry set with black pearls together with precious stones. Artist/proprietress Karen Lei Noland opened her first shop some years ago on the porch of her grandfather's ranch house up the road, then later built the gallery.

Moonbow Tropics

Locations 300 Maalaea Road, Maalaea; 20 and 36 Baldwin Avenue, Paia; 612 Front St., Lahaina.

Contact ☎ 808-243-9577, 808-579-8775, or 808-579-8592.

Hours Monday–Saturday, 10 a.m.–7 p.m.; Sunday 10 a.m.–6 p.m.

DESCRIPTION Men seem to be comfortable shopping here, browsing through classy aloha shirts and other clothes for men and women, as well as other appointments of the tropical good life, including CDs. Stores include one by the Maui Ocean Center and two on Paia's main shopping street, Baldwin Avenue, one for men and one for women's clothes, and a new spot in Lahaina.

Precision Goldsmiths

Location 16 North Market Street, Wailuku.

Contact ☎ 808-986-8282, **www.precisiongoldsmiths.com.**

Hours Monday–Friday, 9 a.m.–5 p.m.

DESCRIPTION Tasteful inspirations by master goldsmith Brian Thomsen, who can create something just for you.

Sig Zane Designs

Location 53 North Market Street, Wailuku.

Contact ☎ 808-249-8997.

Hours Monday–Friday, 9:30 a.m.–5:50 p.m.; Saturday, 9 a.m.–3 p.m.

DESCRIPTION Hawaiian style men's and women's clothing and fabrics for interiors, in bold Hawaiian graphics and striking colors, by Hawaii designer Sig Zane.

South Maui

Blue Ginger

Location Shops at Wailea, Kaahumanu Center, Kahului, Lahaina Cannery Mall, and Whalers Village, Kaanapali (also Blue Ginger Kids).

Contact ☎ 808-891-0772, ☎ 808-871-7002, ☎ 808-667-5433, ☎ 808-667-5793

Hours Daily, 9:30 a.m.–9 p.m.

DESCRIPTION Soft cotton and rayon batiks in pastel print resort wear for the family, primarily women and children, designed by its owner-operator founders.

Kii Gallery

Location The Shops at Wailea.

Contact ☎ 808-874-1181.

Hours Daily, 9:30 a.m.–9 p.m.

DESCRIPTION Remarkable collection of brilliantly colorful glass sculptures of all hues, sizes, and shapes, sharing the space with wood art objects and unlikely Greek marble statuary, bronze lamps, and the like, by American artists.

Dolphin Galleries

Location The Shops at Wailea, 728 Front Street in Lahaina and Whalers Village, Kaanapali.

Contact ☎ 808-891-8000, 808-661-5000, or 808-661-3223.

Hours Daily, 9:30 a.m.–9 p.m.

DESCRIPTION Jewelry and art, some familiar, some extraordinary in well-designed galleries where "just looking" is a pleasure. Modern cloisonné set in gold, kinetic gemstone rings, and dolphins galore are among the works.

Elephant Walk, A Gallery of Life

Location The Shops at Wailea

Contact ☎ 808-891-8684.

Hours Daily 9:30 a.m.–9 p.m.

DESCRIPTION Artisan gifts and crafts from Hawaii and elsewhere, some to wear and some to display.

Kihei Wine and Spirits

Location 300 Ohukai Road, Kihei.

Contact ☎ 808-879-0555.

Hours Tuesday–Friday, 10 a.m.–6 p.m.; Saturday, 10 a.m.–6 p.m.

DESCRIPTION A selection of more than 500 wines, premium liquors and liqueurs, Hawaiian microbrews, gourmet foods, and cigars.

Na Hoku

Location Shops at Wailea among eight Maui locations and 66 stores nationwide

Contact ☎ 800-260-3912 or ☎ 808-891-8040; **www.nahoku.com.**

Hours Daily, 9:30 a.m.–9 p.m.

DESCRIPTION An exception to our no-chain rule, Na Hoku is worth seeking out. This is a Hawaii-based chain, the state's oldest and largest jewelry maker and the nation's 17th largest fine jewelry retailer. Their fresh designs feature symbols of Island lifestyle, such as flowers, palm trees or Hawaiian slippers, rendered in pendants and earrings of white, yellow or rose gold decorated with diamonds and other inlays.

Serendipity

Location Shops at Wailea; Lahaina Cannery Mall, Kaahumanu Center, Kihei.

Contact ☎ 808-871-1116.

Hours Daily, 9:30 a.m.–9 p.m.

DESCRIPTION Women's clothing in the form of tasteful Indonesian imports, tropical-weight rayon, and other breezy fabrics and styles, including silk sarongs; just right for Maui moods. Also in some stores are Javanese teak furnishings and accents. Serendipity's owner does the design and buying.

Upcountry Maui

David Warren Gallery

Location 3625 Baldwin Avenue, Makawao.

Contact ☎ 877-572-1288 or 808-572-1288.

Hours Daily except Sunday 10:30 a.m.–5 p.m.

DESCRIPTION This small, eclectic family gallery is dedicated to the late David Warren, who painted scenes of the lovely place where he lived—Upcountry Maui—abloom with blue jacaranda trees, and of human figures dancing, often hula. When Warren died in 1998, his wife, sons, and friends took over the gallery, selling his works and their own, including handcrafted placemats and fine woodcraft, as well as framing and jewelry.

Hui Noeau Visual Arts Center

Location 2841 Baldwin Avenue, Makawao.

Contact ☎ 808-572-6560, **www.huinoeau.com.**

Hours Monday–Saturday, 10 a.m.–4 p.m.

DESCRIPTION This beautiful, old 10-acre estate with its 1917 mansion is the heart of Maui's art colony. Devoted to art education, with classes, demonstrations, and exhibitions, the Hui provides studios for artists and a fine shop for their wares.

Kula Marketplace

Location 15200 Haleakala Highway, Kula

Contact ☎ 808-878-2135, **www.kulamarketplace.com.**

Hours Daily 8 a.m.–7 p.m.

DESCRIPTION Gourmet foods and art, some of it homegrown in cool Upcountry Kula. Ask for the addictive coconut candy, little chunks of dried coconut rolled in raw sugar. Pleasant store, reasonable prices. Plantation style building neighbors Kula Lodge and the little flower stand where you can buy bizarre protea flowers—pincushions, fuzzy black and pink blooms, spiky thistle-like blooms and other varieties thrive on the cool mountain slope.

Maui Hands

Location 84 Hana Highway, Paia; 3620 Baldwin Avenue, Makawao; 612 Front Street, Lahaina; and Hyatt Regency Hotel, Kaanapali Beach Resort.

Contact ☎ 800-352-4278, ☎ 808-579-9245, ☎ 808-572-5194, ☎ 808-667-9898 or ☎ 808-667-7997; **www.mauihands.com.**

Hours Monday–Saturday, 10 a.m.–7 p.m.; Sunday, 10 a.m.–6 p.m. in Paia.

DESCRIPTION Works by more than 300 Maui artists, designers, and artisans are featured, including fine arts, wood bowls and sculptures, home furnishings, jewelry, glass and pottery, baskets, and accessories. Good website choices as well as appealing galleries. Prices range from $2–$10,000.

Tropo

Location 3643 Baldwin Avenue, Makawao.

Contact ☎ 808-573-0356.

Hours Monday-Saturday, 10 a.m.–6 p.m., 11 a.m.–5 p.m. Sunday.

DESCRIPTION Guy things—men's designer aloha shirts, of silk and other fine fabrics, name-brand tropical wear, and tasteful informal clothing; also books, jazz CDs, Swiss Army knives, binoculars, accessories, and Crabtree and Evelyn cosmetics.

Hana

Hana Coast Gallery

Location Hotel Hana-Maui.

Contact ☎ 800-637-0188 or ☎ 808-248-8636, **www.hanacoast.com.**

Hours Daily, 9 a.m.–5 p.m.

DESCRIPTION Visit here to see the exquisite collection of Maui artists' works as you might in a small museum, because it's that committed to the culture and it's that good. Oil, watercolors, woods, feathers, stone, prints, glass, and fibers are among the media used to interpret the beauty of Hana and Maui by famous and lesser-known artists in artworks, furniture, and jewelry. If you want to purchase some excellent local pieces for your collection, don't miss this gallery.

Hasegawa General Store

Location 5165 Hana Highway, Hana.

Contact ☎ 808-248-8231.

Hours Monday–Saturday, 7 a.m.–7 p.m.; Sunday, 8 a.m.–6 p.m.

DESCRIPTION An old-fashioned general merchandise store, so beloved that a song was written about it ("You can get anything you want/At the Hasegawa General Store..."). Founded in 1910, rebuilt in 1991 after a fire, and with plans to build a new store soon to add a bakery, deli and laundromat, this family-run store sells gas and other necessities and some frills for residents and visitors in faraway Hana. Hana-related music, art and books, T-shirts, specially blended coffee, dried fruit, and other gifts are among the wares.

Molokai

Big Wind Kite Factory

Location 120 Maunaloa Highway, Maunaloa.

Contact ☎ 808-552-2364.

Hours Monday–Saturday, 8:30 a.m.–5 p.m.; Sunday, 10 a.m.–2 p.m.

DESCRIPTION Kites of all shapes, sizes, and designs, some made on-site; plus imported gifts. The friendly owner provides free kite-flying lessons (at an adjacent open field) with "no strings attached."

Molokai Artists & Crafters Guild

Location Above American Savings Bank, 40 Ala Malama, the main street of Kaunakakai town.

Contact ☎ 808-553-8018

Hours Monday–Friday, 9:30 a.m.–4:30 p.m.; Saturday, 9:30 a.m.–1 p.m.; closed Sunday.

DESCRIPTION Gallery and gift shop cooperative featuring local artists' works.

Lanai

Dis 'N Dat

Location 418 8th Street, Lanai City

Contact ☎ 808-565-9170, **www.suzieo.com**/

Hours Monday–Saturday, 10 a.m.–5 p.m.; closed Sunday.

DESCRIPTION Among the wind chimes, garden décor and T-shirts, Suzie O's fun jewelry offers plumeria, petroglyph, pineapple and slipper pendants of silver and crystal for a fraction of the cost of their gold-and-diamond cousins over in Lahaina. She also creates enameled barrel-shaped beads to wear threaded onto chains, including a pink-ribbon circle-of-life barrel.

Gifts with Aloha

Location 7th Street, Lanai City.

Contact ☎ 808-565-6589.

Hours Monday–Saturday, 9:30 a.m.–5:30 p.m.

DESCRIPTION Made-in-Hawaii gifts, including koa-wood products, scented candles, books, hand-quilted pillow covers.

Local Gentry

Location 363 7th Street, Lanai City.

Contact ☎ 808-565-9130.

Hours Monday–Saturday, 10 a.m.–6 p.m.

DESCRIPTION Apparel for men and (mostly) women in a tiny boutique that marks a coming-of-age of sorts in Lanai City—at last, enough customers, resident or passing through, to support a clothing store. Choices include lightweight sweaters for anyone who didn't believe Upcountry Lanai could be chilly.

Richard's Market

Location 434 8th Street, Lanai City.

Contact ☎ 808-565-6047.

Hours Monday–Saturday, 8:30 a.m.–6:30 p.m.

DESCRIPTION This 1946 plantation store sells groceries, fishing gear, kitchen utensils, cold drinks and ice cream treats, beach mats, and other stuff you need on an island. With the changing nature of Lanai residents, it now also features a substantial wine section and some gourmet and fresh foods.

SHOPPING CENTERS

West Maui

505 Front Street

Location Front Street, Lahaina.

Contact ☎ 808-667-2514, **www.505frontstreet.com**

Hours Monday–Saturday, 10 a.m.–9 p.m.; Sunday, 10 a.m.–6 p.m.

Number of stores and restaurants 25+.

DESCRIPTION Oceanfront boutique mall at the quieter, southern end of Lahaina. Clapboard village of storefronts houses made-on-Maui products, needlework and Hawaiian quilt supplies, spa cosmetics, clothing, souvenirs, art and gifts, and surfing schools. Waterfront restaurants include IO and PacificO. The Feast at Lele Luau takes place here. Live jazz is played here on weekends.

Lahaina Center and Old Lahaina Center (adjacent, across Papalaua Street)

Location 900 Front Street, Lahaina.

Contact ☎ 808-667-9216, **www.lahainacenter.com** (coupons available for download)

Hours Monday–Saturday, 9 a.m.–10 p.m.; Sunday, 9 a.m.–6 p.m. (Store hours vary.)

Number of stores and restaurants 70.

DESCRIPTION Stores feature aloha wear and other apparel, gifts, sundries, T-shirts, swimwear, children's wear, jewelry, ice cream, Mexican takeout, burgers, movie and live performance theaters and clubs, and microbrews. Free hula shows are held Wednesday and Friday, at 2 and 6 p.m. Purchases good for two-hour parking validation at Lsahina Center; free parking at Old Lahina Center.

Lahaina Cannery Mall

Location 1221 Honoapiilani Highway, Lahaina

Contact ☎ 808-661-4411, **www.lahainacannerymall.com** (coupons available for download)

Hours Daily 9:30 a.m.–9 p.m.

Number of stores and restaurants 50.

DESCRIPTION Onetime pineapple cannery is now air-conditioned mall frequented by residents and tourists alike with plentiful free parking and food court. Stores include jewelry, aloha wear, tropical gifts, surf shop, hat shop, toys, shoes, pharmacy and 24-hour supermarket. Hula performed (free) Tuesday and Thursday evenings at 7 p.m. and Saturdays and Sundays at 1 p.m. Watch for free special concerts and events.

Whalers Village

Location 2435 Kaanapali Parkway, Kaanapali Beach Resort.

Contact ☎ 808-661-4567, **www.whalersvillage.com.**

Hours Daily, 9:30 a.m.–10 p.m.

Number of stores and restaurants 90.

DESCRIPTION Upscale European and American boutiques, jewelry, scrimshaw, Hawaiian koa furniture, gifts, art galleries, Island apparel, and general goods are all available here. Waterfront restaurants include casual outdoor cafés Hula Grill and Leilani's.

Napili Plaza

Location 5095 Napilihau Street, Napili.

Contact ☎ 808-661-5304.

Hours 9 a.m.–9 p.m., market until 11 p.m.

Number of stores and restaurants 17.

DESCRIPTION Napili Plaza serves surrounding residents and visitor condos with supermarket; surf shop, bank, informal plate lunch, pizza, sub, and taco eateries; coffee store that roasts beans, jeweler, florist, day spa, and mailing-services store where you can mail a coconut, hand-decorated, for less than $10 postage. Tongan family demonstrates and sells crafts on Mondays.

South Maui

Azeka Place Shopping Center

Location 1279 and 1280 South Kihei Road, Kihei.

Contact ☎ 808-879-5000.

Hours Daily, 8:30 a.m.–10 p.m.

Number of stores and restaurants 50+.

DESCRIPTION That traffic snarl at the southern end of Kihei is due largely to this shopping conglomeration of specialty stores, markets, and restaurants serving residents and visitors.

Kihei Kalama Village

Location 1941 South Kihei Road, Kihei.

Contact ☎ 808-879-6610.

Hours Daily, 9 a.m.–9 p.m.

Number of stores and restaurants 50.

DESCRIPTION Collection of specialty stores and restaurants, including an adult novelty store, aloha wear, gifts and souvenirs, tropical tattoo shop, barber, coffee, free parking.

The Shops at Wailea

Location 3750 Wailea Alanui Drive, Wailea Resort.

Contact ☎ 808-879-4474.

Hours Daily, 9:30a.m.–9 p.m.

Number of stores and restaurants 25+.

DESCRIPTION This new $24 million cluster is the swankiest shopping center you're likely to find. Four restaurants offer alternatives to hotel dining: Longhi's (American food); Tommy Bahama's Tropical Café and Emporium (attached to a clothing and home store); Cheeseburger Island Style; and Ruth's Chris Steak House, not to mention Honolulu Coffee Company's Cafe Wailea, which opens at 7 a.m. (8 a.m. on Sundays) with espresso drinks and breakfast breads. Retail vendors include Tiffany's,

Fendi, Gucci, and the like, along with the Gap, Banana Republic, Tommy Bahama, Chico's and local clothing firms Crazyshirts, Serendipity, and Blue Ginger. Martin & McArthur features Hawaiian koa furniture and other crafts. Galleries include works ranging from Wyland seascapes and celebrity art to extraordinary glass, jewelry, and sculpture at Dolphin Galleries and Kii Galleries. In sum, you'll find resort wear, upscale boutiques, gifts, art, wood crafts and furniture, toys, camera shops, sundries, ice cream, and beachwear. Watch for special events like food festivals. Every Wednesday night, you'll find restaurant specials and live entertainment, fashion, and art events.

Piilani Village Center

Location 225 Piikea Avenue, Kihei.

Contact ☎ 808-874-8900.

Hours Daily, 10 a.m.–10 p.m.

Number of stores and restaurants 25+.

DESCRIPTION This new shopping complex, built for a newly created Kihei neighborhood, describes itself as the place visitors shop when they actually need something—groceries, haircuts, lattes, dry-cleaning, beachwear, music, smoothies, medical services, photo printing, video rentals, and the like. Unlikely spot to find a great restaurant, Roy's Kihei Bar & Grill, specializing in East/West Island fusion cuisine masterminded by chef Roy Yamaguchi. It's located just off Piilani Highway on the southern end of Kihei.

Central Maui

Queen Kaahumanu Center

Location 275 West Kaahumanu Avenue, Kahului.

Contact ☎ 808-877-3369.

Hours Monday–Saturday, 9:30 a.m–9 p.m.; Sunday, 10 a.m.–5 p.m.

Number of stores and restaurants About 75.

DESCRIPTION This is the island's principal mall, recently redone, and a good place to get a sense of the scope of goods available on Maui. Several of the local stores have other outlets in the resort shopping centers, such as Serendipity, which sells Indonesian clothes and furniture. Department stores (including Macy's), books, gifts, toys, cards, jewelry, cartoon logos, coffee, shoes, apparel, photo processing, movies, and restaurants are included here, along with frequent community events.

PART TEN

ENTERTAINMENT *and* NIGHTLIFE

YOU CAME *to* MAUI *for* *the* NIGHTLIFE?

YOU MUST BE MISINFORMED. Wait, don't go away. Actually, there is life after sundown on Maui, but it isn't always what you might expect. It may even surprise you.

If you came to Hawaii to escape the ordinary and experience something new and different, even exotic, now is your chance. The Islands of Hawaii were once an independent kingdom, and nowhere is that legacy more obvious than in music and dance. Even in this age of mass media and world culture, Hawaii has its own popular music and star performers, its own cultural dance and theater tradition based on the chant, its own language and legends, its own style of dress and casual speech, and its own killer cocktails, headlined by the mai tai.

Islanders don't just pack up their native sounds and moves until a cultural holiday comes along. Hawaiian music, be it traditional or reggae-hiphop, is the daily music of choice for people of all ages. Many kids today take hula classes at some stage or another, much like piano class elsewhere, and learn ukulele from their elders at backyard family gatherings. This is not to say you'll find only Hawaiian entertainment on Maui, Molokai, and Lanai. But you won't find it at all in most other places, so this is the best chance to sample it. Hotels usually feature live Hawaiian entertainment sometime during the day, and some of the clubs star popular contemporary Hawaiian musicians and singers, often with a bit of sensual hula thrown in. Several clubs, mostly in Kihei and Lahaina, feature rock and pop music live for dancing and late-night fun.

The Islands are full of gifted musicians and singers, such as Maui's Kealii Reichel, Willie K., Amy Hanaialii Gilliom, her brother Eric Gilliom, Hookena, Makaha Sons of Niihau, Robbie Kahakalau, and Na Leo Pumehana, to name a few. Check the *Maui News,* or the free *Maui Time* and *Maui Weekly,* for dates and venues.

It doesn't take much originality to go to the Hard Rock Cafe and get another T-shirt, but you can, right on Front Street in Lahaina. You can also seek out what makes Maui different from other islands.

A few caveats: The legal drinking age is 21. Keep in mind the State of Hawaii has tough drunk-driving laws (the legal blood-alcohol limit is 0.08 percent), and police set up roadblocks on weekends and holidays to check the sobriety of motorists. If you drink, don't drive; take a taxi.

Maui nightlife action is centered in Kihei and Lahaina, where a variety of clubs draws crowds, and the action gets interesting after 10 p.m. Some biker bars in Kahului and Wailuku have become all the rage with unlikely patrons—holiday boomers on rental hogs.

The state's best live theatrical production runs nightly in Lahaina: *Ulalena,* a *Cirque du Soleil*–inspired, must-see rendition of Hawaii's fabled history at the high-tech **Maui Myth and Magic Theater.** The diversity of the percussive band alone is worth the price of a ticket.

Otherwise, nightlife is limited to hotel lounge acts (some quite good) and commercial luau, and yes, you should certainly attend at least one luau during your stay. The best, in our view: **Old Lahaina Luau, The Feast at Lele,** and **Wailea's Finest Luau** at the Marriott Wailea Beach Resort, which features world champion fire knife dancer Ifi Soo.

If your timing's good, you may see Willie Nelson (who has a home on Maui), the Beach Boys, or even Tony Bennett at Maui Arts and Cultural Center, and for a lot less than on the Mainland. It's just a question of when you will be there. Maui Arts and Cultural Center, the crossroads of lively arts, features a diverse year-round schedule. Check out who's there when you are at **www.mauiarts.org.**

Someone's always strumming a ukulele or singing a Hawaiian song at **Kaanapali Beach Hotel.** Maui's "most Hawaiian hotel" celebrates **Aloha Friday** not only every Friday but every day of the week in song and dance; the hotel employees' choir even created a local Kahili award–winning compact disc, *E Hoomau I Ka Pookela.*

The attractions are stellar up on the roof at the Hyatt Regency Maui Resort and Spa, where at the three-times-nightly **Tour of the Stars** astronomers show guests how to find astral phenomena by peering through high-powered, computer-operated telescopes to scan Maui's incredible night sky. After finding the Big Dipper, you may see the rings of Saturn, the moons of Jupiter, the Southern Cross, and other timely celestial sights, or look into the beyond, to distant stars and new planets. This popular after-dark activity began more than a decade ago and continues to attract stargazers and junior stargazers up to the roof at 8, 9, and 10 p.m. nightly. On weekends, the late-night Tour of the Stars, popular with honeymooners, starts at 11 p.m. and includes chocolate-dipped strawberries and champagne.

Sea Adventures after Dark

NIGHT DIVES

And, no, we don't mean the biker bars. This after-dark-on-Maui adventure is for certified divers only and on certain dates only, in the spring and early summer. Take a chartered night dive off Maui with Mike Severns Diving to observe a rare phenomenon, coral spawning. Coral is a living organism, and in a few places, including Maui and the Great Barrier Reef in Australia, you can see it propagate. Divers say it's an amazing sight when hundreds of coral colonies release orange globes that rise to the surface in curtains, then break apart and mix to spawn.

Contact **Mike Severns Diving** at P.O. Box 627, Kihei; **www .mikesevernsdiving.com**; ☎ 808-879-6596.

DIVE AT DUSK

Ed Robinson takes you down at dusk on two-tank dives to watch the shift change on the reef, observing crabs, shrimp, lobsters, octopus, Spanish Dancer nudibranchs, and reef fish as some species shut down and others come awake.

"Dusk is a unique time of change for the reef animals," he says. "Some perform mating rituals, others display feeding activity, and some are easy to approach as they become sleepy." Then, after dinner, divers submerge again to see a new world of active night creatures. It's "night life as you've never seen it before," says Robinson.

Contact **Ed Robinson Diving Adventures** at **www.mauiscuba.com/ erda3.htm** or ☎ 808-879-3584.

The Maui Ocean Center may not be at the top of your mind as a hot nightspot, but after sundown, big pelagic fish like sharks show their nocturnal side at the **Aquarium After Dark;** it's safer than the night dives certified divers do.

Nighttime, when it's cooler, is the right time to play tennis on Maui. You can play after dark on world-class courts at the **Wailea Tennis Club** (☎ 808-879-1958), which has 14 courts, including four lighted for night play, or **The Tennis Garden** at Kapalua, with ten Plexipave courts, four of them lighted for night play (☎ 808-669-5677).

And the bright lights of Waikiki are only 30 minutes away by jet, in case you need to hear more than the sound of surf and wind in the palm trees. You did come to Maui to relax, didn't you?

BIG-TIME PERFORMERS

SOONER OR LATER, ENTERTAINERS FROM ELSEWHERE come to Maui to perform, as diverse as rock's Melissa Etheridge, country's Crystal Gayle, New Age music guru George Winston, pop artist

> ### SUNSET ON HALEAKALA
>
> Everyone goes up to the volcano's summit at sunrise, but sunsets on Haleakala are just as spectacular. And less crowded. After the sun sinks in the Pacific, you can watch the moon rise over Haleakala, another surreal act of nature, and then the inky-black night sky shines with a million points of light. Bring a sleeping bag; you may not want to leave. You can crash at the park's nearby Hosmer Grove Campground, often full of other starry-eyed campers.
>
> There's a reason the U.S. Air Force maintains its Maui Space Surveillance Site up here on Haleakala, and it isn't only to monitor spacecraft (ours and maybe theirs). It's off-limits, but otherwise the night is yours up here. To reach the summit, take Haleakala Highway 378. Bring a coat.

Prince, and the New Shanghai Circus, all of whom appeared on-island recently.

The **Maui Arts and Cultural Center,** the island's premier venue in Kahului, has a lively schedule of Hawaiian and other entertainment. For information call ☎ 808-242-7469 or visit **www.mauiarts.org.**

MOLOKAI AND LANAI AFTER DARK

IF YOU'RE STAYING ON MOLOKAI OR LANAI, bring a good book and your iPod, or plan to revive the lost art of charades. Resort sundry stores usually have some beach-reading, old paperbacks, last month's magazines, and day-late city newspapers from the West Coast, as well as the *Maui News*. The major hotels provide a daily fax version of the *New York Times* if you want to stay abreast of current events. The resort libraries are often libraries in name only, with shelves full of gilt-edged leather-bound books, mostly in German, bought by the yard from interior decorators. Maui does have a Borders (call ☎ 808-877-6160), two Waldenbooks (call ☎ 808-661-8672 or 808-667-6712), and the Old Lahaina Book Emporium (call ☎ 808-661-1999), with hard-to-find and collectible Hawaii books.

The hot spot for live music on Molokai's East End is **Hula Shores** at Hotel Molokai. Otherwise the island has a bar or two where *pau hana* (work's end, like TGIF) is celebrated over beer and *pipikaula* (beef jerky) and, sometimes, a loud boogie band or even local entertainer Darrell Labrado, whose "Shaka Da Moon" gives a faint hint of nightlife on a tropical island. Be careful which pretty lady you ask to dance or you may get more than you thought. Molokai is noted for its drag queens, transsexuals, and *mahu* (boys raised as girls, a Polynesian tradition that still endures in some families).

On Molokai, if the lights are out at Kaunakakai's **Mitchell Pauole Stadium,** home of local softball games, your next best shot is star-gazing, an old Polynesian pastime, considered excellent since night skies in the mid-Pacific are clear and distracting ground lights nearly nonexistent.

Finally, if you are really desperate for diversion, there are always movies—on demand in your hotel room, in video rentals, at multiplexes on Maui (in Lahaina, Kahului, and Kihei) and at the restored 1930s **Lanai Theatre,** which also features live programs and special events.

LIVE ENTERTAINMENT

Note: Look for show discount ads in Maui's myriad tourist magazines. Some are worth $10 a person off your tab.

Ulalena
Maui Myth and Magic Theater, 878 Front Street, Lahaina; ☎ 877-688-4800 or 808-661-9913; www.ulalena.com

Show times Tuesday–Saturday, 6:30 p.m.; may vary seasonally.

Length 90 minutes.

Cost Standard seating, adults, $59.50; children ages 3–15, $39.50. Add $10 per ticket for premium seating and $20 per ticket for a package that includes VIP seats, drink, photos, and an after-show session with cast. Dinner and show packages are $129.50 for adults and $84.50 for children ages 3–15.

Discounts None.

Type of seating $10 million, state-of-the-art theater with stadium seating, features live Hawaiian chant and music with 8-channel surround sound.

Food Snack bar in lobby.

Beverages Beer, wine, soft drinks, juice, coffee.

DESCRIPTION AND COMMENTS Best original, creative show in Hawaii. Excellent entertainment. A *Cirque du Soleil*–style production blends Island myth and fact in a culturally keen live theatrical performance. If you go to Maui, you must see *Ulalena.*

Masters of Hawaiian Slack Key Guitar Concert Series
Napili Kai Beach Resort Hale Aloha Paviolion, Kapalua Resort;
☎ 888-669-5838 or 808-669-5838; www.slackkey.com

Show times Wednesday, 7:30 p.m.

Length 90 minutes.

Cost $45 per person plus tax.

DESCRIPTION AND COMMENTS This is music close to the Hawaiian soul. And these concerts are your most authentic Hawaiian entertainment choice on Wednesday nights on Maui. They were performed at the Ritz-Carlton, Kapalua until the hotel closed for renovations in 2007, then the series moved next door to the Napili Kai. Virtuoso performances of slack-key guitar, that magical Hawaiian invention of rich, full, and intricately tumbling notes like a musical waterfall, feature different artists each week. George Kahumoku Jr. is the emcee for the concerts as well as an accomplished performer. Slack-key (*kihoalu*) literally means the guitar strings have been loosened from classical tuning and retuned to the player's own fingering style, in ways passed down through families. The tradition was born in the 1800s, when Mexican vaqueros (*paniolo* in Hawaiian) were hired to train Hawaiians to handle royal cattle herds. The visiting cowboys brought their six-string guitars, taught Hawaiians how to play, and left the instruments behind when they returned home. Hawaiians blended Spanish ways with Hawaiian songs and created new music. They developed a method to play melody, bass, and chords all together, getting the most sound out of the few instruments and trained players available. Slack-key was born. Artists appear weekly to share music and talk story in an intimate setting. A Grammy Award–winning 2006 CD recorded live (*Masters of Hawaiian Slack Key Guitar, Volume 1*) preserves these special moments. A second compilation CD, Legends of Hawaiian Slack Key Guitar–Live from Maui, is available at **www.slackkey.com.**

Kupanaha
Kaanapali Beach Hotel, 2525 Kaanapali Parkway, Lahaina;
☎ **808-667-0128**

Show times Tuesday–Saturday, 4:30 p.m.

Length 2.5 hours.

Cost Gold Circle seating, $89; general adult seating, $79; teenagers, $55; children ages 6–12, $39.

Food 3-course dinner.

Beverages Mai tai, wine, beer, soft drinks, coffee.

DESCRIPTION AND COMMENTS The name *Kupanaha* is Hawaiian for magical and mystical. Illusionists Jody and Kathleen Baran present a magic show based on Hawaiian legends about Kekaa, the Black Rock that is Kaanapali Beach's famous landmark. Keep an eye on this cast of magicians (if you can); this fast-paced family show features sleight of hand, along with traditional hula and chant, in a good dinner show.

Warren and Annabelle's
900 Front Street, Lahaina; ☎ **808-667-6244;**
www.warrenandannabelles.com

Show times 2 shows Monday–Saturday, 5 p.m. check-in; second show at 7:30 p.m. on nights when first show sells out.

Length 3.5 hours, including 2-hour magic show.

Cost $56 general admission (adults only), $94.50 adds 2 cocktails, pupu, and dessert, tips included.

Discounts Coupons offering a 20 percent discount are available in hotel lobbies.

Type of seating Table seating for pupu and cocktails. Intimate 78-seat theater (stadium seating) for show. First come, first served.

Food Unless you order pupu, everything is à la carte. Menu includes spicy crab cakes, coconut-battered shrimp, chicken satay, and pork wrap. Desserts include chocolate truffle cake, key lime pie, crème brûlée, apple pie, and 2 types of cheesecake. Vegetarians should request alternatives in advance.

Beverages Tropical drinks, specialty drinks, beer, wine, soft drinks.

DESCRIPTION AND COMMENTS "Close-up" magician Warren Gibson performs sleight-of-hand tricks in cozy theater with Annabelle, a piano-playing ghost who takes requests.

BEFORE- AND AFTER-DINNER LOUNGES

MAJOR RESORT HOTELS ON ALL THE ISLANDS offer good Hawaiian music, jazz, and a place to dance or relax with a drink, before or after dinner, and enjoy the sunset and balmy evening. Here are some favorites:

Maui

Wailea Beach Marriott Resort & Spa, ☎ 808-875-9394. Mala Wailea Lounge is a great perch for comparing the finer points of Maui sunsets.
Ritz-Carlton, Kapalua, ☎ 808-669-6200. Alaloa Lounge enlivens the lobby with a great ocean view (watch whales on winter days, stars at night). Interesting decor features a ribbon of red light flowing across the lava-rock backdrop behind the bar, homage to volcanic origins. Where else will you find a bar made of inky black onyx and a

---

WHERE TO FIND THE PERFECT MAI TAI

Bright as a tropical moon, smooth as summer surf, rich as old *S.S. Lurline* passengers, cool and fresh as green limes, the mai tai is Hawaii's favorite drink. One sip and it's paradise. Or should be. Most mai tais served in Hawaii today are too strong, too sweet, and, at $7 and up, too expensive. Some taste like gasoline, others like cough syrup. They burn the throat, produce terrible headaches, and generally give Hawaii a bad name. These tacky concoctions have little in common with a real mai tai and should be avoided at all costs. Some variations on the original theme are excellent because they don't alter the basic ingredients. The classic mai tai is an unforgettable cocktail, an icy Jamaican rum and fresh lime juice drink with a subtle hint of oranges and almonds and a sprig of fresh mint for garnish. Now, that's a mai tai. Where you sip a mai tai is almost as important as the ingredients. This tropical drink always tastes better in a thatch hut on a lagoon with coco palms lining the shore.

Here's where to find and enjoy the best mai tai on Maui today:

Fairmont Kea Lani swim-up bar, Wailea, South Maui Maui may be the Chardonnay capital of Hawaii (all those ex-pat California winebibbers), but you can sip a great mai tai at the swim-up bar under a waterfall in the upper pool, Polo Beach Grille & Bar. Only drawback is the bar closes at 6 p.m.

Maui Nightlife

NAME	DESCRIPTION	REGION
Casanova	Restaurant with bar and dancing	Central Maui
Hard Rock Café	Music-themed restaurant and bar	West Maui
Jacques Northshore Restaurant/Bistro	Restaurant and bar	Central Maui
Life's A Beach	Beach bar with dancing	South Maui
Longhi's Lahaina	2nd-floor dancing and live entertainment on Friday nights	West Maui
Mulligan's on the Blue	Irish pub	South Maui
Sports Page Grill & Bar	Sports bar	South Maui

scrumptious menu of pupu (appetizers) until 10 p.m. (in case you missed dinner). Live music on weekend nights.

Westin Maui Resort & Spa, ☎808-667-2525. You have from 3 p.m. until 10 p.m. every night to cast your vote for the island's best martini, or so it was declared by Maui No Ka Oi readers. Or choose another concoction at this bar by the sea. Happy hour, 3–5 p.m.; live music, 6–9 p.m. with dinner.

Molokai

Hotel Molokai, ☎ 808-553-5347. Hula Shores restaurant and bar features live Hawaiian entertainment seven nights a week from "about 6–7 p.m., sometimes until 9 p.m., just depends."

Lanai

Hale Aheahe Lounge, Four Seasons Resort Lanai at Manele Bay, ☎ 808-565-7700. The lounge features a pianist or Hawaiian music most evenings.

Lanai Theatre, 465 Seventh Street, Lanai City; ☎ 808-565-7500. Live local performances, including school plays, art programs, movies, and special events.

The Lodge at Koele, ☎ 808-565-7300. Hawaiian music most evenings in the Great Hall.

NIGHTLIFE

PROFILED CLUBS AND NIGHTSPOTS

YOU CAN FIND LATE-NIGHT AMUSEMENT ON Lahaina's Front Street and Kihei's main drag, but don't expect much of a scene elsewhere. The legal drinking age is 21.

Below are the island's hotspots, grouped by region. Clubs come and go; schedules and formats change often, as determined by which places are hot or not. Check with your hotel concierge for up-to-the-minute details.

WEST MAUI

Hard Rock Café

INTERNATIONALLY KNOWN MUSIC-THEMED RESTAURANT

900 Front Street, Lahaina; ☎ 808-667-7400; www.hardrock.com

Cover None.

Minimum None.

Dress Casual.

Beverages Beer, wine, mixed drinks.

Food available Pig sandwiches, pot roast, grilled fajitas, burgers, and barbecue chicken.

Hours Dining: daily, 11 a.m.–10 p.m. Bar: open until midnight.

WHO GOES THERE 18–50; tourists, music lovers, T-shirt collectors.

WHAT GOES ON Live entertainment late on Friday, Art Night on Front Street.

COMMENTS Same place, different artifacts, including a wall devoted to local surfer heroes.

IF YOU GO Expect a wait to eat.

CENTRAL MAUI

Casanova

ITALIAN DINING AND LATE-NIGHT DANCING

188 Makawao Avenue, Makawao; ☎ 808-572-0220; www.casanovamaui.com

Cover Varies according to night and live or recorded format.

Minimum None.

Dress Resort casual.

Beverages Beer, wine, soft drinks, and other nonalcoholic drinks.

Food available The main dining room boasts extensive Italian menus at lunch and dinner; a separate deli offers breakfast, lunch, and takeout.

Hours Daily, 11:30 a.m.–9:30 p.m. Bar: Wednesday, Friday, and Saturday, 10 p.m.–2 a.m.

WHO GOES THERE Women from all over Maui on Ladies' Night (Wild Wahine Wednesday), club crawlers who seek live or recorded contemporary Hawaiian and reggae on weekends; or anyone still awake after 10 in Makawao.

COMMENTS Keep an eye on the Web site or entertainment roster; big-name entertainers have been known to show up here over the years. The brightest lights in sleepy Makawao promise late-night fun in any event, but be careful driving home.

Jacques Northshore Restaurant

INDOOR AND OUTDOOR BISTRO AND SOCIAL HUB

120 Hana Highway, Paia; ☎ 808-579-8844

Cover None.

Minimum None.

Dress Surfer casual (T-shirts, board shorts, slippers, lots of tan skin).

Beverages Beer, wine, soft drinks, juice, coffee.

Food available Fresh seafood, salads, sushi, for lunch and dinner.

Hours Daily, 5–10 p.m.

WHO GOES THERE Sooner or later everyone goes to Jacques, the perfect tropo bistro, but it's known as a surfer hangout.

WHAT GOES ON You can dine inside (at a fish-themed sushi bar) or out on an open-air lanai with a bandstand where, after dinner on Fridays, Jacques rocks with late-night dancing under the stars. No matter where you are at Jacques, you are part of an in-crowd of North Shore surfers, unreconstructed hippies, and wandering tourists. It's the best place to see and be seen by the sea.

COMMENTS Off the beaten path for tourists, this is the local hangout for windsurfers, with jazz on Monday nights, Hawaiian music early on Aloha Friday, and lively fun every night; the food's good, too. Seating is available indoors and outdoors under a banyan tree in the tropical garden.

IF YOU GO Be prepared to make new pals in old Paia town.

SOUTH MAUI

Life's A Beach

BAR AND HANGOUT WITH MEXICAN OVERTONES

1913 South Kihei Road (Next to Foodland), Kihei; ☎ 808-891-8010; www.mauibars.com

Cover None.

Minimum None.

Dress Casual.

Beverages Beer, wine, mixed drinks, 50 kinds of margaritas.

Food available Burgers, appetizers, Mexican, kids' menu, daily specials.

Hours Daily, 11 a.m.–2 a.m.; kitchen closes at midnight.

WHO GOES THERE Beachgoers, partyers.

WHAT GOES ON Nightly live entertainment, karaoke on Sunday, open mike on Monday, and a daily happy hour, 4–7 p.m.

COMMENTS A regular watering hole with cheap drinks and food that won't break your budget; real working people go here for pau hana.

IF YOU GO Get ready to party with locals in Kihei. Aim for Sunday nights when Mexican food and drinks are half price and entertainment starts at 9 p.m.

Mulligan's on the Blue

Wailea's Blue Course Clubhouse, 120 Kaukahi Street; ☎ 808-874-1131; www.mulligansontheblue.com

Cover None.

Minimum None.

Dress Casual.

Beverages Guinness and 24 other international beers, wine, Irish coffee, mixed drinks.

Food available Breakfast (all day), lunch, dinner.

Hours Daily, 8 a.m.–1 a.m.

WHO GOES THERE Locals, tourists, resort workers late (after their shifts at the golf course).

WHAT GOES ON Nightly live music and dancing; local stars Eric Gilliom and Barry Flanagan perform at dinner on Thursday and Friday; Saturday and Sunday nights feature a traditional Irish jam session, 7–10 p.m., followed by dancing. Monday and Tuesday it's local jazz groups and Wednesday, anybody's guess.

COMMENTS 200-seat indoor/outdoor restaurant with genuine Irish flair is, as advertised, the only place to have rowdy fun at night in Wailea. Lawn settings can be arranged for weddings and special parties. If dancing's not your gig, sneak away to the satellite sports screens to watch pro football and basketball.

IF YOU GO Wailea nightlife is an oxymoron. Mulligan's by day doubles as the Blue Course Clubhouse, and after dark may either be a full-tilt boogie scene or a bore. You never know what high tide will bring; the Guinness is far more dependable.

Sports Page Grill & Bar

2411 South Kihei Road, Kihei; ☎ 808-879-0602; www.sportspagemaui.com

Cover None.

Minimum None.

Dress As you are.

Beverages Beer, wine, mixed drinks.

Food available Burgers and hot dogs, sandwiches, plate lunches, baby-back ribs;

Sunday NFL special breakfast. College and pro football games start early in the morning in Hawaii (which is in its own time zone, Hawaiian Standard Time), so you can catch almost all the action before noon and spend the day at the beach.

Hours Daily, 11 a.m.–1:30 a.m. (8 a.m.–2 a.m. on football weekends).

WHO GOES THERE Are you ready for some fearless spectators?

WHAT GOES ON Live music several nights a week; games on a big-screen TV and 17 little ones; 2 satellite dishes and nine televisions provide a full sports roster. Pool tables, video games, and foosball also available.

COMMENTS Heavy pupu and sandwiches, burgers, chicken wings. This is Kihei's sports center every Sunday in football season. Games start in the morning in Hawaii due to the time difference with the Mainland.

IF YOU GO Be careful which team you cheer—the big, nasty guy full of Bud Light behind you roots for the other side.

ACCOMMODATIONS INDEX

Note: Page numbers in **bold face** type indicate accommodation profiles.

RESTAURANT INDEX

Note: Page numbers in **bold face** type indicate restaurant profiles.

SUBJECT INDEX

Unofficial Guide Reader Survey

If you'd like to express your opinion about traveling in Maui or this guidebook, complete the following survey and mail it to:

Unofficial Guide Reader Survey
P.O. Box 43673
Birmingham, AL 35243

Inclusive dates of your visit: _____

Members of your party:

	Person 1	Person 2	Person 3	Person 4	Person 5
Gender:	M F	M F	M F	M F	M F
Age:					

How many times have you been to Maui? _____
On your most recent trip, where did you stay? _____

Concerning your accommodations, on a scale of 100 as best and 0 as worst, how would you rate:

The quality of your room?   The value of your room?
The quietness of your room?   Check-in/checkout efficiency?
Shuttle service to the airport?   Swimming-pool facilities?

Did you rent a car?_____   From whom?_____

Concerning your rental car, on a scale of 100 as best and 0 as worst, how would you rate:

Pickup-processing efficiency?_____   Return-processing efficiency?____
Condition of the car?____   Cleanliness of the car?____
Airport-shuttle efficiency?_____

Concerning your dining experiences:

Estimate your meals in restaurants per day? _____
Approximately how much did your party spend on meals per day? ____

_____

Favorite restaurants in Maui: _____

_____

Did you buy this guide before leaving? _____ While on your trip?_____

How did you hear about this guide? (check all that apply)

Loaned or recommended by a friend ☐   Radio or TV ☐
Newspaper or magazine ☐   Bookstore salesperson ☐
Just picked it out on my own ☐   Library ☐
Internet ☐

What other guidebooks did you use on this trip? _____

_____

_____

_____

On a scale of 100 as best and 0 as worst, how would you rate them?

_____

_____

_____

Using the same scale, how would you rate the _Unofficial Guide_(s)?

_____

Are _Unofficial Guides_ readily available at bookstores in your area? _____

Have you used other _Unofficial Guides_? _____

Which one(s)? _____

_____

_____

Comments about your Maui trip or the _Unofficial Guide_(s):

_____

_____

_____

_____

_____

_____

_____

_____

_____

_____

_____

_____

_____

_____

_____

_____

_____

_____